SOUTHEASTERN MESOAMERICA

© 2021 by University Press of Colorado

Published by University Press of Colorado
245 Century Circle, Suite 202
Louisville, Colorado 80027

 The University Press of Colorado is a proud member of
the Association of University Presses.

The University Press of Colorado is a cooperative publishing enterprise supported, in part, by Adams State University, Colorado State University, Fort Lewis College, Metropolitan State University of Denver, Regis University, University of Colorado, University of Northern Colorado, University of Wyoming, Utah State University, and Western State Colorado University.

∞ This paper meets the requirements of the ANSI/NISO Z39.48–1992 (Permanence of Paper).

ISBN: 978-1-64642-096-4 (cloth)
ISBN: 978-1-64642-097-1 (ebook)
DOI: https://doi.org/10.5876/9781646420971

Library of Congress Cataloging-in-Publication Data

Names: 1 Goodwin, Whitney A., edi | 1 Johnson, Erlend, edi | 1 Figueroa, Alejandro J., edi
Title: Southeastern Mesoamerica : indigenous interaction, resilience, and change / edited by Whitney A. Goodwin, Erlend Johnson, and Alejandro J. Figueroa.
Description: Louisville : University Press of Colorado, [2020] | Includes bibliographical references and index.
Identifiers: LCCN 2020051349 (print) | LCCN 202005 (ebook) | ISBN 9781646420964 (hardback) | ISBN 9781646420971 (ebook)
Subjects:
Classification: LCC F1434.2.S62 S68 2020 (print) | LCC F1434.2.S62 (ebook) | DDC 972.8/01—dc23
LC record available at https://lccn.loc.gov/2020051349
LC ebook record available at https://lccn.loc.gov/2020051350

Cover illustration: "La Buena Cosecha" (1986) by Ezequiel Padilla Ayestas.

SOUTHEASTERN MESOAMERICA

1

Southeastern Mesoamerica has for decades been a shifting archaeological and geographical concept used to refer to an area that encompasses modern-day eastern Guatemala, western Honduras, and most of El Salvador (figure 1.1). While even the earliest definitions were tenuous, as detailed below, decades of sustained research have complicated, and thus advanced, our understanding of the region even further. As evidence of this progress, the chapters in this volume do not espouse a singular view of the region or rely on one particular theory or methodological approach to the study of its past. Rather, these chapters draw on new concepts, techniques, or records, both archaeological and historic, to add to the increasingly complex picture of the lives of the indigenous peoples who inhabited the region and who continue to call it home today. By expanding our view deeper into the past than previous volumes on the subject and drawing out the histories of the region into the period after European contact, together the chapters in the volume trace the related processes of interaction, resilience, and change that shaped the trajectories of the varied indigenous groups in the region over millennia. The underlying goal of the volume as a whole remains similar, however, to many works that came before it: to demonstrate the universal utility of the case studies from this region to archaeological and anthropological understandings of intercultural interaction among diverse populations along fluid, ever-changing frontiers and borders.

Introduction

Whitney A. Goodwin,
Alejandro J. Figueroa,
and Erlend Johnson

DOI: 10.5876/9781646420971.c001

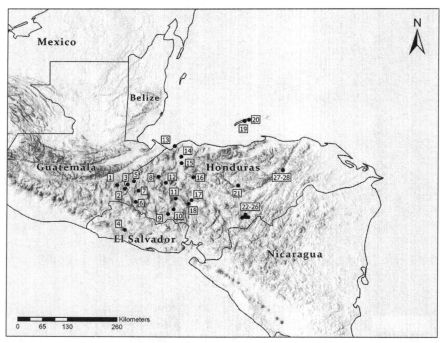

FIGURE 1.1. *Map of Southeastern Mesoamerica with key sites mentioned in this volume (see table 1.1). Our omission of a physical boundary to delineate the region is deliberate and in keeping with the spirit of this volume.*

TABLE 1.1. Key sites mentioned in the text and included in figure 1.1

Site No.	Site	Site No.	Site	Site No.	Site
1	Jocotán	11	Sinsimbla	21	Silca
2	Jupilingo	12	Tencoa	22	Santa Rosalia
3	Copán	13	San Fernando de Omoa	23	La Cañera
4	Cuscatlan	14	Ticamaya	24	Calpules
5	Río Amarillo	15	Travesia	25	El Zapotillo
6	San Marcos	16	Salitrón Viejo	26	Rancho Rosa
7	La Union	17	Comayagua	27	La Cooperativa
8	Yamala	18	Lejamani	28	Suyapita
9	La Pintada	19	El Antigual		
10	El Gigante	20	Augusta		

This volume's editors and contributors represent a range of senior and junior scholars in the fields of archaeology, anthropology, and ethnohistory, with decades of combined research in Southeastern Mesoamerica. The chapters in this volume are representative of the most recent theoretically driven and socially relevant research on the past indigenous peoples of this region and encompass the entire temporal depth of past human occupation in this area—from the latest Pleistocene to the ethnohistoric and historic periods—as well as the vast spatial and cultural breadth that is encompassed within the area. The majority of these contributions are the culmination of multiyear projects, which have continued to expand our understanding of the cultural diversity present in the geographic area that lies between Mesoamerica and the Intermediate Area.

SOUTHEASTERN MESOAMERICA AS AN OBJECT OF STUDY

Just as the concept of Southeastern Mesoamerica has changed, the southern "border" of Mesoamerica was at various times placed along the Ulúa and Lempa Rivers of western Honduras and El Salvador (Fox 1981; Lange and Stone 1984), the Choluteca River in southern Honduras (Glass 1966), and the Nicoya Peninsula in northwestern Costa Rica (Fowler 1991; Lange 1979). This same geographic area also received interchangeable titles including *Middle America*, *Central America*, and *Lower Central America* by various scholars over the years. One additional factor that has significantly contributed to the diffuse definition of this area is its ecological, geophysical, and cultural heterogeneity (Willey 1984). However, this diversity is one of Southeastern Mesoamerica's most defining characteristics. The spatial proximity of varied landforms and ecosystems, each with its own suite of resources, led to the early development of localized traditions that were both isolated and at the same time intricately linked in various ways with those of groups near and far. The history of how these groups and their interactions have been studied is long and complex, and beyond the purview of this introduction, and we present but a brief summary of it below in an effort to situate our volume within it.

This region originally encompassed the southernmost limit of the Mesoamerican culture area, a concept developed by Paul Kirchhoff (1943, 1952, 1960) and operationalized by Willey et al. (1964) to delimit a geographic area of shared languages and cultural traits. As its name suggests, this region was originally thought of as the cultural periphery or fringe of the larger and more economically and sociopolitically centralized societies in Mesoamerica. It was for a long time referred to as the *Southeastern Maya Periphery* (Lothrop

1939), since it was believed that the Maya represented the evolutionary end-point towards which other smaller and less complex societies aspired to or were headed towards. Consequently, and following the culture area approach espoused by Kroeber (1939), groups in this area were defined almost exclusively by the presence or absence of cultural traits characteristic of more complex societies (Baudez 1970; Hay et al. 1940; Sauer 1959; Spinden 1924).

While some early research acknowledged that populations in Southeastern Mesoamerica were not solely reliant on external influences for their social and cultural development (Strong 1935; Stone 1957), the periphery was nevertheless often viewed as being in the shadow of Maya polities and their histories (i.e., Baudez 1970:133). Because this region was analyzed for so long in comparison with or as a reflection of its Maya neighbors, studies of interaction and diffusion were predominant, and these focused primarily on stylistic, ideational, and sociopolitical influences and similarities (Hay et al. 1940; Kroeber 1939; Longyear 1947; Lothrop 1939; Thompson 1970). The goal of these studies was to identify where certain traits were present or absent, with the ultimate aim of defining the area of influence of particular cultures. As such, Southeastern Mesoamerica was often seen as a transitional or buffer zone, where Mesoamerican traditions "thinned out" and traces of Lower Central American or Intermediate Area traditions began to appear (Baudez 1970; Lange 1979). Despite the shortcomings of this approach, and as pointed out by others in the past (Schortman and Urban 1986), this research was the product of early twentieth-century archaeology, which focused largely on state-level societies such as the Maya and was thus part of a common historical narrative in our field.

This trend shifted markedly in the 1970s and 1980s with the onset of large-scale projects across much of Guatemala, Honduras, and El Salvador, and a shift in focus towards examining the nuanced and mutualistic nature of the interaction between state- and nonstate-level societies and local sociopolitical developments (e.g., Andrews 1976; Boone and Willey 1988; Creamer 1987; Creamer and Haas 1985; Demarest 1988; Healy 1984; Helms and Loveland 1976; Hirth et al. 1989; Lange 1984, 1992; Lange and Stone 1984; Linares 1979; Robinson 1987; Schortman and Ashmore 2012; Schortman et al. 1986; Sharer 1974, 1978, 1984; Sheets 1979, 1982; Urban and Schortman 1986, 1988). This research questioned the marginal status of the region and exploited its potential for providing detailed understandings of the relationships between states and nonstates and highlighted the relevance that these insights could have in similar areas around the globe. In Honduras, the Honduran Institute of Anthropology and History (IHAH) began to organize symposia that allowed researchers to share results and interpretations from projects taking place across the country. This work was expanded upon in subsequent seminars, meetings, and symposia in the United States, leading to the publication of a number of edited volumes (e.g., Boone and Willey 1988; Fowler 1991; Graham 1993; Helms and Loveland 1976; Henderson and Beaudry-Corbett 1993; Robinson 1987).

During this time, some authors (e.g., Schortman and Urban 1986) proposed the usage of the term *periphery* rather than *frontier*, as it signified a more porous boundary that more adequately explained the multidirectional nature of the interactions taking place between Southeast Mesoamerican populations and those to the north and south. Other scholars (e.g., Fox 1981) redefined the concept of frontier to mean not a boundary but a distinct cultural entity with its own internal history and traits that combine Mesoamerican and non-Mesoamerican elements. Frederick Lange (1976, 1979), on the other hand, advocated the use of the term *buffer*, which implies a zone composed of at least two frontiers or boundaries with more developed cultures and an area of internal developments. This concept emphasized the "outstanding feature" of this area: the maintenance of long-term indigenous traditions in spite of constant interaction with outside forces (Lange 1976).

Researchers in the 1980s also advocated a variety of models and approaches to the study of the prehispanic peoples of Southeastern Mesoamerica. The interaction sphere or network model (Joyce 1988; Smith and Heath-Smith 1980; Urban and Schortman 1988) was developed to allow for the examination of the relationships between societies with different sociopolitical configurations without requiring the delimitation of rigid geographic boundaries. Researchers applied this model to bring attention to the diverse strategies used by local populations to tap into various inter- and intraregional networks at different points in time for a variety of purposes. A third model expanded upon the interaction-sphere approach and focused on acculturation and the changes produced by the different kinds of relationships taking place between neighboring groups (Ashmore et al. 1982; Urban and Schortman 1986). This acculturation model viewed geographical boundaries as dynamic and did not limit itself to a single dimension of interaction (e.g., economic, political, social), which allowed for the integration of large amounts of data.

Research in the 1990s continued adding to our understanding of the region and addressed the limitations of ongoing research, namely the homogenization of cultures and a unidirectional view of intersocietal interactions that assumed the domination of state-level societies (Graham 1993; Lange 1993, 1996; Schortman and Nakamura 1991; Schortman and Urban 1994, 1996;

Sharer 1992; Sheets 1992). This research showed how the peoples of Southeast Mesoamerica—and aspiring individuals within these societies—constantly shifted and manipulated their identities to project their independence from their neighbors to the north, in some instances playing polities against each other to gain access to particular resources or networks of exchange. This work also began simultaneously to parse out the political, economic, and ideological dimensions of interaction between state- and nonstate-level societies and to show how these did not always overlap (Schortman and Urban 1994, 1996). In the 1990s archaeologists working in Southeastern Mesoamerica adopted world-systems theory, originally developed by Wallerstein (1976, 1980), to better examine the nuanced and multidirectional ways in which cores—large hierarchical societies, namely Maya polities—interacted with their hinterlands or peripheries (Joyce 1996; Schortman and Urban 1994, 1999). This research showed that Maya polities had in many cases strong and long-lasting connections with polities and societies in the region; however, these larger polities never established long-term economic, political, or ideological dominance over other polities in the region, did not have direct or indirect control over these, and were thus forced to interact with these societies in a wide variety of forms (Joyce 1996; Schortman and Urban 1999).

Archaeologists in this decade also dropped the term *periphery* and adopted the more neutral term *Southeastern Mesoamerica* to address this area without focusing on a particular chronological period (usually the Late Classic), to move away from an emphasis on interregional interaction, and to emphasize the dualistic nature of interactions between this and neighboring regions (Fowler 1991; Schortman and Urban 1994). Moreover, research began to focus on the internal trajectories and dynamics of Southeastern Mesoamerican societies, including the emic factors and processes that led to the development and relative stability of the sociopolitical complexity and economic independence of these groups (Joyce 1993; Lange 1992, 1993, 1996; Sheets 1992). It was also at this time that researchers once again began to "look south" and examine the relationships between groups in this region with groups in Nicaragua, Costa Rica, Panama, and Colombia (e.g., Healy 1992; Healy et al. 1996; Joyce 1993; Lange 1992, 1993). The book *Los indios de Centroamérica* by Hasemann and colleagues (1996) marked the apogee of research at this time and synthesized the current state of knowledge of past and present indigenous societies through the lenses of archaeology, ethnohistory, and cultural anthropology. These authors called on future researchers to keep the far-reaching history of indigenous populations in mind when studying the mosaic of cultures that have characterized this region.

Research at the turn of the twenty-first century continued to expand in depth and breadth across Southeastern Mesoamerica. The IHAH once again hosted research symposia in the late 1990s and early 2000s, resulting in two edited volumes (Fajardo and Ávalos 2004; Martínez 2012) and an electronic conference proceedings (Fajardo and Figueroa 2004). Sessions organized at international meetings also brought together scholars working in the region to share their latest results, though these did not result in edited volumes but rather individual articles and monographs, too numerous to cite here. Research in the past two decades expanded our knowledge of periods outside the Classic, namely the Preceramic and colonial periods, which had up to then remained largely unexplored. These efforts also sought to address explicitly the relevance of archaeological research to contemporary issues of identity, sustainability, and cultural-heritage management (Martínez 2012).

The research presented in this volume continues to highlight the diversity and dynamism of the indigenous groups that inhabited and continue to inhabit its borders. Alongside continuity in cultural, linguistic, social, and political processes, sweeping changes that have shaped the broad history of the region are also identified. This research echoes what previous studies in the region have argued for decades: that cultures living in Southeastern Mesoamerica were not marginal at all, but rather defined their own goals and lives according to their own premises and principles, while selectively and strategically borrowing from cultural traditions to the north and south. These peoples had their own forms of monumental architecture, long-term human-environment relations, and routes and methods of exchange, but also social, cultural, political, and economic traits that were wholly their own, and the result of internal creativity and inspiration influenced by local social and natural trajectories.

NEW APPROACHES TO SOUTHEASTERN MESOAMERICA

Collectively, the chapters in this volume call upon scholars working in Mesoamerica, the Intermediate Area, and other cultural border areas around the world to reexamine the roles that indigenous resilience and agency play in the so-called margins or peripheries of better known cultures and the cultural developments and interactions that occur within them. At the local level, these chapters continue to move beyond defining this region and its history not by what it lacks or with respect to its better-known cultural neighbors to the north and south, but rather by its local histories and developments.

The contributions included in this volume present data and interpretations that are necessary to expand the discussion of what social complexity entails, particularly in a region neighboring a large cultural group that personifies the traditional definition of a complex society, the Maya. The various contributors to this volume, despite their call for a new framework of analysis, acknowledge the difficulty of abandoning old terminologies because of their history of use and because they serve as points of reference to entities and processes that are better understood, which is why the term *Southeast Mesoamerica* is retained. This limitation, however, is a challenge for future researchers of the region, who should seek to fill the gaps in our knowledge of the prehistory and history of the area in order to better understand it. It is our hope that the research presented in this volume will inspire others to establish new frameworks for describing the phenomena we are observing in Southeastern Mesoamerica; not simply new definitions of old terms, but a new language that will allow researchers in this area to describe the realities we are witnessing and struggling to define using previous approaches and their related conceptual baggage. This process of change is gradual and difficult, and at this stage we cannot change our conceptual framework without changing our interpretations, and vice versa. As a result, some of the chapters in this volume focus on new ways to collect data, others on new ways to interpret it, and still others on new ways to discuss both data and our interpretations of it. Together, they move us forward, increasing the lexicon with which we describe and discuss archaeological phenomena.

Like the edited volumes that preceded and inspired it (e.g., Boone and Willey 1988; Fajardo and Ávalos 2004; Fowler 1991; Graham 1993; Henderson and Beaudry-Corbett 1993; Lange 1992; Lange and Stone 1984; Robinson 1987; Urban and Schortman 1986), this compilation aims to provide archaeologists, anthropologists, historians, and ethnohistorians working in Mesoamerica, the Intermediate Area, and beyond with new theoretical perspectives and unique case studies on how indigenous groups in these areas mitigated, negotiated, and sidestepped natural, cultural, economic, and sociopolitical changes within and outside their borders during the prehistoric and historic periods. We are at a point in time when we have the critical mass of data necessary to make a systematic comparison of the actions and reactions of the groups along Southeastern Mesoamerica in relation to each other, rather than solely with distant groups, which will lead to a better understanding of the history of the region in its own right. As the history of research in the area shows well, this is a joint effort, and can only be accomplished through working alongside living communities (the subject of a separate recent edited volume: see Martínez 2012) and Central American students and scholars. As such, the chapters in this volume serve as a bridge from the pioneering research that has transformed our understanding of Southeastern Mesoamerica to research that is forthcoming, shaped by local capacities and international collaboration. By combining Central American and foreign voices and experiences, this book places itself at a key juncture in the way archaeology and anthropology are conducted in Southeastern Mesoamerica and Central America in general.

ORGANIZATION OF THE VOLUME

The volume is organized into fourteen chapters including an introduction and a conclusion. The main body of the book is organized both chronologically and spatially: the chapters transition from the deep to the recent past and move roughly from west to east and back as the volume moves through time. Generally, the first half of the volume deals with projects that rely strictly on archaeological evidence while those in the second half either incorporate or focus solely on historic documents. The chapter by Joyce is an exception to these generalizations, for reasons expanded upon below.

The volume begins with an overview in chapter 2 of the Preceramic period of Southeastern Mesoamerica (ca. 11,000–5,000 cal BP). Using data gathered over 16 years of pedestrian surveys in the highlands of southwestern Honduras, Alejandro Figueroa and Timothy Scheffler highlight how behavioral and environmental changes and developments taking place during this period helped bring about the region's well-known cultural markers, such as domestication, agriculture, and locally distinctive social relationships. This chapter provides a unique contribution by pushing the scope of time coverage in the volume into the deep past. Focusing on the Preceramic/Formative transition in southwestern Honduras, and particularly on data from the well-preserved remains of the El Gigante rockshelter, Figueroa and Scheffler outline the interplay between the natural and social landscapes of the area and how these factors led to the relatively late adoption of Mesoamerican cultivars. The patterns of domestication here were apparently heavily dependent on the natural landscape, which provided a relatively marginal environment for farming. Instead of intensive farming, experimentation with agroforestry occurred early and persisted late in this area, as evidenced by the changing morphometric qualities of avocado remains from the macrobotanical assemblage at El Gigante. Rather than suggesting the region was isolated, however, Figueroa and Scheffler show that the eventual adoption of Mesoamerican cultivars took place alongside continued use of a wide variety of locally available resources, suggesting that the shift was voluntary rather than necessary for survival, highlighting local ties to wider social networks throughout Southeastern Mesoamerica. In turn, the limits of the landscape may have helped shape the social and political processes of early Lenca groups in the area, given that only limited and likely unreliable surpluses of crops could be amassed. The authors suggest that this lack of predictable resources was one of several needs that fostered early ties between groups.

Throughout their chapter, Figueroa and Scheffler return to the cultural significance of caves and rockshelters over time as well, arguing that the uses of caves and rockshelters in this area suggest deep roots for common Mesoamerican ritual practices, ranging from practical needs for shelter for early populations to ossuaries of the Classic period and locations for wakes in the present day. The association between caves and the dead was surely shaped throughout the period in which locals made these locations their home. The ritual and symbolic importance of caves and rockshelters is underscored by the presence of rich displays of art at these locales. The admittedly tenuous links between the motifs present in the rock art and the ethnohistorically recorded practices of local groups is an avenue for future research here. Overall, this chapter sets the model followed by several other chapters in the book by laying out the connectedness of Southeastern Mesoamerican groups, apparent even this far into the past, and demonstrating the persistence of traditions over many millennia.

Chapter 3 by Erlend Johnson moves the focus of the volume into western Honduras and later in time. His work adds to our understanding of the reach and influence of the Copán polity along the Southeastern Mesoamerican border. By tracing the political development of settlements in the Cucuyagua and Sensenti Valleys from the Protoclassic to the Late Classic periods, he outlines divergent histories in the types of relationships enjoyed and the strategies employed by local residents in their dealings with the Copán elite. In line with other research at sites along the edge of the Copán polity, Johnson suggests that Copán's influence in the political processes that unfolded in the neighboring valleys was filtered not only by distance but by the particular response of the existing populations in those areas and possibly by the nature of the existing settlements. With data from extensive survey and mapping of both the Cucuyagua and Sensenti Valleys, Johnson uses settlement patterns and monumental architecture as proxies for political organization and collective action to trace the political trajectories of each area. Ceramic and architectural data from excavations are used to bolster local chronologies from these little-known areas and to assess the nature of the relationship between distant settlements and the Copán elite. While settlements in the further afield Sensenti Valley were precocious during the Protohistoric period, interaction with Copán seems to have been relatively limited in comparison with the central site of La Union in the Cucuyagua Valley during the Late Classic period. Although influence from Copán is evident at later settlements in the Sensenti Valley, evidence from La Union demonstrates what was likely a more direct, mutually beneficial relationship between local elites and those at Copán that resulted in a more definitively hierarchical political organization in the traditional lowland Maya style and suggests direct political integration within the broader Copán polity in the Late Classic period. In addition to calling attention to the diverse range of political strategies and resulting organizations that existed along the border, this study adds evidence of long-lived settlements in both valleys, highlighting the cultural continuity of many of the groups in the region. Johnson's work echoes the sentiment of decades of research along Southeastern Mesoamerica and reminds us that while few settlements in this region were untouched by the founding of the Copán polity and its expansion during the Late Classic period, local responses to shifting political structures are not predictable and cannot be assumed.

In chapter 4, Cameron McNeil and colleagues move us even closer to the polity of Copán by presenting their recent findings from excavations at the site of Río Amarillo, located within the Copán Valley. Drawing on what is known of the complex history of the ruling dynasty of Copán, they expertly weave the fate of rulers and the extent of their political reach with the history of this particular site, demonstrating the interconnectedness of the two. The authors then turn to the possible role and attraction of Río Amarillo—that of breadbasket to feed the populations of Copán as the center grew during the Late Classic period. In addition to its strategic location for trade, the authors argue that its proximity to fertile lands did indeed contribute to its importance and likely explains the continued interest and investment in the settlement by the Copán elite. Furthermore, they note that the location of Río Amarillo near diverse ecological zones likely played a sustaining role in this relationship. The authors provide an in-depth history of the site from the limited Preclassic settlement, through its most-intensive occupation during the Late Classic, and into the Terminal Classic and Postclassic periods. Using architectural and artifactual data, they outline the long-term interaction between the Copán elites and residents at Río Amarillo as well as highlighting the often-overlooked interactions between the site and their central Honduran neighbors. This is an important contribution in that it extends the examination of settlement histories both spatially and temporally within the Copán Valley, as they are often limited to the site core itself, and also draws on a familiarity of the researchers with the cultural practices of other areas of Honduras to demonstrate the significant ties to those regions that may not have been considered otherwise. This perfectly demonstrates the need for researchers to possess broad familiarity with both Southeastern Mesoamerican cultural histories and an understanding of the populations that lived beyond this imaginary border.

William McFarlane and Miranda Stockett Suri's chapter 5 explicitly argues for, and convincingly demonstrates, the potential of Southeastern Mesoamerican datasets to address broader questions about the nature of political, social, and economic responses to interaction on a politically diverse landscape. Drawing on data from valley-wide survey and excavations at the Late Classic site of Sinsimbla, the authors consider intra- and intervalley patterns in settlement, architecture, and artifacts across the Jesús de Otoro Valley in relation to patterns seen in neighboring valleys. At this scale, differences in seemingly homogenous ceramic traditions can tease out diverse but overlapping networks of interaction among this and neighboring valleys. Consistent site planning at contemporaneous settlements within a limited portion of the valley, when considered in conjunction with the settlement-pattern data demonstrating the lack of primary centers, suggests heterarchical organization. How and why this organization came to be will require further investigation within the valley. In any case, documenting the way in which the populations of the Jesús de Otoro valley organized themselves during the Late Classic period adds an essential piece to the puzzle that is Southeastern Mesoamerica—a piece that could only now take shape, given that interpretations relied heavily on the availability of increasingly robust datasets from nearby regions. As the authors note, this scale of interpretation, in between the restrictive intravalley confines of a single project's data, and one step below a broad regional interpretation, is precisely the type of foundational research that is necessary to piece together a solid understanding of diversity and continuity in central Honduras and beyond. Only by comparing the actions and reactions of the groups along Southeastern Mesoamerica in a systematic way will we be able to discover the broader truths about the history of Southeastern Mesoamerica as a whole.

In chapter 6, Eva Martínez, working in the previously unstudied Jamastrán Valley of southeastern Honduras, uses survey data to model demographic patterns to gain an understanding of the multiscalar social and political organization of its prehispanic inhabitants during its brief history of occupation from AD 600 to 1000. Martínez mapped ceramic-sherd distributions across the entire valley and transformed these data into densities that reflect socially meaningful units and imply certain levels of interaction among residents that may correspond with certain categories of settlement like households, farmsteads, hamlets, or villages. Like others, she finds that settlement patterns within the valley do not support the presence of hierarchically organized populations. Instead, over 60 percent of the valley's inhabitants were shown to have been clustered into two relatively equally populated settlement areas that contained the majority of cross-community interactions within their respective boundaries, suggesting two autonomous social and/or political systems operating within the valley. The author argues that prestige-oriented economic strategies, focused on controlled access to prime agricultural lands, local craft production and exchange, or interregional exchange, were either not employed or not entirely successful in the valley. Despite not being directly involved in strategies of hierarchical power, however, local populations were significantly connected to social and political networks centered farther west, which resulted in local decentralization in conjunction with similar processes occurring throughout much of Southeastern Mesoamerica.

In chapter 7, Christopher Begley discusses the ways in which prominent members of eastern Honduran populations utilized certain symbolic elements from neighboring areas, especially site planning from Mesoamerica, to materialize their claim to power, while otherwise maintaining minimal interactions with neighboring cultures. Begley's work, much like that of Martínez, demonstrates the difficulty in drawing a singular or certain border for Southeastern Mesoamerica. Building on a long but often overlooked history of research in the Mosquitia, Begley traces the development of complexity among groups settled in interior valleys from AD 500 to 1000 through extensive archaeological survey and excavation. While local groups share cultural traits and ties with groups in Lower Central America to the south, Begley argues that emerging elites used their ties to Mesoamerican groups not to exploit commodity-based trade networks but rather to tap into networks of power that relied on restricted access to esoteric knowledge. Most important, however, were the ways in which that knowledge was used to shape internal political and social relations. The creation and maintenance of internal inequalities relied on the ability of elites to transform their knowledge into concrete, material means of power that could be understood and experienced by many but controlled by few. Begley sees these relationships manifested in the unexpected construction of ballcourts at multiple sites within the region at a time in which the first traces of complexity also emerged. Ballcourts, he argues, in addition to being symbolically related to distant powers, were a well-defined arena for political competition that served as a stage for local aggrandizers. Additionally, despite its distance from the Maya frontier, this region underwent similar shifts in population and decentralization as seen in the rest of Southeastern Mesoamerica, supporting the idea that ties to the north were significant in maintaining these local political structures. Begley's work shares central underlying tenets with many other researchers working along this border: that the nature and importance of broad, external influences can truly be understand only by looking at local processes.

Chapters 8–12 discuss the challenges and possibilities inherent in studying indigenous populations through ethnohistoric documents and archaeological excavations, and the intersection between these complementary datasets. These chapters highlight how the combination of ethnohistoric documents and archaeological investigations can lead to a better understanding of the continuity of communities of practice and the ethnogenesis of hybrid identities and communities resulting from indigenous and African groups that were displaced and forced to adapt and coexist.

The first of these chapters, chapter 8, by Lorena Mihok and colleagues, bridges the artificial divide between prehispanic and colonial archaeology in the region. The authors examine the overlapping histories of the indigenous Pech, the Miskitu—whose identity cannot be succinctly defined or delineated in time or space—and the European colonizers of the Bay Islands and the north coast of Honduras. Mirroring the present-day situation, this area has long been a crossroads where many groups came into contact. Beginning with Columbus's arrival in 1502, the Bay Islands in particular were a contested locale, battled over by English and Spanish forces over the following centuries. The authors argue that differences in the royalization strategies employed by European colonizers played a role in shaping different long-term demographic processes of these two local groups. The Spanish, looking to discourage settlement on the Bay Islands, forcibly resettled the majority of Pech populations to the mainland. The English, however, opted to encourage the adoption of a distinctly Miskitu identity that relied heavily on both symbolic and material elements borrowed from English society in order to solidify alliances with that group. Using archaeological data from the island of Roatán, the authors examine Postclassic-period Pech sites and an eighteenth-century Miskitu-English settlement as case studies for how these broad strategies played out locally and were shaped by existing social, political, and environmental circumstances. Notably, they also draw connections between their research and ongoing debates about Bay Islander identities today, highlighting the central role of knowledge from history and prehistory in modern issues of group identity and heritage preservation.

In chapter 9, Russell Sheptak also seeks to mend the divide between prehispanic and historic archaeology, but also speaks explicitly to the importance of doing so and the inherent difficulties involved, both theoretically and methodologically. Sheptak begins by laying out the central challenges to this work: establishing chronologies, understanding site-formation processes, and using appropriate units and scales of analysis. Rather than simply laying out these problems, however, Sheptak offers solutions that range from practical methodological goals to improved frameworks for bringing together data from excavation and historical documents that take as central the consideration of the movement of people and things across landscapes. Using case studies from contemporaneous northern Honduran indigenous and European colonial settlements, Sheptak demonstrates the essential utility of his approach. Patterns in the production and use of materials recovered from excavation are compared within and among towns that are known from historical documents to have been connected by the movement of people and things. The creation of new identities—ethnogenesis—from new, mixed populations is recorded in the similarities in material assemblages across these sites, but only a landscape scale of analysis, guided in its investigation of connections by the documentary evidence, provides this insight. His perspective offers not just hope but proof that carefully executed research on Honduran colonial settlements can overcome past difficulties and produce fascinating new, otherwise unattainable, and strikingly rich understandings of this period that are not limited to European settlements.

Moving back towards the western portion of the country, chapter 10 by Gloria Lara-Pinto provides a rich history of the complex Lenca-Chortí-Nahua frontier in southwestern Honduras through an extensive analysis of historic texts from the region. This chapter poses questions about how and why the conquest played out in this area as it did, particularly by exploring the ways in which the existing social and political ties and histories among and within local groups influenced how events unfolded. Lara-Pinto begins by laying out the deep history of the Lenca in the area, relying primarily on linguistic and documentary analyses, and highlighting the long-contested nature of this region as a united territory. She then continues to outline the complex trajectory of the local processes of segmentation and integration among the Lenca prior to contact. These include intense internal politics, but also the use of ethnic ties in the maintenance of the Lenca's "floating frontier," wherein ethnically Lenca groups experiencing internal conflict would unite against outside threats. Eventually, this strategy helped the Lenca to preserve their ancestral territories, even in the face of the encroaching migrations of Chortí and eventually Nahua-Pipil populations into the region. This series of events in the precontact history of the Lenca clearly set a precedent for strategies of resistance, which helped the Lenca maintain ancestral territories despite Spanish conquests into the region. Ultimately, Lara-Pinto's work serves to remind us that the social and political landscapes of the indigenous territories into which the Spanish marched were not static or simplistic. Nor were the events that unfolded reliant only on the history of outside forces, but rather were heavily influenced by the long-term histories of indigenous groups like the Lenca. The Spanish were not the first or the last challenge faced by the Lenca, and that reality had as much consequence and importance then as it does today.

In chapter 11, Pastor Gómez provides a new view on the political geography of the Lenca of western and southwestern Honduras. He argues that the use of the term *province* to describe the political configuration of the region has been assumed in previous ethnohistorical analyses to imply political unity. In the Lenca area, this has led to an assumption that vast territories were united under a single ruler. Gómez contends that the nature of the political structure among the Lenca prior to and immediately following contact is understood to have been composed of an elite class of chiefs and priests, but that the extent of such politically integrated units was small and centralization of power was weak. Using examples from newly discovered sixteenth-century texts, he demonstrates ambiguities in the use of the word *province*, which can range in meaning from an area united by politics to one united by language, ethnicity, or even one in which settlements are simply geographically proximate. He then discusses specific examples from the Lenca area that support his claim that previously outlined provinces are not actually representative of integrated units, at least not politically. More than semantics, Gómez's argument is that a monolithic interpretation of the word *province* in historical documents has limited the ways in which we consider Lenca political organization and overshadowed complexities in the arrangement and interaction of their settlements. This conclusion has far-reaching implications for the use of historic texts in understanding social and political integration across the region and serves as a cautionary tale for other ethnohistorians.

William Fowler examines similar political relationships from a broader perspective in chapter 12, using ethnohistoric documents as a way to infer the region's far-reaching prehistoric networks of exchange and interaction. Fowler draws attention to the considerable amount of data that can be gleaned concerning prehispanic networks of communication, interaction, and migration through a thorough analysis of early historical accounts. By studying the movements of early Spanish conquistadors and their native allies in El Salvador, Honduras, and Nicaragua, he argues that we may develop better understandings of the level and manner of interconnectedness across these regions. While Spaniards and their particular motivations were ultimately driving the movement of troops across the landscape, the logistics of those movements were likely heavily reliant on indigenous allies familiar with existing routes that may have been in use for thousands of years prior to contact. Using three case studies, he presents evidence for specific routes that likely represented longstanding networks of interaction that were appropriated by the Spaniards in their military conquests across Southeastern Mesoamerica. Additionally, Fowler suggests that current models of prehispanic troop movements are likely underestimating the ability of native armies to move large numbers of people great distances in relatively short amounts of time. Using examples from the early colonial period, he demonstrates the occurrence of such large-scale troop movements that involved large numbers of native allies. While Fowler cautions that such routes and movements should not be assumed to be directly analogous to indigenous migrations and interactions, his model highlights the central role and agency of native allies in choices made about Spanish military operations. In doing so, he has laid out several avenues of inquiry into networks for prehispanic interaction that can be borne out by future archaeological investigations.

The final two chapters of the book are dedicated to addressing the state and future of research in Southeastern Mesoamerica. In chapter 13, Rosemary Joyce calls for the adoption of a new framework for analyzing indigenous societies in the area, particularly in Honduras. Joyce argues that the archaeological record of Honduras provides a rare opportunity to document forms of social organization that restrained inequality, yet traditional frameworks are hindering our understandings and interpretations. By adopting a social framework based on tracing *communities of practice*, we can begin to detect and describe the repeated, shared practices that brought groups together at varied and often overlapping scales across space and time. This allows us to look at differences from the household to the settlement to the region in ways that are complementary, not conflicting, in order to explain complicated realities where communities of practice cross-cut the types of groups defined by characteristics such as ethnicity or language that we typically rely on. Drawing on data synthesized from over 30 years of fieldwork in western Honduras, Joyce first traces the communities of practice involved in the production and consumption of Ulúa Polychrome and Ulúa marble vessels. She uses these examples to demonstrate how patronage of craft skills and spirituality were both integrating forces among communities who participated in events that necessitated the use of these items, but that they were also used in multiple ways by multiple actors so that the same item or type of item may have been part of several communities of practice. By recognizing that communities of practice may share deep-rooted similarities across space and time, comprising a constellation of practice, this framework also allows flexibility in describing and explaining the arrangement of and interaction between actors at varying scales. This is essential, Joyce argues, in a region characterized by heterogenous settlements that reflect the simultaneous operation of multiple forms of organization. Additionally, and significantly, it was precisely this heterogeneity that allowed for the constraining of inequality that is so unique to the region. To illustrate this point, Joyce contrasts processes of inequality development at Copán with those at Cerro Palenque and Travesia in northwestern Honduras. While inequality existed at the latter two sites, relative inequality—that is, the degree of difference between classes—was less. Heterogeneity—that is, the distribution of populations between social groups—indicates that the structure of power was heterarchical: instead of expanding the hierarchy by creating new levels within a single power structure, new hierarchies of power were created. Ultimately, it was the differentiation of power, and the independence of those domains, that restrained inequality across the region and led to greater stability among Honduran societies than their Maya neighbors during the Late/Terminal Classic.

The volume concludes with chapter 14, written by Edward Schortman and Patricia Urban, who were among the first to examine Southeastern Mesoamerica under a new light in a series of articles and an edited volume (Schortman and Urban 1994; Schortman et al. 1986; Urban and Schortman 1986). Their work has inspired and challenged many others working in the region. In this concluding synthesis, Schortman and Urban summarize the common goals and themes of the other chapters in the volume, pointing to collective advances in methods and theory as well as enduring problems in Southeastern Mesoamerican research. They argue that many of the lingering issues facing the region are a result of how early work drew the southeast border and led to assumptions that not much was to be learned from the small-scale societies located beyond it, resulting in the lag in research in comparison to the Maya region that is still apparent today. Relatedly, groups beyond the border, as well as the scholars who study them, are still often defined only relative to the Maya. In defining groups in their own right, they argue, contributors to the volume are helping to shed light on the varied social and political forms and strategies that existed in the region at various levels and were enacted by different players, resulting in the material patterns we find today. This ties into Schortman and Urban's broader point that our units of analysis are crucial to shaping how we conceptualize these interactions and the material patterns they produce. While previous work in the region has tended to privilege the importance of hierarchically structured relations, contributions to this volume emphasize the importance and prevalence of heterarchically organized political and social interactions. This encourages multiscalar perspectives that are better able to detect and describe networks and identities that cross-cut traditionally understood groups and boundaries. To accompany these new understandings, and to be able to trace and discuss them effectively, new terms and definitions are required to be able to capture the unfolding complexity of the past as it is revealed through new investigations. While these steps are difficult, Schortman and Urban contend that they are necessary for moving research forward and making it more achievable through the collection and sharing of comparable data across the region. As we work towards this goal, scholars in the region are collectively contributing to understanding broad questions concerning Southeastern Mesoamerica—ones that have evolved from simplistic notions of who was and was not Maya, to anthropologically significant concerns with how small-scale societies act and react to large and expansive states in ways that shaped their local trajectories in meaningful ways, particularly where they were able to avoid the development of local political centralization and hierarchies. Schortman and Urban's chapter makes clear that while our understanding of the region has changed in significant ways, the central tenet of the work here has remained the same: Southeastern Mesoamerica has lessons to teach us about the nature of frontier and border interactions that are relevant beyond the region.

ACKNOWLEDGMENTS

We would first like to thank all of those who participated in the original SAA symposium. While the participants were too numerous for all to have contributed to the volume, we believe the gathering together of so many active scholars in the region resulted in important sharing of data and lively discussions that helped to produce this volume. We would especially like to thank all of the contributors to the volume, who patiently worked with us, and often guided us, throughout this long process and who took to heart our goal of having the individual chapters speak to each other. We are also grateful to Edward Schortman and Patricia Urban for inspiring the original symposium and for taking on the task of writing the conclusion to the volume. We also wish to thank the Honduran Institute of Anthropology and History (IHAH) for the various forms of support given to the authors of the book, including IHAH directors Margarita Durón, Vito Véliz, Ricardo Agurcia, Darío Euraque, and Virgilio Paredes. Finally, we extend our thanks to Jessica d'Arbonne, Charlotte Steinhardt, and Darrin Pratt at the University Press of Colorado for seeing value in our volume and for their constant encouragement throughout this long process.

WORKS CITED

Andrews, E. Wyllys. 1976. *The Archaeology of Quelepa, El Salvador*. New Orleans, LA: Middle American Research Institute.

Ashmore, Wendy, Edward M. Schortman, and Patricia A. Urban. 1982. The Classic Maya Fringe: Cultural Boundaries in the Southeast Mesoamerican Periphery. Paper presented at the 81st meeting of the American Anthropological Association, Washington, DC.

Baudez, Claude. 1970. *Central America*. Geneva, Switzerland: Nagel Publishers.

Boone, Elizabeth Hill, and Gordon R. Willey. 1988. *The Southeast Classic Maya Zone*. Washington, DC: Dumbarton Oaks Research Library and Collection.

Creamer, Winifred. 1987. "Mesoamerica as a Concept: An Archaeological View from Central America." *Latin American Research Review* 22(1):35–62.

Creamer, Winifred, and Jonathan Haas. 1985. "Tribe vs. Chiefdom in Lower Central America." *American Antiquity* 50(4):738–754.

Demarest, Arthur A. 1988. "Political Evolution in the Maya Borderlands: The Salvadoran Frontier." In *The Southeast Classic Maya Zone*, ed. Elizabeth Hill Boone and Gordon R. Willey, 335–394. Washington, DC: Dumbarton Oaks Research Library and Collection.

Fajardo, Carmen Julia, and Kevin Ávalos, eds. 2004. *Memoria del VII Seminario de antropología de Honduras "Dr. George Hasemann."* Tegucigalpa, Honduras: Instituto Hondureño de Antropología e Historia.

Fajardo, Carmen Julia, and Alejandro J. Figueroa. 2004. *Memoria del VIII Seminario de antropología de Honduras*. CD-ROM. Tegucigalpa, Honduras: Instituto Hondureño de Antropología e Historia.

Fowler, William R., ed. 1991. *The Formation of Complex Society in Southeastern Mesoamerica*. Boca Raton, FL: CRC Press.

Fox, John W. 1981. "The Late Postclassic Eastern Frontier of Mesoamerica: Cultural Innovation Along the Periphery." *Current Anthropology* 22(4):321–346.

Glass, John B. 1966. "Archaeological Survey of Western Honduras." In *Archaeological Frontiers and External Connections*, ed. Gordon F. Ekholm and Gordon R. Willey, 157–179. *Handbook of Middle American Indians*, Volume 4, gen. ed. Robert Wauchope. Austin: University of Texas Press.

Graham, Mark Miller, ed. 1993 *Reinterpreting the Prehistory of Central America*. Niwot, CO: University Press of Colorado.

Hasemann, George, Gloria Lara-Pinto, and Fernando Cruz Sandoval. 1996. *Los indios de Centroamérica*. Madrid, Spain: Editorial MAPFRE.

Hay, Clarence L., Samuel K. Lothrop, Ralph L. Linton, Harry L. Shapiro, and George C. Vaillant, eds. 1940. *The Maya and Their Neighbors*. New York: Appleton-Century.

Healy, Paul F. 1984. "Northeast Honduras: A Pre-Columbian Frontier Zone." In *Recent Developments in Isthmian Archaeology: Advances in the Prehistory of Lower Central America*, ed. Frederick W. Lange, 227–242. Oxford, UK: BAR.

Healy, Paul F. 1992. "Ancient Honduras: Power, Wealth, and Rank in Early Chiefdoms." In *Wealth and Hierarchy in the Intermediate Area*, ed. Frederick W. Lange, 85–108. Washington, DC: Dumbarton Oaks Research Library and Collection.

Healy, Paul F., Frank Asaro, Fred Stross, and Helen Michel. 1996. "Precolumbian Obsidian Trade in the Northern Intermediate Area: Elemental Analysis of Artifacts from Honduras and Nicaragua." In *Paths to Central American Prehistory*, ed. Frederick W. Lange, 271–284. Niwot, CO: University Press of Colorado.

Helms, Mary W., and Franklin O. Loveland, eds. 1976. *Frontier Adaptations in Lower Central America*. Philadelphia, PA: Institute for the Study of Human Issues.

Henderson, John S., and Marilyn Beaudry-Corbett. 1993. *Pottery of Prehistoric Honduras: Regional Classification and Analysis*. Los Angeles, CA: UCLA Institute of Archaeology.

Hirth, Kenneth, Gloria Lara-Pinto, and George Hasemann, eds. 1989. *Archaeological Research in the El Cajón Region*. Tegucigalpa, Honduras: Instituto Hondureño de Antropología e Historia.

Joyce, Rosemary A. 1988. "The Ulua Valley and the Coastal Maya Lowlands: The View from Cerro Palenque." In *The Southeast Classic Maya Zone*, ed. Elizabeth Hill Boone and Gordon R. Willey, 269–296. Washington, DC: Dumbarton Oaks Research Library and Collection.

Joyce, Rosemary A. 1993. "The Construction of the Mesoamerican Frontier and the Mayoid Image of Honduran Polychromes." In *Reinterpreting the Prehistory of Central America*, ed. Mark Miller Graham, 51–102. Niwot, CO: University Press of Colorado.

Joyce, Rosemary A. 1996. "Social Dynamics of Exchange: Changing Patterns in the Honduran Archaeological Record." In *Chieftains, Power and Trade: Regional Interaction in the Intermediate Area of the Americas*, ed. Carl Henrik Langeback and Felipe Cardenas-Arroyo, 31–46. Bogota, Colombia: Departamento de Antropologia, Universidad de los Andes.

Kirchoff, Paul. 1943. "Mesoamerica." *Acta Americana* 1(1):92–107.

Kirchoff, Paul. 1952. "Mesoamerica: Its Geographic Limits, Ethnic Composition and Cultural Characteristics." In *Heritage of Conquest: The Ethnology of Middle America*, ed. Sol Tax, 17–30. Glencoe: Free Press.

Kirchoff, Paul. 1960. "Mesoamérica: Sus límites geográficos, composición étnica y caracteres culturales." Suplemento de la revista *Tlatoani* 3:1–12.

Kroeber, Alfred L. 1939. *Cultural and Natural Areas of Native North America*. Berkeley: University of California Press.

Lange, Frederick W. 1976. "The Northern Central American Buffer: A Current Perspective." *Latin American Research Review* 11(2):177–183.

Lange, Frederick W. 1979. "Theoretical and Descriptive Aspects of Frontier Studies." *Latin American Research Review* 14(1):221–227.

Lange, Frederick W., ed. 1984. *Recent Developments in Isthmian Archaeology: Advances in the Prehistory of Lower Central America*. Oxford, UK: BAR.

Lange, Frederick W. 1992. *Wealth and Hierarchy in the Intermediate Area* Washington, DC: Dumbarton Oaks Research Library and Collection.

Lange, Frederick W. 1993. "The Conceptual Structure in Lower Central American Studies: A Central American View." In *Reinterpreting the Prehistory of Central America*, ed. Mark Miller Graham, 277–324. Niwot, CO: University Press of Colorado.

Lange, Frederick W. 1996. *Paths to Central American Prehistory*. Niwot, CO: University Press of Colorado.

Lange, Frederick W., and Doris S. Stone, eds. 1984. *The Archaeology of Lower Central America*. Albuquerque: University of New Mexico Press.

Linares, Olga F. 1979. "What Is Lower Central American Archaeology?" *Annual Review of Anthropology* 8:21–43.

Longyear, John M., III. 1947. *Cultures and Peoples of the Southeastern Maya Frontier*. Washington, DC: Carnegie Institution of Washington.

Lothrop, Samuel K. 1939. "The Southeastern Frontier of the Maya." *American Anthropologist* 41(1):42–54.

Martínez, Eva, ed. 2012. *Arqueología y comunidades en Honduras*. Tegucigalpa, Honduras: Instituto Hondureño de Antropología e Historia.

Robinson, Eugenia J., ed. 1987. *Interaction on the Southeast Mesoamerican Frontier: Prehistoric and Historic Honduras and El Salvador*. Oxford, UK: BAR.

Sauer, Carl O. 1959. "Middle America as Culture Historical Location." In *Actas del XXXIII Congreso de Americanistas*, 115–22. San José, Costa Rica: Lehmann.

Schortman, Edward M., and Wendy Ashmore. 2012. "History, Networks, and the Quest for Power: Ancient Political Competition in the Lower Motagua Valley, Guatemala." *Journal of the Royal Anthropological Institute* 18(1):1–21.

Schortman, Edward M., and Seiichi Nakamura. 1991. "A Crisis of Identity: Late Classic Competition and Interaction on the Southeast Maya Periphery." *Latin American Antiquity* 2(4):311–336.

Schortman, Edward M., and Patricia A. Urban. 1986. "Introduction." In *The Southeast Maya Periphery*, ed. Patricia A. Urban and Edward M. Schortman, 1–16. Austin: University of Texas Press.

Schortman, Edward M., and Patricia A. Urban. 1994. "Living on the Edge: Core/Periphery Relations in Ancient Southeastern Mesoamerica." *Current Anthropology* 35(4):401–430.

Schortman, Edward M., and Patricia A. Urban. 1996. "Actions at a Distance, Impacts at Home: Prestige Good Theory and a Pre-Columbian Polity in Southeastern Mesoamerica." *Pre-Columbian World Systems*, ed. Peter N. Peregrine, 97–114. Madison, WI: Prehistory Press.

Schortman, Edward M., and Patricia A. Urban. 1999. "Thoughts on the Periphery: The Ideological Consequences of Core/Periphery Relations." In *World-Systems Theory in Practice: Leadership, Production, and Exchange*, ed. Nick P. Kardulias, 125–152. Lanham, MD: Rowman and Littlefield.

Schortman, Edward M., Patricia A. Urban, Wendy Ashmore, and Julie Benyo. 1986. "Interregional Interaction in the SE Maya Periphery: The Santa Barbara Archaeological Project." *Journal of Field Archaeology* 13(3):259–272.

Sharer, Robert J. 1974. "The Prehistory of the Southeastern Maya Periphery." *Current Anthropology* 15(2):165–187.

Sharer, Robert J. 1978. *The Prehistory of Chalchuapa, El Salvador*. Philadelphia: University of Pennsylvania Press.

Sharer, Robert J. 1984. "Lower Central America as Seen from Mesoamerica." In *The Archaeology of Lower Central America*, ed. Frederick W. Lange and Doris S. Stone, 63–84. Albuquerque: University of New Mexico Press.

Sharer, Robert J. 1992. "Variations of a Theme: A Frontier View of Maya Civilization." In *New Theories on the Ancient Maya*, ed. Eric C. Danien and Robert J. Sharer, 161–171. Philadelphia: University of Pennsylvania University Museum.

Sheets, Payson D. 1979. "Maya Recovery from Volcanic Disasters: Ilopango and Cerén." *Archaeology* 32(1):32–42.

Sheets, Payson D. 1982. *Volcanism and the Archaeology of Central America*. New York: Academic Press.

Sheets, Payson D. 1992. "The Pervasive Pejorative in Intermediate Area Studies." In *Wealth and Hierarchy in the Intermediate Area*, ed. Frederick W. Lange, 15–42. Washington, DC: Dumbarton Oaks Research Library and Collection.

Smith, Michael E., and Cynthia M. Heath-Smith. 1980. "Waves of Influence in Postclassic Mesoamerica? A Critique of the Mixteca-Puebla Concept." *Anthropology* 4(2):15–50.

Spinden, Herbert J. 1924. "The Chorotegan Culture Area." In *Proceedings of the Twenty-First International Congress of Americanists*, 529–545. The Hague, Netherlands: Kraus.

Stone, Doris Z. 1957. *The Archaeology of Central and Southern Honduras*. Cambridge, MA: Peabody Museum.

Strong, William Duncan. 1935. *Archaeological investigations in the Bay Islands, Spanish Honduras*. Smithsonian Institution, Washington, DC.

Thompson, J. Eric S. 1970. "The Eastern Boundary of the Maya Area: Placements and Displacements." In *Maya History and Religion*, ed. J. Eric S. Thompson, 84–102. Washington, DC: Smithsonian Institution.

Urban, Patricia A., and Edward M. Schortman, eds. 1986. *The Southeast Maya Periphery*. Austin: University of Texas Press.

Urban, Patricia A., and Edward M. Schortman. 1988. "The Southeast Zone Viewed from the East: Lower Motagua-Naco Valleys." In *The Southeast Classic Maya Zone*, ed. Elizabeth Hill Boone and Gordon R. Willey, 223–268. Washington, DC: Dumbarton Oaks Research Library and Collection.

Wallerstein, Immanuel. 1976. *The Modern World System I: Capitalist Agriculture and the Origins of the European World-Economy in the Sixteenth Century*. New York: Academic Press.

Wallerstein, Immanuel. 1980. *The Modern World System II: Mercantilism and the Consolidation of the European World-Economy, 1600–1750*. New York: Academic Press.

Willey, Gordon R. 1984. "A Summary of the Archaeology of Lower Central America." In *The Archaeology of Lower Central America*, ed. Frederick W. Lange and Doris S. Stone, 341–378. Albuquerque: University of New Mexico Press.

Willey, Gordon R., Gordon F. Ekholm, and Rene F. Millon. 1964. "The Patterns of Farming Life and Civilization." In *Handbook of Middle American Indians*, ed. Robert Wauchope and Robert C. West, 446–498. Austin: University of Texas Press.

2

This chapter assesses the long-term history of use of the highlands of southwestern Honduras as it relates to the transition from Preceramic foragers to Formative Lenca farmers. The focus is environmentally possibilistic (Kormondy and Brown 1998:44), and our discussion emphasizes the reflexive relationship between human behavior and the total (physical and social) environment. In this view, subsistence adaptation is a form of niche construction (Odling-Smee et al. 2003), an idea that has been promoted for some time (Yen 2014). We seek this approach to give a holistic picture of Honduras's deep past, integrating the economic practices, resource heterogeneity, and belief systems into a dynamic vision of an "ethnographic landscape" (Egan 2003:260). Moreover, our evidence supports the assertion that Southeastern Mesoamerica, and indeed much of the Americas, share common biocultural elements of subsistence and ritual behavior that can tentatively be traced back to the early Holocene.

Our research in southwestern Honduras suggests that people are not only a product of their surroundings but also the producers of landscapes. In this context, the landscape is the significant human niche. A landscape-level analysis has been presented previously by Lara-Pinto and Hasemann (2000) with respect to Honduran prehistory, and we seek to provide a similar analysis of the oldest occupied landscape in Honduras known to date. Cultural landscapes are composed of physical characteristics and available resources, the

Integrating the Prehistoric Natural and Social Landscapes of the Highlands of Southwest Honduras

A Deep History

ALEJANDRO J. FIGUEROA
AND TIMOTHY SCHEFFLER

DOI: 10.5876/9781646420971.c002

dynamic yet historically contingent ecological configuration of the land, and, most important, the social relationships that frame and are framed by these physical elements (Anschuetz et al. 2001; Basso 1996; David and Thomas 2008; David and Wilson 2002). In this sense, the line between a culture's concept of the ritual landscape and the subsistence landscape is blurred. Using the cumulative results of recent surveys and excavations in the highlands of southwestern Honduras, we integrate independent lines of evidence to shed light on both the ritual and subsistence aspects of the landscape of this area.

What we know about the Preceramic period in Honduras—which encompasses the Paleoindian and Archaic periods (11,000–4,000 BP, or 9000–2000 BC)—has been defined on the one hand by opportunistic and isolated finds throughout the country, and on the other, by a series of systematic research projects conducted in southwestern Honduras. Outside of this area, evidence of human activity predating the Formative period (3,500–2,000 BP) is limited to undated contexts that either lack ceramics or are stratigraphically below early ceramic contexts, as in the case of a subceramic stratum at Copán (Longyear 1948). Another example is Bullen and Plowden's (1963) survey of aceramic sites near the city of La Esperanza, which recovered the fluted base of a biface, described by some as a possible Clovis-like point (Sheets et al. 1990:145). Because little is known regarding the diagnostic artifacts of the Preceramic period in Mesoamerica and much of Central America, absolute dates remain the sole indicator of this period in Honduras.

Despite significant research in southeastern Mesoamerica, the Archaic and Paleoindian periods have received little attention. However, as emphasized recently for the broader lowland Maya region (Lohse 2010), the precursors to the central cultural, economic, and demographic markers of later "Classic" civilizations lie in these early millennia. These behavioral changes included the development of sedentism and the diversification of the diet, which in some places resulted in the region's earliest domesticates. While we know these significant shifts took place both here and in several other areas of the globe, questions remain as to the specific contexts and circumstances of this process in southwestern Honduras. Were populations here pushed to settle down and take up agriculture, and if so, by what factors? Or, conversely, were these major behavioral changes proactive choices as a result of long-term knowledge of the surrounding landscape? What role did environmental change, demographic change (i.e., population growth), and human agency (e.g., through landscape modification) play? Our goal with this chapter is to begin to address these questions by proposing some possible factors and contexts that led to and conditioned these major cultural and environmental changes in southwestern

Honduras during the Preceramic period, and how these changes were expressed locally later in prehistory.

THE PHYSICAL LANDSCAPE

The defining physiographic feature of southwestern Honduras is the Chinacla River, a major system that belongs to the Río Lempa drainage, which runs to the Southwest towards El Salvador and empties into the Pacific coast. The bedrock of this area is composed of a geological unit formed by Miocene and Pliocene eruptions known as the "Grupo Padre Miguel," which contributes geomorphologically to the undercutting and scouring of deep tuff formations. The Chinacla and its various tributaries downcut this volcanic substrate for millennia, resulting in a series of sharp mountains (known as the Sierra de La Paz), steep cliffs, and small intermontane valleys (Kozuch 1991). Because of this high topographic relief and dynamic erosional processes, these highlands are considered a marginal landscape for intensive agriculture and large-scale settlement, with none of the enriching benefits of flood-derived soils of lower elevations. However, as a function of its unique volcanic geology and hydrology, the area is rife with habitable caves and rockshelters, which are natural sites for the accumulation and concentration of human activities (Collins 1991). When combined with the proximity to sources of water and other desirable resources, these sites can become central places (*sensu* Cannon 2003; Winterhalder and Kennett 2006; Zeanah 2000) on the landscape where human populations can meet their everyday needs.

One final but critical physiographic feature of the landscape is an abundance of high-quality lithic sources, the most important of which is the La Esperanza obsidian source (Sorensen and Hirth 1984; see also Aoyama et al. 1999; Saunders 2001; Sheets 1989; Sheets et al. 1990). This source is unique in the region because it is widespread and heterogeneous, with the possibility of several outcrops existing throughout the southwest highlands. This landscape also has localized outcrops of other high-quality cryptocrystalline stone such as chert, jasper, and chalcedony, all of which appear to have been used by local populations as far back as the earliest Holocene (Figueroa 2014; Scheffler 1998, 1999, 2001, 2008; Scheffler et al. 2012).

THE ECOLOGICAL LANDSCAPE

Fine-grained paleoecological and paleoenvironmental data are currently unavailable for southwestern Honduras and the highlands of southern

Mesoamerica. However, paleoclimatic and paleoenvironmental research in the tropical forests spanning southern Mexico to western Colombia suggests that the Pleistocene/Holocene transition was characterized by a shift from dry and cold to wet and warm conditions (Correa-Metrio et al. 2012; Hodell et al. 2000; Markgraf 1989; Schmidt et al. 2004). In the lowlands of Central America, these climatic changes resulted in a reduction of grasslands-savannah-forest mosaics in favor of denser and more homogeneous tropical and subtropical forests, which are less productive environments for humans because the majority of their biomass is inedible and because they support lower densities of animal prey (Bernal et al. 2011; Pérez et al. 2013; Piperno and Pearsall 1998). In the lesser-known highlands, these climatic and ecological changes could have been more heterogeneous, as we explain below.

Modern ecological work in southwestern Honduras has classified it as a "tropical evergreen seasonal montane forest" (Vreugdenhil et al. 2002:51), with a high degree of biodiversity given its diverse herbaceous understory and relatively intact watercourses (House et al. 2002). Pedestrian surveys of the area conducted by Scheffler (1998, 1999, 2001) and Figueroa (2006, 2014) recorded moderate to strong relief, shallow volcanic soils, large swaths of exposed bedrock, and a highly marked seasonal rain cycle, all of which are conducive to both dense and relatively patchy tropical and subtropical forests (Castellanos et al. 1962). Variations in elevation, topography, soil composition, and rainfall could have combined to form pine-oak parklands, alpine savannahs, cloud forests, and riverine habitats, all closely packed together starting in the Pleistocene/ Holocene transition, though this remains to be evaluated (Castellanos et al. 1962; Holdridge 1962).

Our survey work in the southwestern highlands has thus far identified 38 caves and rockshelters in an area of less than 350 km^2 (figure 2.1). Culturally derived materials indicating human occupation and/or ritual use were present in every single one of them (Figueroa 2006, 2014; Scheffler 1998). While we have carried out test excavations at several of these sites, the El Gigante rockshelter is the only site in this area that has been the subject of systematic archaeological research, and excavations within it show it has exceptional preservation and time depth (table 2.1; Kennett et al. 2017; Scheffler 1999, 2001, 2008; Scheffler et al. 2012).

Initial analyses of El Gigante's lithic, faunal, and botanical assemblages (Scheffler 2008) concluded that its inhabitants practiced a resilient subsistence regime in an area not classified as a center of domestication (Harlan 1971). The diet of its inhabitants included as major components perennial crops such as avocado (*Persea americana*), bottle gourd (*Lagenaria siceraria*),

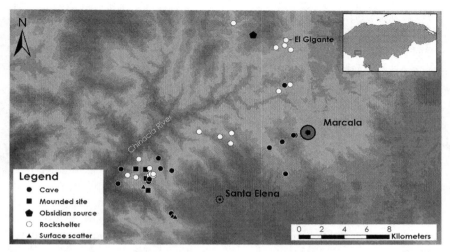

FIGURE 2.1. *Archaeological sites recorded in the highlands of southwestern Honduras.*

TABLE 2.1. Cultural horizons at El Gigante (EG)

Date Range (cal BP)	Cultural Horizon (EG)	Cultural Horizon (Mesoamerica)
11,010–10,220	Early Esperanza	Paleoindian
10,160–9550	Late Esperanza	Paleoindian
8990–7670	Early Marcala	Paleoindian/Archaic
7610–7430	Middle Marcala	Archaic
4340–4020	Late Marcala	Archaic
3390–2780	Early Estanzuela	Middle Formative
2350–1820	Middle Estanzuela	Late Formative
1280–980	Late Estanzuela	Classic

hog plum or ciruela (*Spondias* sp.), sapotaceae (*Manilkara* sp. and *Sideroxylon* sp.), and maguey or agave (*Agave americana*), alongside a wide variety of faunal resources from terrestrial and aquatic habitats. This mixed and extensive subsistence strategy was adaptively stable for millennia, as evidenced by the relatively late introduction of agriculture in this area (Kennett et al. 2017). Interestingly, these results are consistent with climate trends towards more-humid forested habitats. Given the trophic structure and resulting distribution of biomass, these circumstances would favor a shift to lower-rank, vegetable foods that could be foraged more efficiently.

To date, 51 direct AMS dates have been run on the maize samples from El Gigante (Blake and Benz 2010; Kennett et al. 2017). Results confirm that domesticated corn was introduced to the area no earlier than ca. 4300 BP These dates indicate a late introduction of permanent field crops to the highlands of southwestern Honduras. This is especially true if compared with other documented cases across Mesoamerica. In the Río Balsas Valley of Mexico, for example, believed to be the center of maize domestication, microbotanical analysis suggests a domesticated introduction by ca. 8700 BP (Piperno et al. 2009). In early agricultural centers in highland Mexico, such as Guila Naquitz (Piperno and Flannery 2001), the earliest dates for maize established by direct AMS dates are ca. 6250 BP, while maize specimens at Tehuacan have been redated directly to 5450 BP (Long et al. 1989). Further south, maize pollen at Cob Swamp in Belize was dated to 5000 BP (Pohl et al. 1996). Early dates have also been established south in Costa Rica at 5500 BP (Horn 2016), in Colombia at around 7000 BP (Aceituno and Loaiza 2014), and in highland and lowland contexts of Ecuador to 6000 BP (Athens et al. 2016). The dates obtained from the El Gigante specimens are more consistent with the estimates provided for the Copán and Yojoa regions, which place the introduction of maize at Copán to 4600–4700 BP and at Yojoa to ca. 4500–3000 BP (Rue 1989; Rue et al. 2002; Webster et al. 2005).

Research suggests the initial focus on maize as a cultivar may have been for purposes other than its inflorescence, for example as a hardy and reliable source of sugary juices (Iltis 2000, 2006; Smalley and Blake 2003). In this scenario, commonly known as the "Iltis hypothesis," the intensive selection and resulting domestication of maize may have been in the context of an agricultural supplement, since the appearance of maize often predates the onset of intensive agriculture and sedentism in paleoenvironmental records (Blake et al. 1992; Iltis 2000, 2006). We believe existing data from El Gigante may support this scenario, given the relatively late appearance of maize and its gradual inclusion within the varied and stable economy of the mixed foraging and horticultural subsistence system of the area's inhabitants.

The maize specimens discussed above are only a small part of the large and well-preserved macrobotanical assemblage recovered from El Gigante. The materials recovered from the main block of excavations at this site have only been preliminarily analyzed (Scheffler 2008), though an in-depth analysis is presently ongoing at the Pennsylvania State University (see Hirth et al. 2018). Preliminary analyses identified 19,419 specimens, including 16 taxa and 49 unidentified morphotypes. These analyses show there is a high degree of

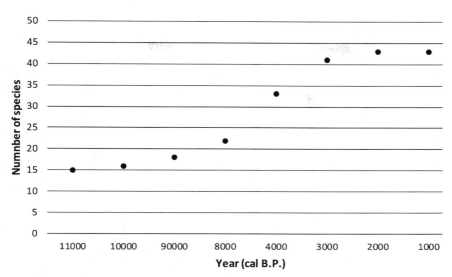

FIGURE 2.2. *Macrobotanical assemblage richness from El Gigante.*

correlation (r = 0.834) between the macrobotanical NISP and the species richness (total number of species present) through time (figure 2.2). This is not
surprising, because preservation and taphonomy both act to reduce the numbers of identifiable specimens over time. Also, nearly 3,000 specimens were
represented in the materials belonging to the late Formative, while only 70
individual specimens represent the earliest chronological phase.

In order to assess patterns in diet through time as represented by the archae-
ological assemblage, the inverse of Simpson's diversity index, or $D = 1 - \Sigma(pi)^2$
(Simpson 1949) was calculated for each discrete cultural period (figure 2.3).
This diversity index measures the *evenness* of an assemblage, which is the relative or proportional importance (p) of each species represented in the diet (i).
As such, it has been utilized as a proxy for diet breadth (e.g., Stiner et al. 2012).
A full discussion of the middle-range theory and confounding factors inherent in the application of diversity measures to archaeological assemblages is
beyond the scope of this chapter (see Leonard and Jones 1989; Meltzer et al.
1992). The measure is used here as one strand of multiple lines of independent
evidence supporting our thesis.

One of the advantages of the Simpson diversity index is that it controls—to
a certain degree—for variable sample sizes, such as those in our dataset.
Typically, a high index value signals a rich and diverse diet, while a low index

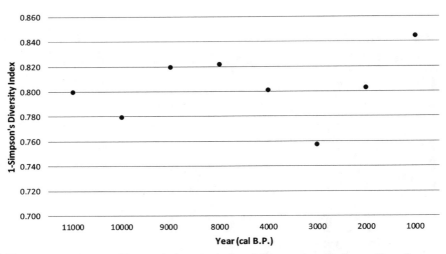

Figure 2.3. *Inverse of Simpson's diversity index of the macrobotanical assemblage from El Gigante.*

value is indicative of a less diverse or narrower diet. In contrast to the richness of the assemblage, the diversity of El Gigante's botanical assemblage is much less significantly correlated with total recovery numbers (r = 0.294), lending significance to the emerging pattern, which we discuss below.

The Simpson diversity index for the El Gigante macrobotanical assemblage shows an early rising trend followed by a steep decline beginning in the Early Marcala phase. It reaches its lowest point during the Early Estanzuela phase (ca. 3000 cal BP), which follows the earliest available date for maize at ca. 4230 cal BP and climbs again in the Middle and Late Estanzuela phases. The data and results we present are preliminary, and many factors likely played a role in the decline and subsequent rise in the diversity of El Gigante's macrobotanical assemblage. We offer several scenarios that are congruent with other lines of evidence obtained from the site and its surrounding region, though these will need to be evaluated by future studies.

First, it is plausible that botanical diversity near El Gigante was affected by local or regional climatic patterns, which led to a decrease in ecological diversity in the region (Piperno and Pearsall 1998). This, however, remains to be tested. Perhaps most likely, drops in assemblage diversity might be the result of gaps in the occupational history of the rockshelter, since they are chronologically coincident with these. However, occupational gaps aside, the diversity of the assemblage generally increases over time. Scheffler (2008:227) has previously noted that El Gigante's inhabitants continuously added items to their diet without making any obvious replacements. Maize, in this case, could have been one more item added to a dietary regime which continued to grow in diversity over time as local populations learned to utilize more resources. This pattern of increased use of local resources over time has also been observed in preliminary analyses of the site's faunal and lithic materials (Scheffler 2008).

Based on these results, we hypothesize that during the latter half of the Marcala phase, local populations maintained a high-quality diet by transitioning to a more intensive, field-based economy, achievable through the planting of the maize-beans-squash triad. The political economy of these groups could have been reoriented towards the potential for surplus production following regional trends (Lentz et al. 1997; Rue 1989). This could have led to even more permanent attachments to the land and the rise of ascribed status and the association of certain groups to permanent plots, which is indicative of contact-period Lenca groups (Chapman 1978; Gómez, chapter 11, this volume; Lara-Pinto 1991; chapter 10, this volume). This process is envisaged as having operated as a sort of feedback loop, where even minor incremental changes in either landscape configuration or diet affected the balance of the other. In addition, we believe this was conditioned in part by the agricultural marginality of the highlands landscape, which directed energy towards risk-averse strategies rather than surplus-maximizing ones (*sensu* Winterhalder 1986). These strategies included the maintenance of a mixed foraging and horticultural way of life, which the Lenca inhabitants of the area largely maintain to this day (Figueroa 2014; Scheffler 1998).

Arboriculture and Landscape Modification at El Gigante

Among the myriad taxa recovered from El Gigante, the avocado (*Persea americana*) remains the best evidence for the practice of agroforestry and for the operation of selective pressures and domestication occurring throughout the entire history of occupation of this shelter. This tree has been of particular interest for some time because of its economic importance, and avocado research has continued in the agronomic and ethnoecological fields (Galindo-Tovar et al. 2007; Galindo-Tovar et al. 2008; Gama-Campillo and Gómez-Pompa 1992; Landon 2009). Avocado remains have been found in Preceramic contexts in highland Colombia dating to ca. 10,000 BP (Gnecco 2000). Based on these and other results, it has been hypothesized that Preceramic populations cultivated and domesticated avocado because of its resilience and high nutritional value (Piperno and Pearsall 1998).

There are three horticultural varieties of avocado: a Mexican (*Persea americana* var. *drymifolia* Blake), a Guatemalan (*P. americana* var. *guatemalensis* Williams), and a West Indian (*P. americana* var. *americana* Miller) variety. Genetic studies of 33 modern cultivars derived from these three stocks confirm this classification (Chen et al. 2009). These studies have shown that the wild ancestral populations of these modern cultivars were polymorphic and geographically widespread. Given the southwestern-highland context of El Gigante, it is likely that the specimens from this site are cultivars ancestral to the Guatemalan variety (see Hamilton and Reichard 1992 for taxonomic distinction between cultivars and varieties).

At El Gigante, the entire dicot seed, single cotyledons, as well as stem and rind fragments of avocados were commonly recovered. The first of these occurred in stratum VIIa, dated to the initial occupation of the shelter (Esperanza phase, 11,010–10,220 BP). Avocado remained a consistent component of the macrobotanical assemblage through the earliest of Archaic times until the Formative, a span of 9,450 years. A sample of 42 whole seeds and/or cotyledon fragments were measured for morphometric analysis by Scheffler (2008). These came from 15 distinct strata, spanning the entire cultural sequence of the site. Two standard metrics were recorded: the length of the long axis and the diameter at the midsection. A seed-size index, the product of these two measurements and a robust indicator of overall fruit volume (*sensu* Smith 1967), was calculated for 30 intact specimens (table 2.2; figure 2.4).

A simple one-way analysis of variance, which compares the means of multiple samples, shows that there are statistically significant differences between the four chronologically ordered data sets ($p = .05$). With such small sample sizes, a normal distribution could not necessarily be assumed. Therefore, a nonparametric Kruskall-Wallis test was performed. This test, emphasizing the modal characteristics of the samples, resulted in a similar significance ($p = .05$). Assessing the distribution in this manner substantiates the overall trend towards larger cotyledon size through time. However, as can be seen in table 2.2, the coefficients of variation (CV) for size indices show no significant change over time. CV's in the range of 30 percent emphasize the polymorphic and variable nature of this tree species.

Variation in the cotyledon-length measurement was modeled using parametric linear regression methods. When age is modeled against length a significant relationship is revealed ($p = .009$). The R^2 value (.175) indicates that nearly a fifth of the variance in the assemblage is explained by the passage of time and a significant slope (β) indicates positive selection for seed length (a proxy for fruit size).

TABLE 2.2. El Gigante avocado seed-size index results and descriptive statistics

Cultural Horizon	n (= 30)	Mean	Std dev	Min	Max	CV (%)
Esperanza	6	457.04	125.39	345.24	689.59	27.44
Marcala	4	367.28	111.01	249.57	496.93	30.22
Early Estanzuela	6	411.75	126.15	248.75	556.93	30.64
Late Estanzuela	14	552.21	136.43	355.6	793.9	24.71
Mean		480.43	142.88	248.75	793.9	29.74

Source: Scheffler 2008.

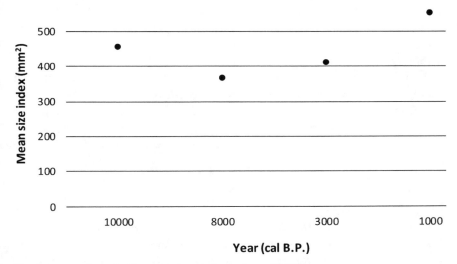

FIGURE 2.4. *Avocado (*Persea *sp.) seed-size index at El Gigante.*

Based on these results we conclude that avocados were subject to artificial and disruptive selection (Pianka 2000) at El Gigante since their initial use in the early Holocene. The plants' mean phenotype is shown to have shifted. Several implications can be derived from these results. First, avocado trees are "small-gap specialists" (Wolstenholme and Whiley 1999:9) and thrive in early successional habitats such as those following tree falls, selective clearings, or burns. Burning and clearing are two activities that began as early as the Terminal Pleistocene in the tropical forests of Chiapas, Panama, and western Colombia (Acosta Ochoa 2008; Gnecco and Aceituno 2006; Piperno 2011; Piperno et al. 1990). Anthropogenic burning has been detected in later periods in Honduras (Rue 1989; Rue et al. 2002; Webster et al. 2005), yet its occurrence in early Honduran prehistory has yet to be verified. Second, the long-term selection of avocado trees would have made them more predictable and abundant in particular areas. This would have made avocado trees a predictable resource on the landscape of the southwest highlands, reducing the time it took populations to find a nutrient-rich source of food. As resources such as avocado became more predictable, longer stays at El Gigante would have been more advantageous and would have resulted in more-intensive occupations of the shelter over time, a behavior that is supported by existing studies of El Gigante's assemblage.

The archaeological data obtained from El Gigante has enriched our understanding of the peoples who occupied, modified, and lived off the mountainous landscape of southwestern Honduras. The heterogeneous nature of this landscape, in which a variety of ecosystems and their resources overlap and vary within a relatively small area, allowed populations to maintain a rich, varied, and stable diet over millennia as long as extensive tracts of land were available, between which foragers could move and seasonally exploit. The manipulation of tree crops at El Gigante, not exclusively limited to avocado (see Scheffler 2008), was part of a broader resilient and stable subsistence strategy based on the mutualistic and long-term interaction between these populations and their surroundings.

THE RITUAL LANDSCAPE

It is easy to surmise that long-term interactions between people and the landscape of southwestern Honduras led to the development of attachments and relationships to the land that transcended the physical and economic. To assess these areas of past human experience we must rely on a more ethnohistoric approach that extends ethnographically documented practice into the deeper past as evidence permits. At El Gigante, social and ritual behavior was materialized in human burials and rock art (Scheffler 2008). Our research has shown that these two cultural markers of territoriality and of belonging to the land—ossuaries and rock art—are widespread in this area and are a product of the unique local physiography and the Mesoamerican cultures that have occupied it in the past and the present.

Evidence for the use of caves as conduits or portals to the underworld, the world of the dead, in Mesoamerica dates as early as 2600 BP (Brady 2005; Healy 2007; Heyden 2005; Moyes 2012; Prufer and Brady 2005; Stone 1995; Wrobel 2014). For these societies, caves and shelters became important locations for the performance of rituals and other spiritual acts related to the origin and termination of life, namely burials. Long-term research into the use of caves in Mesoamerica shows these groups had a bimodal use for these localities: larger, deeper caves were often reserved for the society's elite, while smaller outlying caves were used by the lower classes (Michael 2016; Moyes and Brady 2012). Over time, caves became shrines for ancestor worship tied to a particular lineage, a practice that continues in the Maya area today (Brown 2005).

Roughly a quarter (*n* = 10) of recorded caves and shelters in the Sierra de La Paz contain human remains, and half of those (*n* = 5) contain the remains of multiple individuals. Human remains are often associated with high-quality imported items such as jadeite and shell beads and polychrome ceramics, all indicative of Classic-period Lenca groups. The ceramics associated with these remains include Ulúa Polychromes belonging to the Yojoa and Nebla classes and date to ca. AD 650–800 (Rosemary Joyce, personal communication, 2018). The study of cave burials in the highlands of southwestern Honduras is very much in its infancy, and no systematic investigations have been carried out in these sites or on these remains. Our interpretations of this material assemblage are therefore preliminary and based solely on surface contexts, which are often disturbed.

Doris Stone (1957:114) called the placement of multiple individuals in ossuaries within caves and rockshelters in southwestern Honduras "the outstanding trait in this area." We believe the burials and ossuaries of the southwestern highlands of Honduras represent a local manifestation of the more general Mesoamerican worldview that tied specific ancestral group identity (and therefore status) to specific aspects of place and memorialized it in significant physical locations. The presence of multiple ossuaries within a relatively small area hints at the importance of collective intra- and intercommunity negotiation of social identity. In addition, the fact that the majority of these burials are of adult individuals suggests that ritual access to these localities was limited to certain parts of the population. Both of these patterns might be a product of the sociopolitical hierarchy of prehispanic Lenca societies, which previous research suggests inhabited this area (Chapman 1978; Lara-Pinto 1991). According to contact-period accounts, Lenca society consisted of chiefs or *señores*, religious and military specialists or *principales*, commoners or *maceguales*, and slaves (Chapman 1978; Gómez, chapter 11, this volume; Lara-Pinto 1991; chapter 10, this volume). Because power relations were not well developed, they resembled a heterarchy (Crumley 1987, 1995; Crumley and Marquardt 1987) in which power and authority were wielded not solely by chiefs but by their *principales* as well, an observation made by several other authors in this volume (Gómez, chapter 11, this volume; Joyce, chapter 13, this

volume; McFarlane and Stockett Suri, chapter 5, this volume). Burials of multiple individuals, in this case, would embody a system that prevented upward
social mobility and emphasized the importance of kin groups by restricting
the use of certain spaces to part of the population, which ongoing studies of
the rock-art sites in the area corroborate (Figueroa 2016).

In the Sierra de La Paz, caves and shelters continue to be sites charged with
ritual meaning and importance. According to the cosmology of thise who
inhabit this area today, caves are the dwelling places of *duendes*, magical creatures who are caretakers and owners of a delimited area—such as a mountain,
pond, or cave—and the plants and animals within it (Chapman 1985). *Duendes*
are either benign or malicious and come in a variety of forms, one of which is
a *Tacayo* or *Litacayo*, a *duende* who inhabits mountains and caves. The Lenca
today also speak of "the people of the past" (*la gente de antes*), who lived in
caves and buried their deceased within them (Chapman 1986:22).

One of the rockshelters recorded during a survey of the area by Figueroa
(2006) had recently been the site of a wake ceremony according to local informants and evidence found within it (figure 2.5). This rockshelter had several
elements that are common in Lenca rituals (Chapman 1985, 1986), including
two wooden crosses decorated with flower bundles and the remains of a small
fire and a meal composed of corn cobs, gourds or *guacales* for drinking *chicha*,
and squash rinds. In addition, two other prehispanic ossuaries recorded in
this area had bones that had been recently rearranged. In one of these, all
of the long bones had been piled together and a palm leaf had been placed
on top. While the palm offering is a typical Lenca practice (Chapman 1985),
the rearrangement of bones does not have a modern analog, though it bears
resemblance to Lacandon Maya rituals in Chiapas (Cucina and Tiesler 2014).
The second ossuary had been originally recorded by Figueroa (2006), and the
bones had been rearranged when the site was revisited in 2013 (Figueroa 2014).

While a significant number of sheltered sites contain human remains, an
even larger number (*n* = 13, or 34%) contain paintings and petroglyphs. The
dating of the rock art in this area is relative and based on image superimpositions, surface associations, and iconography, all of which suggest some
antiquity and the continued reutilization of space. Rock-art sites in the central
Honduran highlands such as Santa Rosa de Tenampúa, Yarales, Las Pintadas,
and Santa Elena de Izopo have been associated with Classic-period societies
due to their symbolic connection and influence from Teotihuacan (Agurcia
1976; Reyes-Mazzoni 1977a, 1977b; Stone 1957). The style and execution of
the rock art in the Sierra de La Paz mountains is incredibly rich and varied.
It depicts pan-Mesoamerican motifs such as an emphasis on serpentiforms

FIGURE 2.5. *Rockshelter where a wake was held: (left) cross with flower bundle and sleeping arrangements for the deceased; (right) sleeping arrangement for the attending.*

(including feathered serpents) and felines, and depictions of maize alongside geometric motifs and zoomorphs with no known cultural affiliation.

A summary of the various rock-art sites found in the Sierra de La Paz mountains is beyond the scope of this chapter. We focus instead on describing the rock art and context of one site, La Pintada de Azacualpa, to highlight some of the stylistic and behavioral patterns we believe are representative of how human populations in this area interacted with and marked their surroundings. At this site, perhaps the largest rock-art site in Honduras with over 200 individual motifs, the number and diversity of images, superimpositions, and material assemblages suggest it was used repeatedly over generations as a place where a community or, more likely, different communities, congregated. La Pintada is composed of a large rock overhang that runs 40 m southwest–northeast and is approximately 13 m high. The site has several levels, each composed of natural incisions into the rock, several of which contain rock art. In terms of its natural context, La Pintada has a relatively large flat surface adjacent to the rock overhang, effectively making this a large rockshelter. Archaeological materials including ceramics and both chipped and ground stone are found on this surface and eroding into the adjacent slope. There is also a small perennial source of water—a small spring—approximately 5 m to the southwest of the shelter. Because of its size, La Pintada can be identified from a distance, and the site is in fact periodically visited by local residents and travelers, who have defaced the rock art and left garbage at the site.

La Pintada has over 200 individual motifs spread across seven different panels (Figueroa 2016; Scheffler 1998). Roughly half of these motifs are of anthropomorphic figures, and the rest are zoomorphs, anthropozoomorphs, and abstract or geometric figures. What calls the most attention to this site is its central panel, composed of a small recess where motifs appear to celebrate the convergence of groups of people at different times and for different motives. The most recent phase of this panel—defined by the superposition of motifs atop earlier ones—includes, on the right side, anthropomorphic figures playing a variety of musical instruments, and on the left side of the panel two anthropomorphic figures with different geometric motifs atop each head (figure 2.6). These figures are painted in the same color—green, which is very rare in the rock art of this area—and we interpret them as representing two groups that are different yet share some common traits. Both the music players and the emblem-carriers are surrounded by dancing zoomorph and anthropozoomorph figures. While we recognize the limitations of ethnographic analogy and our own limited interpretation of the iconography of a single site, we hypothesize that this panel might be a representation of the Lenca *guancasco* ceremony. This is a ritualized practice wherein warring parties established a period of peaceful relations (Chapman 1978; Lara-Pinto, chapter 10, this volume). This practice was limited to groups who spoke the same language, and it served to secure internal peace and strengthen ties between these groups. Interestingly, ethnohistoric documents recount that Santa Elena used to hold a *guancasco* with the town of Eramaní, which no longer exists but which was located near the modern city of La Esperanza (Chapman 1986).

Although our interpretations of the ritual use of the highlands of southwestern Honduras are preliminary and incomplete, we believe these are the practices of populations with deep roots in prehistory and strong attachments to their surroundings. These cultural traditions are also the product of a unique landscape whose rough topography is conducive to cultural isolation and conflict (Gómez, chapter 11, this volume; Lara-Pinto, chapter 10, this volume). The economic defensibility model (Dyson-Hudson and Smith 1978) suggests that systems of territoriality (i.e., defense of a territory and its resources) are conditioned by the density and dependability of resources on a landscape. This model predicts that dense and predictable resource distributions lead to stable and highly territorial systems. On the other hand, a sparse yet predictable resource base—such as that found in the southwestern highlands—is more likely to lead to less-strict territorial systems with populations that have overlapping home-ranges and institutions that hinge on social reciprocity and intergroup collaboration and communication. This configuration is consistent with the prehistoric context of the southwestern highlands outlined in the first half of this chapter and is thus far supported by our survey data.

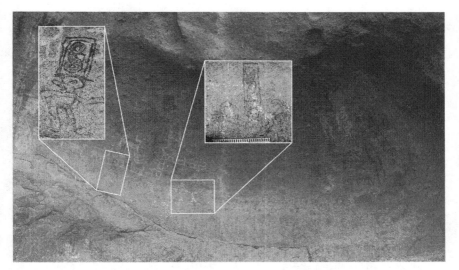

FIGURE 2.6. *Emblem-bearing anthropomorphs in the central panel at La Pintada de Azacualpa.*

In the case of the Sierra de La Paz, our research suggests that intergroup conflict was mediated by the need to maintain genetically healthy and well-provisioned populations, which made the trade and exchange of goods, people, and ideas necessary. Evidence of these relationships includes the widespread use and exchange of La Esperanza obsidian and nonlocal polychromes across this area. Additionally, the rock art in the Sierra de La Paz has iconography that is similar to that of sites in the highlands to the west and southwest of the Comayagua Valley (Rodríguez Mota 2007) and the north of the Department of Morazán, El Salvador (Coladan 1998; Coladan and Amaroli 2003; Haberland 1991). Of note, the area covered by this exchange of materials, iconography, and ritual traditions falls within the proposed boundaries for the sixteenth-century province of the Care Lenca, which might have had a shared dialect of the Lenca language (Chapman 1978; Lara-Pinto 1991; chapter 10, this volume).

CONCLUSIONS

In this chapter, we have attempted to reconstruct the deep history of the ritual, economic, and physical landscape of the highlands of southwestern Honduras. In presenting a holistic view of the landscape, which incorporates aspects of the environment into human experience and relationships, and vice versa, we seek to further explore those social relations and their development at a broad scale. The setting for the human-landscape relations we are attempting to reconstruct—the Sierra de La Paz—is a mosaic of mountains, small valleys, and sheltered sites prone to isolation but suffused by networks of exchange, meaning, and significance that were shared across this area and extended to broader Southeastern Mesoamerica. It is within this setting that we have explored broad patterns of cultural change while keeping in mind that every site—be it a cave, rockshelter, mounded village, or lithic scatter—is its own unit, with material remains that are the product of unique combinations of geology, ecology, settlement, and culture (Moyes and Brady 2012). Given the limited nature of our available datasets and our lack of absolute dates for sites other than El Gigante, our goal has been to offer hypotheses to be evaluated by further research in this and neighboring areas.

Evidence from El Gigante and elsewhere consistently suggests that a broad-based and arboriculturally focused adaptation spans the entire Preceramic period in the neotropics (Lentz 2000; Lentz et al. 1997; McKillop 1994; Miller and Schaal 2005; Peters 2000). Foraging populations exploited a variety of habitats and resources and over time increased the diversity of resources consumed as they settled more into the landscape and began utilizing it more intensively, fostering stronger connections to their surroundings. It is in this context that imported maize and beans and other Mesoamerican crops were integrated into the diet and took on a central role. This suggests a widening interaction sphere and a similar, though delayed, metastasis towards ascribed status and the stratification of authority. We hypothesize that this transition happened much later at El Gigante—and purportedly across the highlands of southwestern Honduras—than at other Mesoamerican centers. Nevertheless, we argue that the inhabitants of the Sierra de La Paz were active participants in processes of domestication and non-domesticating cultivation (Piperno 2011) that cumulatively conditioned the development of agriculture there and in neighboring regions. Under this scenario, local economies were subject to new forms of competition and new levels of surplus production were sought by ever more powerful "big-men" aspiring to be hereditary chiefs. Ritual activities shifted from forms of communal, domestic ceremony (at El Gigante shelter, for example) to more exclusive centralized rituals performed in special and restricted spaces (local ossuaries later in prehistory). However, in both cases these acts personalizing and mythologizing local group identity were essential. This empowerment of place is also attested to in the creation of multitudinous and elaborate rock-art sites.

The shifts outlined above represent a profound change in the concept of and the perception of the landscape. It is beyond the scope of this chapter to explore other aspects of the Classic and Postclassic periods, such as the few but important permanent mounded settlements recorded in the highlands. Future research needs to investigate the intersections between these mounded sites and caves and rockshelters in order to articulate local chronologies and patterns of landscape use, as it has been done elsewhere (Awe 1998; Moyes and Brady 2012). What remains clear is that the stage was set in the Preceramic. Areas marginal to large-scale settlement such as the highlands of Honduras were fertile experimental grounds, and it should be our goal to explore and emphasize the flow of plants, information, and possibly people across all of Mesoamerica and even between continents.

Our research thus far, while preliminary, suggests that the populations of highland southwest Honduras left and continue to leave their long-term marks on the landscape in every sense—ecologically, ritually, culturally, even physically. Under this view, the landscape is more than just geological formations and natural resources—it tells the story of a people and their beliefs about the world going back millennia. It is the anchor to an incredibly rich oral history among the Lenca who continue to use this landscape for every aspect of their lives, from shelters to places of ritual and spiritual significance for their community.

WORKS CITED

Aceituno, Francisco J., and Nicolás Loaiza. 2014. "Early and Middle Holocene Evidence for Plant Use and Cultivation in the Middle Cauca River Basin, Cordillera Central (Colombia)." *Quaternary Science Reviews* 86(1):49–62.

Acosta Ochoa, Guillermo. 2008. *La Cueva de Santa Marta: y los cazadores-recolectores del Pleistoceno final—Holoceno temprano en las regiones tropicales de México.* Tésis doctoral, Universidad Nacional Autónoma de México, Mexico City, Mexico.

Agurcia Fasquelle, Ricardo. 1976. "Los petroglifos de Valladolid, Comayagua. (Honduras)" In *Las fronteras de Mesoamérica*, Tomo 2: *XIV Mesa Redonda*, ed. Sociedad Mexicana de Antropología, 211–219. Sociedad Mexicana de Antropología, Mexico City, Mexico.

Anschuetz, Kurt F., Richard H. Wilshusen, and Cherie L. Scheick. 2001. "An Archaeology of Landscapes: Perspectives and Directions." *Journal of Archaeological Research* 9(2):157–211.

Aoyama, Kazuo, Toshibaru Tashiro, and Michael D. Glascock. 1999. "A Pre-Colombian Obsidian Source in San Luis, Honduras: Implications for the

Relationship between Late Classic Maya Political Boundaries and the Boundaries of Obsidian Exchange Networks." *Ancient Mesoamerica* 10(2):237–249.

Athens, Steve, Jerome V. Ward, Deborah M. Pearsall, Karol Chanlder-Ezell, Dean W. Blinn, and Alex E. Morrison. 2016. "Early Prehistoric Maize in Northern Highland Ecuador." *Latin American Antiquity* 27(1):3–19.

Awe, Jaime, ed. 1998. *The Western Belize Regional Cave Project: A Report of the 1997 Field Season.* Durham: University of New Hampshire, Department of Anthropology,

Basso, Keith. 1996. *Wisdom Sits in Places: Landscape and Language among the Western Apache.* Albuquerque: University of New Mexico Press.

Bernal, Juan Pablo, Matthew Lachniet, Malcolm McCulloch, Graham Mortimer, Pedro Morales, and Edith Cienfuegos. 2011. "A Speleothem Record of Holocene Climate Variability from Southwestern Mexico." *Quaternary Research* 75(1):104–113.

Blake, Michael, and Bruce Benz. 2010. AMS Radiocarbon Dates for Maize Samples from El Gigante Rockshelter, Honduras. Report submitted to Kenneth Hirth and David Webster, Department of Anthropology, Pennsylvania State University, University Park, PA.

Blake, Michael, Brian S. Chrisholm, John E. Clark, and Karen Mudar. 1992. "Non-Agricultural Staples and Agricultural Supplements: Early Formative Subsistence in the Soconusco Region, Mexico." In *Transitions to Agriculture in Prehistory*, ed. Anne B. Gebauer and Theron D. Price, 133–151. Madison, WI: Prehistory Press.

Brady, James E. 2005. *In the Maw of the Earth Monster: Mesoamerican Ritual Cave Use.* Austin: University of Texas Press.

Brown, Clifford T. 2005. "Caves, Karst, and Settlement at Mayapán, Yucatán." In *In the Maw of the Earth Monster: Mesoamerican Ritual Cave Use*, ed. James E. Brady, 373–402. Austin: University of Texas Press.

Bullen, Ripley P., and William W. Plowden, Jr. 1963. "Preceramic Sites in the Highlands of Honduras." *American Antiquity* 28(3):382–385.

Cannon, Michael D. 2003. "A Model of Central Place Forager Prey Choice and an Application to Faunal Remains from the Mimbres Valley, New Mexico." *Journal of Anthropological Archaeology* 22(1):1–25.

Castellanos, Vladimiro, Charles S. Summons, and Kirk P. Rodgers. 1962. "Mapa Parcial de Honduras: Clasificacion de Tierras." Washington, DC: Organizacion de los Estados Americanos.

Chapman, Anne. 1978. *Los Lencas de Honduras en el Siglo XVI.* Tegucigalpa, Honduras: Instituto Hondureño de Antropología e Historia.

Chapman, Anne. 1985. *Los Hijos del Copal y la Candela: Ritos agrarios y tradición oral de los Lencas de Honduras*, Tomo I. Mexico City: Universidad Nacional Autónoma de México,

Chapman, Anne. 1986. *Los Hijos del Copal y la Candela: Ritos agrarios y tradición oral de los Lencas de Honduras,* Tomo II. Mexico City: Universidad Nacional Autónoma de México.

Chen, Haofeng, Peter L. Morrell, Vanessa E.T.M. Ashworth, Marlene de la Cruz, and Michael T. Clegg. 2009. "Tracing the Geographic Origins of Major Avocado Cultivars." *Journal of Heredity* 100(1):56–65.

Coladan, Elisenda. 1998. "Las pinturas rupestres del oriente de El Salvador." In *XI Simposio de Investigaciones Arqueológicas en Guatemala,* 1997, ed. Juan Pedro Laporte, Hector Escobedo, and Sandra Villagrán de Brady, 660–671. Guatemala City, Guatemala: Museo Nacional de Arqueología y Etnología.

Coladan, Elisenda, and Paul Amaroli. 2003. "Las representaciones rupestres de El Salvador." In *Arte Rupestre de Mexico Oriental y Centro América,* ed. Martin Künne and Matthias Strecker, 143–162. Berlin, Germany: Gebr. Mann Verlag.

Collins, Michael B. 1991. "Rock Shelters and the Early Archaeological Record in the Americas." In *The First Americans: Search and Research,* ed. Tom D. Dillehay and David J. Meltzer, 157–182. Boca Raton, FL: CRC Press.

Correa-Metrio, Alexander, Mark B. Bush, Kenneth R. Cabrera, Shannon Sully, Mark Brenner, David A. Hodell, Jaime Escobar, and Tom Guilderson. 2012. "Rapid Climate Change and No-analog Vegetation in Lowland Central America During the Last 86,000 Years." *Quaternary Science Reviews* 38:63–75.

Crumley, Carole L. 1987. *A Dialectical Critique of Hierarchy.* In *Power Relations and State Formation,* ed. Thomas Patterson and Christine W. Gailey, 155–169. Washington, DC: American Anthropological Association.

Crumley, Carole L. 1995. "Heterarchy and the Analysis of Complex Societies." *Archeological Papers of the American Anthropological Association* 6(1):1–5.

Crumley, Carole L., and William Marquardt, eds. 1987. "Regional Dynamics: Burgundian Landscapes in Historical Perspective." Orlando, FL: Academic Press.

Cucina, Andrea, and Vera Tiesler. 2014. "Mortuary Pathways and Ritual Meanings Related to Maya Human Bone Deposits in Subterranean Contexts." In *The Bioarchaeology of Space and Place,* ed. Gabriel D. Wrobel, 225–254. New York: Springer.

David, Bruno, and Julian Thomas, eds. 2008. *Handbook of Landscape Archaeology.* Walnut Creek, CA: Left Coast Press.

David, Bruno, and Meredith Wilson, eds. 2002. *Inscribed Landscapes: Marking and Making Place.* Honolulu: University of Hawai'i Press.

Dyson-Hudson, Rada, and Eric Alden Smith. 1978. "Human Territoriality: An Ecological Reassessment." *American Anthropologist* 80(1):21–41.

Egan, Dave. 2003. "Defining Cultural and Ethnographic Landscapes." *Ecological Restoration* 21(4):258–260.

Figueroa, Alejandro. 2006. Proyecto de Arte Rupestre (PARUP), Temporada 2005–2006: Informe Final. Tegucigalpa, Honduras: Archives of the Honduran Institute of Anthropology and History (IHAH).

Figueroa, Alejandro. 2014. Informe Final, Proyecto Paleoindio de Honduras (PRO-PALEOH): Temporada 2013. Final field report submitted to Honduran Institute of Anthropology and History. Tegucigalpa, Honduras; Archives of the Honduran Institute of Anthropology and History (IHAH),

Figueroa, Alejandro. 2016. Mountain Doorways: Caves, Shelters, and Rock Art in Past and Present Southwestern Honduras. Paper presented at the 81st annual meeting of the Society for American Archaeology, Orlando, FL.

Galindo-Tovar, María Elena, Amaury M. Arzate-Fernández, Nisao Ogata-Aguilar, and Ivonne Landero-Torres. 2007. "The Avocado (*Persea americana*, Lauraceae) Crop in Mesoamerica: 10,000 Years of History." *Harvard Papers in Botany* 12(2):325–334.

Galindo-Tovar, María Elena, Nisao Ogata-Aguilar, and Amaury M. Arzate-Fernández. 2008. "Some Aspects of Avocado (*Persea americana* Mill.) Diversity and Domestication in Mesoamerica." *Genetic Resources and Crop Evolution* 55(3):441–450.

Gama-Campillo, Lilia, and Gómez-Pompa, Arturo. 1992. "An Ethnoecological Approach for the Study of *Persea*: A Case Study in the Maya Area." In *Proceedings of the Second World Avocado Congress: The Shape of Things to Come*, ed. Carol J. Lovatt, Peter A. Holthe, and Mary Lu Arpaia, 11–18. Riverside: University of California Press.

Gnecco, Cristóbal. 2000. *Ocupación temprana de bosques tropicales de montaña*. Popayán, Colombia: Editorial Universidad del Cauca.

Gnecco, Cristóbal, and Francisco Javier Aceituno. 2006. "Early Humanized Landscapes in Northern South America." In *Paleoindian Archaeology: A Hemispheric Perspective*, ed. Juliet E. Morrow and Cristóbal Gnecco, 86–104. Gainesville: University Press of Florida.

Haberland, Wolfgang. 1991. "Informe preliminar de investigaciones arqueológicas en la gruta de Corinto y sus alrededores." *Mesoamérica* 12(21):95–104.

Hamilton, Clement W., and Sarah H. Reichard. 1992. "Current Practice in the Use of Subspecies, Variety, and Forma in the Classification of Wild Plants." *Taxon* 41(3):485–498.

Harlan, Jack R. 1971. "Agricultural Origins: Centers and Noncenters" *Science*, Volume 174:468–474.

Healy, Paul F. 2007. "The Anthropology of Mesoamerican Caves." *Reviews in Anthropology* 36(3):245–278.

Heyden, Doris. 2005. "Rites of Passage and Other Ceremonies in Caves." In *The Maw of the Earth Monster: Mesoamerican Ritual Cave Use*, ed. James E. Brady, 21–34. Austin: University of Texas Press.

Hirth, Kenneth G., Alejandro J. Figueroa, Alejandra Domic, Harry Iceland, Timothy Scheffler, Eric Dyrdahl, Heather Thakar, Amber VanDerwarker, and Douglas Kennett. 2018. "The Esperanza to Middle Marcala Phase Subsistence Practices at El Gigante Rockshelter (11,000–7,400 cal B.P.)." Paper presented at the 83rd annual meeting of the Society for American Archaeology, Washington, DC.

Hodell, David A., Mark Brenner, and Jason H. Curtis. 2000. "Climate Change in the Northern American Tropics and Subtropics Since the Last Ice Age: Implications for Environment and Culture." In *Imperfect Balance: Landscape Transformations in the Precolombian Americas*, ed. D. Lentz, 13–38. New York: Columbia University Press.

Holdridge, Leslie R. 1962. *Mapa Ecológico de Honduras*. Washington, DC: Organization of American States.

Horn, Sally P. 2016. "Pre-Columbian Maize Agriculture in Costa Rica." In *Histories of Maize in Mesoamerica: Multidisciplinary Approaches*, ed. John E. Staller, Robert H. Tykot, and Bruce F. Benz, 104–117. London: Routledge.

House, Paul, Carlos Cerrato, and Daan Vreugdenhil. 2002. *Rationalization of the Protected Areas System of Honduras*, Volume II: *Biodiversity of Honduras*. Washington, DC: World Bank.

Iltis, Hugh H. 2000. "Homeotic Sexual Translocations and the Origin of Maize (*Zea mays*, Poaceae): A New Look at an Old Problem." *Economic Botany* 54(1): 7–42.

Iltis, Hugh H. 2006. "Origin of Polystichy in Maize." In *Histories of Maize: Multidisciplinary Approaches to the Prehistory, Linguistics, Biogeography, Domestication, and Evolution of Maize*, ed. John Staller, Robert Tykot, and Bruce Benz, 21–53. Walnut Creek, CA: Left Coast Press.

Kennett, Douglas J., Heather B. Thakar, Amber M. VanDerwarker, David L. Webster, Brendan J. Culleton, Thomas K. Harper, Logan Kistler, Timothy E. Scheffler, and Kenneth Hirth. 2017. "High-precision Chronology for Central American Maize Diversification from El GiganteRrockshelter, Honduras." *PNAS* 114(34):9026–9031.

Kormondy, Edward John, and Daniel E. Brown. 1998. *Fundamentals of Human Ecology*. Upper Saddle River, NJ: Prentice Hall.

Kozuch, Michael J. 1991. *Mapa Geológico de Honduras*. Tegucigalpa, Honduras: Instituto Geográfico Nacional.

Landon, Amanda J. 2009. "Domestication and Significance of *Persea americana*, the Avocado, in Mesoamerica." *Nebraska Anthropologist*, Paper 47.

Lara-Pinto, Gloria. 1991. "Sociopolitical Organization in Central and Southwest Honduras at the Time of the Conquest: A Model for the Formation of Complex Society." In *The Formation of Complex Society in Southeastern Mesoamerica*, ed. William Fowler, Jr., 215–236. Boca Raton, FL: CRC Press:

Lara-Pinto, Gloria, and George Hasemann. 2000. Rock Shelters of Central Honduras: The Setting of a Prehistoric Landscape. Paper presented at the Annual Meeting of the Society for American Archaeology, Philadelphia, PA.

Lentz, David. 2000. "Anthropocentric Food Webs in the Precolumbian Americas." In *Imperfect Balance: Landscape Transformations in the Precolumbian Americas*, ed. David L. Lentz, 89–119. New York: Columbia University Press.

Lentz, David, Carlos R. Ramirez, and Bronson W. Griscom. 1997. "Formative-Period Subsistence and Forest-Product Extraction at the Yarumela Site, Honduras." *Ancient Mesoamerica* 8(1):63–74.

Leonard, Robert D., and George T. Jones, eds. 1989. *Quantifying Diversity in Archaeology*. Cambridge, UK: Cambridge University Press.

Lohse, Jon, C. 2010. "Archaic Origins of the Lowland Maya." *Latin American Antiquity* 21(3):312–352.

Long, Austin, Bruce F. Benz, Douglas J. Donahue, A. J. Timothy Jull, and Lawrence J. Toolin. 1989. "First Direct AMS Dates on Early Maize from Tehuacán, Mexico." *Radiocarbon* 31(03):1035–1040.

Longyear, John M., III. 1948. "A Sub-Pottery Deposit at Copán, Honduras." *American Antiquity* 13(3):248–249.

Markgraf, Vera. 1989. "Palaeoclimates in Central and South America since 18,000 BP Based on Pollen and Lake-level Records." *Quaternary Science Reviews* 8(1):1–24.

McKillop, Heather. 1994. "Ancient Maya Tree Cropping, a Viable Subsistence Adaptation for the Island Maya." *Ancient Mesoamerica* 5(1):129–140.

Meltzer, David J., Robert D. Leonard, and Susan K. Stratton. 1992. "The Relationship Between Sample Size and Diversity in Archaeological Assemblages." *Journal of Archaeological Science* 19(4):375–387.

Michael, Amy R. 2016. "Histological Analysis of Dentition in Rockshelter Burials from Two Sites in Central Belize." *Dental Anthropology* 29(1):32–40.

Miller, Alison, and Barbara Schaal. 2005. "Domestication of a Mesoamerican Cultivated Fruit Tree, *Spondias pupurea*." *PNAS* 102(36):12801–12806.

Moyes, Holley, ed. 2012. *Sacred Darkness: A Global Perspective on the Ritual Use of Caves*. Boulder: University Press of Colorado.

Moyes, Holley, and James E. Brady. 2012. "Caves as Sacred Space in Mesoamerica." In *Sacred Darkness: A Global Perspective on the Ritual Use of Caves*, ed. Holley Moyes, 151–170. Boulder: University Press of Colorado.

Odling-Smee, F. John, Kevin N. Laland, and Marcus W. Feldman. 2003. *Niche Construction: The Neglected Process in Evolution*. Princeton, NJ: Princeton University Press.

Pérez, Liseth, Jason Curtis, Mark Brenner, David Hodell, Jaime Escobar, Socorro Lozano, and Antje Schwalb. 2013 "Stable Isotope Values (δ 18 O and δ 13 C) of

Multiple Ostracode Species in a Large Neotropical Lake as Indicators of Past Changes in Hydrology." *Quaternary Science Reviews* 66(1):96–111.

Peters, Charles M. 2000. "Precolumbian Silviculture and Indigenous Management of Neotropical Forests." In *Imperfect Balance: Landscape Transformations in the Precolumbian Americas*, ed. David L. Lentz, 203–223. New York: Columbia University Press.

Pianka, Eric R. 2000. *Evolutionary Ecology*. 6th ed. San Francisco, CA: Addison Wesley Educational Publishers.

Piperno, Dolores R. 2011. "The Origins of Plant Cultivation and Domestication in the New World Tropics, Patterns Process and New Developments." *Current Anthropology* 52(4):453–470.

Piperno, Dolores R., Mark B. Bush, and Paul A. Colinvaux. 1990. "Paleoenvironments and Human Occupation in Late-Glacial Panama." *Quaternary Research* 33(1):108–116.

Piperno, Dolores R., and Kent V. Flannery. 2001. "The Earliest Archaeological Maize (*Zea mays* L.) from Highland Mexico: New Accelerator Mass Spectrometry Dates and Their Implications." *PNAS* 98(4):2101–2103.

Piperno, Dolores R., and Deborah M. Pearsall. 1998. *The Origins of Agriculture in the Lowland Neotropics*. San Diego, CA: Academic Press.

Piperno, Dolores R., Anthony J. Ranere, Irene Holst, Jose Iriarte, and Ruth Dickau. 2009. "Starch Grain and Phytolith Evidence for Early Ninth Millennium BP Maize from the Central Balsas River Valley, Mexico." *PNAS* 106(13):5019–5024.

Pohl, Mary D., Kevin O. Pope, John G. Jones, John S. Jacob, Dolores R. Piperno, Susan D. DeFrance, David L. Lentz, John A. Gifford, Marie E. Danforth, and J. Kathryn Josserand. 1996. "Early Agriculture in the Maya Lowlands." *Latin American Antiquity* 7(4):355–372.

Prufer, Keith Malcolm, and James Edward Brady, eds. 2005. *Stone Houses and Earth Lords: Maya Religion in the Cave Context*. Boulder: University Press of Colorado.

Reyes-Mazzoni, Roberto R. 1977a. "Influencias mayas y mexicanas en los petroglifos de la quebrada de Santa Rosa Tenampua, Honduras." *Katunob* 9(3):38–51.

Reyes-Mazzoni, Roberto R. 1977b. "Posibles influencias Epi-Teotihuacanas en petroglifos de Honduras." *Vinculos* 3(1–2):47–65.

Rodríguez Mota, Francisco. 2007. Informe del Proyecto de Arte Rupestre 2007: Valle de Comayagua. Tegucigalpa, Honduras: Archives of the Honduran Institute of Anthropology and History (IHAH).

Rue, David. 1989. "Archaic Middle American Agriculture and Settlement: Recent Pollen Data from Honduras." *Journal of Field Archaeology* 16(2):177–184.

Rue, David, David Webster, and Anthony Traverse. 2002. "Late Holocene Fire and Agriculture in the Copán Valley, Honduras." *Ancient Mesoamerica* 13(2):267–272.

Saunders, Nicholas J. 2001. "A Dark Light: Reflections on Obsidian in Mesoamerica." *World Archaeology* 33(2):220–236.

Scheffler, Timothy E. 1998. El Gigante 1998: Key Site Survey in the Marcala, La Paz Area: May 14–June 3. Tegucigalpa, Honduras: Archives of the Honduran Institute of Anthropology and History (IHAH).

Scheffler, Timothy E. 1999. "Cuevas y abrigos del suroeste de Honduras: Hallazgos e inferencias del recorrido 'El Gigante' 1998." In *VIII Seminario de antropología de Honduras, "Dr. George Hasemann,"* ed. Carmen Julia Fajardo and Kevin Rubén Avalos, 251–265. Tegucigalpa, Honduras: Instituto Hondureño de Antropología e Historia.

Scheffler, Timothy E. 2001. "Research Report on the Proyecto Cueva El Gigante 2000, La Paz, Honduras." *Mexicon* 23(1):115–123.

Scheffler, Timothy E. 2008. "The El Gigante Rockshelter, Honduras." Unpublished PhD dissertation, Pennsylvania State University, University Park, PA.

Scheffler, Timothy E., Kenneth G. Hirth, and George Hasemann. 2012. "The El Gigante Rockshelter: Preliminary Observations on an Early to Late Holocene Occupation in Southern Honduras." *Latin American Antiquity* 23(4):597–610.

Schmidt, Matthew W., Howard J. Spero, and David W. Lea. 2004. "Links Between Salinity Variation in the Caribbean and North Atlantic Thermohaline Circulation." *Letters to Nature* 428(6979):160–163.

Sheets, Payson D. 1989. "Recent Research on Obsidian in the Zapotitan Valley, El Salvador." In *La Obsidiana en Mesoamerica*, ed. Margarita Gaxiola and John E. Clark, 419–425. Mexico City, Mexico: Instituto Nacional de Antropologia e Historia.

Sheets, Payson D., Kenneth G. Hirth, Fred W. Lange, Fred Stross, Frank Asaro and Helen Michel. 1990. "Obsidian Sources and Elemental Analysis of Artifacts in Southern Mesoamerica and the Northern Intermediate Area." *American Antiquity* 55(1):144–158.

Simpson, Edward H. 1949. "Measurement of Diversity." *Nature* 163:688.

Smalley, John, and Michael Blake. 2003. "Sweet Beginnings: Stalk Sugar and the Domestication of Maize." *Current Anthropology*, 44(5):675–703.

Smith, C. Earle., Jr. 1967. "Plant Remains." In *The Prehistory of the Tehuacan Valley*, Volume 1: *Environment and Subsistence*, ed. Douglas S. Byers, 220–255. Austin: University of Texas Press.

Sorensen, Jerrel, and Kenneth G. Hirth. 1984. "Minas Precolumbianas y Talleres de Obsidiana en La Esperanza, Depto. de Intibuca." *Yaxkin* 7(1):31–45.

Stiner, Mary C., Natalie D. Munro, and Britt M. Starkovich. 2012. "Material Input Rates and Dietary Breadth During the Upper Paleolithic through Mesolithic at Franchthi and Klissoura 1 Caves" (Peloponnese, Greece). *Quaternary International* 275(1):30–42.

Stone, Andrea J. 1995. *Images from the Underworld: Naj Tunich and the Tradition of Maya Cave Painting*. Austin: University of Texas Press.

Stone, Doris. 1957. *The Archaeology of Central and Southern Honduras*. Cambridge, MA: Peabody Museum.

Vreugdenhil, Daan, Jan Meerman, Alain Meyrat, Luis Diego Gómez, and Douglas J. Graham. 2002. *Map of the Ecosystems of Central America: Final Report*. Washington, DC: World Bank.

Webster, David. R., David Rue, and Anthony Traverse. 2005. "Early *Zea* Cultivation in Honduras: Implications for the Iltis Hypothesis." *Economic Botany* 59:101–111.

Winterhalder, Bruce. 1986. "Diet Choice, Risk, and Food Sharing in a Stochastic Environment." *Journal of Anthropological Archaeology* 5(4):369–392.

Winterhalder, Bruce, and Douglas J. Kennett. 2006. "Behavioral Ecology and the Transition from Hunting and Gathering to Agriculture." In *Behavioral Ecology and the Transition to Agriculture*, ed. Douglas J. Kennett and Bruce Winterhalder, 1–21. Berkeley: University of California Press.

Wolstenholme, B. Nigel, and Anthony W. Whiley. 1999. "Ecophysiology of the Avocado (*Persea americana* Mill.) Tree as a Basis for Pre-Harvest Management." *Revista Chapingo Serie Horticultura* 5(1):77–88.

Wrobel, Gabriel D., ed. 2014. *The Bioarchaeology of Space and Place*. New York: Springer,

Yen, Douglas. E. 2014. "The Domestication of Environment." In *Foraging and Farming: The Evolution of Plant Exploitation*, ed. David R. Harris and Gordon C. Hillman, 55–75. London: Routledge.

Zeanah, David W. 2000. "Transport Costs, Central Place Foraging, and Hunter-Gatherer Alpine Land Use Strategies." In *Intermountain Archaeology*, ed. David B. Madsen and Michael D. Metcalf, 1–14. Salt Lake City: University of Utah Press.

3

Evaluating the Size, Limits, and Influence of the Copán Polity in Western Honduras

Protoclassic to Late Classic Transformations in the Cucuyagua and Sensenti Valleys

ERLEND JOHNSON

DOI: 10.5876/9781646420971.c003

Our perspectives on the influence that Classic Copán and the Maya culture had on neighboring southeastern groups have undergone significant changes over the last 100 years. Research today indicates both that the number and extent of Maya populations in Southeastern Mesoamerica (Andrews and Fash 2004; Canuto and Bell 2013; Fash and Fash 2006; Sharer 2004) and the influence of the Copán Maya on this region (Hendon 2009; Joyce 1993; Schortman and Urban 1994) were less than once thought (Lothrop 1939; Stone 1941; Thompson 1970). Current models recognize multi-ethnic populations were present in Copán (Andrews and Fash 2004; Fash and Fash 2006; Sharer 2004) and in surrounding valleys (Canuto and Bell 2013; Inomata and Aoyama 1996; Saturno 2000) rather than attempting to delineate Maya and non-Maya regions. Furthermore, scholars have critiqued earlier core/periphery models, inspired by world-systems theory that overemphasized the impact of Copán on surrounding areas (Joyce 1993; Schortman and Urban 1994). Scholars of central Honduras point out that Copán's interactions with and influences on many parts of Southeastern Mesoamerica were limited, as few artifacts or styles from Copán are found in regions such as the lower Ulúa Valley (Joyce 1993) and the Naco Valley (Schortman and Urban 1994). However, while it is clear now that the Classic-period Copán polity was not the core of

Southeastern Mesoamerica, its rulers effected significant changes in a more limited area of western Honduras. This essay seeks to highlight the ways that Copán's rulers transformed nearby regions as well as to outline the limits of that power.

This chapter compares political institutions via settlement pattern and artifact data from the Protoclassic period (AD 100–400), the period preceding Copán's rise as a regional power, through the Late Classic period (AD 650–800), when Copán was a mature polity. This discussion examines broader trends in Copán's periphery, using case studies from the Cucuyagua and Sensenti Valleys, a region southeast of the Copán Valley. Researchers suggest (Hall and Viel 2004; Manahan and Canuto 2009; Sharer et al. 2009; Stuart 2004) that a Maya population may have been present in the Copán Valley from the Protoclassic period but that non-Maya, likely proto-Lenca populations, occupied the Copán Valley and surrounding regions prior to that point. However, there is no evidence that Maya peoples either settled in or exerted influence over peoples in surrounding valleys (Canuto and Bell 2013; Nakamura et al. 1991:90) before Copán's dynastic founding in the Early Classic (AD 400–650). By comparing settlement, architecture, and artifactual data from these two periods it will be possible to determine whether Copán's interactions with its neighbors were informal, consisting of the use of art or architecture from Copán by semiautonomous neighbors, or alternatively whether these regions were more closely integrated within and transformed by the Copán polity, and to demonstrate how these close ties may have shifted over time. Convergences in political institutions, visible when surrounding valleys adopted structures and styles from the Copán polity, provide the best evidence for examining these relationships. Such studies may also examine how distance and accompanying logistical challenges may have affected the formation and maintenance of political relationships between the Copán polity and its neighbors.

The Cucuyagua and Sensenti Valleys are situated 30 km and 50 km southeast of Copán, respectively, and each contains centers from the Protoclassic and Late Classic periods. They are well situated to study how political relations between the Copán polity and both more-proximate and more-distant neighbors shifted over time (figure 3.1). This chapter first presents recently collected survey and excavation data from the Cucuyagua and Sensenti Valleys in order to discuss political changes in each valley during the Classic period. These data are then discussed together with data from previous investigations in order to examine the nature and extent of Copán's political influence in Southeastern Mesoamerica.

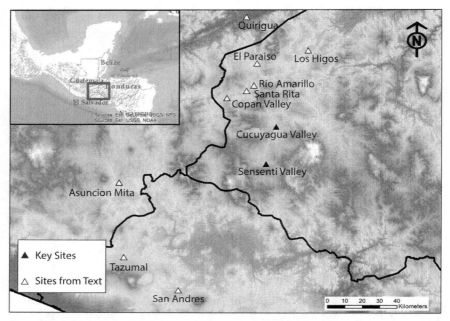

FIGURE 3.1. *Significant Southeastern Mesoamerican sites discussed in the text.*

HIERARCHY, HETERARCHY, AND COOPERATION: POLITICAL MODELS IN SOUTHEASTERN MESOAMERICA

As new research in Mesoamerica is published and we move beyond earlier neoevolutionary political models, it is clear that a diverse array of political organizations were employed by Mesoamerican peoples (Fargher et al. 2010a; Fargher et al. 2010b; Joyce and Hendon 2000). New research suggests that both the ability to cooperate (Blanton and Fargher 2008, 2012; Carballo 2013; Carballo et al. 2014, Fargher et al. 2010a) and the modes by which past peoples made political decisions (Crumley 1987, 1995; Joyce and Hendon 2000; Zagarell 1995) greatly varied from place to place. This chapter characterizes both lowland Maya and Southeastern Mesoamerican political institutions using measures of collective action and political centralization. An understanding of norms from each system will allow us to compare and contrast lowland Maya and Southeastern Mesoamerican political influences in the context of the Cucuyagua and Sensenti Valleys.

Cooperation refers to the ability of individuals to band together in order to meet group goals (Blanton and Fargher 2008, 2012; Carballo 2013; Carballo et al. 2014; Fargher et al. 2010a). Archaeologists can, although somewhat crudely, measure and compare the differing abilities of past groups to cooperate by examining the energetics of construction projects (Abrams 1994; Blitz and Livingood 2004; Carelli 2004; Kolb 1997; Murakami 2015; Torres 2014) and measuring the spatial capacities of communal spaces (Inomata 2006; Inomata and Tsukamoto 2014; Murakami 2014). This study uses mound volumes and plaza capacities in order to compare the capacity for collective action in the study area over time and space.

In addition to cooperation, this chapter also uses the concepts of heterarchy and hierarchy (Crumley 1987, 1995; Zagarell 1995) in order to evaluate political centralization. Carol Crumley (1987) first employed the concept of heterarchy as an alternative to the hierarchical models of political organization that dominated discourses in contemporary archaeology. She contrasted *hierarchy*, which she defined as "elements which based on certain factors are subordinate to others and may be ranked," and *heterarchy*, defined as "relations of elements to one another where they are unranked or possess the potential to be ranked in multiple ways" (1977:144). Archaeologists have most commonly used settlement-pattern data and site-layout data as proxies for hierarchical and heterarchical decision-making structures (Crumley 1987; Joyce and Hendon 2000; Zagarell 1995). Multitier settlement hierarchies with central places surrounded by smaller centers and residential sites are often associated with hierarchical political structures (Wright 1994; Wright and Johnson 1975). Unequal access to prestige and wealth often accompany political hierarchies as well, which may be visible in unequal access to labor and material for residential constructions and tombs (Flannery 1999).

While there is much debate about the nature of Classic-period, lowland-Maya political organization (Chase and Chase 1996; Foias 2013; Fox 1988; LeCount and Yaeger 2010; Marken and Fitzsimmons 2015), there is little doubt that hierarchical political institutions and stratified social structures, both capable of mobilizing significant collective action, were employed by the Classic-period lowland Maya. At the apex of this structure was the *kuhul ajaw* or divine lord, a figure who led both secular and religious institutions (Friedel 2008; Houston and Stuart 1996; Martin and Grube 2008). The prominence of these *ajaws* is supported by the archaeological evidence, which shows *ajaws* were celebrated on monuments (Houston and Stuart 1996; Martin and Grube 2008), lived in ornate palaces (Harrison and Andrews 2004; Inomata and Houston 2000), and were buried with rich assemblages in prominent tombs (Bell et al. 2004; Carrasco Vargas et al. 1999; Tiesler and Cucina 2006). Maya archaeologists recognize significant variations in the degree of centralized power and the size of territories that specific ajaws ruled over (Foias 2013; Marken and Fitzsimmons 2015; Martin and Grube 2008). However, even relatively modest kingdoms, such as Pusilha (Braswell and Prufer 2009) contained hierarchical political structures capable of constructing monumental pyramids and plazas.

Lowland Maya–style political institutions were in place in the Copán polity by the Early Classic period. Retrospective texts referring to early kings (Stuart 2004), as well as evidence of hydraulic engineering projects (Hall and Viel 2004), hint that hierarchical, Maya-style political institutions may have been established in the Protoclassic period. However, the first examples of royal tombs, such as the Yehnal and Margarita tombs (Bell et al. 2004), hieroglyphic monuments (Stuart 2004), and early palace complexes and large-scale construction projects (Carelli 2004), appear in the Early Classic period (Sharer 2004).

As previous research shows, including this volume (see Begley, chapter 7; Joyce, chapter 13; Martínez, chapter 6; McFarlane and Suri, chapter 5; and McNeil et al., chapter 4), there was likely a range of political structures in this diverse area that included a variety of groups in the Classic period. Data from Classic-period centers in western El Salvador suggest that it contained centralized political institutions similar to those at Copán (Card and Zender 2016; Demarest 1988; Sharer 1978). Tazumal and San Andres were primate centers in local settlement hierarchies (Black 1983; Sharer 1978). Additionally, Tazumal contained several elite tombs with elaborate jade and ceramic offerings (Boggs 1963; Card and Zender 2016; Murano et al. 2011).

Central and northwestern Honduran sites, such as La Sierra (Schortman and Urban 2011, 2012; Schortman et al. 2004), El Coyote (Urban 2016), Gualjoquito (Schortman et al. 1986), Salitrón Viejo (Hasemann 1998; Hirth 1996), and Tenampua (Dixon 1992), have also been identified as central places ruled by hierarchical political institutions. These sites are all large centers at the apex of local settlement hierarchies and all contain both large public spaces and monumental constructions. However, these sites lack extravagant elite tombs. Sites like Travesia, Cerro Palenque, and Curruste in the lower Ulúa Valley seem to have had developed social, if not political, hierarchies as well (Joyce, chapter 13, this volume). Joyce argues that prominent houses, who were patrons of craft production, especially of marble vases, existed at these sites but that no site in the region dominated a significant hinterland area.

Finally, research from the Cuyumapa (Joyce and Hendon 2000), Lake Yojoa (Baudez and Becquelin 1973), and Jesús de Otoro Valleys (McFarlane and Suri, chapter 5, this volume) suggest the existence of heterarchical political organizations. These regions lack a primate center and/or elaborate residences and tombs. The Cuyumapa region (Joyce and Hendon 2000), for example, contains only modest monumental architecture, most notably ballcourts (Fox 1996), and lacks large formal plazas. Other settlements, in particular sites in the Jesús de Otoro Valley (McFarlane and Suri, this volume), contained several closely spaced monumental architectural groups of similar size with no single center.

While it is impossible to characterize a dominant southeastern political model within the region, it is important to highlight the diversity of political models that existed there. A diachronic examination of political structures in a region near the Copán Valley may be informative as it can highlight how and to what degree these surrounding populations adopted Maya political institutions or developed autochthonous political traditions. Such measures in turn may suggest the scale of integrative practices employed by the Copán polity at different points in the Classic period.

RESEARCH IN THE CUCUYAGUA AND SENSENTI VALLEYS

The Cucuyagua and Sensenti Valleys are formed by the Alax River, a tributary of the Ulúa River. The presence of the Panamerican Highway and the earlier royal road, linking the Atlantic and Pacific coasts, highlights the region's role as a vital communication corridor. Fertile and extensive bottomlands of 50 km^2 and 40 km^2 also suggest that this region could potentially have supported large populations and surplus agriculture. Despite these features, no systematic exploration had been conducted in either the Cucuyagua or Sensenti Valley until this study (Cruz and Heredia 2002; Girard 1949; Nakamura 1996; Richardson 1938; Sanchez 2003, 2010; Stone 1957; Stromsvik 1952). Investigations of the Cucuyagua Valley were previously limited to the site of La Union, where both Gustav Stromsvik (1952) and Carleen Sanchez (2003) mapped and excavated. Previous explorations of the Sensenti Valley consist of brief visits to key sites (Stone 1957) and a survey along the route of a power line (Cruz and Heredia 2002).

The author began the Proyecto Arqueologico Regional Cucuyagua Sensenti in 2011 in order to reconstruct settlement patterns in each valley. Survey strategies consisted of visiting a 10-percent sample of mountain, hill, and river terrace environments within the survey area (using Turner et al. 1983 definitions from Copán), pedestrian survey of the river terraces along the Alax River, and data from local informants on the locations of key sites. All sites containing more than one patio group were mapped using an electronic distance measurer and GPS. These techniques documented 105 sites with a total of 965 mounds in both valleys (figure 3.2). Over the course of two seasons in 2015 and 2016, the author also dug test excavations at 11 sites in order to reconstruct local settlement chronology. This sample included all key sites, as well as an example of a secondary and a residential site from the Classic and Protoclassic periods of each valley. The following sections examine shifting settlement patterns first in the Cucuyagua and then in the Sensenti Valley in order to discuss the nature and limits of Copán's political influence over time in each. The diachronic change in settlement patterns from the Cucuyagua Valley, which is closer to Copán, is described first, followed by a description of shifts in settlement in the Sensenti Valley.

AUTOCHTHONOUS SETTLEMENT IN THE CUCUYAGUA VALLEY FROM THE PROTOCLASSIC/ EARLY CLASSIC PERIODS

The survey identified Late Preclassic and Protoclassic sites. The

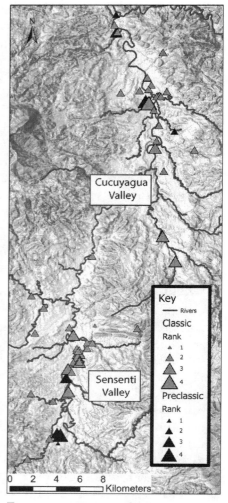

FIGURE 3.2. *Classic and Preclassic settlement in the Cucuyagua and Sensenti Valleys.*

first true center to be built in the valley, the site of La Union, was constructed in the Protoclassic period. The site contains five earth-and-cobble mounds arranged around an informal plaza. Both the layout and the architecture of this group in La Union are similar to contemporary sites elsewhere, such as Los Naranjos (Baudez and Becquelin 1973), El Guayabal (Sharer et al. 2009), and La Florida (figure 3.3).

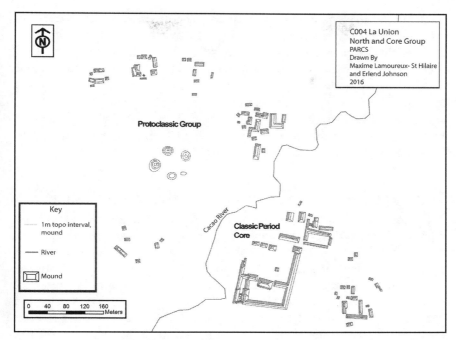

FIGURE 3.3. *Protoclassic and Classic site cores at La Union in the Cucuyagua Valley.*

Many features of La Union's political organization remain unclear, due to our limited understanding of Late Preclassic political institutions in Southeastern Mesoamerica and to limited investigations at the site. The people of La Union were able to organize sufficiently to complete monumental, though relatively modest, public architecture. The informal plaza at this group, which measured 1,667 m², would have been able to fit 463 people using Inomata's (2006) most-conservative capacity coefficient. Furthermore, three of the group's mounds measured over 4 m tall and contained over 1,000 m³ of fill, each representing a significant energetic investment. If a hierarchy existed at La Union, it was not complex, as La Union was only at the head of a two-tiered settlement hierarchy, with the only other known Protoclassic sites in the valley consisting of more modest, likely residential, sites.

Data collected as part of this study suggest that settlement at this early group may have endured longer than once thought. Carleen Sanchez suggested that the site was abandoned during the Protoclassic period and then resettled in the Early Classic, based upon the limited evidence available to her (2003:250–251). The author encountered both Protoclassic and Early Classic modal material, including two annular base sherds and a comal fragment in a midden context in a stratum underneath bajareque wall fall from structure LAN55. This diagnostic material suggests that the group continued to be in use until the Early Classic period and contradict Sanchez's earlier conclusions and its broader implications by suggesting that occupation of the earlier and later cores overlapped. The fact that La Union's earlier earthen mounded core continued to be preserved by later people despite its desirable location on higher and less floodable ground indicates that later inhabitants continued to draw meaning from and connect themselves to this group.

CULTURAL SHIFTS AND MEMBERSHIP IN THE COPÁN POLITY

The construction of a new site core in the Early Classic period at La Union represents a shift in local traditions and political institutions that would eventually establish La Union as a secondary center of Copán and situate the Cucuyagua Valley within the Copán polity (figure 3.3). Ceramics from the earliest phases of this new site core date to the Cuevas subphase (AD 500–650) of the Early Classic period and include ceramic markers such as Chilanga and Melano pottery types. While test excavations by Sanchez and myself uncovered Early Classic material in LUC1 and LUC2, the largest plazas of the site core, a better understanding of the size and elaboration of early architecture and any architectural connections to the Copán polity in this group will require future probing excavations beneath final-phase Late Classic architecture. The presence of a few examples of Melano, a type rare outside of Copán, may indicate early interaction between La Union and Copán.

Settlement in the Cucuyagua Valley reached its greatest height during the Late Classic period, when 25 sites containing 387 mounds were occupied. A four-tiered settlement hierarchy centered at La Union and local minor centers at El Barro, Jopopo and Cucuyagua existed during this period. However, settlement was highly nucleated at La Union as 254 of the 387 mounds documented were at La Union.

Previous research at La Union highlights clear ties between it and the Copán polity during the Late Classic period. Specifically, La Union's ballcourt emulated Ballcourt III at Copán, as it was of similar dimensions and construction and was decorated with similar macaw-head ballcourt markers (Sanchez 2003; Stromsvik 1952). Three of these markers survive today, though six markers may have originally existed (Sanchez 2003:89). The similarities in style and carving techniques between La Union and Ballcourt III's markers suggest that they were both carved during the eighth century (Sanchez 2003:83).

Macaw imagery recalls both dynastic imagery and Maya mythological beliefs from Copán. The macaw or *mo'* is part of Copán's dynastic founder's name and as such macaw imagery is featured on several versions of Copán's ancestral shrine (Fash et al. 2001; Taube 2004:264), as well as on early jade jewelry from acropolis tombs (Bell and Johnson 2015). However, as Fash and Fash (2016) have noted, macaw imagery at ballcourts may also reference interactions between the Hero Twins and the Principal Bird Deity.

Similarities can also be seen between the site layouts of La Union and Copán. Like Copán, La Union is oriented north–south and contains a southern elite complex and a central open ritual plaza area with a ballcourt to the north. Unlike Copán, La Union lacks a monumental great plaza north of its ballcourt.

Large public spaces and monumental architecture at La Union's Late Classic core affirms that its rulers could draw on significant collective action. The plaza capacity of LUC2 at La Union would have been sufficient to accommodate over 1,800 people for gatherings, trade, or ritual using Inoamata's (2006) most-conservative calculation. The aggregate volumes of all the structures surrounding plaza LUC2 were over 4,000 m³, though construction histories remain unknown.

Both La Union's elite residential group, made up of LUC1 and LUC8, and its position at the apex of a three-tiered settlement hierarchy affirm the hierarchical lowland Maya–style political institutions employed at the site. Sanchez (2003) proposed that LUC1 and LUC8 contained the residences of La Union's paramount elites. Findings of comal fragments, grinding stones, and utilitarian storage jars in the test excavations dug around this group by Sanchez (2003) and myself suggest that domestic activities took place in this group. The size and elaboration of LUC1 and LUC8 dwarfed residential patio groups elsewhere at La Union, with LUC1 covering twice the area of the next-largest residential patio group. Furthermore, this group contained elaborations, including a stucco-finished plaza floor and cut-stone architecture, which are absent in other domestic contexts. Finally, the prominent location of the group highlights the status of its occupants (Sanchez 2003).

While there are significant symbolic and structural links between La Union and Copán, there are many distinctly local features as well. Much of the architecture at La Union, including portions of the Late Classic site core, was built with unshaped river cobbles. Differences also exist between the aggregate ceramic assemblage from the Cucuyagua Valley and Copán. While Copador Polychrome is common both in the Cucuyagua Valley and Copán, other fineware types, such as Surlo Group sherds, have a markedly lower frequency at La Union's site core and elite compound (>1%, N = 2) than at Copán (4–6%)

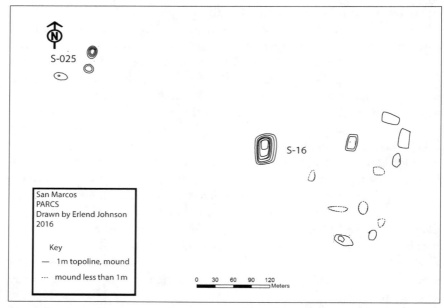

FIGURE 3.4. *San Marcos, a Protoclassic center in the Sensenti Valley.*

and are absent from smaller Late Classic sites (Bill 1997; Viel 1993). Utilitarian types, such as Casaca and Rual Red, which are common in Copán and present at some secondary sites like El Paraíso (Canuto and Bell 2013), are completely absent from the Cucuyagua Valley assemblages. Most telling, however, strong stylistic and ceramic links, exist between the Cucuyagua Valley and contemporary settlement in the Sensenti Valley to the south, including the shared use of Talquesalapa incised sherds as a primary decorated utilitarian type. These features, combined with the continual settlement history of the site, suggest that the local population was probably Lenca rather than lowland Maya throughout the Classic period.

PROTOCLASSIC SETTLEMENT IN THE SENSENTI VALLEY

The earliest settlement in the Sensenti Valley dates to the Protoclassic period. Four sites dating to this time period have been identified in the south of the valley, including a monumental center at San Marcos, two mounded sites, and a concentration of artifacts. The political center of the valley in this period was at the site of San Marcos (figure 3.4).

The site of San Marcos is located within the eponymous modern town in the southernmost limit of the Sensenti Valley. This area is strategically located to control mountain passes into El Salvador to the south and is well watered by two rivers. While large portions of the site have been destroyed by modern development, an 8-m-tall earthen mound, with a 50 m × 30 m base and a volume of 5,140 m³, and 13 additional mounds in three informal plazas were documented by the author. A second group of three mounds, separated from the main group by 300 m of highway and other development, may originally have been part of the same site. Surface scatter extends 400 m east of the principal group as well, though no mounds are preserved in this area. Finally, Protoclassic remains have been found in house lots in town 900 m south of the main group. Together, this evidence suggests that San Marcos was one of the largest sites encountered during survey in either valley.

San Marcos's residents created both large places for public gatherings and collaborated in large-scale construction projects. Plazas at San Marcos provided large public spaces that would have been capable of holding over 1,000 people, using Inomata's (2006) conservative coefficient. Similarly, Structure 1, with its volume of 5,140 m³, was the largest construction created in the prehistory of either valley.

Based on available evidence, less can be said about the political structure of the site. San Marcos was part of a four-tiered settlement hierarchy and had at least one secondary center. However, these initial investigations have not identified elite tombs or residential complexes. It is plausible that large structures, such as Structure 10, which was 32 m × 26 m, and 1.2 m high, may have been elite residences. Ceramic analysis from the two test pits dug behind Structure 10 identified parts of jars, bowls, and plates, which may have been domestic refuse. However, more excavations would be necessary at Structure 10 and surrounding mounds to test this hypothesis. Ceramic seriation suggests that San Marcos was abandoned by the end of the Protoclassic period. It is unclear why the site was abandoned. However, later precolumbian peoples avoided the area despite its prime location.

CLASSIC-PERIOD PATTERNS IN THE SENSENTI VALLEY

Survey identified 35 sites with a total of 528 mounds dating to the Classic period in the Sensenti Valley. As of yet no site with Early Classic material has been found and this represents a significant gap in the valley's settlement history. The earliest phases of the sites of Sensenti and La Joya, two large sites that reached their peak in the Late Classic period, date to the transition between the Early Classic and the Late Classic (AD 550–650), and can be identified by stratigraphic layers containing Gualpopa cream-paste pottery and Talqueslapa of the deep-incised variety. The extent of these early occupations is limited to Plazuela F in Sensenti and the area around Plazuelas F and G at La Joya. This suggests that both sites began as smaller rural settlements during the Early/Late Classic transition.

As the population of the Sensenti Valley grew in the Late Classic period, a political system developed that was distinct from earlier Protoclassic traditions and lowland Maya–style hierarchical systems. Both the ability to mobilize collective action and signs of hierarchical organization in site and settlement patterns decreased in the Late Classic, mirroring changes in the Cuyumapa Valley (Joyce and Hendon 2000) and Lake Yojoa (Baudez and Becquelin 1973) areas of central Honduras.

Most notably, there is a significant decrease in both the size of public spaces and the monumentality of architecture in the Sensenti Valley. Plaza capacities decreased from over 1,000 people at San Marcos in the Protoclassic to under 600 individuals at the site of Sensenti in the Late Classic period. Also, the size of monumental architecture notably decreased from Mound 1 at San Marcos (8 m tall, 5,140-m³ volume) to the largest pyramidal structure at the site of Sensenti (3 m tall, 250 m³ volume) in the Late Classic period. These indices suggest that local groups were capable of less cooperation than in past periods.

Furthermore, where clear settlement and spatial hierarchies existed in the Sensenti valley during the Protoclassic period, Late Classic settlements lack similarly developed hierarchies. There is only a three-tiered settlement hierarchy, and while two concentrations of residential structures existed at the site of Sensenti with 120 mounds and the site of La Joya containing 97 mounds, neither site contained formalized public spaces. Finally, unlike the Late Classic settlement patterns of the Cucuyagua Valley, settlement is not nucleated around one site but is regularly spaced along a broader stretch of river in the central Sensenti Valley.

Large but restricted-access residential plazuelas represent the most elaborate architectural groups known at Late Classic sites in the Sensenti Valley (figure 3.5). There are multiple plazuelas, ranging in area from 400 m² to 600 m² at the largest Late Classic sites. Three of these plazuelas existed at Sensenti and two plazuelas existed at La Joya. Other similarly sized but singular plazuelas are present at smaller sites such as Chocoyuco, El Comedero, Marquetado, El Madereado, and La Cancira. The presence of cut-stone architecture at many of these groups, and known stone-tomb chambers at the sites of El Comedero and Marquetado set them apart from more modest nearby constructions.

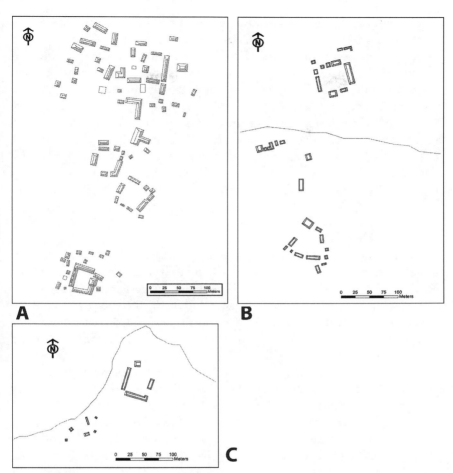

FIGURE 3.5. *Late Classic sites with plazuelas in the Sensenti Valley: (a) Sensenti, (b) Marquetado, and (c) El Comedero.*

However, the ubiquity of these groups, the domestic nature of finds from excavations, where manos and metates, jars, and comales as well as serving dishes and plates were found in middens, suggest that these groups were residential. These patterns more closely resemble trends in the Cuyumapa (Joyce and Hendon 2000), Lake Yojoa (Baudez and Becquelin 1973), and Comayagua (Dixon 1992) Valleys than lowland Maya norms.

Copán's elite culture did influence local elites in the Sensenti Valley. The cut-stone tombs found there more closely resemble traditions at Copán (Bell et al. 2004; Fash et al. 2001) than elsewhere in Southeastern Mesoamerica. Stone (1957) documented two pieces of Copán-style architectural sculpture on her visit to the Sensenti Valley as well. Furthermore, Sensenti's elite residents, like the elites in Copán, had access to similar fineware styles of pottery, with examples of Copador, Surlo Group pottery, and Ulúa polychromes all being found at the sites of Sensenti and La Joya. However, the quantities of Surlo Group (N = 28) and Ulúa (N = 4) ceramics are less than 1 percent of the overall assemblage and are present in notably lower quantities than at Copán (Bill 1997; Viel 1993). The lack of a clear administrative center and evidence for a distinctly non-Maya political system in the Sensenti Valley suggest that this region was outside of the Copán polity's direct control during the Late Classic period.

DISCUSSION

Together, data from the Cucuyagua and Sensenti Valleys provide new insights into the nature of interactions between the Copán polity and non-Maya peoples in western Honduras. These data suggest that Copán's rulers were capable of spurring lasting transformations in the social and political structures of the peoples in nearby valleys as they expanded the boundaries of their polity. This is also supported from recent discoveries at other secondary sites around Copán.

Though Protoclassic data are sparse in the valleys surrounding Copán, there is evidence that centers existed in the La Florida and La Venta Valleys (Nakamura et al. 1991) at La Florida, Los Higos, and Las Pilas, as well as in the El Paraíso Valley (Sharer et al. 2009) at El Cafetal (Canuto and Bell 2013), and in the Cucuyagua and Sensenti Valleys. Architecture from La Florida in particular suggests that these earlier peoples were capable of collectively constructing monumental structures (Nakamura et al. 1991). However, there is still too little evidence to determine whether or not these Protoclassic populations had hierarchical structures with paramount rulers or whether they were governed by other political systems. Certainly, recovered art and sculpture, including an alter-ego pedestal sculpture from La Florida (Nakamura et al. 1991), do not clearly depict rulers. However, more investigation will be needed in order to better understand political structures in this period.

By the late Classic period, a hierarchical lowland Maya–style political system had been adopted both at La Union and other major centers surrounding Copán. This conclusion is well supported by the presence of elaborate residential compounds linked to local paramounts. The elite residential group of LUC1 and LUC8 at La Union compares with throne-room structures from

El Cafetal in the El Paraíso Valley (Canuto and Bell 2013) and El Puente in the La Florida Valley (Shuichiro Terasaki, personal communication, 2015). These throne rooms include benches and niches that mimic structure 10L-22 at Copán (Bell and Canuto 2013) and may have been where local paramounts received guests. However, unlike at Copán, these throne rooms were integrated within more open plaza areas. The rise of these types of elite architecture in Copán's periphery likely represented an active strategy of support for local elite allies that allowed Copán's rulers to more efficiently extract labor and resources through a hierarchically stratified system.

The macaw-head sculptures from La Union fit within a broader campaign of sculptural elaboration that celebrates Copán's ruling dynasty. As Von Schwerin (2010) has pointed out, dynastic imagery is one of the major themes portrayed in sculpture at Copán's secondary centers. Such imagery mainly consists of images of turbaned individuals, as is present at Los Higos and El Puente, as well as images of individuals containing costume elements consistent with rulers from Copán, as is seen at El Paraíso and Las Pilas (Von Schwerin 2010). Dynastic imagery at these secondary sites represents unambiguous statements of membership within the Copán polity and allegiance to its rulers within a lowland Maya–style political hierarchy.

Data from valleys farther afield, such as the Sensenti Valley, also clearly indicate that the Copán polity, at the zenith of its power, incorporated an area more or less within 50 km^2 to its north, south, and east. Sites like El Roncador in the La Venta Valley (Inomata and Aoyama 1996; Nakamura et al. 1991), and Las Quebradas in the Lower Motagua Valley (Ashmore and Schortman 2012), are identified as outside of Copán or Quirigua's direct rule. These sites lack the decorative sculpture typical of Copán (Nakamura and Schortman 1991). Roncador in particular lacked access to Ixtepeque obsidian, which was controlled by Copán (Inomata and Aoyama 1996). In addition, the presence of multiple, similarly sized, enclosed plaza groups at lower–Motagua Valley sites in particular may suggest that a heterarchical political system, distinct from lowland Maya norms, was practiced in these areas (Ashmore and Schortman 2012). Altogether, less is known about the boundaries of the Copán polity to the west, though sites like Asuncion Mita, over 90 km away from Copán (Stromsvik 1952; Wauchope and Bond 1989), may have been allied with or integrated within the Copán polity. Finally, while relatively little has been published on the Classic-period remains from Tazumal and San Andres, intriguing finds, such as the poison bottle reported by Card and Zender (2016) from Tazumal, suggest that these regions south of Copán may have been allied with Copán as well.

CONCLUSIONS

Data from the Sensenti and Cucuyagua Valleys reinforces the fact that the Copán polity played an important, though limited, role as a regional power within the western portion of Southeastern Mesoamerica in the Late Classic period. Local settlements in both the Sensenti and Cucuyagua Valleys had few links to either Copán or the lowland Maya in the Protoclassic period. However, during the Late Classic period, transformations were implemented in the political institutions of the Cucuyagua Valley that closely mirrored lowland Maya political norms. The new site core of La Union was remodeled to mirror that of Copán's and included a prominent residential compound for the local paramount's lineage. Such transformations reflect the establishment of a lowland Maya–style political hierarchy. Dynastic imagery, such as La Union's macaw-head ballcourt markers, may have been adopted by local paramounts in order to both legitimize their own local privilege and pay homage to distant rulers.

The presence of distinctly non-Maya political institutions, as typified by the settlement patterns of the Late Classic–period Sensenti Valley, also indicate that the Copán polity's direct rule only extended over a limited area. As has been argued elsewhere (Ashmore and Schortman 2012; Inomata and Aoyama 1996; Nakamura and Schortman 1991), some of Copán's neighbors could and did choose less-intense relations or active resistance towards the Copán polity and lowland Maya cultural developments. In fact, as can be seen in the Sensenti Valley, these border areas were often also influenced by political and social developments from central Honduras and El Salvador. Together, work from the Cucuyagua and Sensenti Valleys adds to our overall understandings of the nature and limits of Copán's influence in Southeastern Mesoamerica during the Late Classic period.

WORKS CITED

Abrams, Elliot M. 1994. *How the Maya Built Their World: Energetics and Ancient Architecture*. Austin: University of Texas Press.

Andrews, E. Wyllys, III., and William A. Fash. 2004. "Issues in Copán Archaeology." In *Copán: The History of an Ancient Maya Kingdom*, ed. W.E Andrews and W.L. Fash, 395–426. Santa Fe, NM: SAR Press.

Ashmore, Wendy, and Edward Schortman. 2012. "History, Networks, and the Quest for Power: Ancient Political Competition in the Lower Motagua Valley, Guatemala." *Journal of the Royal Anthropological Institute* 18:1–21.

Baudez, Claude F., and Pierre Becquelin. 1973. "Archeologie de Los Naranjos, Honduras." Mexico City, Mexico: Mission Archeologique et Ethnologique Francaise au Mexique.

Bell, Ellen, and Erlend Johnson. 2015. *Classic Period Political Organization on the Southeast Edge of the Maya Area: Case Studies from Western Honduras*. Paper Presented at the 114th Annual Meeting of the American Anthropological Association, Denver, CO.

Bell, Ellen E., Robert J. Sharer, Loa P. Traxler, David W. Sedat, Christine W. Carelli and Lynn A. Grant. 2004. "Tombs and Burials in the Early Classic Acropolis at Copán." In *Understanding Early Classic Copán*, ed. E. E. Bell, M. A. Canuto, and R. J. Sharer, 131–158. Philadelphia: University of Pennsylvania Museum of Archaeology and Anthropology.

Bill, Cassandra R. 1997. "Patterns of Variation and Change in Dynastic Period Ceramics and Ceramic Production at Copán, Honduras." Unpublished PhD dissertation, Department of Anthropology, Tulane University, New Orleans, LA.

Black, Kevin D. 1983. "The Zapotitan Archaeological Survey." In *Archaeology and Volcanism in Central America: The Zapotitan Valley of El Salvador*, ed. P. D. Sheets, 83–84. Austin: University of Texas Press.

Blanton, Richard E., and Lane F. Fargher. 2008. *Collective Action in the Formation of Pre-Modern States*. New York: Springer.

Blanton, Richard E., and Lane F. Fargher. 2012. "Neighborhoods and the Civic Constitutions of Premodern Cities as Seen from the Perspective of Collective Action." In *The Neighborhood as a Social and Spatial Unit in Mesoamerican Cities*, ed. M. C. Arnauld, L. R. Manzanilla and M. E. Smith, 27–54. Tucson: University of Arizona Press.

Blitz, John H., and Patrick Livingood. 2004. "Sociopolitical Implications of Mississippian Mound Volume." *American Antiquity* 69(2):291–301.

Boggs, Stanley H. 1963. "Excavations at Tazumal, El Salvador." *Yearbook of the American Philosophical Society* 1(1):505–507.

Braswell, Geoffery, and Keith Prufer. 2009. "Political Organization and Interconnections in Southern Belize." In *Research Reports in Belizean Archaeology: Papers of the 2008 Belize Archaeology Symposium*, ed. J. Morris, J. Awe, G. Thompson, and C. Helmke, 43–55. Belmopan, Belize: Institute of Archaeology, National Institute of Culture and History.

Canuto, Marcello A., and Ellen E. Bell. 2013. "Archaeological Investigations in the El Paraíso Valley: The Role of Secondary Centers in the Multiethnic Landscape of Classic Period Copán." *Ancient Mesoamerica* 24(1):1–24.

Carballo, David M. 2013. "Cultural Evolutionary Dynamics of Cooperation in Archaeological Perspective." In *Cooperation and Collective Action Archaeological Perspectives*, ed. D. M. Carballo, 3–34. Boulder: University Press of Colorado.

Carballo, David M., Paul Roscoe, and Gary M. Feinman. 2014. "Cooperation and Collective Action in the Cultural Evolution of Societies." *Journal of Archaeological Method and Theory* 21(1):98–133.

Card, Jeb, and Marc Zender. 2016. "A Seventh-Century Inscribed Miniature Flask from Copán found at Tazumal, El Salvador." *Ancient Mesoamerica* 27(2):279–292.

Carelli, Christine W. 2004. "Measures of Power: The Energetics of Construction at Early Classic Copán." In *Understanding Early Classic Copán*, ed. E. E. Bell, M. A. Canuto, and R. J. Sharer, 113–130. Philadelphia: University of Pennsylvania Museum of Archaeology and Anthropology.

Carrasco Vargas, Ramon, Sylviane Boucher, Paula Alvarez Gonzalez, Vera Tiesler Blos, Valeria Garcia Vierna, Renata Garcia Moreno, and Javier Vazquez Negrete. 1999. "A Dynastic Tomb from Campeche: New Evidence on Jaguar Paw, A Ruler of Calakmul." *Latin American Antiquity* 10(1):47–58.

Chase, Arlen F., and Diane Z. Chase. 1996. "More than Kin and King: Centralized Political Organization among the Late Classic Maya." *Current Anthropology* 37(5):803–811.

Crumley, Carole L. 1987. "A Dialectical Critique of Hierarchy." In *Power Relations and State Formation*, ed. Thomas Patterson and Christine W. Gailey, 155–169. Washington, DC: American Anthropological Association.

Crumley, Carole L. 1995. "Heterarchy and the Analysis of Complex Societies." *Archaeological Papers of the American Anthropological Society* 6(1):1–5.

Cruz Castillo, Oscar N., and Victor F. Heredia Guillen. 2002. "Proyecto reconocimiento de superficie de la linea de transmision electrica Puerto Cortes-El Poy. Resultados preliminares." *Yaxkin* 20(1):77–97.

Demarest, Arthur A. 1988. "Political Evolution in the Maya Borderlands." In *The Southeast Classic Maya Zone*, ed. E. H. Boone and G. R. Willey, 335–395. Washington, DC: Dumbarton Oaks.

Dixon, Boyd. 1992. "Prehistoric Political Change on the Southeast Mesoamerican Periphery." *Ancient Mesoamerica* 3:11–25.

Fargher, Lane F., Richard E. Blanton, and Verenice Y. Heredia Espinoza. 2010a. "Egalitarian Ideology and Political Power in Prehispanic Central Mexico." *Latin American Antiquity* 21(3):227–251.

Fargher, Lane F., Richard E. Blanton, Verenice Y. Heredia Espinoza, John Millhauser, Nezehualcoyotl Xiuhtecutli, and Lisa Overholtzer. 2010b. "Tlaxcallan: The Archaeology of an Ancient Republic in the New World." *Antiquity* 85(327):172–186.

Fash, William L., Harriet F. Beaubien, Catherine E. Magee, Barbara W. Fash, and Richard V. Williamson. 2001. "The Trappings of Kingship among the Classic Maya: Ritual and Identity in a Royal Tomb from Copán." In *Fleeting Identities: Perishable Material Culture in Archaeological Research*, ed. P. B. Drooker, 152–169.

Carbondale: Center for Archaeological Investigations, Southern Illinois University, Carbondale.

Fash William L, and Barbara W. Fash. 2006. "Ritos de Fundacion en Una Cuidad Pluri-Etnica: Cuevas y Lugares Sagrados Lejanos en la Reivindicación del Pasado en Copán." In *Nuevas Ciudades, Nuevas Patrias: Fundacion y Relocalizacion de Ciudades en Mesoamerica y el Mediterraneo Antiguo*, ed. M. J. Iglesias Ponce de Leon, R. Valencia Rivera, and A. Cuidad Ruiz, 105–129. Madrid, Spain: Sociedad Española de Estudios Mayas.

Fash William L, and Barbara W. Fash. 2016. *Mythological Markers, Shifting Boundaries and Exchange in the Late Classic Copán Kingdom*. Paper presented at the 81st annual meeting of the Society for American Archaeology, Orlando, FL.

Flannery, Kent. 1999. "Process and Agency in Early State Formation." *Cambridge Journal of Archaeology* 9(1):3–21.

Foias, Antonia. 2013. *Maya Political Dynamics*. Gainesville: University of Florida Press.

Fox, John G. 1996. "Playing with Power: Ballcourts and Political Ritual in Southern Mesoamerica." *American Anthropologist* 37(3):483–509.

Fox, John W. 1988. "Hierarchization in Maya Segmentary State." In *State and Society: The Emergence and Development of Social Hierarchy and Political Organization*, ed. J. Gledhill, B. Bender, and L. T. Larsen, 103–112. London, UK: Unwin Hyman.

Friedel, David. 2008. "Maya Divine Kingship." In *Religion and Power: Divine Kingship in the Ancient World and Beyond*, ed. N. Brisch, 191–206. Chicago, IL: University of Chicago Press.

Girard, Raphael. 1949. "Los Chortís Ante el Problema Maya: Historia de las Culturas Indígenas de América desde su Origen hasta Hoy." Mexico City, Mexico: Antigua Libreria Robredo.

Hall, Jay, and Rene Viel. 2004. "The Early Classic Copán Landscape: A View from the Preclassic." In *Understanding Early Classic Copán*, ed. E. E. Bell, M. A. Canuto, and R. J. Sharer, 17–28. Philadelphia: University of Pennsylvania Museum of Archaeology.

Harrison, Peter D., and E. Wyllys Andrews. 2004. "Palaces of Tikal and Copán." In *Palaces of the Ancient New World*, ed. S. T. Evans and J. Pillsbury, 113–148. Washington, DC: Dumbarton Oaks.

Hasemann, George E. 1998. "Regional Settlement History on the Lower Sulaco River, West Central Honduras: Rural Settlement Theory and Ancient Settlement Patterns in the Honduran Highlands." Unpublished PhD dissertation, Department of Anthropology, University of Kentucky, Lexington, KY.

Hendon, Julia A. 2009. *Houses in an Everyday Landscape: Memory and Everyday Life in Mesoamerica*. Durham: University of North Carolina Press.

Hirth, Kenneth G. 1996. "Community and Society in a Central Honduran Chiefdom: Inferences from the Built Environment." In *Arqueologia Mesoamericana: Homenaje a William T. Sanders*, ed. W. T. Sanders and A. G. Mastache de Escobar, 169–191. Mexico City, Mexico: Instituto Nacional de Antropologia e Historia.

Houston, Stephen, and David Stuart. 1996. "Of Gods, Glyphs and Kings: Divinity and Rulership among the Classic Maya." *Antiquity* 70(268):289–312.

Inomata, Takeshi. 2006. "Plazas, Performers and Spectators: Political Theaters of the Classic Maya." *Current Anthropology* 47(5):805–842.

Inomata, Takeshi, and Kazuo Aayoma. 1996. "Central-Place Analyses in the la Entrada Region, Honduras: Implications for Understanding the Classic Maya Political Economic Systems." *Latin American Antiquity* 7(4):291–312.

Inomata, Takeshi, and Stephen D. Houston. 2000. "Opening the Royal Maya Court." In *Royal Courts of the Ancient Maya*, ed. T. Inomata and S. D. Houston, 3–26. Boulder, CO: Westview Press.

Inomata, Takeshi, and Kenichiro Tsukamato. 2014. "Gathering in an Open Space: Introduction to Mesoamerican Plazas." In *Mesoamerican Plazas: Arenas of Community Power*, ed. K. Tsukamoto and T. Inomata, 3–18. Tuscon: University of Arizona Press.

Joyce, Rosemary A. 1993. "The Construction of the Mesoamerican Frontier and the Mayoid Image of Honduran Polychromes." In *Reinterpreting Prehistory of Central America*, ed. Mark Miller Graham, 51–103. Boulder: University of Colorado Press.

Joyce, Rosemary A., and Julia A. Hendon. 2000. "Heterarchy, History, and Material Reality: 'Communities' in Late Classic Honduras." In *The Archaeology of Communities: A New World Perspective*, ed. J. Yaeger and M. Canuto, 143–159. New York: Routledge.

Kolb, Michael J. 1997. "Labor Mobilization, Ethnohistory, and the Archaeology of Community in Hawai'i." *Journal of Archaeological Method and Theory* 4(3):265–285.

LeCount, Lisa, and Jason Yaeger. 2010. "Provincial Politics and Current Models of the Maya State." In *Classic Maya Provincial Politics*, ed. L. Lecount and J. Yaeger, 20–45. Tucson: University of Arizona Press.

Lothrop, Samuel K. 1939. "The Southeastern Frontier of the Maya." *American Anthropologist* 41(1):42–54.

Manahan, T. Kam, and Marcello A. Canuto. 2009. "Bracketing the Copán Dynasty: Late Preclassic and Early Postclassic Settlements at Copán, Honduras." *Latin American Antiquity* 20(4):553–580.

Marken, Damien B., and James L. Fitzsimmons. 2015. "Introducing Maya Polities: Models and Definitions." In *Classic Maya Polities of the Southern Lowlands*, ed. D. B. Marken and J. L. Fitzsimmons, 1–42. Boulder: University of Colorado Press.

Martin, Simon, and Nikolai Grube. 2008. *The Chronicle of Maya Kings and Queens*. New York: Thames and Hudson.

Murakami, Tatsuya. 2014. "Social Identities, Power Relations, and Urban Transformations: Politics of Plaza Construction at Teotihuacan." In *Mesoamerican Plazas: Arenas of Community and Power*, ed. K. Tsukamoto and T. Inomata, 34–49. Tucson: University of Arizona Press.

Murakami, Tatsuya. 2015. "Replicative Construction Experiments at Teotihuacan Mexico: Assessing the Duration and Timing of Monumental Construction." *Journal of Field Archaeology* 40(3):263–282.

Murano, Masakage, Masashi Kudo, Akira Ichikawa, Nobuyuki Ito, and Shione Shibata. 2011. "Los Entierros Encontrados en Tazumal, Chalchuapa, un studio de practicas mortuorias." In *Procedimentos del 24 Simposio de Investigaciones Arqueologicas de Guatemala*, ed. B Arroyo, L. Paiz, A. Linares, and A. Arroyave, 697–716. Guatemala City, Guatemala: Museo Nacional de Arqueologia y Etnologia.

Nakamura, Seiichi. 1996. *Informe de la Fundación Toyota*. Unpublished research report. Tokyo, Japan: Toyota Foundation.

Nakamura, Seiichi, Kazou Aoyama, and Eiji Uratsuji. 1991. *Investigaciones Arqueológicas en La Región de La Entrada, Primera Fase*. Tegucigalpa, Honduras: Servicio de Voluntarios Japoneses para la Cooperación con el Extranjero.

Nakamura, Seiichi, and Edward E. Schortman. 1991A. "Crisis in Identity: Late Classic Competition and Interaction on the Southeast Maya Periphery." *Latin American Antiquity* 2(4):311–336.

Richardson, Frederick B. 1938. *Study of Maya Sculpture*. Carnegie *Year Book* 37:154–162. Washington, DC: Carnegie Institution of Washington.

Sanchez, Carleen D. 2003. "Topographies of Power: The Political Landscape of the Southeast Maya Region." Unpublished PhD dissertation, Department of Anthropology, University of California, Santa Barbara.

Sanchez, Carleen D. 2010. "Monumental Architecture and Preclassic Occupation at La Union in Western Honduras." *Mexicon* 23(5):109–114.

Saturno, William A. 2000. "In the Shadow of the Acropolis: Rio Amarillo and Its Role in the Copán Polity." Unpublished PhD dissertation, Department of Anthropology, Harvard University, Cambridge, MA.

Schortman, Edward M., and Patricia A. Urban. 1994. "Living on the Edge: Core/Periphery Relations in Ancient Southeastern Mesoamerica." *Current Anthropology* 35(4):401–430.

Schortman, Edward M., and Patricia A. Urban. 2011. "Power, Memory, and Prehistory: Constructing and Erasing Political Landscapes in the Naco Valley, Northwestern Honduras." *American Anthropologist* 113(1):5–21.

Schortman, Edward M., and Patricia A. Urban. 2012. "Enacting Power through Networks." *Journal of Anthropological Archaeology* 31(4):500–514.

Schortman, Edward M., Patricia A. Urban, Wendy Ashmore, and Julie Benyo. 1986. "Interregional Interaction in the SE Maya Periphery: The Santa Barbara Archaeological Project." *Journal of Field Archaeology* 13(3):259–272.

Schortman, Edward M., Patricia A. Urban, and Marne Ausec. 2004. "Politics with Style: Identity Formation in Prehispanic Southeastern Mesoamerica." *American Anthropologist* 103(2):312–330.

Sharer, Robert J. 1978. *The Prehistory of Chalchuapa, El Salvador*. Philadelphia: University of Pennsylvania Press.

Sharer, Robert J. 2004. "External Interaction in Early Classic Copán." In *Understanding Early Classic Copán*, ed. E. E. Bell, M. A. Canuto, and R. J. Sharer, 297–318. Philadelphia: University of Pennsylvania Museum of Archaeology and Anthropology.

Sharer, Robert J., Marcello A. Canuto, and Ellen E. Bell. 2009. "The Classic in the Southeastern Area: Issues of Organizational and Ethnic Diversity in the Copán Valley." In *The Southern Maya in the Late Preclassic: Identity, Urbanism, and State Formation*, ed. J. Kaplan and M. Love, 502–538. Boulder: University Press of Colorado.

Stone, Doris. 1941. *Archaeology of the North Coast of Honduras*. Cambridge, MA: Peabody Museum.

Stone, Doris. 1957. *The Archaeology of Central and Southern Honduras*. Cambridge, MA: Peabody Museum.

Stromsvik, Gustav. 1952. The Ballcourts of Copán with Notes on Courts at La Union, Quirigua, San Pedro Pinula and Asuncion Mita. Washington, DC: Carnegie Institute.

Stuart, David. 2004. "The Beginning of the Copán Dynasty: A Review of the Hieroglyphic and Historic Evidence." In *Understanding Early Classic Copán*, ed. E. E. Bell, M. A. Canuto, and R. J. Sharer, 215–248. Philadelphia: University of Pennsylvania Museum of Archaeology.

Taube, Karl. 2004. "Structure 10L-16 and Its Early Classic Antecedents: Fire and the Evocation and Resurrection of K'inich Yax K'uk' Mo'." In *Understanding Early Classic Copán*, ed. E. E. Bell, M. A. Canuto, and R. J. Sharer, 265–295. Philadelphia: University of Pennsylvania Museum of Archaeology.

Thompson, J. Eric. 1970. *Maya History and Religion*. Oklahoma City: University of Oklahoma Press.

Tiesler, Vera, and Andrea Cucina. 2006. "Studying Janaab' Pakal and Reconstructing Maya Dynastic History." In *Janaab' Pakal of Palenque*, ed. V. Tiesler and A. Cucina, 3–20. Tucson: University of Arizona Press.

Torres, Joshua. 2014. "Of Flesh and Stone: Labor Investment and Regional Sociopolitical Implications of Plaza/Batey Construction at the Ceremonial Center of Tibes (AD 600-1200), Puerto Rico." *Latin American Antiquity* 25(2):125–151.

Turner, B. L., II., William Johnson, Gail Mahood, Frederick M. Wiseman, B. L. Turner, and Jackie Poole. 1983. "Habitat y Agricultura en la Region de Copán." In *Introduccion a la Arqueologia de Copán*, ed. Claude F. Baudez, 35–102. Tegucigalpa, Honduras: Secretaria de Estado en el Despacho de Cultura y Turismo.

Urban, Patricia A. 2016. "Political Economy in the Late and Terminal Classic Southeastern Mesoamerica: Putting the El Coyote Copper Smelting Workshop in Its Regional Context." *Economic Anthropology* 3(2):240–253.

Viel, Rene. 1993. *Evolucion de la Ceramica de Copán*. Tegucigalpa, Honduras: Instituto Hondureño de Antropologia e Historia.

Von Schwerin, Jennifer. 2010. "The Problem of the 'Copán Style' and Political Identity: The Architectural Sculpture of El Paraíso, Honduras in a Regional Context." *Mexicon* 32(3):56–66.

Wauchope, Robert, and Margaret N. Bond. 1989. *Archaeological Investigations in the Department of Jutiapa, Guatemala*. New Orleans, LA: Middle American Research Institute, Tulane University.

Wright, Henry T. 1994. "Prestate Political Formations." In *Chiefdoms and Early States in the Near East*, ed. G. Stein and M. S. Rothman, 68–84. Madison, WI: Prehistory Press.

Wright, Henry T., and Gregory A. Johnson. 1975. "Population, Exchange, and Early State Formation in Southwestern Iran." *American Anthropologist* 77(2):267–289.

Zagarell, Allen. 1995. "Hierarchy and Heterarchy: The Unity of Opposites." *Archaeological Papers of the American Anthropological Association* 6(1):87–100.

4

Río Amarillo

*A Community on the
Margins of Ancient Copán*

Cameron L. McNeil,
Edy Barrios,
Walter Burgos,
Antolín Velásquez, and
Mauricio Díaz García

DOI: 10.5876/9781646420971.c004

Considerable scholarship has been devoted to investigating the relationships between Maya peoples and their neighbors along the southeastern periphery of their lands (Canuto and Bell 2013; Gerstle 1988; Inomata and Aoyama 1996; Manahan and Canuto 2009; Miller 2014; Schortman 1986; Schortman and Nakamura 1991; Schortman and Urban 2004; Sheets 2009; Stone 1957; Thompson 1970; Von Schwerin 2010). This research has helped to define cultural and ethnic differences between polities expressing a Copán identity, those copying certain aspects of Copán (or a more generalized Maya identity) (Von Schwerin 2010), and those that resolutely retain an identity expressive of other cultural traditions (Canuto and Bell 2013). To this large body of scholarship we add some detailed information on the site of Río Amarillo, which while closely connected to the polity of Copán during the Late Classic period, also demonstrates some links to Honduran cultures outside of the Maya area.

The Proyecto Arqueológico Río Amarillo, Copán (PARAC) has conducted extensive excavations of Late Classic and Postclassic contexts at the site of Río Amarillo, which is located in the Copán Valley of Honduras (figure 4.1). This work has revised and refined previous hypotheses about the site—in particular, its relationship with ancient Copán—and revealed some architectural traditions and ceramic types from the interior of Honduras. Río Amarillo's allegiances during the Early Classic are obscured

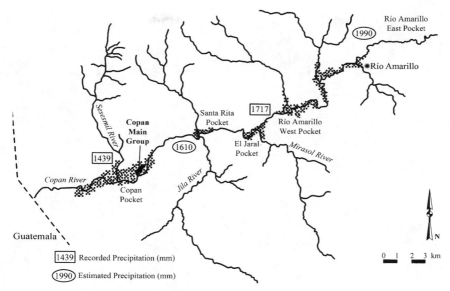

FIGURE 4.1. *Map of the Copán Valley. (Map by Edy Barrios after Turner et al. 1983:54, figure T-13.)*

by the layers of dirt and later structures covering them, but during the Late Classic period the appearance of altars with hieroglyphic inscriptions, one of which mentions Copán rulers, and a building with mosaic sculpture, imply that Río Amarillo had become a secondary center to Copán. Within the ceremonial core and in the residential area to its immediate east (figure 4.2) are found Maya-style architecture and artifact assemblages that echo patterns found in neighborhoods of the city of Copán. Towards the end of the Late Classic period the ceramic assemblages contain some Ulúa polychromes, although in smaller amounts than are found in Copán's center (Bill 2014). In Río Amarillo's East Group, and to the north of Río Amarillo's core at Site 5, the use of stepped ramps (an architectural form not documented elsewhere in the Copán Valley) tie strongly into patterns of construction from Los Naranjos. These construction choices may be linked to increasing trade with the interior of Honduras during the Late Classic, which continued to some degree into the Postclassic period.

In this chapter, we first briefly review evidence of Copán's connections to central and western Honduran cultures in the Preclassic period, followed by a discussion of Copán rulers salient to the interaction of Copán and Río Amarillo

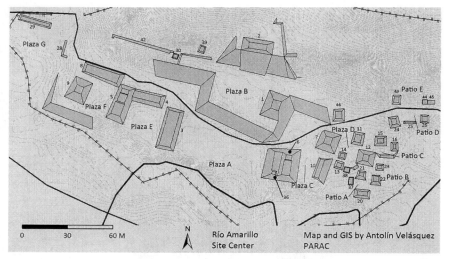

FIGURE 4.2. *Río Amarillo. (Map by Antolín Velásquez, PARAC.)*

during the Classic period. We then present results from PARAC excavations of household contexts and the initial survey of natural resources in the Río Amarillo East Pocket. Finally, we evaluate evidence for interactions between greater Honduras and Río Amarillo in the Late Classic and Postclassic periods.

THE DYNAMIC EBB AND FLOW OF THE MAYA IN THE COPÁN VALLEY

To understand our discussion of the ancient town of Río Amarillo and its interactions with the city of Copán, one must understand the settlement history of the valley and be familiar with at least four of the Copán Maya rulers: Ruler 1 (K'inich Yax K'uk' Mo'), Ruler 12 (K'ahk' Uti' Witz' K'awiil), Ruler 13 (Waxaklajuun Ubaah K'awiil), and Ruler 16 (Yax Pasaj Chan Yopaat). Settlement patterns and ceramics associated with the Preclassic population of Copán have led scholars to conclude that these individuals were not Maya (Manahan and Canuto 2009; Sharer 2009). The first evidence for Maya settlements is found during the second century AD (Sharer 2009:130–131). The impetus behind this influx of Maya migrants may have been the shrinking size of Lake Miraflores (Valdés 1997), the primary source of water for the important center of Kaminaljuyu, in highland Guatemala, which was occupied during the Preclassic and Early Classic periods.

While Maya settlement patterns are found in the Protoclassic (AD 100–300) at Copán, Maya-style architecture, art, and artifacts increased dramatically with the arrival of K'inich Yax K'uk' Mo', "the founder" of Copán's Maya dynasty in AD 427. A tomb found in the Hunal Structure (Burial 95-2) is believed to hold the remains of this lord. The burial lies far beneath the last manifestation of Temple 16, and just below the royal tomb in the Margarita structure (Burial 93-2), which holds a royal lady of local birth, hypothesized to be his spouse (Bell et al. 2004; Price et al. 2010). The apex of the Late Classic Acropolis is marked by Temple 16, whose superstructure bore images of the first ruler (Ramos 2006), and was most certainly seen as a place where this powerful founder and ancestor could be called upon for assistance by his descendants.

On the Late Classic Altar Q, the text records that K'inich Yax K'uk' Mo' came to Copán after "taking the K'awiil" elsewhere in AD 426 (Stuart 2004:233), possibly at Teotihuacan. Stuart (2004) links the ritual of "taking the K'awiil" to an ascension to a new status. In this case, it would seem one that enabled him to enter Copán, whether through agreement or force, as a polity leader. His headdress on Altar Q contains the emblem glyph for the Maya center of Caracol, and it is assumed that he was a prince from this locale (Stuart 2007). In Yax K'uk' Mo's earliest depiction on the Mot Mot marker (ca. AD 441), which most likely dates to the reign of Ruler 2, Yax K'uk' Mo' appears in the garb of a Maya lord (Martin and Grube 2008; Stuart 2004). In later depictions, including on Altar Q, he takes on the guise of a ruler with strong connections to the highland Mexican city of Teotihuacan, particularly through the use of "goggles" around his eyes that link him to the storm god Tlaloc. A pile of broken censers found outside of the tomb of Ruler 12 were upon reconstruction found to be censer lids (and their associated bases), each taking the form of one of the twelve Maya rulers of Copán up to that date (Fash 2001). The figure that represents K'inich Yax K'uk' Mo' has goggle-eyes and a Copán-style elite turban. The specter of the first ruler in this Teotihuacanized form can be seen on monuments and artifacts from at least the time of Ruler 12 through to the reign of Ruler 16, and may appear even earlier on Vessel 1 from the offering platform of Tomb 93–2 (Fash 2001). Under the reign of K'inich Yax K'uk' Mo' significant new constructions within the Acropolis were undertaken (Sharer et al. 1999). However, Yax K'uk' Mo' was the head of a chiefdom, not a state and much of the valley remained outside of his control.

Credit for the transition of Copán to state-level complexity is given to K'ahk' Uti' Witz' K'awiil, the longest-reigning (AD 628–695) member of Copán's Maya dynasty (Fash 2001). Ruler 12 greatly expanded the reach of Copán's power during his reign of 67 years. He erected five stelae outside of the Principal Group, and he is the only ruler to have erected monuments outside of the polity center (Fash 2001; Martin and Grube 2008). He is also featured on Altar L at the site of Quirigua (Fash 2001:104), which some scholars believe is evidence of the hegemony of Copán over Quirigua at this time.

References to Ruler 12 have been found as far away as Chalchuapa, El Salvador, in the Tazumal Complex (Card and Zender 2016:284–285), where an inscribed flask was found bearing an image of a small figure paying a tribute of highly valued quetzal birds to God D, the creator deity. The flask, likely for tobacco snuff, bears a hieroglyphic inscription implying that it was produced at the behest of Ruler 12. Card and Zender (2016:287, 289) propose that the gift signifies that Ruler 12 was of a higher status than the Chalchuapa lord and that the presence of the flask may support a larger range of political influence for Ruler 12 than has previously been realized.

Ruler 12 was followed by another long-reigning leader and powerful ruler, Waxaklajuun Ubaah K'awiil, whose governance of the polity ended when his head was cut off by the leader of Quirigua after a failed trip to garner captives for sacrifice (Martin and Grube 2008). The impact of Ruler 13's death to the integrity of the kingdom remains unknown. Did secondary centers under his control break away? Or was the status quo of the previous hundred years maintained under Ruler 14?

The last great ruler of the Copán polity was the sixteenth, Yax Pasaj Chan Yopaat, who governed from AD 763 to 820. While he did not erect freestanding stelae, he built important structures in the Acropolis center, and dedicated some elaborate altars (Martin and Grube 2008). Altar Q, one such monument, shows Yax Pasaj Chan Yopaat receiving power directly from K'inich Yax K'uk' Mo' (Fash 2001). His fate is also linked to "the founder's" on Stela 11, which may mention the political fall of the Maya dynasty at Copán (Martin and Grube 2008:212).

Sometime shortly following the death of Copán's Ruler 16, if not before, the polity experienced a dramatic demographic and political collapse. Many structures in the Acropolis were sacked and burned, as were structures in the palace complex, El Cementerio, to its south (Fash et al. 2004). Pollen data shows a rapid increase in forestation around this time (McNeil et al. 2010). Later groups, possibly unrelated to the Maya, reinhabited and reused Late Classic structures. Only limited evidence has been found of their settlements in the Main Group and El Bosque area (Longyear 1952; Manahan 2004).

A range of causes have been blamed for the collapse, but the most popular prime mover has been environmental mismanagement (Abrams et al. 1996; Fash 2001; Martin and Grube 2008; Webster et al. 2000). It was proposed in the 1980s that as the population increased around the Copán Pocket the city was not able to feed itself with the arable land at hand, and in response fallow times were shortened and the soil was gradually depleted of nutrients. Following this hypothesis, fuel and construction needs also led to widescale deforestation to the point where no pine trees remained in the Copán Pocket. Abrams et al. (1996) proposed that this pattern of overexploitation would have continued throughout the valley. Analysis of a sediment core from a body of water 6 km from Copán's center by McNeil (2006) and McNeil et al. (2010) found that, contrary to earlier proposals, the Late Classic ratio between fields and forests was more stable in the latter half of Copán's Classic history. And yet, the population in the Late Classic was much higher than in earlier periods and structures were built on the best lands, limiting the availability of rich agricultural soils (Abrams at al. 1996; Fash 2001; Webster and Freter 1990; Webster et al. 2000).

If the inhabitants of the Copán Pocket experienced shortfalls in their ability to produce sufficient foodstuffs to support the Late Classic population, as some scholars have proposed (Fash 2001; Webster and Freter 1990; Webster et al. 2000), the access to products of other areas in the valley and beyond could have been a necessity for the burgeoning Late Classic city. The Río Amarillo East Pocket contains the second-largest amount of low-lying agricultural fields in the valley after the Copán Pocket. Food imported from Río Amarillo (as well as from other areas), either as tribute or trade, may have mitigated the inability of the Copán Pocket to support its population, if there was actually a problem. The idea that Río Amarillo could have acted as a bread basket for Copán's center is not a new one and has been previously suggested by Aoyama (2001), Bill (1997), and Saturno (2000). To follow out this hypothesis, a project was undertaken in the eastern section of the valley to examine its history of settlement, architecture, trade, land-use patterns, and ecological context.

RÍO AMARILLO

BACKGROUND

The site of Río Amarillo is found in the "Río Amarillo East Pocket," at the opposite end of the valley from the center of Copán (figure 4.1). Its position on the periphery of Copán influenced its fortunes. It lies approximately 20 km from the city's center, and rests amidst a natural geographic corridor between Copán and El Paraíso (see Canuto and Bell 2013), and between Copán and the La Entrada region. Its position along the path to El Paraíso also places it along one of two trade routes between Copán and Quirigua. Its strategic location

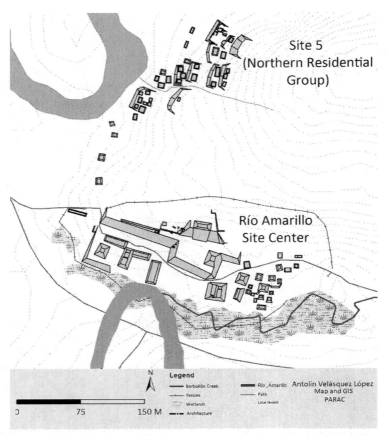

FIGURE 4.3. *Río Amarillo and Site 5. (Map by Antolín Velásquez, PARAC.)*

would have made it appealing to Maya elites at Copán, but potentially more important were the wet fertile bajos that lay along the Río Amarillo and its various tributaries such as the Río Blanco, the Quebrada Piedras Negras, and the Quebrada Borbollón, as well as some seasonal waterways.

The center of Río Amarillo was built into the incline of Cerro Canteada, unlike other large centers in the valley during the Late Classic period that rest on the floodplains of the valley floor (figure 4.3). It is set amidst a confluence of the Río Amarillo, which flows along both its western and southern sides, and the more intermittent Quebrada Borbollón. Archaeologists (McNeil et al. 2015; Pahl 1987; Saturno 2000) have documented 31 mounds at the site, which represent both ceremonial and household structures.

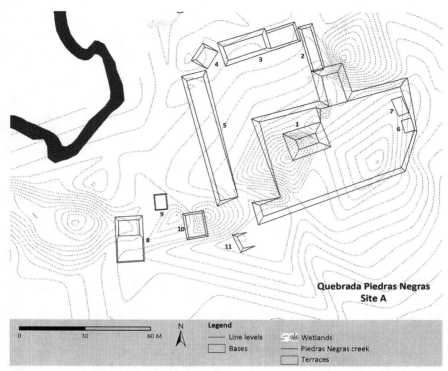

FIGURE 4.4. *Quebrada Piedras Negras. (Map by Antolin Velásquez, PARAC.)*

Small house mounds once connected the Río Amarillo site to Site 5, which lies to the north and was likely considered an extension of the community living around the ceremonial core. At Site 5, 33 house mounds have been mapped (McNeil at al. 2015). Another large group, Site 4, is found to the east of the town, consisting of at least 18 house mounds that have been mapped but not investigated. The inhabitants of Site 4 and Site 5 likely interacted daily with the activities and individuals within Río Amarillo's core.

Río Amarillo contains the tallest structure found outside of Copán's Acropolis (Saturno 2000:157), Structure 2, a pyramidal platform that had a river-cobble base and a superstructure topped by walls of bajareque (figure 4.2). This platform gains much of its height through the use of the natural topography and thus its monumentality is deceptively achieved.

The Río Amarillo East section of the valley had a relatively large Late Classic–period population (Freter 1988; Pahl 1987:237). The largest nearby center is Quebrada Piedras Negras, a Type 3 site (following Willey and Leventhal

1979), which is found 1,800 m to the north of Río Amarillo (figure 4.4). Smaller groups and individual house mounds dot the landscape around both sites.

The Environmental Context of the Community

The climate and natural resources of the Río Amarillo East Pocket are somewhat different from that of the Copán Pocket. This area receives approximately 1,990 mm of rain annually in comparison with Copán's 1,439 mm of rain (Turner et al. 1983:54, figure T-13) (figure 4.1). This area is also frequently fogged over in the mornings and late afternoons. It contains both a remnant of a cloud forest, Cerro Negro, and a rain forest, El Gobiado, which may have been far more extensive in the precolumbian period. These forest types are not found elsewhere in the Copán Valley and would have increased the overall biodiversity of the area. Cloud forests are one habitat favored by the quetzal, the value of whose feathers is well-illustrated on the flask discussed earlier from Tazumal, El Salvador.

El Gobiado looms over the site of Quebrada Piedras Negras, currently covering 600 ha (Komar et al. 2006). Collection and description of vegetation in El Gobiado has also been conducted by Komar et al. (2006) and Paul House (McNeil and Barrios 2012). The extent of this rainforest during the precolumbian period is being investigated by the first author through the analysis of sediment cores. Locals say that only 50 years ago, when the population was much lower, the floor of the valley was also covered in tropical forest and inhabited by a diversity of animal species, including jaguars, which are now unknown in the valley. Today, the surviving rainforest is predominantly reduced to the one hill where it is a refuge for howler monkeys, birds, and a diversity of botanical species.

Managed well, the lowlands of Río Amarillo could have produced food surpluses of maize, beans, and squash, among other field crops, and the uplands might have provided a diversity of forest resources such as animals for consumption or sacrifice, feathers, pelts, medicinal plants, wood, and tree fruits, all of which would have been appealing to the elites of Copán.

Evidence for the Preclassic and Early Classic Period

Río Amarillo's lowest levels have architecture dating back to the Early Classic period (McNeil et al. 2013; Pahl 1987; Saturno 2000). No excavations conducted at the site have found dwellings predating the Early Classic. A small number of Preclassic sherds have been identified by Mauricio Diaz among sherds from test pits made by Saturno and beneath structures in both the East Group and Site 5, but all of these have been mixed with ceramics from later periods and could have arrived at the site from nearby areas through the introduction of sediment for construction. A Preclassic greenstone avian-celt pendant with a convex back emerged from a midden in Site 5, but it also could have been carried to the area in a later period.

Excavations by both Pahl (1987) and Saturno (2000) found Early Classic construction underlying the Late Classic structures within Río Amarillo. PARAC also found the remnants of an Early Classic building underlying Late Classic construction at Site 5 (McNeil et al. 2012). Pahl (1987:figure 6) created a reconstruction of Early Classic structures in Plaza 1 from data gained during the excavation of a trench. Pahl's (1987:243) excavations determined that Río Amarillo was "under-developed" during the Early Classic period, consisting of a humble community. He found that during the Late Classic the settlement of Río Amarillo became dramatically larger, suggesting that this could have been a product of investment on the part of Copán. Pahl (1987:243) found that Structures 3–5 (see figure 4.2) were likely built towards the end of the Late Classic and that they directly overlay an earlier Late Classic residential structure. Pahl (1987) hypothesized that by the Late Classic the leaders of Río Amarillo would have had a familial relationship to Copán's elites.

LATE CLASSIC CONTEXTS AT RÍO AMARILLO

In the Late Classic contexts, Copán's influence can clearly be seen at the site in the form of two altars with hieroglyphic inscriptions; two impressive stairways of cut-stone blocks; the West Platform, which is faced in cut-stone blocks and has a seven-stepped stairway at its center; and Structures 1–5, the last of which bore a sculpture that recalls a number of buildings produced by Yax Pasaj Chan Yopaat (Ruler 16).

Altars 1 and 2 are currently housed at the Centro Regional de Investigaciones Arqueológicas (CRIA). Each of these altars has hieroglyphic inscriptions and each likely dates from some time in the Late Classic period. Both have suffered damage over the years. Work by Schele (1987) suggests that Altar 1, the more intact of the two, was most likely dedicated during the reign of Ruler 12. If borne out by further study, then Copán's influence at Río Amarillo was first marked on the ritual center of the site during a period when Copán is believed to have dramatically expanded its control under the rulership of K'ahk' Uti' Witz' K'awiil, Ruler 12.

By the Late Classic, at least some inhabitants of the town embraced important aspects of the ideology and identity of the Maya city of Copán, including the veneration of K'inich Yax K'uk' Mo', the first Copán Maya king. References to Copán's dynastic founder were uncovered by Pahl's excavation of Structure 5 in the form of "cross bundle fire signs" with the "te" and "naah" glyph affixes (Stuart 2004:272). These signs label the structure an "Origin House," tied to the "root" of the Maya dynasty at Copán, K'inich Yax K'uk' Mo' (Stuart 2004:238). Structure 5 also bore Mexican Year Signs, and warriors dressed in Teotihuacan-style regalia, connecting it to the same foreign associations to which K'inich Yax K'uk' Mo' was tied by the time of K'ahk' Uti' Witz' K'awiil (Fash 2011; Saturno 2000; Stuart 2004). Stuart (2004:273) believes that the crossed bundles may specifically signify Teotihuacan and New Fire Ceremonies; however, in the case of Copán, the symbol is also used as a referent for K'inich Yax K'uk Mo' (Taube 2004). The cross-bundle fire sign is also found on Altar 1 at Río Amarillo (Schele 1987). In the last manifestation of the Copán Acropolis, Temple 16 was conceived of as a "crossed-bundles place" (Taube 2004).

Structure 5 also bore Witz Monster masks. Von Schwerin (2010) has demonstrated that many Late Classic sites, either within or close to the Copán Valley, had such motifs and that while some were likely finely produced by Copán sculptors, others were crudely copied. The dearth of sculpture at Río Amarillo—with the exception of Altars 1 and 2, and Structure 5—and the fact that the sculpture is artfully produced, together suggest that the sculptors were not native to the town but instead came from elsewhere. Saturno (2000) notes that the sculptural elements on Structure 5 are identical to elements found on Temple 16, Temple 22, and Temple 26, in the Acropolis of Copán, and 10L-29 in El Cementerio (Copán's royal palace complex), supporting the supposition that artisans came from the city to adorn the building at Río Amarillo, marking it with a style and ideology attached to the hegemony of ancient Copán. The input of skilled artisans imported from Copán appears to signal the community's importance to the ancient city, or specifically the importance of what it could offer.

THE EAST GROUP, RÍO AMARILLO

Immediately east of the main plaza in the center of Río Amarillo, a high concentration of structures occupy a confined space (figure 4.2). The perceived lack of organization within the settlement pattern of the structures here has led to popular (although, not published) suggestions that this area reflects a non-Maya settlement pattern. Saturno (2000:158) dismissed this idea upon a limited investigation of the area, since the material culture is similar not only to the rest of the site but also to that of Copán during the Late Classic period. More-extensive excavations by PARAC also found that the individuals living in the area were engaged in domestic behaviors similar to those found in neighborhoods of Copán, although some architectural choices echoed traditions from the interior of Honduras. Excavations by PARAC of this area in 2012–2014 determined that rather than a disorganized group of residences, this area is composed of four small residential courtyards packed into a constrained area lying immediately east of the ritual core of Río Amarillo.

PARAC investigated Patios A, C, and D, as well as Plaza D, and some of their structures. Plaza D has a layout that is similar to Patios A, C, and D, but some of its structures are larger. However, Plaza D shares certain characteristics with the patios, such as closely spaced buildings, structures that do not have fine masonry, and construction predominantly of river cobbles, with wattle-and-daub superstructures.

In Patio A, Structures 20, 21, 22, and 37 were excavated. Structure 21 with its small size and shape could be a family shrine built in the later phase of the group. Like structures documented by Becker (1999) on his Plaza Plan 2 at Tikal, it is too narrow to have held a house. Structure 22 is larger and had two construction phases, the first made with cut stones and large river rocks. Overall, Structure 22 had an average height of 1.50 m, and could be entered by climbing a well-built river-cobblestone staircase. Some period after its construction, two small platforms were built to each side of the original building, creating new rooms.

Structures 20 and 37 have basically the same layout as each other, with a front platform—also called a "porch" or "lower terrace" by Wauchope (1938)—covering the entire façade of each building with a room behind it. These buildings are also similar to Structure 16 from Site 5 (Barrios et al. 2013). This architectural form has been documented in several sites of the Maya lowlands, such as at Uaxactun, and at Valladolid in the Yucatán (Wauchope 1938:13, figuress 4d and 4e.). Next to the back (northwest) corner of Structure 37, some rustic walls were located, consisting of one line of cobbles. The space created by these basic walls was small and filled with burned remains, including charcoal, burned soil, and ceramics. This area appears to have served as a kitchen for the patio group. Outside the kitchen lay a large midden that included thousands of ceramic sherds and artifacts as well as hundreds of obsidian and chert flakes.

Patio C is singular within the East Group, because superficially the courtyard space has an unusual inclination. A trench was excavated from south to north up to the southwestern corner of Structure 15 in order to better understand construction. The trench revealed that the patio does not have a flat surface. Instead the patio is occupied by a stepped platform, and each of its steps is produced with an inclination that creates a series of small ramps, all of which were built with local clay and without the use of stones. This stepped ramp leads up to the platform of Structure 15 and 16. Such earthen platforms, produced without masonry, are not common in the Copán Valley. They are, however, found at Los Naranjos, a monumental site with a long history of occupation. Los Naranjos is located on the west bank of Lake Yojoa, which lies to the east of Copán and outside the Maya area (Baudez and Bequelin 1973).

Of the two structures on the top of the ramp, only Structure 15 has been investigated. It is a simple building, constructed with a base of river stones and a few blocks of volcanic tuff. It has a front staircase, which allows entry to a room that has a bench of simple masonry, next to which were three *alujadores* (wide but thin river stones, which locals say were used to smooth tobacco leaves in the process of producing cigars). Along with these was found a quartz pendant. Off the southwestern corner of the structure, the remains of a smashed censer lid in the form of K'inich Yax K'uk' Mo' were found near the surface (figure 4.5). The construction fill of Structure 15 contains ceramics from the Acbi/Coner transition, but those overlying it and associated with the censer date to the Late Coner (AD 750–820). Due to its location, it is likely that the censer was smashed towards the end of the Late Classic period. The ritual materials found in this structure suggest that it was either a god-house, or possibly the residence of a ritual practitioner.

The discovery of this censer, which bears some similarity to the one found outside of the tomb of Ruler 12 (Fash 2001:107, figure 63), demonstrates that individuals living in the East Group of the site were also involved in revering the first king of Copán, and that an adherence to Copán's ideology was not limited to the more elaborate structures in the ceremonial core.

Patio D from the East Group was formed by Structures 24, 25, and 26. Of these, only Structures 25 and 26 were investigated. Both of these appear to be residential buildings that also engaged in household rituals. In Structure 26 an elaborate censer was recovered that is decorated with thorns and seeds of a ceiba tree. Such censers have been found in Copán's Main Group and associated neighborhoods such as Las Sepulturas (Willey et al. 1994). Like the censer found in front of Structure 15, this censer was also smashed on front of the steps of the structure.

All of the structures in the East Group differ in the quality of their construction from those of Las Sepulturas in that, while Sepulturas had structures with

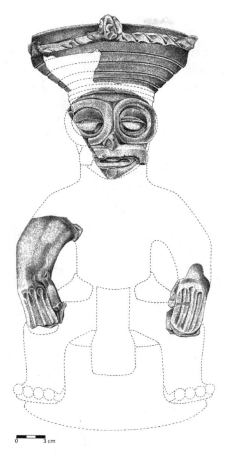

FIGURE 4.5. *Censer lid in the form of K'inich Yax K'uk' Mo', the founder of the Maya Copán dynasty. (Drawing by Elvin Arias. Excavated by the Proyecto Arqueológico Río Amarillo, Copán. Collection of the Instituto Hondureño de Antropología e Historia.)*

masonry walls, Río Amarillo's were made of wattle and daub, although in some cases their architectural layouts are similar. The foundation of Structure 25 is similar to the foundation of the smallest structures found in Plazas D and K at Las Sepulturas. In the case of Structure 26, a new room was added using the platform walls as part of a room. This construction method also bears some similarity to Structure 111, and possibly also to Structure 96 in Plaza E at Las Sepulturas, although it is smaller in size.

In all three patios discussed above, the surfaces were earthen, without any sign of paving or stucco. The buildings were of reduced dimensions when compared with those of Las Sepulturas and were predominantly made of uncut stones collected locally from the river, but their layouts and general design reflect Maya structures, with some local adaptations and perhaps foreign elements. The ceramics in this area are predominantly Maya, but less than 1 percent (.59%) of the ceramics analyzed are Ulúa Polychromes, including one nearly complete vessel. Rosemary Joyce (personal communication, 2014) describes this cylinder vase as a Yojoa class, subclass Molinero, with tripod lug feet dating between AD 650 and 750, which would have been produced somewhere between Lake Yojoa and Comayagua. She further states that the vessel was most likely made as a "presentation piece for someone outside the Ulúa marble circulation zone."

Structure 2, the West Platform, and the Western Section of Plaza B

Structure 2 was the highest structure in the site (figure 4.2). The lower two platforms of Structure 2 were built using blocks made out of volcanic tuff and cobblestones, while the upper platform was entirely built with cobblestones. The upper surface of the platform had a paved floor, or *emplantillado*, with abundant remains of burnt clay. A substantial portion of *barro quemado* complete with wood impressions was found on the back side of the structure, suggesting that the upper level of the structure was wattle and daub and that at least some of the building was burned and fell to the north.

PARAC excavations discovered the existence of the West Platform extending out from the pyramidal platform of Structure 2. The West Platform has a cut-stone block face to its south and west, and a formal stairway in the middle of the south side that connects its upper surface with Plaza B at its base (figure 4.2). The cut-stone blocks that form the West Platform suggest that it may be a product of a time when Copán had hegemony over the site—whether that time falls under the earlier or the later part of the Late Classic has yet to be determined. At one point, part of the West Platform's western wall collapsed and it was later rebuilt.

At the southwestern corner of the West Platform, steps connect its side with a stone walkway that runs a short distance along the northern side of a 35-m-long wall. This wall, or wall base, stretches out to the west end of the promontory of the upper section of the ceremonial core. The wall may have had a defensive purpose. Perhaps it was used to protect the upper section of the ceremonial core, although it is peculiar that no vestiges of a wall have been found running north–south along the western section of the promontory if it was meant to be defensive. Intriguingly, the wall at one time had an entryway near the West Platform, which was closed off at some point. Evidence suggests that the river-cobble wall had an upper wall of bajareque, which was burned and fell to the south. The burned adobe found both behind Structure 2 and to the south of the wall could be a product of a willful sacking of the center like that found by Fash et al. (2004) in Copán's core, or at El Paraíso and El Cafetal by Canuto and Bell (2013), or of a ceremonial cancellation ritual.

The Northern Residential Area (Site 5)

Research was begun in 2011 in the Northern Residential Area (NRA), also called Site 5, in the hopes that this part of Río Amarillo would reveal

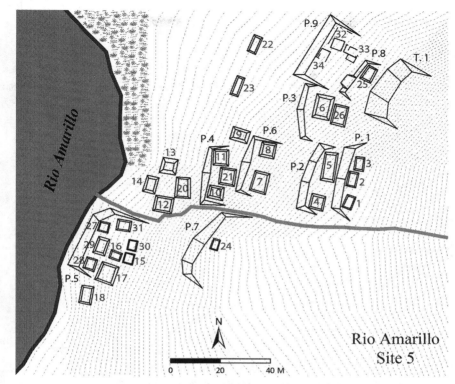

FIGURE 4.6. *Site 5, Río Amarillo. (Map by Antolín Velásquez, PARAC.)*

information on the Late Classic/Postclassic transition, and particularly on the ties between Río Amarillo and Copán's center. These residential groups predominantly rest on a steep incline (figure 4.6) and are supported with platforms anchored with stone-lined boxes filled with river cobbles.

On the lower section of the hill, the Late Classic Structure 10, resting on Platform 4, was excavated and found to have earthen-stepped terraces with cobble retaining walls (figure 4.6). This style of construction is similar to that of Los Naranjos's Structure IV, a large pyramidal platform (Barrios et al. 2013; Cruz Castillo and Valles 2002:52), although Structure 10 is of modest dimensions and was a house. The building on top of the platform is similar to other superstructures at Site 5, although the design is a bit more elaborate. What remains of the walls is mostly river cobbles, but some volcanic tuff blocks are found on the corners and the steps. It has multiple rooms and a central bench in the principal room.

Further up the hill in the eastern portion of the site are found Platforms 1–3 and 8–9 (figure 4.6). The house mounds in this area are predominantly associated with Late Classic, Terminal Classic, and Postclassic ceramics. Sixty percent of the northern half of Platform 9 was excavated through a meticulous grid that had 70 excavation units. Three small buildings and two long retaining walls on the west and north ends of the platform were uncovered. In each case all that remained were foundations made with river stones lying over an earthen floor. The landowner had cleared much of the area to grow young coffee shrubs and may have removed some parts of the structure walls. Over 10,000 ceramic sherds were recovered from this platform, with utilitarian ceramics composing the greatest numbers of sherds, including Plumbate (part of the Postclassic Ejar Complex). Also in this assemblage were some *comal* fragments caked with burned food remains. Sixty projectile points made out of chert or obsidian, as well as cores, flakes and microdebitage were found on the platform. Obsidian blades were predominantly Ixtepeque, but smaller quantities of El Chayal and Pachuca from highland Mexico were also found. The lithic assemblage allows us to document the process of production and preparation of lithic artifacts by the inhabitants of this community as well as to learn something about their trading partners.

A ramp connects Platforms 8 and 9 (see figure 4.6). Ramps have not previously been found in the Copán Valley. This construction, like the stepped-clay section in the East Group, and the stepped terraces of Structure 10 below it, echoes the ramps at Los Naranjos in the interior of Honduras, but those are from the Preclassic and Early Classic periods and this ramp dates to the Late Classic, Terminal Classic, or Postclassic. Postclassic ramps have been found at Río Claro in the Aguan Valley of northeastern Honduras (Healy 1978), but they are produced of stone and the one in the northern residential group is predominantly of clay and garbage with a layer of stone lining the surface in the form of an *emplantillado*. An offering centered in the ramp contained a fragmented polychrome vase with a pedestal base, which Rosemary Joyce identified from photographs as most likely to be Travesia Bombero, an Ulúa Polychrome type produced in the lower Ulúa Valley between AD 650 and 750 (Rosemary Joyce, personal communication, 2017; McNeil et al. 2013). The ramp itself was filled in with debris such as (predominantly) Ixtepeque obsidian flakes, chert, and ceramics (including Copador).

To the south of the ramp entrance is Structure 6, whose backside meets with Platform 9. Structure 6 consists of a stone platform with basal walls of river cobbles. *Barro quemado* distributed throughout the mound indicates that it once had a wattle-and-daub superstructure. The entrance of the structure faces south towards the ceremonial core of Río Amarillo. Excavations of the building revealed two offerings. The first consisted of two nested vessels resting under the southern end of the building and located near the stairs, which were likely placed there when the building was constructed. Both vessels date to the Late Classic: the first is a small jar and the second is a red-on-orange Chilanga bowl. The second offering was found on the steps of the building and consisted of a greenstone axe resting under two cut-stone blocks that would have effectively stopped entry to the building. The offering on the steps is particularly interesting as it indicates that the inhabitants left intentionally and had the time and energy to perform a cancelation ritual. Classic, Terminal Classic, and Postclassic ceramics were found in association with this structure, suggesting it was in use prior to and after the abandonment of Copán.

On Platform 1, two structures (1 and 2) were excavated (see figure 4.6). They contained both Late Classic and Postclassic ceramics. Structure 1 is a very small building. Structure 2 contained the remains of a round oven with burned bones inside. One partially complete vessel was found on what may have been the pathway used to enter these structures. This vessel—which is a red-slipped hemispherical bowl made of a coarse, dark, reddish-brown paste—has no known correlates in the Copán Pocket and is thus likely of local manufacture (McNeil et al. 2013). Several sherds belonging to the same type of vessel were recovered from other final occupation contexts in and around Structures 1 and 2, in association with probable Early Postclassic pottery. Unlike the multipurpose Postclassic structures in the El Bosque area of Copán, which were excavated and described by Manahan (2004), this grouping consists of three small Postclassic buildings, each with likely a specific purpose: 1 was a small storage area or sleeping space; 2 was a kitchen; and 3 has yet to be investigated. Manahan (2004) judged such a settlement pattern to be reflective of a Maya household.

In all the groups of Site 5, PARAC found offerings either within or outside of the buildings. In some cases they contained exotic goods imported from distant regions, such as Pachuca obsidian from central Mexico, or obsidian from the Lenca region's La Esperanza source, providing information on the trade networks of Río Amarillo's inhabitants that stretched beyond Maya lands. Like the East Group, Site 5 residences also contain Ulúa Polychromes, but only .30 percent of the sherds were of this type, a smaller amount than the households found closer to the ritual center of Río Amarillo.

The Postclassic occupation of Site 5 is focused in its eastern section and is higher up on the hillside than the more elaborate Late Classic structures produced of cut-stone blocks and river cobbles that are found closer to the base, on Platform 5. This reflects a pattern whereby Postclassic populations chose to locate themselves at higher elevations, perhaps for safety reasons in a postcollapse world where the might of Copán's military could no longer protect them. The later contexts were also associated with a larger number of projectile points, like Postclassic-period contexts excavated by Manahan in the El Bosque neighborhood of Copán (2004).

CONCLUSIONS

Excavations of Late Classic contexts at Río Amarillo have revealed a community tightly tied into the exchange networks and ideology of Copán from at least the reign of K'ahk Uti' Witz' K'awiil through the reign of Yax Pasaj Chan Yopaat. Some contexts, particularly in Site 5, appear to have outlasted the collapse, demonstrating a greater degree of resilience than has been found in some of Copán's groups. While the overall affiliations at Río Amarillo are Maya even in the Postclassic period, architectural styles associated with the interior of Honduras demonstrate that there were other cultural influences in the lives of this ancient town's inhabitants.

Consistent with the findings of excavations at the sites of El Puente, El Abra, and El Paraíso (Canuto and Bell 2013; Schortman and Nakamura 1991; Von Schwerin 2010), by the Late Classic period the inhabitants of Río Amarillo employed important symbols of Copán's hegemony within its center, particularly in the form of K'inich Yax K'uk' Mo' and referents to him. And like their Copán neighbors (Bill 2014), in the latter half of the Late Classic they also used small amounts of fine ceramics from communities from the interior of Honduras (Burgos et al. 2015; McNeil et al. 2013).

The use of earthen-ramped steps and ramps, both in the East Group and at Site 5 during the Late Classic, Terminal Classic, and Postclassic periods strongly suggests that at least some of the people inhabiting Río Amarillo had significant cultural links to the interior of Honduras, where this architectural practice has a long tradition. None of the other sites mentioned above has documented this type of Los Naranjos–style architecture, nor is it known elsewhere in the Copán Valley. While its appearance at Río Amarillo therefore is significant, it is impossible with so little evidence to determine the meaning of it. Did some occupants of Río Amarillo hail from the area of Lake Yojoa? Or was this style learned by Maya visitors to production sites of Ulúa Polychromes? Future research at the site may provide more nuanced answers to these questions.

ACKNOWLEDGMENTS

We are thankful to the Instituto Hondureño de Antropología e Historia for their support. Our work would not have been possible without a grant from the National Science Foundation and additional funding from PSC-CUNY. We are grateful to the PARAC laboratory technicians at CRIA, the wonderful workers from the community of La Castellona and from some of the other *aldeas* around Río Amarillo, and our current laboratory directory Mauricio Díaz. Their hard work has made the data in this chapter possible. We also appreciate comments from Erlend Johnson, Alejandro Figueroa, and Whitney Goodwin.

WORKS CITED

Abrams, Elliot M., AnnCorinne Freter, David Rue, and John Wingard. 1996. "The Role of Deforestation in the Collapse of the Late Classic Copán State." In *Tropical Deforestation: The Human Dimension*, ed. Leslie E. Sponsel, Thomas N. Headland, and Robert C. Bailey, 55–75. New York: Columbia University.

Aoyama, Kazuo. 2001. "Classic Maya State, Urbanism, and Exchange: Chipped Stone Evidence of the Valley and Its Hinterland." *American Anthropologist* 103(2):346–360.

Barrios, Edy, Cameron L. McNeil, Walter Burgos, Kristin Landau, Raquel Macario, Roberto Ramírez, and Justin Bracken. 2013. "La Vida en la Vega del Río Copán: Investigaciones en Áreas Residenciales de Río Amarillo, Copán, Honduras." Simposio de Investigaciones Arqueológicas de Guatemala 26:405–420.

Baudez, Claude, and Pierre Bequelin. 1973. *Arqueologie de Los Naranjos, Honduras*. Mexico City, Mexico: Mission Arqueologique et Ethnologique Fracaise au Mexique.

Becker, Marshall. 1999. *Excavations in Residential Areas of Tikal: Groups with Shrines*. Tikal Report 21. Philadelphia: University of Pennsylvania Museum of Archaeology and Anthropology.

Bell, Ellen E., Robert J. Sharer, Loa P. Traxler, David W. Sedat, Christine W. Carrelli, and Lynn A. Grant. 2004. "Tombs and Burials in the Early Classic Acropolis at Copán." In *Understanding Early Classic Copán*, ed. Ellen E. Bell, Marcello A. Canuto, and Robert J. Sharer, 131–158. Philadelphia: University of Pennsylvania Museum of Archaeology and Anthropology.

Bill, Cassandra R. 1997. "Patterns of Variation and Change in Dynastic Period Ceramics and Ceramic Production at Copán, Honduras." Unpublished PhD dissertation, Department of Anthropology, Tulane University, New Orleans, LA.

Bill, Cassandra R. 2014. "Shifting Fortunes and Affiliations on the Edge of Ruin: A Ceramic Perspective on the Classic Maya Collapse and Its Aftermath at Copán."

In *The Maya and Their Central American Neighbors*, ed. Geoffrey E. Braswell, 83–111. London: Routledge.

Burgos, Walter, Cameron L. McNeil, Edy Barrios, Paula Torres, and Antolín Velásquez. 2015. "Nuevos resultados de las investigaciones en el Área Central del Sitio Río Amarillo, Copán, Honduras." In *XXVIII Simposio de Investigaciones Arqueológicas en Guatemala 2014*, ed. B. Arroyo, L. Méndez Salinas, and L. Paiz, 441-452. Guatemala City, Guatemala: Asociación Tikal, Museo Nacional de Arqueología y Etnología.

Canuto, Marcello A., and Ellen E. Bell. 2013. "Archaeological Investigations in the El Paraíso Valley: The Role of Secondary Centers in the Multiethnic Landscape of Classic Period Copán." *Ancient Mesoamerica* 24(1):1–24.

Card, Jeb J., and Marc Zender. 2016. "A Seventh-Century Inscribed Miniature Flask from Copán Found at Tazumal, El Salvador." *Ancient Mesoamerica* 27(2):279–292.

Cruz Castillo, Oscar, and Erick Valles. 2002. "Proyecto Arqueólogico Los Naranjos 2001. Excavaciones en las Estructura IV del Conjunto Principal." *Yaxkin* 21(1):45–62.

Fash, Barbara. 2011. *The Copán Sculpture Museum: Ancient Maya Artistry in Stucco and Stone*. Cambridge, MA: Peabody Museum Press.

Fash, William L. 2001. *Scribes, Warriors, and Kings*. London: Thames and Hudson.

Fash, William L., E. Wyllys Andrews, and T. Kam Manahan. 2004. "Political Decentralization, Dynastic Collapse, and the Early Postclassic in the Urban Center of Copán, Honduras." In *The Terminal Classic in the Maya Lowlands: Collapse, Transition, and Transformation*, ed. Arthur A. Demarest, Prudence M. Rice, and Don S. Rice, 260–287. Boulder: University Press of Colorado.

Freter, AnnCorinne. 1988. "Classic Maya Collapse at Copán, Honduras: A Regional Settlement Perspective." Unpublished PhD dissertation, Department of Anthropology, University of Pennsylvania, Philadelphia, PA.

Gerstle, Andrea I. 1988. "Maya-Lenca Ethnic Relations in Late Classic Period Copán, Honduras." Unpublished PhD dissertation, Department of Anthropology, University of California Santa Barbara.

Healy, Paul F. 1978. "Excavations at Río Claro, Northeast Honduras: Preliminary Report." *Journal of Field Archaeology*. 5(1):15–28.

Inomata, Takeshi, and Kazuo Aoyama. 1996. "Central-Place Analysis in the La Entrada Region, Honduras: Implications of Understanding the Classic Maya Political and Economic Systems." *Latin American Antiquity* 7(4):291–312.

Komar, Oliver, Juan Pablo Arce, Christopher Begley, Franklin E. Castañeda, Knut Eiserman, Robert J. Gallardo, and Leonel Marineros. 2006. *Informe Final: Evaluación de la Biodiversidad del Parque Arqueologico y Reserva Forestal Río Amarillo (Copán, Honduras)*. San Salvador, El Salvador: SalvaNATURA Programa de Ciencias para la Conservación.

Longyear, John M., III. 1952. *Copán Ceramics: A Study of Southeastern Maya Ceramics.* Washington, DC: Carnegie Institution of Washington.

Manahan, T. Kam. 2004. "The Way Things Fall Apart: Social Organization and the Classic Maya Collapse of Copán." *Ancient Mesoamerica.* 15(1):107–125.

Manahan, T. Kam, and Marcello A. Canuto. 2009. "Bracketing the Copán Dynasty." *Latin American Antiquity* 20(4):553–580.

Martin, Simon, and Nikolai Grube. 2008. *Chronicle of the Maya Kings and Queens.* London: Thames and Hudson.

McNeil, Cameron. 2006. "Maya Interactions with the Natural World: Landscape Transformation and Ritual Plant Use at Copán, Honduras." Unpublished PhD dissertation, Department of Anthropology, City University of New York, New York, NY.

McNeil, Cameron L., and Edy Barrios, eds. 2012. *Informe Final de la 1era Temporada de Investigaciones en Río Amarillo. Proyecto Arqueológico Río Amarillo, Copán (PARAC).* Tegucigalpa, Honduras: Archives of the Instituto Hondureño de Antropología e Historia.

McNeil, Cameron L., Edy Barrios, Cassandra Bill, Walter Burgos, and Raquel Macario. 2013. "Investigando el colapso maya y periodo Postclásico en Río Amarillo, Copán, Honduras." In *XXVI Simposio de Investigaciones Arqueológicas en Guatemala 2012,* ed. Barbara Arroyo and Luis Méndez Salinas, 421–432. Guatemala City, Guatemala: Museo Nacional de Arqueología y Etnología.

McNeil, Cameron L., Edy Barrios, and Walter Burgos. 2015. "Rio Amarillo: Un Pueblo en la Cercanías de Copán." En *V Congreso Centroamericano de Arqueología en El Salvador,* ed. Heriberto Erquicia and Shioni Shibata, 54–70. San Salvador, El Salvador: Secretaría de Cultura de la Presidencia.

McNeil, Cameron L., Edy Barrios, Walter Burgos, and Raquel Macario. 2012. "Investigando canales, terrazas, lluvia y el medio ambiente en el sitio Río Amarillo, en el Valle de Copán." In *Los Investigadores de la Cultura Maya 20, Tomo II,* 9–22. México: Universidad Autónoma de Campeche.

McNeil, Cameron L., David Burney, and Lida Pigott Burney. 2010. "Evidence Disputing Deforestation as the Cause for the Collapse of the Ancient Maya Polity of Copán, Honduras." *PNAS* 107(3):1017–1022.

Miller, Kathryn. 2014. "Family, Foreigners, and Fictive Kinship: A Bioarchaeological Approach to Social Organization at Late Classic Copán." Unpublished PhD dissertation, Department of Anthropology, Arizona State University, Tempe, AZ.

Pahl, Gary W. 1987. "Survey and Excavation of La Canteada, Copán, Honduras: Preliminary Report, 1975 Season." In *The Periphery of the Southeastern Classic Maya Realm,* ed. Gary Pahl, 227–261. Los Angeles, CA: UCLA Latin American Publications.

Price, T. Douglas, James H. Burton, Robert J. Sharer, Jane E. Buikstra, Lori E. Wright, Loa P. Traxler, and Katherine A. Miller. 2010. "Kings and Commoners at Copán: Isotopic Evidence for Origins and Movement in the Classic Maya Period." *Journal of Anthropological Archaeology* 29(1):15–32.

Ramos, Jorge H. 2006. "The Iconography of Temple 16: Yax Pasaj and the Evocation or a 'Foreign' Identity at Copán." Unpublished PhD dissertation, Department of Anthropology, University of California, Riverside.

Saturno, William A. 2000. "In the Shadow of the Acropolis: Río Amarillo and its Role in the Copán Polity." Unpublished PhD dissertation, Department of Anthropology, Harvard University, Cambridge, MA.

Schele, Linda. 1987. *Notes on the Río Amarillo Altars*. Austin, TX: Copán Mosaic Project.

Schortman, Edward M. 1986. "Interaction between the Maya and non-Maya along the Late Classic Southeast Maya Periphery: The View from the Lower Motaqua Valley, Guatemala." In *The Southeast Maya Periphery*, ed. Patricia Urban and Edward Schortman, 114–137. Austin: University Press of Texas Press.

Schortman, Edward, and Seiichi Nakamura. 1991. "A Crisis of Identity: Late Classic Competition and Interaction on the Southeastern Maya Periphery." In *Latin American Antiquity* 2(4):311–336.

Schortman, Edward, and Patricia Urban. 2004. "Marching Out of Step: Early Classic Copán and Its Honduran Neighbors." In *Understanding Early Classic Copán*, ed. Ellen E. Bell, Marcello A. Canuto, and Robert J. Sharer, 319–335. Philadelphia: University of Pennsylvania Museum of Archaeology and Anthropology.

Sharer, Robert J. 2009. "The Ch'orti' Past: An Archaeological Perspective." In *The Ch'orti' Maya Area: Past and Present*, ed. Brent E. Metz, Cameron L. McNeil, and Kerry M. Hull, 124–133. Gainesville: University Press of Florida.

Sharer, Robert J., Loa P. Traxler, David W. Sedat, Ellen E. Bell, Marcello A. Canuto, and Christopher Powell. 1999. "Early Classic Architecture Beneath the Copán Acropolis: A Research Update." *Ancient Mesoamerica* 10(1):3–23.

Sheets, Payson. 2009. "Who Were Those Classic Period Immigrants into the Zapotitlán Valley, El Salvador?" In *The Ch'orti' Maya Area: Past and Present*, ed. Brent E. Metz, Cameron L. McNeil, and Kerry M. Hull, 61–77. Gainesville: University Press of Florida.

Stone, Doris. 1957. *The Archaeology of Central and Southern Honduras*. Cambridge, MA: Peabody Museum of Archaeology and Ethnology.

Stuart, David. 2004. "The Beginnings of the Copán Dynasty: A Review of the Hieroglyphic and Historical Evidence." In *Understanding Early Classic Copán*, ed. Ellen E. Bell, Marcello A. Canuto, and Robert J. Sharer, 215–247. Philadelphia: University of Pennsylvania Museum of Archaeology and Anthropology.

Stuart, David. 2007. "The Origin of Copán's Founder." *Maya Decipherment*: decipherment.wordpress.com/2007/06/25/the-origin-of-Copáns-founder/.

Taube, Karl. 2004. "Structure 10L-16 and Its Early Classic Antecedents: Fire and the Evocation and Resurrection of K'inich Yax K'uk' Mo'." In *Understanding Early Classic Copán*, ed. Ellen E. Bell, Marcello A. Canuto, and Robert J. Sharer, 215–247. Philadelphia: University of Pennsylvania Museum of Archaeology and Anthropology.

Thompson, J. Eric S. 1970. *Maya History and Religion*. Norman: University of Oklahoma Press.

Turner, B. L., II, W. Johnson, G. Mahood, F. Wiseman, and J. Poole. 1983. "Habitat y agricultura en la region de Copán." In *Introducción a la Arqueología de Copán, Honduras*, Tomo I, ed. Claude Baudez, 35–142. Tegucigalpa, Honduras: Instituto Hondureño de Antropología e Historia.

Valdés, Juan Antonio. 1997. "Kaminaljuyú, Guatemala: Descubrimientos recientes sobre poder y manejo hidráulico." In *Memorias de Tercer Congreso Internacional de Mayistas, 1995*, 752–770. Mexico City, Mexico: Centro de Estudios Mayas, Universidad Nacional Autónoma de México.

Von Schwerin, Jennifer. 2010. "The Problem of the 'Copán Style' and Political Identity: The Architectural Sculpture of El Paraíso, Honduras in Regional Context." *Mexicon* 32(3):56–65.

Wauchope, Robert. 1938. *Modern Maya Houses: A Study of Their Archaeological Significance*. Publication 502. Washington, DC: Carnegie Institution of Washington.

Webster, David L., and AnnCorinne Freter. 1990. "The Demography of Late Classic Copán." In *Precolumbian Population History in the Maya Lowlands*, ed. Don S. Rice and T. Patrick Culbert, 37–61. Albuquerque: University of New Mexico Press.

Webster, David, AnnCorinne Freter, and Nancy Gonlin. 2000. *Copán: The Rise and Fall of an Ancient Maya Kingdom*. Fort Worth, TX: Harcourt College Publishers.

Willey, Gordon R., and Richard M. Leventhal. 1979. "Prehistoric Settlement at Copán." In *Maya Archaeology and Ethnohistory*, ed. Norman Hammond, 75–102. Austin: University of Texas Press.

Willey, Gordon R., Richard M. Leventhal, Arthur A. Demarest, and William L. Fash. 1994. *Ceramics and Artifacts from Excavations in the Copán Residential Zone*. Cambridge, MA: Peabody Museum of Archaeology and Ethnology.

5

The Archaeology of
Jesús de Otoro and
Intervalley Variation
in Central Honduras

WILLIAM J. McFARLANE AND
MIRANDA STOCKETT SURI

Southeast Mesoamerica is an often-used label for
the contiguous national borders of Guatemala, El
Salvador, and Honduras (figure 5.1). With few exceptions, these modern borders demarcate the southern limits of the research area for most Mayanists.
So too do these borders mark the northern limits
for the archaeologists of Central America. Indeed,
Southeast Mesoamerica as a concept is problematic
because it glosses over the differences of the peoples
living along these cultural demarcations. This is especially the case for the ancient inhabitants who lived
in northwestern and central Honduras. For the contributors to this volume, the edges of these culture
areas are central to our research, and the dynamic
interactions of the peoples and polities across this
region are exceedingly interesting because they do
not conform to neatly constrained labels imposed
from the outside.

The precolumbian peoples in this area are culturally united by a suite of shared material traits and are
also marked by an absence of more traditional "Maya"
characteristics. For example, much like their Maya
neighbors, Southeast Mesoamericans built platforms
of stone and earth, often organized loosely around
centralized patios and sometimes exhibiting similar principles of cosmic/spatial layout and aesthetic
design (Ashmore 1987, 1991). Likewise, although
there is a dizzying abundance of ceramic types in
Southeastern Mesoamerica, some ceramics closely

DOI: 10.5876/9781646420971.c005

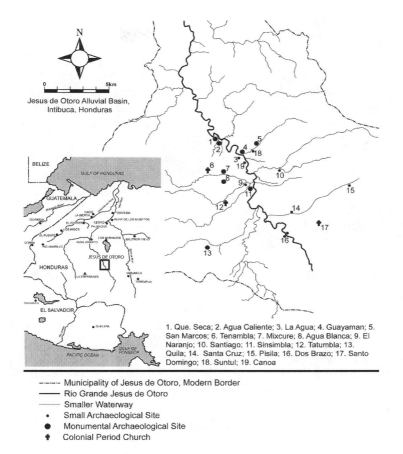

FIGURE 5.1. *Southeastern Mesoamerica (inset) and settlement map of the Jesús de Otoro Valley.*

mimic Maya forms of decoration, incorporating human figures and "pseudo-glyphs" (Joyce 1993a).

Although similarity in rituals, construction practices, and other aspects of material culture attest to interaction with the Maya, Southeast Mesoamericans are also marked as culturally distinct. They left behind no hieroglyphic inscriptions or definitive evidence of written languages. They typically eschewed cut-stone masonry in favor of more expedient cobble-and-earth constructions. They engaged in arguably less complex—and certainly more varied—forms of sociopolitical organization than their Maya neighbors.

Here, we call attention to these differences during a time of rapid transformation, the Late Classic period. Explosive growth is characteristic of this period, as central Honduras is filled with increasingly complex polities and rising populations (see Healy 1984 for a concise but now somewhat outdated synthesis). A shift in material culture also accompanies this transition, in which monumental constructions become more common, distinctive polychrome traditions emerge, and obsidian-exchange networks are stabilized. All of this signals changes in the organization of the local and regional economy.

Historically, explanations for this transformation looked to the role of the Copán polity. Others (Boone and Wiley 1988; Urban and Schortman 1986) have put forth a strong case that early interpretations with Copán as an instigator for change among the less-developed peoples to the east were flawed. Such outdated models often portrayed non-Maya peoples beyond the frontier as passive recipients of the ideological sophistication and statecraft of the more-complex Maya.

Of course, the numerous large-scale research efforts spanning the 1970s through 1990s have demonstrated older core-periphery models to be ill-suited to explaining the rise of complexity in the Southeast (Robinson 1987; Schortman and Urban 1994, 1996). In advancing theoretical models of interregional interaction, these efforts revealed that some polities, such as Gualjoquito in the middle Ulúa drainage, were indeed intimately connected with the Copán polity (Ashmore 1987; Schortman and Urban 1987; Schortman et al. 1986). Other communities, such as those across the Sula plain, were engaged with distant Maya centers along the coast of Belize (Joyce 1986). More important, it is now clear that many polities in central Honduras were only marginally related to the Maya, and others, seemingly not at all (Hirth 1988).

While the notion of more autonomous and self-guided interactions replaced earlier core-periphery sentiments, questions of intraregional concern captured the attention of scholars working along the border of Guatemala and Honduras. With few exceptions (Aoyama 1994, 2001; Canuto and Bell 2008, 2013; Inomata and Aoyama 1996; Johnson, chapter 3, this volume; Schortman and Nakamura 1991), these efforts have focused on polities constrained by valleys, which coincidentally define the limits of research permits issued by the Instituto Hondureño de Antropología y Historia (IHAH). Although the particular research agendas and theoretical perspectives of these scholars vary, the collective results point again to the profound variation and continuity of these Late Classic cultures.

Although explanations for this pattern are of course contingent on local developments, we propose that alternative strategies employed to interact with agents of societies in neighboring valleys had a significant influence on these local trajectories. Indeed, by focusing on intervalley interactions among the polities in central Honduras, there is great potential to highlight one of the most interesting facets of this region.

Recently, Menzies and Haller (2012) have amply demonstrated the utility of adopting a similar "macroregional" perspective (following Flannery 1976:5; Redmond et al. 1999:110) to compare contemporary developments across the Late Ceramic political landscape of central Panama. We are not the first to call attention to the utility of such an approach (Beaudry-Corbett and Henderson 1993; Hirth et al. 1993:230), but we do think that comparable and robust data-sets from this region are now widely available.

To that end, in this chapter we consider the nature of intervalley variation in the Late Classic remains of central Honduras as an outcome of alternative interaction strategies. We accomplish this by placing the findings of our research in the Jesús de Otoro Valley within the broader context of the region. We first present the initial findings of our archaeological efforts at Sinsimbla, a previously uninvestigated Late Classic monumental site centrally located in the valley. We then compare three lines of evidence—ceramic assemblages, site layout, and settlement concentrations—across Late Classic contexts in central Honduras. We conclude with a discussion of how this distinctive pattern may result from differing strategies for exchange, competition, and emulation enacted by Southeast Mesoamericans beginning in the fifth century.

SINSIMBLA AND THE JESÚS DE OTORO VALLEY

Our investigations contribute another piece to the emerging picture of the variation and continuity exhibited by precolumbian peoples in central Honduras. The Jesús de Otoro Valley is located in west-central Honduras, roughly 30 km south of Lake Yojoa (figure 5.1). The valley is topographically defined by a centrally located alluvial basin surrounded to the east, south, and west by mountains. The Río Otoro is formed by several tributaries and drains to the north, becoming the Ulúa River. Considering the substantial research efforts to the north and west, the Jesús de Otoro Valley completes the southern portion of a well-documented region elsewhere referred to as the Central Honduran Corridor (Dixon 1989a).

The floor of the modern Jesús de Otoro basin is taken up with the cultivation of rice, corn, beans, chiles, and coffee, as well as fields dedicated to cattle ranching. As a result of the modern agroeconomy, most of the valley is deforested and clear of significant vegetation, facilitating archaeological survey but increasing damage to archaeological remains. The archaeological remains in the valley include abundant precolumbian settlements dominated by several monumental centers, mostly clustered along the Río Otoro. The contemporaneity of these monumental centers is unclear, as settlement chronologies have not been confirmed.

Although the archaeological heritage of the Jesús de Otoro Valley was first documented more than half a century ago (Lunardi 1943), systematic research in the valley did not begin until 2004. In collaboration with local informants, IHAH produced site maps for most of the 19 precolumbian and colonial-period sites in the valley (Cruz Castillo 2004). When this was coupled with a settlement map produced by a local informant, Nery Fiallos, the extent and distribution of the archaeological remains in the valley began to take shape. To date, a complete pedestrian survey of the valley floor has not been completed. However, based on the extent of clearing and development of the valley floor, it is unlikely that many sites with surface-visible architecture remain unrecorded.

Two brief visits to the valley in 2004 and 2006 provided us with several initial impressions. First, while monumental constructions were easily identified, smaller mounds were not abundant, likely a consequence of modern farming activities. It is worth noting that ballcourts, a feature common to the neighboring valleys (see Begley, chapter 7, this volume), are conspicuously absent in the valley. Second, given the size of the valley floor, settlement within the Jesús de Otoro was surprisingly concentrated. The valley floor covers 72 km² yet the bulk of the known sites are located within a 12-km² area (Cruz Castillo 2004:16). This pattern is indicative of a potentially complicated sociopolitical, ethnic, and/or functional relationship among the sites (Crumley 1995; Joyce and Hendon 2000:154–155; Yaeger and Canuto 2000).

Finally, the precolumbian sites with monumental architecture exhibited strikingly similar site-planning principles. While some monumental sites exhibit more rectilinear organization and greater restricted access than others, a fascinating pattern was noted. Of the largest visited, all five of the top-tier sites shared a large plaza bordered on the east by a monumental platform and superstructure (figure 5.2). Although the site layouts of this region are exceptionally diverse (Dixon 1989a, Joyce and Hendon 2000; Robinson 1986; Stockett 2010; Urban 1986), this particular east-focused pattern seems unique to the Jesús de Otoro valley.

Taken together, these factors braise the question: how does the cultural pattern exhibited by the remains from Jesús de Otoro compare with emerging models from neighboring areas in Southeastern Mesoamerica? We explore this question by looking closer at the site of Sinsimbla, which was the focus of

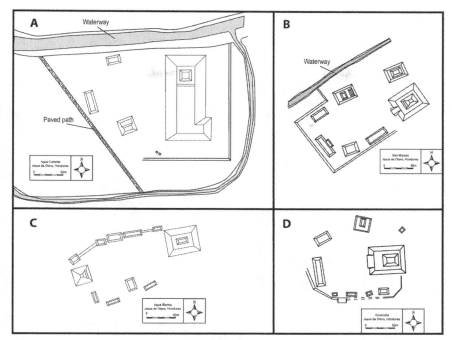

FIGURE 5.2. *Common site plans for precolumbian sites in the Jesús de Otoro Valley. (A) Agua Caliente, (B) San Marcos, (C) Agua Blanca, (D) Sinsimbla.*

our work in the Jesús de Otoro valley from 2007 through 2011 (McFarlane and Suri 2012; Stockett and McFarlane 2007, 2008).

ARCHAEOLOGICAL RESEARCH AT SINSIMBLA

Our formal investigations began at Sinsimbla with a pedestrian survey, which revealed several dense artifact scatters within the surrounding plowed agricultural fields (see figure 5.3). In most cases, these exhibited concentrations of artifacts mixed with river-rounded cobbles atop barely visible rises. The artifact assemblage from surface collections are predominantly Late Classic pottery types with trace amounts of Early Classic and Terminal Classic types accompanied by assorted chipped-chert and obsidian artifacts. These scatters are all that remain of damaged ancient residential architecture.

The layout of the Main Plaza at Sinsimbla (designated as Operation 1) is representative of the east-focused site-planning principle of monumental

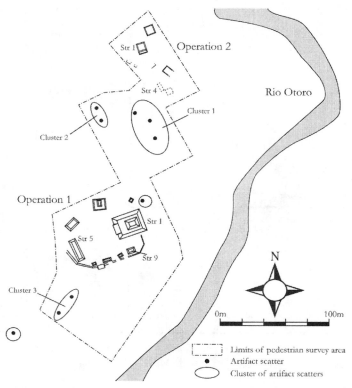

FIGURE 5.3. *Limits of pedestrian survey and sampled structures at Sinsimbla, Jesús de Otoro Valley.*

settlements in the Jesús de Otoro Valley. The expansive plaza is defined by nine surface-visible structures. The largest of these is Structure 1, a monumental platform at the eastern edge of the plaza with an outset stair facing west and a superstructure with a total elevation of 10 m above the modern ground surface. The topography surrounding the Main Plaza is demarcated by a steep but short decline to the west and south, then gradually dropping to the southeast and the Río Otoro.

To the north of the Main Plaza lies a smaller complex of five modestly sized surface-visible structures atop a slight topographic rise. This residential complex was designated as Operation 2. Three additional features were noted, but poor preservation precluded clear classification as architectural or nonstructural elements. Unlike at Operation 1, there were no clearly formed patios or plazas identified in this small northern group.

Test excavations in association with the better-preserved structures of Operation 1 and Operation 2 yielded key information regarding construction techniques, a history of modification and expansion, and distribution of material remains. All excavated contexts revealed a common practice of utilizing unmodified cobbles as fill for basal platforms, and no cut-stone blocks were encountered in any context. Most excavations exposed collapsed walls of basal platforms and debris associated with fallen superstructures.

OPERATION 1

Although lacking evidence for modification to the platform or superstructure, the stratigraphic sequence identified in association with the monumental eastern pyramid revealed a history of cultural modifications to the surface of the Main Plaza. On at least two occasions the surface of the plaza was leveled and finished with a compacted clay-like soil. If these relatively thick deposits (each 20 cm thick) are representative of treatment to the entire Main Plaza surface, then each episode would have required a significant investment of resources and labor. The absence of material remains in association with these deposits indicates that the plaza surface was swept clean.

A test probe east of Structure 9, a smaller mound immediately south of the principal pyramid, revealed an alternative enhancement of the plaza surface. Here, the building material that raised the surface consisted primarily of dry core fill of unmodified cobbles built atop the ancient ground surface. A thin layer of packed soil was later deposited on top of the fill to create a smooth surface. Its location adjacent to the southeastern corner of the Main Plaza created a relatively private space and this may account for the different application of construction methods.

Test excavations along the western base of this smaller mound exposed fragmentary evidence of *bajareque* from the collapsed superstructure. Of some interest were large fragments of burnt clay, presumably utilized as a plaster-like treatment to cover the exterior of the cobble-filled basal platform. It also served as a medium for modeled decoration. In particular, one large fragment exhibited a curling sculpted design reminiscent of depictions of floral elements (figure 5.4).

OPERATION 2

The best-preserved archaeological remains were recovered from the northern residential group, Operation 2. Here, along the north side of the largest

FIGURE 5.4. *Decorative element of burnt clay, exterior treatment of Structure 9, Operation 1, Sinsimbla, Jesús de Otoro Valley.*

edifice, Structure 1, we exposed a low cobble terrace faced with burnt clay similar to that recovered from the Main Plaza. The clay was used as an exterior surface for the cobble terrace as well as applied as a formal plaster-like treatment to the ground surface. This "flooring" extends north roughly 30 cm from the base of the platform and likely extends further (although no formal termination of the surface was identified).

This clay surface sealed a stratified midden. One of two radiocarbon dates was extracted from this context, placing activities associated with this structure to the Late Classic (1320 ± 30; Beta-338857, charred material; $\delta^{13}C$ = -26.6‰; 2σ cal AD 660 to 780). A second radiocarbon date was recovered from a midden in association with a smaller structure near the southern end of Operation 2 (1430 ± 30; Beta-338858, charred material; $\delta^{13}C$ = -24.4‰; 2σ cal AD 570–650). These Late Classic designations correspond well with the vast majority of ceramic types recovered from these contexts. We argue that the founding and occupation of Sinsimbla falls within the Late Classic–period transformations noted throughout the region.

Artifact Classification

The ceramic, lithic, and special-find data based on samples taken from the entire assemblage from Operations 1 and 2 are summarized in table 5.1. For ceramics, specific classes based on slight differences in surface treatment have been combined into diagnostic groups. Well-known diagnostic types associated with the Late Classic Honduran Polychrome Tradition (Henderson and Beaudry-Corbett 1993; Joyce 1993a), such as Ulúa Polychrome, Monte Grande, and Cancique, were noted in the assemblage. The Red-on-Natural varieties are a utilitarian ware local to the Jesús de Otoro Valley. Our Early Classic category combines Usulutan wares and a contemporary red-painted variety. The Terminal Classic category consists almost exclusively of sherds classified as Las Vegas Polychrome. Miscellaneous polychrome, slipped, or undecorated types constitute the remaining category. Specimens for which no surface treatment remains have been excluded. These ceramic classes are summarized by context in table 5.2.

Technological analysis of the chipped-stone assemblage (following Clark 1997; Clark and Bryant 1997; Sheets 1975) revealed that unspecialized expedient percussion was the most commonly utilized reduction technique at Sinsimbla. To a lesser extent, pressure flaking and retouch were utilized in the manufacture of bifacial tools and in the modification of expedient flakes. Prismatic blades were present in all excavated contexts, but lacking evidence for blade production debris it is unclear where (or if) blade production took place at Sinsimbla.

Special finds were recovered in limited amounts at Sinsimbla. Various types of incensario fragments were the most commonly encountered special artifacts. Ladle-style censers with hollow-tube, solid, or strap handles were found in contexts at Operation 2 and Operation 1. Remaining paint on these incensarios was red in color. Modeled incensarios were also recovered from Operation 2, including a noteworthy fragment of an effigy incensario with a life-sized modeled human face.

Remaining special finds include two worked sherds, two heavily eroded figurine fragments, two metate fragments, and a fragmentary bark beater. A single incomplete earspool is the only item of ornamentation or jewelry recovered from Sinsimbla. Finally, two metate fragments are noteworthy as the only special finds recovered in association with the artifact scatters between Operations 1 and 2.

Summary of Findings

Our work at Sinsimbla allows tentative construction of a cultural and chronological framework for the site, which may in turn further our understanding

TABLE 5.1. Artifact counts and excavation volume from all excavated contexts at Sinsimbla, Jesús de Otoro Valley

Structure: Stratum	Pottery	Chipped Stone	Bajareque (g)	Figurines	Incensarios	Worked Sherd	Ear Spool	Bark Beater	Ground Stone
Op. 1: Str. 1	235.0	193.0	1,886.2	0.0	3.0	1.0	1.0	0.0	0.0
3.1 m³	*75.8*	*62.3*	*608.4*	*0.0*	*1.0*	*0.3*	*0.3*	*0.0*	*0.0*
Op. 1: Str. 5	248.0	55.0	3,115.6	0.0	0.0	0.0	0.0	1.0	0.0
1.1 m³	*225.5*	*50.0*	*2,832.4*	*0.0*	*0.0*	*0.0*	*0.0*	*0.9*	*0.0*
Op. 1: Str. 9	930.0	312.0	4,051.0	1.0	1.0	0.0	0.0	0.0	0.0
3.2 m³	*290.6*	*97.5*	*1,265.9*	*0.3*	*0.3*	*0.0*	*0.0*	*0.0*	*0.0*
All Op. 1	1,413.0	560.0	9,052.8	1.0	4.0	1.0	1.0	1.0	0.0
7.4 m³	*190.9*	*75.7*	*1,223.4*	*0.1*	*0.5*	*0.1*	*0.1*	*0.1*	*0.0*
Op. 2: Str. 1	2708.0	637.0	117.0	1.0	14.0	1.0	0.0	0.0	1.0
2.5 m³	*1,083.2*	*254.8*	*46.8*	*0.4*	*5.6*	*0.4*	*0.0*	*0.0*	*0.4*
Op. 2: Str. 4	789.0	132.0	425.0	3.0	5.0	0.0	0.0	0.0	1.0
1.0 m³	*789.0*	*132.0*	*425.0*	*3.0*	*5.0*	*0.0*	*0.0*	*0.0*	*1.0*
All Op. 2	3497.0	769.0	542.0	4.0	19.0	1.0	0.0	0.0	2.0
3.5 m³	*999.1*	*219.7*	*154.9*	*1.1*	*5.4*	*0.3*	*0.0*	*0.0*	*0.6*
All Excavated Contexts	4,910.0	1,329.0	9,594.8	5.0	23.0	2.0	1.0	1.0	2.0
10.9 m³	*450.5*	*121.9*	*880.3*	*0.5*	*2.1*	*0.2*	*0.1*	*0.1*	*0.2*

Note: Italics signify artifact counts adjusted by volume.

TABLE 5.2. Classified ceramics from excavated contexts at Sinsimbla, Jesús de Otoro Valley

Structure: Stratum	Honduras Polychrome		Red-on-Natural		Early Classic		Terminal Classic		Other		Subtotal	
	N	mass (g)	N	mass (g)	N	mass (g)	N	mass (g)	N	mass (g)	N	mass (g)
Op. 1: Str. 1	30.0	127.4	56.0	308.3	7.0	20.3	3.0	9.4	28.0	158.6	124.0	624.0
	24.2%	20.4%	45.2%	49.4%	5.6%	3.3%	2.4%	1.5%	22.6%	25.4%		
Op. 1: Str. 5	27.0	78.8	83.0	277.1	4.0	18.2	0.0	0.0	39.0	96.2	153.0	470.3
	17.6%	16.8%	54.2%	58.9%	2.6%	3.9%	0.0%	0.0%	25.5%	20.5%		
Op. 1: Str. 9	87.0	220.6	71.0	366.0	77.0	369.8	0.0	0.0	158.0	579.4	393.0	1,535.8
	22.1%	14.4%	18.1%	23.8%	19.6%	24.1%	0.0%	0.0%	40.2%	37.7%		
All Op. 1	144.0	426.8	210.0	951.4	88.0	408.3	3.0	9.4	225.0	834.2	670.0	2630.1
	21.5%	16.2%	31.3%	36.2%	13.1%	15.5%	0.4%	0.4%	33.6%	31.7%		
Op. 2: Str. 1	217.0		157.0		25.0		1.0		84.0		484.0	
	44.8%		32.4%		5.2%		0.2%		17.4%			
Op. 2: Str. 4	72.0		82.0		7.0		0.0		21.0		182.0	
	39.6%		45.1%		3.8%		0.0%		11.5%			
All Op. 2	289.0		239.0		32.0		1.0		105.0		666.0	
	43.4%		35.9%		4.8%		0.2%		15.8%			
All Excavated Contexts	433.0		449.0		120.0		4.0		330.0		1,336.0	
	32.4%		33.6%		9.0%		0.3%		24.7%			

of the Jesús de Otoro Valley. Limited occupation appears to have begun at both the monumental core and surrounding residential compounds during the Early Classic. Subsequently, the Sinsimbla community underwent significant sociopolitical changes, evidenced by construction of the monumental Structure 1 in Operation 1 and smaller structures bordering the Main Plaza.

Ulúa Polychromes, diagnostic for the Late Classic, were recovered from all structures, small and large. The relative scarcity of Terminal Classic types suggests site abandonment began prior to the tenth century AD. Therefore, the majority of cultural activity appears to date to the Late Classic. Further, the inhabitants of Sinsimbla were engaged in intraregional interactions across central Honduras; evidence suggests that they were producing and/or acquiring recognizable Ulúa Polychrome types and varieties.

The Sinsimbla ceramic assemblage conforms most frequently with the Ulúa Polychrome Red Group (Joyce 1993b:260–261). Other decorative types include Monte Grandes and Canciques. Together these ceramics clearly place Sinsimbla's occupants within a wider exchange network extending across Southeastern Mesoamerica from the Comayagua Valley to the Sula plain. Perhaps not surprisingly, the decorative forms found at Sinsimbla exhibit the greatest similarity with the Jesús de Otoro Valley's nearest neighbors: the regions adjoining Lake Yojoa (see Baudez and Becquelin 1973; Beaudry-Corbett 1993).

Although there are slight variations in the frequency of Late Classic types between the civic-ceremonial and residential areas, we attribute this distribution to the nature of contexts sampled. The artifact assemblage from Operation 2 originated from dense midden deposits in association with residential activities, and similarly dense deposits remained elusive at Operation 1. Notably, sherd counts of Honduran Polychrome types constitute 45 and 40 percent of the analyzed sample from excavated contexts at Operation 2. Similar types were noted in much lower frequencies in excavated contexts at Operation 1.

Given the difference in types of contexts, this disparity in frequency cannot be conclusively attributed to restricted access for these wares. Indeed, polychrome vessels were present in all sampled structures, regardless of size or location. The ubiquitous deposition of these wares across the site, and presumably across socially diverse segments of Sinsimbla's community, conforms to a pattern noted in other valleys of central Honduras (Joyce 1993a:52; chapter 13, this volume).

Chipped-stone artifacts reduced from nonlocal resources were also widely and equitably distributed at Sinsimbla. The most commonly used obsidian was from the nearby La Esperanza quarry (Sheets et al. 1990); however, trace amounts of obsidian from other sources were present. Therefore, control over access and distribution of nonlocal resources does not appear to have been limited to a specific segment of the Sinsimbla community. This poses interesting questions about the nature of the local economy, markers of status and differentiation within the valley, and general sociopolitical interactions (*sensu* Blanton et al. 1996, DeMarrais et al. 1996; Roscoe 1993) that can only be answered by future research.

Imported goods were evenly distributed, but we did observe some concentrations of ritual paraphernalia at Sinsimbla. The largest structures in both Operations 1 and 2 appear to be the locus of ritual activities. The terminal debris associated with the monumental pyramid in Operation 1 contained a relatively high frequency of incensario fragments, as did similar contexts associated with the central structure in Operation 2 (see table 5.1). It is possible that the larger size of these structures is a direct outcome of these ritual activities. That is, ritual performance may have been used to co-opt the labor needed to found and expand these structures (Stockett 2007).

The massive size of the eastern pyramid in Operation 1, for example, likely required labor contributions from the entire populace of Sinsimbla, while the more diminutive structure in Operation 2 drew labor from a much smaller segment of the community. Interestingly, this structure in Operation 2 also yielded a wider array of artifacts, suggesting it served a variety of functions including and beyond ritual activities.

Regarding economic organization at Sinsimbla, the limited evidence does suggest that not all segments of the community engaged in similar craft-production activities. In particular, sampled structures from both Operations 1 and 2 revealed concentrations of production debris, particularly from formal chipped-stone tools. Whether the assemblage from these buildings is indicative of domestic or other craft-production activities is not as yet clear. Unfortunately, the analysis of the ceramic assemblage was left at an early stage, and determination of local and imported wares based on paste groups is inconclusive. To date, no formal production locales or workshops have been identified.

Investigations at Sinsimbla, therefore, provide new and preliminary insights into the lives of the precolumbian inhabitants of the Jesús de Otoro Valley. Occupation began with small-scale settlement on the western bank of the central Otoro River near the end of the Early Classic. Soon after, the population expanded, undergoing significant sociopolitical changes. The built environment was transformed dramatically with the construction of the monumental east structure and other edifices along the Main Plaza. The process by which these structures were raised is not yet entirely clear, but it may be that some segment of the community drew on public ritual displays and control over aspects of the political economy to increase their power.

The ceramic assemblage suggests that once Sinsimbla was founded, external trade ties shifted from the Usulután-producing regions in the south toward the lower Ulúa and Lake Yojoa regions in the north. The reasons for this also remain unclear but speak to the dynamic nature of interaction within Southeastern Mesoamerica. Interestingly, there is an absence of familiar Maya types, namely Copador, in the Sinsimbla assemblage. Taken by itself this evidence may suggest that interaction with centers such as Copán was not emphasized.

However, the practice of using plaster as an architectural and decorative element does seem to have been utilized in Operations 1 and 2 at Sinsimbla, albeit through the application of a more humble burnt-clay material. The floral decorative element recovered from excavations in Operation 1 is an unusual and noteworthy example of this practice. It may be the case that people living at Sinsimbla were drawing upon extralocal notions of architectural embellishment and adapting them to suit locally available resources and aesthetics. Simply because there is no evidence for Maya ceramics in the Sinsimbla assemblage does not mean that people within the Jesús de Otoro Valley were completely unaware of other elements of Maya cultural expression. Indeed, the selective incorporation of some traits and rejection of others complicates simplistic and outdated interpretations of passive recipients living beyond the Maya frontier, as well as claims of homogeneity of the strategies employed by populations in this region.

The site-planning principles and settlement of the Jesús de Otoro Valley are significant points of divergence from their more complex neighbors. The layout of monumental architecture at these centers follows a common template and presumably shared affiliations (Ashmore 1991; Schortman and Nakamura 1991). At each site, access to the large plaza is partially restricted through the construction of architectural elements such as a large eastern pyramid, raised platforms, walls, or connected range structures. This pattern is analogous to the layout of the Late Classic site of Cementerio de Yarumela in the neighboring Comayagua Valley, though most contemporary Comayagua sites are dispersed clusters lacking a central plaza (Dixon 1989a, 1989b). Interestingly, some sites in the Jesús de Otoro Valley incorporated rivers as an integral component of the main plaza. Agua Caliente and San Marcos, for example, are well suited to receive waterborne traffic but also exhibit the use of constructed elements that would limit overland access to the central plaza (see figure 5.2).

Ashmore and Sabloff (2002:202) have argued that simplicity in monumental site layout is indicative of a relatively stable political history or short-term occupation. Interestingly, the construction of monumental platforms is a well-established practice of social reproduction in central Honduras and the roots of this practice lie in the Formative period (Dixon et al. 1994; Joyce 2004:23), predating widespread occupation in the Otoro Valley. Whether the use of monumental architecture—and its particular placement within Jesús de Otoro sites—is the result of shared cosmological tenets among Southeast Mesoamerican peoples, political emulation of established neighbors, or some local factors (Ashmore and Sabloff 2002:203; Joyce 2004:7; Joyce et al. 2009; Renfrew 1987:8–9; Stockett 2010; von Schwerin 2011) is not clear from our dataset.

There are also unanswered questions regarding the nature of sociopolitical organization within the Jesús de Otoro Valley itself. Of pressing concern is the question: how does Sinsimbla relate to other settlements within the valley? As described above, the central valley basin is densely packed with 15 precolumbian sites of varying sizes, most of which are located within a 12 km^2 area along the banks of the Otoro River. If the pace of development at Sinsimbla is extended to similarly sized sites, then the Otoro Valley may parallel the rapid development of social complexity noted elsewhere in the region (Schortman and Nakamura 1991; Urban and Schortman 1988).

Despite possible similarities to other regions, the settlement hierarchy of the Jesús de Otoro Valley presents an unusual pattern in which a seeming overabundance of relatively large sites dominates a seeming paucity of small-scale habitation and special-function locales. Of the 16 precolumbian sites in the valley (see figure 5.1), only four are isolated structures or groups of structures with elevation of 2 m or less (La Agua, Santiago, Santa Cruz, and Dos Brazos). Larger sites with multiple structures, arranged around a courtyard with the tallest structures rising 2–3 m above the modern ground surface, are the most common (Suntul, Canoa, El Naranjo, Quebrada Seca, Quila, and Mixcure). Sites at the scale of Sinsimbla are also common, with a large principal structure over 10 m in elevation and smaller structures arranged around a monumental court plaza (Agua Caliente, Guayaman, San Marcos, and Agua Blanca).

Two factors help to explain this pattern. The first is that modern agricultural activities have likely destroyed the surface-visible architecture that would provide evidence of smaller habitation sites. Our pedestrian survey at Sinsimbla supports this argument, as we were able to identify artifact scatters representing destroyed house mounds. Given the extent of farming and use of mechanized plowing, destruction of small habitation sites is likely widespread. Thus, the ancient landscape probably contained far more small sites than are detectable today.

Even accounting for the lack of smaller settlements, the sociopolitical organization of the ancient Jesús de Otoro Valley does not appear to conform to a hierarchical distribution (Johnson, chapter 3, this volume). Most notably, the current evidence suggests there was no single primate center from which activities were coordinated across a valley-wide polity. Rather, multiple centers may have functioned as peer polities or as part of a heterarchically organized polity (Crumley 1979:144; Joyce, chapter 13, this volume; Marquart and Crumley 1987). At the very least, paramount elites do not appear to have been able to influence subordinates to settle nearby. Thus, the local political economy may have exhibited limited disparity among ranked segments (de Montmollin 1989).

Another alternative, which must be verified by further excavation, is the possibility that these larger settlements were occupied consecutively rather than simultaneously. However, due to their similarity in site plan we view it as more likely that they are contemporaneous. If this were the case, it would place the settlement pattern of Jesús de Otoro in line with those identified in the Comayagua Valley (Dixon 1989b) but divergent from most other valleys in Southeastern Mesoamerica. Settlement pattern research undertaken in valleys to the north and west of Jesús de Otoro generally recounts a landscape populated with many small sites supporting a few central places (Joyce et al. 2009; Nakamura 1987; Schortman 1993; Schortman and Nakamura 1991) or a single primate center overseeing a hierarchy of at least three tiers (Hasemann 1987; Pope 1987; Schortman and Urban 1987; Schortman et al. 2001; Urban 1986; Urban et al. 1999; Wells 2003; Willey and Leventhal 1979).

At the current state of research in the Jesús de Otoro Valley, explanations for these patterns are open ended. The ceramic assemblage from Sinsimbla is suggestive of close ties among ceramic producers along the middle and lower Ulúa River to the north. Yet, the acquisition of lowland Maya polychrome wares is not represented in the data. The use of monumental architecture to guide movement and focus diverges from the site layouts described from neighboring valleys. Further, the concentration of similarly sized centers with east-focused main plazas does not align with the more hierarchical political organization found in many of the neighboring valleys. Taken together, these lines of evidence reveal that there is a great deal of heterogeneity of political, economic, and social organization during the Late Classic period in Southeast Mesoamerica. In the following discussion, we consider the role of intervalley interactions as one factor contributing to these patterns of variation in central Honduras.

DISCUSSION

Albeit limited, the archaeological evidence from Sinsimbla and the Jesús de Otoro Valley raises questions about the diversity and continuity of cultural patterns throughout the region. Returning to our central point, we question whether the datasets from these neighboring valleys truly reflect a shared cultural affiliation and concordant identities. We suggest that there are clear differences in the distribution of polychrome wares, site layout, and settlement patterns in the neighboring valleys of central Honduras. Moreover, the variation in material culture reflects alternative if not divergent Late Classic practices. If this is the case, then perhaps we need to develop a new model to understand this region. We believe that one explanation is through the perspective of intervalley interactions.

Ceramic assemblages have long been identified as material expressions of group identity. The incorporation of foreign elements and imported wares provides supporting evidence for the spread of economic exchange networks and shared ideas. Drawing on existing ceramic datasets and chemical source analysis, scholars of the Southeast can begin to fine-tune our understanding of the movement of pottery, as well as the spread of influential ideas about how pottery should be made, decorated, and used from zone to zone within the Southeast. This might shed light on the types of networks uniting or dividing the region and how they changed over time (Joyce, chapter 13, this volume).

The Honduran Polychrome Tradition (Henderson and Beaudry-Corbett 1993) is a prime example of alternative strategies employed in Southeast Mesoamerica. When the Honduran polychromes were described (often disparagingly) in contrast to their Late Classic contemporaries in the Maya area, it is easy to consider them as a homogenous group. However, when an intervalley perspective is adopted, a number of aesthetically complex and symbolically rich varieties emerge (Joyce 1993a).

Bold geometric types, reflecting a Central American influence, are more common in the lower Ulúa and Sulaco Valleys but are rarely documented elsewhere (Hirth 1988). Chamelecon Polychromes exhibit subtle differences in their distribution within the Naco Valley, but are divergent from Ulúa polychromes (Schortman et al. 2001). Ulúa polychromes of any variety are quite rare in the Naco Valley (Urban 1993). Interestingly, the Ulúa polychrome traditions, which are most abundant in the middle and lower Ulúa drainage, Sulaco Valley, and Comayagua Valley, exhibit increasing proliferation of decorative themes among these valleys from the fifth through the ninth centuries (Joyce 1993a). Finally, there is an uneven distribution of Copador and other lowland Maya exports across these valleys. These imports are well represented in the assemblages from the Sula plain and the middle-Ulúa at sites like Gualjoquito, present but uncommon in the Naco Valley, and largely absent in the valleys further to the east (Henderson and Beaudry-Corbett 1993; Henderson et al. 1979; Hirth 1988:315; Joyce 1986). Put simply, polychrome wares are used in quite similar ways throughout the region, but the patterns of variation reveal differing forms of interaction from one valley to the next.

Similarly, intervalley analysis of the built environment may shed light on shared or divergent practices related to political strategizing and architectural vernacular. From the smallest scale of individual site plans, density, and architectural design to larger-scale site size hierarchies, settlement data and landscape perspectives can illuminate both unity and deviation within Southeastern Mesoamerica.

Our data from Jesús de Otoro, suggest an interesting divergence from other documented site-planning principles and settlement distributions in the region. The largest sites in the Jesús de Otoro Valley all share a similar plan: variations on a rectilinear plaza dominated by an east-situated monumental platform. Interestingly, this pattern compares favorably only to the contemporaneous site of Cementerio de Yarumela in the Comayagua Valley (Dixon 1989a:96).

Even more striking is the emphasis on an eastern orientation. At many of the valleys in western and central Honduras, a north–south orientation is emphasized. Ashmore (1991) has persuasively argued that this alignment is entwined with lowland Maya notions of cosmology. From the Honduran evidence, the Principal Group at Copán is a prime example, but these cosmological principles influenced aspiring elites beyond the Maya frontier (Ashmore 1987; Begley, chapter 7, this volume). Joyce and others have offered an alternative explanation for north–south alignments of sites on the landscape of the lower Ulúa Valley. Here, sites are placed with an orientation towards an impressive mountain at the southern limit of the valley (Joyce et al. 2009:60–63). What is especially relevant to our discussion is the revelation pulled from subtle variations in the material patterns from one valley to the next. The reason why Late Classic centers in the Jesús de Otoro Valley are oriented to the east is not yet evident, but we should retain a focus on local contexts and how they vary from their closest neighbors.

Ballcourts in the Jesús de Otoro Valley are noticeably absent. Although there are considerable differences in the size, layout, and orientation of these constructions, they are a common feature of the Southeast Mesoamerican landscape. A sizeable body of literature has demonstrated that ballcourts and the actions they contained served a wide range of political, social, ritual, and even economic functions (Fox 1996; Scarborough and Wilcox 1991). The lack of ballcourts in the Jesús de Otoro settlement presents us with an interpretive challenge. Why did the Late Classic inhabitants of this valley forgo this common approach to normalize intra- and intervalley interactions? And, what alternatives were implemented in place of ballgames and associated activities?

Likewise, the heterarchical settlement pattern in Jesús de Otoro contrasts with the more commonly observed patterns in the Southeast. The lack of one or more dominant centers is unusual for valleys in this region. Nevertheless, emerging research is demonstrating that the Late Classic approaches to consolidating political, social, or economic power and establishing marked inequalities in the Southeast differs significantly from lowland Maya strategies. Beyond these greater interregional differences, more subtle diversity in the changing settlement patterns of central Honduras demonstrates that not all communities followed the same sociopolitical trajectory towards hierarchy.

On one extreme, we cite populations that coalesce around primate centers and the more accentuated hierarchy of "gateway centers." In an influential paper by Hirth (1978), the rise of these centers depends on controlling the movement of people and resources through topographic choke points. Smaller secondary centers develop to support the growth of these centralized communities. It is important to note that different locally contingent circumstances can lead to similar outcomes. For example, Schortman and Urban (1987) describe the rise of Gualjoquito in the middle Ulúa as a consequence of interaction with the Copán network (see also Benyo and Melchionne 1987). Prior to the fifth century there were a number of smaller peer settlements, but they did not grow following contact with the Copán network.

On another extreme, settlement is dispersed and decentralized, reflecting what we suggest are alternative forms of organization and less-extreme forms of inequality. The Late Classic settlement of the Comayagua Valley (Dixon 1989b), along with what we have described in the Jesús de Otoro Valley, serve as examples of this form. The Comayagua Valley is broad and lacks the sort of topography and geographic position that would foster the rise of a gateway center. However, the Jesús de Otoro example seems an ideal candidate: it is located at one of the few passages to the mountains of western Honduras and associated resources. Why then do we see a heterarchical pattern of centers of a similar layout and scale? Did the populations in the Jesús de Otoro Valley opt for shared (or mutually competitive) strategies of political, social, and economic consolidation? We argue that this is exactly the case for the Late Classic and, moreover, reflects diversity in the forms of contemporary interactions across the region.

CONCLUSION

At present, it is important to note that the patterns of variation we identified are anecdotal and unsystematic. If placed in the context of an intervalley analysis drawn from all well-documented Southeast polities, startling insights into differing strategies for the accumulation and expression of power, identity, and authority may be revealed.

We are encouraged to note that our colleagues are beginning to move beyond the poles of intravalley and interregional scales. Some of our colleagues are applying multi-scalar analysis to consider political (Schortman and Urban 2011) or social networks (Joyce this volume). These approaches have shown great success in demonstrating the wide range of human interactions in this region. Here, we have taken an explicitly spatial or geographic approach, from one valley to the next. Rather than emphasizing any single axis of analysis, we train our sights on alternative strategies for dealing with one's neighbors and how this may lead to detectable variation in the archaeological record.

As evident by the essays in this volume, scholars of Southeast Mesoamerica are able to discuss the prehistoric developments of this region with increasing sophistication. We believe our colleagues are beginning to take advantage of the growing body of data from valley-specific and polity-specific projects to undertake a larger effort—one aimed at elucidating the nature of Southeast Mesoamerica as a region and answering the question posed by this volume: was this region truly a reality in precolumbian times?

We see the ultimate goal of this project to be the formulation of specific research questions designed to draw upon data from as many known regions of the Southeast as possible. For example, one might ask: what are the strategies for political development as inferred from the unified or divergent values in the site-planning principles? Or, what do the patterns of integrated or dispersed networks of exchange suggest about interaction and affiliation? And finally, what are the sociopolitical and economic arrangements created by the inhabitants of this region? And, more to the point, what can these alternatives to the hegemonic and hierarchical political arrangements of their neighbors to the west inform us about human organization in the past?

It is these broader goals to which we believe intervalley studies are best suited. By presenting our findings from Sinsimbla and posing questions about their relation to the rest of the region, we hope to stimulate interest in the larger project of intervalley analysis and raise awareness about the potential represented by the datasets of Southeastern Mesoamerica.

ACKNOWLEDGMENTS

The funding for this research was made possible by Johnson County Community College. Much of the fieldwork was completed through the efforts of students participating in the JCCC International Archaeological Field School, and we thank these students for their hard work and dedication. Sandra Moran and Alejandro Figueroa provided invaluable assistance. We are grateful to Patricia Urban and Edward Schortman for their generosity in sharing equipment and expertise. Thanks are also due to Jorge Bueso for his assistance in Honduras. Permission for this research was provided by IHAH and overseen by several representatives, including Raul Johnson. Special thanks are due to Darío Euraque, Eva Martinez, Oscar Cruz Castillo, and Vito Veliz. Without the help and support of innumerable individuals in the community of Jesús de Otoro—including Evelio Inestroza, Dr. Oscar Orellana, and Ricardo Sorto—this work would not have been possible. In particular, we would like single out Nery Fiallos for being a tireless champion of our research. Finally, we would like to thank Whitney A. Goodwin, Erlend Johnson, and Alejandro J. Figueroa for inviting us to participate in this edited volume.

WORKS CITED

Aoyama, Kazuo. 1994. "Socioeconomic Implications of Chipped Stone from the La Entrada Region, Western Honduras." *Journal of field Archaeology* 21(2):133–145.

Aoyama, Kazuo. 2001. "Classic Maya State, Urbanism, and Exchange: Chipped Stone Evidence of the Copán Valley and Its Hinterland" *American Anthropologist* 103(2):346–360.

Ashmore, Wendy. 1987. "Cobble Crossroads: Gualjoquito Architecture and External Elite Ties." In *The Southeast Maya Periphery*, ed. Eugenia J. Robinson, 28–48. BAR International Series 327. Oxford, UK: BAR.

Ashmore, Wendy. 1991. "Site Planning Principles and Concepts of Directionality among the Ancient Maya." *Latin American Antiquity* 2(3):199–226.

Ashmore, Wendy, and Jeremy A. Sabloff. 2002. "Spatial Orders in Maya Civic Plans." *Latin American Antiquity* 13(2):201–215.

Baudez, Claude F., and Pierre Becquelin. 1973. *Archaeologie de los Naranjos, Honduras. Etudes Mesoamericaines*, Volume 2. Mexico, DF: Mission Archéologique et Ethnologique Française au Mexique.

Beaudry-Corbett, Marilyn. 1993. "Lake Yojoa Region." In *Pottery of Prehistoric Honduras: Regional Classification and Analysis*, ed. John S. Henderson and Marilyn Beaudry-Corbett, 180–193. Los Angeles: Institute of Archaeology, University of California, Los Angeles.

Beaudry-Corbett, Marilyn, and John S. Henderson. 1993. "Introduction." In *Pottery of Prehistoric Honduras: Regional Classification and Analysis*, ed. John S. Henderson and Marilyn Beaudry-Corbett, 1–2. Los Angeles: Institute of Archaeology, University of California, Los Angeles.

Benyo, Julie C., and Thomas L. Melchionne. 1987. "Settlement Patterns in the Tencoa Valley, Honduras: An Application of the Coevolutionary Systems Model." In *Interaction on the Southeast Mesoamerican Frontier*, ed. Eugenia J. Robinson, ed., 49–65. BAR International Series 327, Oxford, UK: BAR.

Blanton, Richard E., Gary M. Feinman, Stephen A. Kowalewski, and Peter N. Peregrine. 1996. "A Dual-Processual Theory for the Evolution of Mesoamerican Civilization." *Current Anthropology* 17(1):1–14.

Boone, Elizabeth H., and Gordon R. Willey, eds. 1988. *The Southeast Classic Maya Zone*. Washington, DC: Dumbarton Oaks.

Canuto, Marcello A., and Ellen E. Bell. 2008. "The Ties that Bind: Administrative Strategies in the El Paraiso Valley Department of Copán, Honduras." *Mexicon* 30:10–20.

Canuto, Marcello A. 2013. "Archaeological Investigations in the El Paraíso Valley: The Role of Secondary Centers in the Multiethnic Landscape of Classic Period Copán." *Ancient Mesoamerica* 24(1):1–24.

Clark, John E. 1997. "Prismatic Blademaking, Craftsmanship, and Production: An Analysis of Obsidian Refuse from Ojo de Agua, Chiapas, Mexico." *Ancient Mesoamerica* 8:137–159.

Clark, John E., and Douglas Donne Bryant. 1997. "A Technological Typology of Prismatic Blades and Debitage from Ojo de Agua, Chiapas, Mexico." *Ancient Mesoamerica* 8:111–136.

Crumley, Carole L. 1979. "Three Locational Models: An Epistemological Assessment for Anthropology and Archaeology." In *Advances in Archaeological Method and Theory*, Volume 2, ed. Michael B. Schiffer, 141–173. New York: Academic Press.

Crumley, Carole, L. 1995. "Heterarchy and the Analysis of Complex Societies." In *Heterarchy and the Analysis of Complex Societies*, ed. Robert M. Ehrenreich, Carole L. Crumley, and Janet E. Levy, 1–5. Arlington, VA: American Anthropological Association.

Cruz Castillo, Oscar. 2004. *Patron de Asentamiento Prehispanico de el Valle de Jesús de Otoro*. Manuscript on file, Tegucigalpa, Honduras: Archives of the Instituto Hondureño de Antropológia e Historia.

DeMarrais, Elizabeth, Luis Jamie Castillo, and Timothy Earle. 1996. "Ideology, Materialization, and Power Strategies." *Current Anthropology* 37(1):15–31.

de Montmollin, Olivier. 1989. *The Archaeology of Political Structure: Settlement Analysis in a Classic Maya Polity*. Cambridge, UK: Cambridge University Press.

Dixon, Boyd M. 1989a. "Prehistoric Settlement Patterns on a Cultural Corridor: The Comayagua Valley, Honduras." Unpublished PhD dissertation on file, Department of Anthropology, University of Connecticut, Storrs, CT.

Dixon, Boyd M. 1989b. "A Preliminary Settlement Pattern Study of a Prehistoric Cultural Corridor: The Comayagua Valley, Honduras." *Journal of Field Archaeology* 16:257–271.

Dixon, Boyd, L.R.V. Joesink-Mandeville, Nobukatsu Hasebe, Michael Mucio, William Vincent, David James, and Kenneth Petersen. 1994. "Formative-Period Architecture and the Site of Yarumela, Central Honduras." *Latin American Antiquity* 5(1):70–87.

Flannery, Kent V. 1976. "Research Strategy and Formative Mesoamerica." In *The Early Mesoamerican Village*, ed. Kent V. Flannery, 1–11. New York: Academic Press.

Fox, John G. 1996. "Playing with Power: Ballcourts and Political Ritual in Southern Mesoamerica." *Current Anthropology* 37(3):483–509.

Hasemann, George. 1987. "El Patron de Asentamiento a lo Largo del Río Sulaco Durante el Clasico Tardio, Honduras." *Yaxkin* 19(1):58–77.

Healy, Paul F. 1984. "The Archaeology of Honduras." In *The Archaeology of Lower Central America*, ed. Frederick Lange and Doris Stone, 113–161. Albuquerque: University of New Mexico Press.

Henderson, John S., and Marilyn Beaudry-Corbett, eds. 1993. *Pottery of Prehistoric Honduras: Regional Classification and Analysis*. Los Angeles: Institute of Archaeology, University of California, Los Angeles.

Henderson, John S., Ilene Sterns, Anthony Wonderley, and Patricia Urban. 1979. "Archaeological Investigations in the Valle de Naco, Northwestern Honduras: A Preliminary Report." *Journal of Field Archaeology* 6(2):169–192.

Hirth, Kenneth G. 1978. "Interregional Trade and the Formations of Prehistoric Gateway Communities." *American Antiquity* 43(1):35–45.

Hirth, Kenneth G. 1988. "Beyond the Maya Frontier: Cultural Interaction and Syncretism along the Central Honduran Corridor." In *The Southeast Classic Maya Zone*, ed. Elizabeth Hill Boone and Gordon R. Willey, 297–334. Washington, DC: Dumbarton Oaks.

Hirth, Kenneth, Nedenia Kennedy, and Maynard Cliff. 1993. "El Cajón Region." In *Pottery of Prehistoric Honduras: Regional Classification and Analysis*, ed. John S. Henderson and Marilyn Beaudry-Corbett, 214–232. Los Angeles: Institute of Archaeology, University of California, Los Angeles.

Inomata, Takeshi, and Kazuo Aoyama. 1996. "Central-Place Analyses in the La Entrada Region, Honduras: Implications for Understanding the Classic Maya Political and Economic Systems." *Latin American Antiquity* 7(4):291–312.

Joyce, Rosemary A. 1986. "Terminal Classic Interactions on the Southeastern Maya Periphery." *American Antiquity* 51(2):313–329.

Joyce, Rosemary A. 1993a. "The Construction of the Mesoamerican Frontier and the Mayoid Image of Honduras Polychromes." In *Reinterpreting Prehistory of Central America*, ed. Mark M. Graham, 51–102. Niwot: University Press of Colorado.

Joyce, Rosemary A. 1993b. "A Key to Ulúa Polychromes." In *Pottery of Prehistoric Honduras: Regional Classification and Analysis*, ed. John S. Henderson and Marilyn Beaudry-Corbett, 257–280. Los Angeles: Institute of Archaeology, University of California, Los Angeles.

Joyce, Rosemary A. 2004. "Unintended Consequences? Monumentality as a Novel Experience in Formative Mesoamerica." *Journal of Archaeological Method and Theory* 11(1):5–29.

Joyce, Rosemary A., and Julia A. Hendon. 2000. "Heterarchy, history, and material reality: 'Communities' in Late Classic Honduras." In *The Archaeology of Communities: A New World Perspective*, ed. Marcello A. Canuto, and Jason Yaeger, 44–57. London: Routledge,

Joyce, Rosemary A., Julia A. Hendon, and Jeanne Lopiparo. 2009. "Being in Place: Intersections of Identity and Experience on the Honduran Landscape." In *The Archaeology of Meaningful Places*, ed. Brenda Bowser and Nieves Zedeño, 53–72. Salt Lake City: University of Utah Press.

Lunadri, Federico. 1943. "Los Misteriosos Mayas del Valle de Otoro." *Revista Geografica Americana* 20(118).

Marquardt, William H., and Carole L. Crumley. 1987. "Theoretical Issues in the Analysis of Spatial Patterning." In *Regional Dynamics: Burgundian Landscapes in Historical Perspective*, ed. Carole L. Crumley and William H. Marquardt, 1–17. San Diego, CA: Academic Press.

McFarlane, William J., and Miranda Suri. 2012. *PADO (Proyecto Arqueológico Valle de Jesús de Otoro) Informe 2009 and 2011*. Manuscript on file. Tegucigalpa, Honduras: Archives of the Instituto Hondureño de Antropológia e Historia.

Menzies, Adam C. J., and Mikael J. Haller. 2012. "A Macroregional Perspective on Chiefly Cycling in the Central Region of Panama during the Late Ceramic II Period (AD 700–1522)." *Latin American Antiquity* 23(4):449–466.

Nakamura, Seiichi. 1987. "Archaeology Investigations in the La Entrada Region, Honduras: Preliminary Results and Interregional Interaction." In *Interaction on the Southeast Mesoamerican Frontier*, ed. Eugenia J. Robinson, 129–141. Oxford, UK: BAR.

Pope, Kevin O. 1987. "The Ecology and Economy of the Formative-Classic Transition Along the Ulúa River, Honduras." In *Interaction on the Southeast Mesoamerican Frontier*, ed. Eugenia J. Robinson, 95–128. Oxford, UK: BAR,

Redmond, Elsa M., Rafael A. Gassón, and Charles S. Spencer. 1999. "A Macrore-gional View of Cycling Chiefdoms in the Western Venezuelan Llanos." In *Complexity in the Ancient Tropical World*, ed. Elisabeth Bacus and Lise Lucero, 109–129. Washington, DC: American Anthropological Association.

Renfrew, Colin. 1987. "Introduction: Peer Polity Interaction and Socio-Political Change." *Peer Polity Interaction and Socio-Political Change*, ed. Colin Renfrew and John F. Cherry, 1–18. Cambridge, UK: Cambridge University Press.

Robinson, Eugenia J. 1986. "A Typological Study of the Prehistoric Settlement of the Eastern Alluvial Fans, Sula Valley, Honduras: Comparison to Maya Settlement Forms." In *The Southeast Maya Periphery*, ed. Patricia A. Urban and Edward M. Schortman, 239–261. Austin: University of Texas Press.

Robinson, Eugenia J., ed. 1987. *Interaction on the Southeast Mesoamerican Frontier*. Oxford, UK: BAR.

Roscoe, Paul B. 1993. "Practice and Political Centralization: A New Approach to Political Evolution." *Current Anthropology* 34(2):111–140.

Scarborough, Vernon L., and David Wilcox, eds. 1991. *The Mesoamerican Ballgame*. Tucson University of Arizona Press.

Schortman, Edward M. 1993. *Archaeological Investigations in the Lower Motagua Valley, Izabal, Guatemala: A Study in Monumental Site Function and Interaction*. Quirigua Reports, Volume 3. Philadelphia: University of Pennsylvania, University Museum Press,

Schortman, Edward M., and Seiichi Nakamura. 1991. "A Crisis of Identity: Late Classic Competition and Interaction on the Southeast Maya Periphery." *Latin American Antiquity* 2(4):331–336.

Schortman, Edward M., and Patricia A. Urban. 1987. "Survey Within the Gualjo-quito Hinterland: An Introduction to the Investigations of the Santa Barbara Archaeological Project." In *Interaction on the Southeast Mesoamerican Frontier: Prehistoric and Historic Honduras and El Salvador*, ed. Eugenia J. Robinson, 5–27. Oxford, UK: BAR.

Schortman, Edward M., and Patricia A. Urban. 1994. "Living on the Edge: Core/ Periphery Relations in Ancient Southeastern Mesoamerica." *Current Anthropology* 35(4):401–413.

Schortman, Edward M., and Patricia A. Urban. 1996. "Actions at a Distance, Impacts at Home: Prestige Good Theory and a Pre-Columbian Polity in Southeastern Mesoamerica." In *Pre-Columbian World Systems*, ed. Peter N. Peregrine and Gary M. Feinman, 97–114. Madison, WI: Prehistory Press.

Schortman, Edward M., and Patricia A. Urban. 2011. *Networks of Power: Political Relations in the Late Postclassic Naco Valley, Honduras*. Boulder: University Press of Colorado.

Schortman, Edward M., Patricia A. Urban, Wendy Ashmore, and Julie C. Benyo. 1986. "Interregional Interaction in the Southeast Maya Periphery: The Santa Barbara Archaeological Project 1983–1984 Seasons." *Journal of field Archaeology* 13(3):259–272.

Schortman, Edward M., Patricia A. Urban, and Marne Ausec. 2001. "Politics with Style: Identity Formation in Prehispanic Southeastern Mesoamerica." *American Anthropologist* 103(2):312–330.

Sheets, Payson D. 1975. "Behavioral Analysis and the Structure of a Prehistoric Industry." *Current Anthropology* 16(3):369–391.

Sheets, Payson, Kenneth Hirth, Fred Lange, Fred Stross, Frank Asaro, and Helen Michel. 1990. "Obsidian Sources and Elemental Analyses of Artifacts in Southern Mesoamerica and the Northern Intermediate Area." *American Antiquity* 55(1):144–158.

Stockett, Miranda K. 2007. "Performing Power: Identity, Ritual, and Materiality in a Late Classic Southeast Mesoamerican Crafting Community." *Ancient Mesoamerica* 18(1):91–105.

Stockett, Miranda K. 2010. "Sites of Memory in the Making: Political Strategizing in the Construction and Deconstruction of Place in Late to Terminal Classic Southeastern Mesoamerica." *Ancient Mesoamerica* 21(2):315–330.

Stockett, Miranda K., and William J. McFarlane. 2007. *PADO (Proyecto Arqueológico Valle de Jesús de Otoro) Informe 2007*. Manuscript on file. Tegucigalpa, Honduras: Archives of the Instituto Hondureño de Antropológia e Historia.

Stockett, Miranda K., and William J. McFarlane. 2008. *PADO (Proyecto Arqueológico Valle de Jesús de Otoro) Informe 2008*. Manuscript on file. Tegucigalpa, Honduras: Archives of the Instituto Hondureño de Antropológia e Historia.

Urban, Patricia A. 1986. "Systems of Settlement in the PreColumbian Naco Valley, Northwestern Honduras." Unpublished PhD dissertation, Department of Anthropology, University of Pennsylvania, Philadelphia, PA.

Urban, Patricia A. 1993. "Naco Valley." In *Pottery of Prehistoric Honduras: Regional Classification and Analysis*, ed. John S. Henderson and Marilyn Beaudry-Corbett, 30–63. Los Angeles: Institute of Archaeology, University of California, Los Angeles.

Urban, Patricia A., and Edward M. Schortman, eds. 1986. *The Southeast Maya Periphery*. Austin: University of Texas Press.

Urban, Patricia A. and Edward M. Schortman. 1988. "The Southeast Zone Viewed from the East: Lower Motagua-Naco Valleys." In *The Southeast Classic Maya Zone*, ed. Elizabeth Hill Boone and Gordon R. Willey, 223–267. Washington, DC: Dumbarton Oaks.

Urban, Patricia A., Edward M. Schortman, and Miranda K. Stockett. 1999. *The Proyecto Valle de Cacaulapa, Northwestern Honduras: Archaeological Investigations*

Conducted during the 1999 Field Season. Manuscript on file. Tegucigalpa, Honduras: Archives of the Instituto Hondureño de Antropología e Historia.

von Schwerin, Jennifer. 2011. "The Sacred Mountain in Social Context. Symbolism and History in Maya Architecture: Temple 22 at Copán, Honduras." *Ancient Mesoamerica* 22(2):271–300.

Wells, E. Christian. 2003. "Artisans, Chiefs, and Feasts: Classic Period Social Dynamics at El Coyote, Honduras." Unpublished PhD dissertation, Department of Anthropology, University of Arizona, Tucson, AZ.

Willey, Gordon R., and Richard M. Leventhal. 1979. "Prehistoric Settlement at Copán." In *Maya Archaeology and Ethnohistory*, ed. Norman Hammond and Gordon R. Willey, 75–102. Austin: University of Texas Press.

Yaeger, Jason, and Marcello A. Canuto. 2000. "Introducing an Archaeology of Communities." In *The Archaeology of Communities: A New World Perspective*, ed. Marcello A. Canuto and Jason Yaeger, 1–15. London: Routledge.

6

Archaeological Research in Southeastern Honduras

The Case of the Jamastrán Valley

Eva L. Martínez

DOI: 10.5876/9781646420971.c006

Archaeologists have described the position of Honduras in terms of its frontier-like setting: it lies on the southern periphery of Mesoamerica and on the northern edge of the Intermediate Area (e.g., Baudez 1970; Healy 1984a; Hirth et al. 1989). From this perspective, eastern Honduras has been characterized as a frontier within a frontier area, receiving "filtered" Mesoamerican traditions from the west and Lower Central American influences from the southeast. Nonetheless, eastern Honduras has been typically associated with the Intermediate Area, and most archaeological research in the region has been guided by this assumption. Discussions about the utility of the Intermediate Area as an accurate theoretical construct have been offered amply elsewhere (Drennan 1996; Hoopes 1993; Lange 1984, 1992; Sheets 1992) and expanding on those discussions escapes the purpose of this research. However, this chapter aims to contribute to current efforts to move the discussion from a traditional emphasis on determining cultural affiliation in eastern Honduras to approaches that focus attention on internal social dynamics at regional scales of analysis.

Hasemann (1998:30) summarized the history of research in west-central Honduras by centering his argument on the shift in theoretical and methodological orientations from a "focus almost exclusively of necessity on such pragmatic chores as the identification and inventory of material culture and the basic chronology of culture history, usually linked to the rise, florescence and decline of Mesoamerican traditions, especially the Olmec and the southern Lowland Maya," to more recent studies that have concentrated on the regional distinctiveness of local societies, the transfer of goods and information between regional polities (Ashmore 1987; Dixon 1989; Henderson 1977; Schortman and Urban 1987), the politics of economic organization (Schortman and Urban 1992), the social aspects of political organization and ethnicity (Creamer 1987; Joyce 1991), and the relationship between subsistence resources and the spatial pattering of settlement systems and its implications for the interpretation of sociopolitical organization (Hirth et al. 1989; Pope 1987).

Archaeological research in eastern Honduras has been less intensive, but parallels the general changes in theoretical and methodological interests observed in west-central Honduras and the Intermediate Area. The first non-systematic surveys and excavations carried out in northeastern and eastern Honduras provided data to create a ceramic sequence for the region still utilized today and offered assessments of the cultural affiliation of the prehispanic societies of eastern Honduras (Epstein 1957, 1975; Stone 1941, 1954; Strong 1934, 1935). The first systematic work in the area was conducted by Healy in the 1970s. Healy's research in northeastern Honduras (1974, 1975, 1976, 1978a, 1978b) included subsistence and settlement-pattern studies that were considered at that time new approaches in the archaeology of the country. Alongside those studies, issues of cultural affiliation remained important research questions in the region (Healy 1984b).

Researchers have focused their attention on the nature of interregional interactions between eastern and west-central Honduras, and Lower Central America (Begley 1999; Hasemann and Lara-Pinto 1993; Healy 1980, 1992). Healy (1992) explored the differences in social organization between western and eastern Honduras, pointing out that more-complex levels of social organization are observed late in the cultural sequence of northeastern Honduras, almost coinciding with the appearance of non-Mesoamerican materials in the archaeological record of the region. The implications of such evidence for understanding the development of social complexity in northeastern Honduras, in contrast to other regions, have not been fully investigated yet.

More recent research in eastern Honduras has concentrated on local developments and the emergence of social differentiation in the region. For instance, Begley (1999; chapter 7, this volume), based on Helms's (1979) work, proposed that long-distance relationships of noneconomic nature played a critical part in the social development of eastern Honduras. Specifically, the construction of ballcourts and the adoption of related rituals by the nascent elites of eastern

Honduras are thought to be crucial elements in processes of power acquisition and hierarchy building. The presence of strong Mesoamerican features, such as ballcourts, in eastern Honduras has introduced a different line of inquiry in the region, particularly regarding aspects of interregional interaction and its effect on local social dynamics.

My research attempts to gain an understanding of prehispanic social organization in the Jamastrán Valley of southeastern Honduras. I share the opinion that the study of societies benefits greatly when approached in terms of varying levels of sociopolitical integration (Parkinson 2002; Peterson and Drennan 2005; Steward 1955). Therefore, in order to characterize the processes of political and social organization in the Jamastrán Valley, my investigation explored two interrelated analytical dimensions: political integration and the nature of social interaction.

Survey data were used to address the degree of sociopolitical integration, or autonomy, present in the region and evaluate the occurrence and extent of hierarchical social interactions. The former was assessed by determining the scale and organization of the basic integrative units that make up the social system under study. The latter was studied by exploring contrasting political strategies utilized by aspiring leaders as springboards of social differentiation: economic-oriented strategies, which involve restricted access over basic resources, and/or the control of the production or mobilization of valued items; and prestige-oriented strategies, which involve mechanisms such as restricted access to privileged knowledge, manipulation of symbols and prestige goods, participation in interregional exchange networks, feasting, and so on.

METHODOLOGY

The Jamastrán Valley lies in southeastern Honduras in the Department of El Paraíso (figure 6.1). It is one of several broad valleys scattered throughout the interior rugged mountains of the country and covers approximately 260 km², with a range of elevation from 400 mmsl to 600 mmsl on the valley floor and up to 900–1,200 mmsl in the uplands. The Jamastrán Valley is watered by the Guayambre drainage, which is formed by the El Hato and San Francisco Rivers flowing northward, and the Los Almendros River flowing southward. The Guayambre River joins the Guayape, forming the Patuca River, the second longest river in the country, which crosses eastern Honduras and connects the Jamastrán Valley with the Olancho and La Mosquitia regions. To the east, the valley neighbors part of north-central Nicaragua.

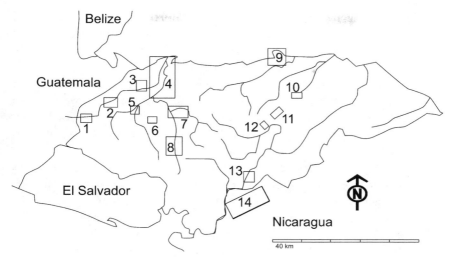

FIGURE 6.1. *The Jamastrán Valley and neighboring regions. 1. Copán Valley, 2. La Venta Valley, 3. Naco Valley, 4. Ulúa Valley, 5. central Santa Bárbara, 6. Lake Yojoa area, 7. Sulaco Valley, 8. Comayagua Valley, 9. northeastern Honduras (Aguan Valley), 10. Culmí Valley, 11. Olancho Valley, 12. Telica Valley, 13. Jamastrán Valley, 14. Las Segovias region. (Modified after Henderson and Beaudry-Corbett 1993:figure 1.1.)*

We conducted a full-coverage systematic regional survey of an area of approximately 250 km² that corresponds roughly to the natural topographic boundaries of the Jamastrán Valley. The survey covered all the ground in the area excepting the slopes too steep to walk. Most of the surveyed area consisted of cultivated plots and pasture lands, and surface visibility was optimal, even during the rainy season. However, in areas where dense vegetation or soil conditions lowered surface visibility (or in order to verify the extent of archaeological sites), 40 cm × 40 cm × 40 cm shovel probes were used at intervals of approximately .5 ha, or closer. All of our shovel probes were negative, so our research relies solely on surface collections.

Archaeological sites were identified by the presence of artifact scatters; two settlements also present earthen mounds, which were not excavated and will be studied in the following stage of the research. The ground surface was carefully examined in order to establish the extent of the artifact concentrations. A collection unit had a maximum of .5 ha. Therefore, if artifacts were scattered over an area of 1 ha, this area would be divided into two .5-ha collection units and a sample would be taken for each one. Conversely, if the artifact concentration was less than .5 ha, only one sample was taken.

Most of our surface collections are systematic; however, we also recovered material from 47 spot findings, which were not incorporated into the final analysis. To standardize artifact-density values, artifacts were collected in circles of 3 m in diameter (7.065 m^2) and assigned to corresponding collection units. On average, we collected 23 sherds for each collection unit. After collecting our samples, the boundaries of each collection unit were drawn in field maps. The settlement maps produced reflect the extent of human occupation in the region expressed through the material remains collected on the surface.

A total of 144 systematic collection units were recorded during the survey. In those systematic collections, ceramics and obsidian were the most common materials, although other lithic artifacts were recovered. Collection units ($n = 114$) yielded information that allowed chronological placement; only these collections were incorporated in our analysis. A total of 3,259 sherds were analyzed. Relative dates were obtained by comparing the ceramic material from the Jamastrán Valley to diagnostic ceramic types from other regions where chronologies have already been established.

Lithic analysis was carried out at the Tegucigalpa laboratory of the Honduran Institute of Anthropology and History (IHAH). We recovered and analyzed 645 flake-stone tools: 34 made of chert and 611 of obsidian. Obsidian sourcing was done through visual examination following Aoyama's (1999) description of obsidian from different sources commonly found in the archaeological record of Honduras. Our material was also compared to a comprehensive obsidian sample located at the IHAH laboratory.

Our ceramic evidence indicates that the occupation of Jamastrán took place between AD 600 and 1000. This relatively late and short occupation of the valley parallels the history of occupation observed in the Culmí Valley and the Talgua drainage (Beaudry-Corbett 1995; Begley 1999) as well as in Dos Quebradas in the Telica Valley in Olancho (Winemiller and Ochoa-Winemiller 2009) and the Las Segovias region in northern Nicaragua (Espinoza et al. 1996).

SOCIAL ORGANIZATION AND POLITICAL INTEGRATION

The main evidence of ancient population presence in the Jamastrán Valley is based on artifactual remains such as lithics and ceramics. Settlement and demographic patterns in the Jamastrán Valley are approached by the analysis of the distribution of ceramics across the survey area as well as by their varying densities in different locations. A starting point for understanding demographic patterns in the Jamastrán Valley consists of analyzing the distribution of ceramics across the survey area.

The number of collection units in the survey area is rather scanty. Most of them are located on high terraces along rivers, which indicate that closeness to permanent water sources might have been important in selecting a settlement location. Despite the general pattern of settlement dispersion, there is a tendency to form clusters of collection units.

To continue exploring settlement and demographic patterns in the Jamastrán Valley, we turn to the density of ceramic materials present in each collection unit. A density area index (DAI) was calculated following the approach proposed by Drennan et al. (2003:152–166). The DAI makes use of two separate categories: occupied area (area of each collection unit) and quantity of material remains (surface density of sherds collected for each unit). The combination of these two sets of information produces a demographic index as the basis for creating surface and contour maps that help us delineate clusters of collection units—that is, to delineate settlements and investigate the presence of local communities and/or other meaningful units of social interaction in the Jamastrán Valley.

DELIMITATION OF SOCIAL UNITS

It was possible to delineate the clusters of settlement identified in the Jamastrán Valley using occupational surfaces based on area-density values that function as archaeological proxy measures of population densities. The methods of analysis carried out here followed the approach proposed by Drennan and Peterson (Drennan and Peterson 2005; Drennan et al. 2003; Peterson 2006; Peterson and Drennan 2005). Their application of distance-interaction principles to smoothed surfaces of occupational distributions allows the delineation of different social units.

Area-density values were calculated for each collection unit included in the analysis, and corresponding values were associated with each digitized collection unit as an independent property of its elevation (z-value). These collection units and their elevation data were then rasterized into a grid of z-values at 100-m intervals (raster layer of ceramics densities at a resolution of 1 ha). Therefore, and also considering that our collection units have an average area of slightly less than half a hectare, more than one collection unit fell within each square 100-m cell in the grid. The values of each cell were mathematically transformed using an inverse distance square logarithm to "smooth" or "pull" the distribution of surface-sherd densities. The distance-interaction effects of the logarithm can be summarized as follows: the greater mathematical power the z-values are raised to, the lesser the effects of distant values, and vice versa. As a result, higher powers will produce less or no smoothing.

Powers 4, 2, 1.5, 1, .50, and .25 were used in this analysis to produce surface maps or "occupation" surfaces. The varying levels of ceramic densities were mapped as they distribute themselves according to each power applied to the dataset. Comparison of these different surfaces along with their corresponding contour maps provided the basis for grouping clusters of collection units into larger inclusive clusters. The formation of such clusters reflects a pattern of closer interaction within them than with other inclusive groupings. Following Drennan and Peterson (Drennan and Peterson 2005; Drennan et al. 2003; Peterson 2006; Peterson and Drennan 2005), the clustering of collection units comes to reflect the clustering of population. As such, the surface maps analyzed here indicate the presence and distribution of spatially discrete occupation units or settlements. Two of these surfaces—the power 4 and power .5 surfaces—are discussed below.

The power 4 surface (figure 6.2) shows a series of peaks that represent higher areas of sherd densities, whereas flat areas represent areas of the survey area where ceramics were not recovered. Naturally, higher peaks represent higher sherd densities. The peaks shown in the surface map are sharply defined and separated from other peaks. A cutoff contour was established to outline the base of each peak. Following this procedure, our 144 collection units were grouped into 15 clusters comprising several collection units with the exception of two particularly dense single-collection units. These 15 settlements range in size from 1.61 ha (130 m across) to 38.62 ha (1,020 m across). A distance of 1 linear km (1,000 m) has been described as the upper threshold for daily face-to-face interaction in small local communities (Peterson and Drennan 2005:10). Thus, we believe that the contour level selected for cutoff is clustering collection units into actual meaningful groupings of social interaction: small local communities or villages and farmsteads.

Besides these 15 areas where collection units clustered, there are 34 isolated single collection units located across the landscape, particularly around larger settlements in the Calpules area in the northern part of the valley. They represent 23.62 percent of the total collection units included in the analysis as opposed to 76.38 percent of collection units clustering within the 15 larger settlements. These 34 isolated settlements range in size from a little less than half a hectare to no more than 20 m across. These small settlements might represent individual households and probably other kinds of occupation areas, such as for special activities and/or areas of sporadic use.

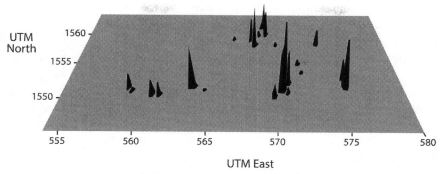

FIGURE 6.2. *Surface representing sherd densities for the Jamastrán Valley, power 4.*

ESTIMATING POPULATIONS

The estimation of absolute population is normally approached by the examination of different lines of evidence, such as ethnohistorical accounts of the region under study or neighboring areas, counts of residential structures when these have been exposed by excavation, and cross-cultural ethnographic studies of demography. The information provided by these sources can be combined with relative demographic indexes to approximate numbers of people. Although we encountered and mapped some mounds during our survey, none of these has been excavated and reliable information about the actual amount of structures is not available for the Jamastrán Valley at this point. As stated earlier, the distribution and quantification of discarded materials left by the ancient inhabitants of the Jamastrán Valley is our best demographic evidence.

The DAI is a relative demographic index; that is, lower values indicate lower population levels and higher values indicate higher ones. Although this index does not by itself provide absolute estimates of population, it is suitable for conversion into such estimates when multiplied by a figure approximating how many people will leave a density of ceramic remains averaging 1 sherd/m² over an area of 1 ha (see Drennan et al. 2003:161 for an expanded rationale for this approach). Therefore, in order to estimate the regional population of the Jamastrán Valley, we summed the DAI values for all the collection units recorded and then multiplied this result by minimum and maximum estimates of the number of people required to produce a fixed surface-sherd density across an area of 1 hea at a particular moment in time. Because no stratigraphic studies exist for the Jamastrán Valley to inform temporal variation in ceramic output, minimum and maximum approximations of absolute population were calculated using a recent demographic analysis for the San Ramon de Alajuela Valley in the western part of the Central Plateau of Costa Rica as a reference (Murillo 2009).

Murillo (2009) created a scale to compare population numbers derived from excavated settlements and population densities (sherd densities) from these settlements with the ones he recorded in San Ramon. This study was chosen due to its relative proximity to eastern Honduras and the demographic and sociopolitical similarities that exist between the prehispanic societies that inhabited both areas. Based on Murillo's scale, a figure can be approximated by which each area-density value needs to be multiplied to obtain the equivalent number of inhabitants in 1 ha. The San Ramon sherd densities presented in Murillo's scale were compared with the Jamastrán sherd densities in order to find a corresponding residential density figure. The top surface-sherd density of Jamastrán is 8.7 (sherds/m²). According to Murillo's scale (2009:72), a sherd density of 8.2 would represent a residential density of about 52 people per hectare. The minimum and maximum figures were also calculated based on the scale discussed here. To account for differences in sherd densities from Jamastrán and San Ramon, both minimum and maximum population figures calculated with Murillo's scale were divided by the equivalent area-density value corresponding to 8.7 sherds/m² from our dataset.

The resulting values are 7 and 15 people per hectare. Therefore, a settlement with a DAI of 1 represents between 7 and 15 people. Based on this numeric relationship, the DAI of each collection unit or series of collection units that make up a settlement can be multiplied by 7 to produce a minimum population estimate and by 15 to produce a maximum population estimate. For instance, the collection unit with a density of 8.7 sherds/m² has an area-density value of 4.39, which equals to 31 people at a minimum and 66 people at a maximum. Then, the average number of people for a sherd density of 8.7 is 48 people.

Applying the factors to the total population index for Jamastrán (DAI:219.29) yields a minimum population estimate for the entire surveyed area of 1,535 people, a maximum estimate of 3,289 and an average of 2,412 people at any given time in the ancient occupation of the valley, from AD 600 to 1000. Population densities in the valley are of 6, 13, and 9 people/km² for minimum, maximum, and mean values, respectively.

Estimating Local Populations

The population of each settlement delimited through the surface and contour maps was calculated by multiplying the DAI values of each settlement (the sum of all DAI values for all collection units composing each settlement) by the minimum and maximum population estimates. This makes it possible to estimate how many people lived in these settlements but also to determine whether a settlement might represent one or three families living together or 10 or 12 families congregating close by. Each settlement was characterized as a given sociopolitical unit according to the population size it hosted.

After estimating the population of the 15 highest "peaks" shown in the surface maps and the 34 isolated settlements that compose our data, it was clear that some of these isolated units represented sporadic occupation areas, since they had population figures of 1 or less than 1 person. We estimated that 30 settlements are considered permanently or continuously occupied, as opposed to the 19 settlements occupied occasionally. Permanent settlements in the Jamastrán Valley sum up to an average of 2,400 people. The minimum and maximum population averages for the permanent settlements are 5 and 530 people, which reflect a wide range of population densities among settlements. It is worth noticing that the 15 settlements with higher population densities (the high peaks in the surface maps) comprise 92 percent of the total population in the valley. The other 8 percent of population is comprised within the 15 remaining smaller settlements.

Based on the population estimates for each settlement, they were classified into households, hamlets, and villages. An average of 2,137 people lived in villages and account for 89 percent of the total population. An average of 200 people lived in hamlets that hosted a minimum of 13 and a maximum of 30 people, and represent 8 percent of the total population. Finally, an average of 63 people lived in individual households that range from a minimum of 5 and a maximum of 11 people, making up 3 percent of the entire population of the Jamastrán Valley.

INTRAVALLEY INTERACTION

Rank-size graphs of the 15 larger settlements (92% of the total population) were created to explore the level of sociopolitical integration in the valley. Rank-size distribution of settlements in a settlement system has been used in archaeology to measure the relative integration of that particular system (Johnson 1977, 1980, 1981). A rank-size distribution is another way of looking at the size-frequency distribution of settlements. Explanations of the rank-size rule and deviations from it have been discussed elsewhere (see Johnson 1980, 1981; Drennan and Peterson 2004); suffice to mention here that a log-normal pattern conforms exactly to the rank-size rule (a settlement of rank 2 is "expected" to be half as large as the rank 1 settlement, the rank 3 settlement to be one-third as large as the rank 1 settlement, and so on) and that two main departures from rank-size linearity have been noted: primate and convex. On one hand, primate distributions produce a rank-size graph with a concave curve dropping below the log-normal line. This pattern is produced by the presence of a significantly large settlement in the system. On the other hand, convex distributions produce a rank-size graph with a convex curve in relation to the log-normal line. This pattern is produced by the presence of several large settlements with similar populations (Johnson 1981).

To go beyond subjective characterizations of rank-size graphs (as primate, convex, primoconvex, or log-normal), Drennan and Peterson (2004) developed a mathematical coefficient for describing the shape of the rank-size curve and establishing levels of confidence. Their coefficient (A) measures the net tendency of a rank-size curve and provides a scale that indicates the strength of the departure of an observed pattern from log-normal. According to the scale, a very highly convex distribution (lack of settlement hierarchy) would have a value of 1.0, a log-normal distribution would have a value of 0.0, and increasingly primate distributions would have increasingly negative values, where -1.00 indicates a pattern of extreme "primateness" (Drennan and Peterson 2004:534; see also Johnson 1980:137–139 and 1981:154–155 for a discussion of a similar index). Moreover, the A coefficient provides the basis for assessing the probability that differences in rank-size patterns could be the result of nothing more than the vagaries of sampling. The basis of such an assessment is accomplished by establishing an error range from the level of the desired statistical confidence (Drennan and Peterson 2004:535).

Figure 6.3 shows a rank-size graph of the 15 largest settlements in the Jamastrán Valley. The rank-size curve is convex, with an associated A value of .173. This pattern indicates the presence of several larger settlements with similar populations; however, their population sizes are not equal enough to create a stronger tendency of the convex curve. We selected a 90-percent confidence level to assess the probability that the pattern observed in the rank-size graph could be the result of the vagaries of sampling. So, we are 90 percent confident that our data represent a settlement dynamic different from that suggested for log-normal patterns.

A convex pattern suggests low political integration in the Jamastrán Valley. This pattern of population distribution coincides with what has been represented in the surface maps: that is, the absence of one central place that congregates high population densities in the region. Instead of one single village clustering a substantial amount of the regional population, there are some

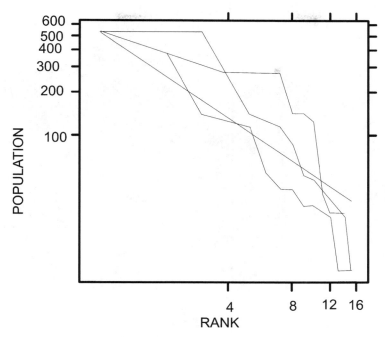

FIGURE 6.3. *Rank-size graph of ancient local communities in the Jamastrán Valley survey area (A = .173, 90% confidence).*

villages of rather similar sizes where populations nucleate. The distribution and size of the population in the valley suggest a regional scenario in which most likely autonomous villages interacted at different levels of intensity.

EXPLORING SUPRAVILLAGE INTERACTION

Surface maps produced with a power of .50 were examined more closely to explore the presence of interactions above the village level. As before, comparison of these different surfaces along with their corresponding contour maps provided the basis for grouping clusters of settlements into larger inclusive clusters. Again, the formation of such clusters reflects a pattern of closer interaction within them than with other inclusive groupings.

In contrast to the surface generated with power 4 (figure 6.2), the map shown in figure 6.4 shows a smoother surface with a series of peaks whose bases extend farther away. A cutoff contour was established to outline the bases of each peak. Following this procedure, five areas of higher population

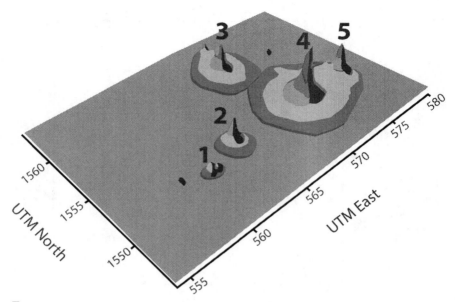

FIGURE 6.4. *Surface representing sherd densities for the Jamastrán Valley, power .5. Peaks represent the following sites: (1) Santa Rosalia, (2) La Cañera, (3) Calpules, (4) El Zapotillo, (5) Rancho Rosa.*

densities can be identified. Two of them (La Cañera and Santa Rosalia, on the western part of the valley) consist of individual villages with mean figures of 273 and 114 people respectively. The other three areas are located in the northern (Calpules), eastern (Rancho Rosa), and central (El Zapotillo) parts of the valley Each of these three areas clusters more than one village and some households and/or hamlets. The Calpules area comprises 28 percent of the population of the valley while the El Zapotillo area makes up 30 percent of the population and the Rancho Rosa area 15 percent of the population.

These clusters are taken to be discrete areas where communication and exchanges among villages and households were closer than with other similar interacting areas in the valley. Johnson (1980:240; 1981:150–151) points out that convex rank-size distributions can be explained as resulting from the "pooling" of settlement systems: that is, from the combination of two or more autonomous or relatively autonomous settlement systems in the same analysis. In these cases, there are significant boundaries between or among settlement systems within an area under study. Following Johnson (1980, 1981), and considering that almost 60 percent of the total population of the Jamastrán Valley nucleated within two of the interacting areas in the valley, it is worth exploring the level of integration within each regional cluster.

The corresponding rank-size graph shows very primate patterns for both the Calpules and El Zapotillo areas. (A = -.801, $n = 9$, and A = -1.34, $n = 5$, respectively). Taking into account the small sample sizes, we selected an 80-percent confidence level to assess the probability that the pattern observed in the rank-size graph could be the result of the vagaries of sampling. So, we are at least 80 percent confident that our data represent a settlement dynamic different from that suggested for log-normal patterns. The patterns observed in the rank-size graphs of the whole region and within the regional clusters support the idea that significant internal interactional boundaries were present in the Jamastrán Valley. We take the regional clusters identified in the surface and contour maps to represent interactional boundaries in the valley. These patterns, in fact, support the notion that more-intensive interaction took place among the local communities within each regional cluster than with communities outside of it.

The "Building Blocks" of the Jamastrán Valley

The first step for assessing social organization in the Jamastrán Valley was to identify the presence and scale of the basic social units in the archaeological record of the society under study. It has been amply pointed out that individuals interact at a variety of levels and as part of a variety of different social units, creating a nested hierarchy of formalized entities of integration and interaction. Therefore, societies are composed of various integrative units, of which the nuclear family is considered the basic social grouping and the genuinely universal one (Murdock 1949:3; Steward 1955:54). Suprafamilial organization and its role as a building block of larger social interactions, however, should not be assumed but verified empirically, given the diversity of forms of social organization found in the archaeological record (Peterson and Drennan 2005).

Our research in the Jamastrán Valley identified three main integrative social units interacting simultaneously in the region: households, small local communities (hamlets and villages), and settlement clusters. Households are composed of nuclear or extended families usually ranging between four and 12 people (Sanders 1977:329; 1984:12). Hamlets and villages correspond to the aggregation of several households into discrete, spatially delineated units forming communities of varying sizes. A community can be defined as the maximal group of persons who normally reside together in face-to-face association

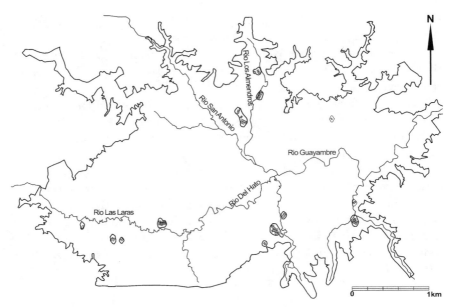

FIGURE 6.5. *Ancient local communities in the Jamastrán Valley.*

(Murdock 1949:79). The community at its lower limit may consist of as few as 15 persons (Carneiro 1998:37), whereas the upper limit is apparently set by "the practical impossibility of establishing close contacts with developing habitual attitudes toward any great number of people" (Murdock 1949:81). Drennan and Peterson (2005:8) point out that a local community is formed when social interactions are intensely concentrated within a single well-defined group of households that interact only much less intensely with households outside the group (figure 6.5).

Despite the dispersed regional distribution in the Jamastrán Valley, population tended to nucleate mainly in two areas of the region under study. Regional settlement clusters in the valley measure as much as 3–4 km across, a spatial scale too large to involve face-to-face interaction on a daily basis but amenable to foster interactions that arise from occasional or less-immediate demands in the small local communities. The presence of larger community structures above the level of the small local community is taken to represent the existence of at least two autonomous systems in the Jamastrán Valley. Within the regional clusters, population tended to concentrate in one local community that hosted a significantly larger population than the other communities integrating the regional cluster (figure 6.6).

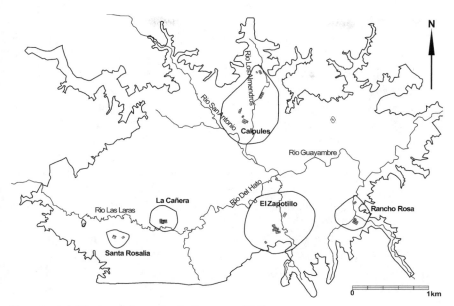

Figure 6.6. *Regional clusters in the Jamastrán Valley.*

ECONOMIC AND PRESTIGE-ORIENTED STRATEGIES

Evidence derived from the analysis of different social trajectories in regions of west-central Honduras (Baudez and Becquelin 1973; Benyo and Melchionne 1987; Dixon 1989; Hasemann 1987, 1998; Healy 1984a, 1992; Henderson et al. 1979; Hirth 1988; Hirth et al. 1989; Schortman and Urban 1987) and north-eastern Honduras (Healy 1978a, 1978b, 1984a, 1984b, 1992), as well as from the north-central region of Nicaragua (Espinoza et al. 1996; Salgado 1996), points to common factors that stand out as key elements that can be used to explain the development of social hierarchies in those regions. For instance, access to prime agricultural land and permanent water sources seem to have been crucial factors in determining settlement location; moreover, early in the sequences of those regions, sedentism is followed by the creation of or participation in already existing interregional exchange networks that mobilized both utilitarian and luxury items, such as obsidian, jade, and pottery.

In light of this information, and building on scholarship regarding the bases of political leadership and subsequent social differentiation, factors such as access to agricultural land, craft specialization, and local and interregional exchange are considered informative to investigate the presence and functioning of economic- and prestige-based strategies in the Jamastrán Valley.

Access to Prime Agricultural Land

Modern and ancient agriculturalists in different areas of Honduras have favored settlement along rivers and within the tropical deciduous forest areas because of higher soil productivity and availability of wild resources in those environments. This selection allowed for maximum resource utilization by providing access to fertile soils for agriculture as well as continuing productivity from fruit trees (Lentz et al. 1997:71). It is likely that agriculturalists in the Jamastrán Valley also relied on this strategy in order to maximize the use of lands with higher agricultural potential and to benefit from other natural resources. The dispersed nature of the communities in Jamastrán suggests that households kept milpas or kitchen gardens adjacent to their dwellings and exploited larger catchment areas to diversify their diet and obtain other resources.

A similar location pattern has been observed in the Culmí Valley and along the Río Talgua in eastern Honduras. In those regions, settlements along the rivers tended to be located on higher terraces where the terrace was narrow, but close to an area where it widened (Begley 1999:197; Hasemann 1995:10). It has been pointed out that in these areas of eastern Honduras the location of dwellings in narrow areas freed the wider terraces for agricultural activities, suggesting that at least some agricultural plots were located in the vicinity of the households. Additionally, this pattern seems to be related to early stages of agriculture during which settlements were initially located on prime agricultural land, within the circumriverine and deciduous-forest environmental zones. Our data from the Jamastrán Valley suggest that the settlement distribution in the region might represent the expression of such an early stage, when access to prime agricultural land might have been favored but control over this resource was not critical for a small population.

Evidence derived from the analysis of the agricultural productivity (annual yield production) of hypothetical catchment areas and the population sizes of each social unit in Jamastrán suggests that communities in the valley were inhabited predominantly by food-producers. This observation is reinforced by the scanty evidence of craft specialization found in the valley. High proportions of basic chipped-stone tools in relation to the total number of artifacts (i.e., proportions of ceramics) among smaller settlements in the valley also suggests that agricultural activities were predominant and occupied most of the time of the inhabitants in the valley. At the same time, it also indicates slight differences among communities with regard to focus on economic activities in the valley.

CRAFT PRODUCTION AND LOCAL EXCHANGE

Our research suggests that some communities and households within them specialized most likely on a part-time basis in the production of prismatic blades. Our data also indicate that the larger villages within the regional clusters were engaged in all steps of blade production, while smaller settlements seem to have concentrated on the finishing steps of blade production. Additionally, all blades produced in the valley were manufactured with obsidian from the La Esperanza source in western Honduras.

Due to the relative closeness of the Jamastrán Valley to the Güinope obsidian source, we had originally assumed that Güinope obsidian would be the predominant source for toolmaking in the region; however, our analysis shows that most of the obsidian (58%) came from an unknown source, followed by obsidian from La Esperanza (32%), whereas Güinope makes up only 10 percent of the obsidian recovered in the survey. Although percentages vary by regional cluster and by area in the valley, the occurrence of obsidian also indicates that Güinope was the least-used source within more spatially discrete areas in the valley. Obsidian from Güinope was more frequently used among communities in the southwestern part of the valley.

Research at the Dos Quebradas archaeological site in Olancho has also challenged the assumption that the Güinope source would be more frequently used in areas of eastern Honduras (Winemiller and Ochoa-Winemiller 2009:8). Obsidian from Güinope has been recovered from other areas in eastern Honduras; however, obsidian in general is a scarce commodity in the archaeological record of eastern Honduras (Begley 1999:224). In the northeast, obsidian has been reported from the site of Selin Farm (AD 300–1000) and Río Claro (AD 1000–1530).

Our data from the Jamastrán Valley suggest that variability in the proportion of different obsidian sources and uses for particular toolmaking might be due to the presence of independent but overlapping procurement strategies. In Jamastrán, obsidian arrived in the form of nodules, macrocores, and polyhedral cores, depending on the distance and availability of the obsidian sources. With the exception of obsidian from the La Esperanza source and its subsequent use for blade production, our data suggest that obsidian procurement, distribution, and production were accessible to all communities in the Jamastrán Valley.

INTERREGIONAL INTERACTION

It has been pointed out that in both northeastern and eastern Honduras no great amount of commodities was mobilized through interregional exchanges with west-central Honduras (Begley 1999; Healy 1992). It has been also suggested that in northeastern Honduras, as in Olancho, interregional commodity exchange with societies in western and central Honduras was not a determinant factor in the development of sociopolitical complexity in the region. For Healy (1984b; 1992:102), the period of greatest political and social complexity in the northeast occurs after AD 1000, when societies in northeast Honduras became increasingly isolated from the chiefdoms in central and western Honduras and commenced contacts with Lower Central American groups. However, Healy (1992) does not attribute the emergence of more-complex forms of social organization in northeastern Honduras to increasing interaction with Lower Central America, at a time when most regions in Honduras are going through processes of political and economic decentralization. Interaction with elite groups from other areas of Central America seems to have strengthened when social differences were already present in northeastern Honduras. Begley (1999; chapter 7, this volume), also supports the idea that interregional economic exchange was not a predominant form of interaction between eastern and central Honduras.

Ceramic evidence from Jamastrán indicates that the inhabitants of the valley were involved in interactions with communities in the Telica Valley in Olancho, suggested by the presence of sherds from the Chichicaste Ceramic Group. The distribution of Chichicaste pottery varies across the regional clusters and areas of the valley. Whereas Calpules and El Zapotillo regional clusters yielded higher proportions of imported ceramics (34% and 38%, respectively), the communities in the southwestern and eastern part of the Jamastrán yielded roughly half of that (15% and 13%, respectively). We consider that differential distributions of imported ceramics in the valley indicate differential access to external interactions and exchanges. As with the mobilization of obsidian, it is likely that the varied distribution of Chichicaste pottery in the valley could be the result of a combination of procurement strategies in the valley, acting independently but operating simultaneously in the region.

Archaeological research at the Dos Quebradas and Chichicaste sites points to a greater degree of commodity exchange with western and central Honduras than has been observed for other areas of eastern Honduras. Research in the Telica Valley suggests that obsidian was an important commodity in the region and that the inhabitants of Dos Quebradas had access to obsidian from distant sources from western Honduras, Guatemala, and the central Mexican highlands (Winemiller and Ochoa Winemiller 2009). More research in the Telica Valley will help us understand the obsidian-procurement strategies in Olancho and Jamastrán. Research at Dos Quebradas has not emphasized the role of interregional interactions in terms of contributing to social complexity in the region (Winemiller and Ochoa-Winemiller 2009).

More research in the Telica Valley will also contribute to our understanding of the role of craft production and elite involvement in its distribution. Our data from the Jamastrán Valley suggests that interaction with that region was direct and apparently constant. A systematic survey of the Telica Valley, where Chichicaste and Dos Quebradas are located, is forthcoming (Winemiller and Ochoa-Winemiller 2009), so there are no concrete data about the relationship among settlements in the region; however, the evidence at hand seems to indicate that Dos Quebradas was an important center in the region at some point of its occupancy. The relationship between the ceramic-producing community of Chichicaste and Dos Quebradas also needs further evaluation in order to explore the presence of Chichicaste polychromes in many areas of eastern Honduras. Were the elites at Dos Quebradas controlling the production and/ or distribution of Chichicaste polychromes? Are Chichicaste polychromes symbols of the "elite etiquette" of some areas in eastern Honduras? Only further research in the Telica Valley and other areas of eastern Honduras would help us answer these questions.

If the Chichicaste polychromes are in fact evidence of elite exchange in eastern Honduras, it is likely that some aspiring local leaders in the Jamastrán Valley were engaging in such interactions in order to bolster their political status or gain social prestige. By the same token, the presence of Chichicaste polychromes in the Jamastrán Valley might reflect the prestige strategies of the elites at Dos Quebradas. The mild positive correlation between settlement sizes and proportion of Chichicaste pottery in Jamastrán could be the result of a combination of procurement strategies that could include redistribution of imported pottery from the larger settlements to neighboring smaller communities, which could be the case of the Calpules regional cluster, or relatively direct access of most communities in the valley to Chichicaste pottery.

CONCLUSION

Survey data, along with ceramic and lithic analysis, suggest that the prehispanic Jamastrán Valley in southeastern Honduras was not politically unified during the period under study (AD 600–1000). At the regional level, the communities in the valley were politically autonomous and economically independent. The presence of discrete areas of closer interaction is taken to represent internal interactional boundaries in the valley. Regional clusters in Jamastrán consist of areas where communication and exchange among communities was closer and more frequent than with other similar interacting areas in the valley. The presence of larger community structures seems to represent the existence of at least two autonomous systems in Jamastrán. Within the regional clusters, population tended to congregate in one village, which hosted a significantly larger population than the other communities integrating the clusters. It is likely that these regional clusters might correspond to more integrated social units in the valley. At this scale, social and economic interdependence could have been established between communities with little social differences.

In contrast to the early establishment of agricultural communities in western and central Honduras, sedentary occupation in eastern Honduras is identified in the archaeological record of different valleys at around AD 300–600. While the emergent central places in northeastern Honduras and the Culmí Valley participated in a rather marginal manner in the well-established commodity-exchange networks of western and central Honduras, emergent centers in the Telica Valley seem to have been more directly involved in those networks. Our current data do not support the idea that interregional interactions between nascent hierarchical communities in the Telica Valley and well-established chiefdoms from west-central Honduras provided the basis for the formation of social complexity in areas of eastern Honduras. However, the disruption of exchange networks in west-central Honduras due to political changes might have had an impact in the local social dynamics of the Telica Valley and other areas in eastern Honduras, including the Jamastrán Valley. It is likely that processes of sociopolitical decentralization observed in areas of west-central Honduras at around AD 800–1000 affected the economic and political land-scape of parts of eastern Honduras where interregional contact with those regions was more constant and direct. The abandonment of centers in the Telica and Jamastrán Valleys might be related to a more generalized process of economic segmentation and population dispersion linked to panregional sociopolitical rearrangements. On the other hand, this political crisis in west-central Honduras had a minimal impact on northeastern Honduras, where communities had maintained a marginal interaction with west-central polities.

As noted before, evidence derived from the comparison of different social trajectories in western, central, and eastern Honduras points to three common factors that stand out as crucial elements for understanding the development of social hierarchies in those regions: access to prime agricultural land, craft production, and local exchange and interregional interactions. It is impossible to single out a sole determining factor responsible for the establishment of institutionalized social differences for each region. Moreover, it is the articula-tion or combination of these factors and the ability to connect economic and prestige strategies to each other that enable the consolidation of permanent forms of social inequality in many regions of prehispanic Honduras, including the Culmí and Telica Valleys and northeastern Honduras, despite different degrees of political centralization.

More than fundamental differences in the social processes leading to social complexity in prehispanic Honduras, comparison of different trajectories seems to indicate that time depth and the pace of social change in each region can better account for the successful establishment of varying forms of political centralization.

The synchronic nature of our data does not allow us, at this moment of our research, to grasp the nuances of social change observed in other social trajectories. It is worth noticing that the late occupation of the Jamastrán Valley coincides with that of other regions in eastern Honduras (the Culmí and Telica Valleys, the Talgua drainage, and northeastern Honduras). Viewed within this larger region, the incipient social differences found among communities in the Jamastrán Valley seem to make sense if understood as part of a wider political system that might have had its center in the Telica Valley. Local aspiring leaders in Jamastrán seem to have failed to articulate in a complementary fashion both economic and prestige-based strategies in order to solidify their social status. The frailty of these hierarchical structures is also reflected in the communities' inability to resist the pressures toward decentralization and population dispersion experienced throughout prehispanic Honduras.

WORKS CITED

Aoyama, Kazuo. 1999. *Ancient Maya State, Urbanism, Exchange, and Craft Specialization: Chipped Stone Evidence from the Copán Valley and the La Entrada Region, Honduras*. Pittsburgh, PA: University of Pittsburgh, Department of Anthropology.

Ashmore, Wendy. 1987. "Cobble Crossroads: Gualjoquito Architecture and External Elite Ties." In *Interaction on the Southeast Mesoamerican Frontier: Prehistoric and Historic Honduras and El Salvador*, ed. Eugenia Robinson, 28–48. Oxford, UK: BAR.

Baudez, Claude F. 1970. *Central America*. Geneva, Switzerland: Nagel Publishers.

Baudez, Claude F., and Pierre Becquelin. 1973. *Archéologie de Los Naranjos, Honduras*. Mexico City, Mexico: Mission Archéologique et Ethnologique Française au Mexique.

Beaudry-Corbett, Marilyn. 1995. *Informe Final Análisis de Cerámica Proyecto Arqueológico Talgua*. Manuscript on File. Tegucigalpa, Honduras: Archives of the Instituto Hondureño de Antropología e Historia.

Begley, Christopher. 1999. "Elite Power Strategies and External Connections in Ancient Eastern Honduras." Unpublished PhD dissertation, Department of Anthropology, University of Kentucky, Laxington, KY.

Benyo, Julie C., and Thomas L. Melchionne. 1987. "Settlement Patterns in the Tencoa Valley, Honduras: An Application of the Coevolutionary Systems Model." In *Interaction on the Southeast Mesoamerican Frontier: Prehistoric and Historic Honduras and El Salvador*, ed. Eugenia J. Robinson, 49–64. Oxford, UK: BAR.

Carneiro, Robert. 1998. "What Happened at the Flashpoint? Conjectures on Chiefdom Formation at the Very Moment of Conception." In *Chiefdoms and Chieftancy in the Americas*, ed. Elsa M. Redmond, 18–42. Gainsville: University Press of Florida.

Creamer, Winifred. 1987. "Evidence for Prehistoric Ethnic Groups in the Sula Valley, Honduras." In *Interaction on the Southeast Mesoamerican Frontier: Prehistoric and Historic Honduras and El Salvador*, ed. Eugenia J. Robinson, 357–384. Oxford, UK: BAR.

Dixon, Boyd. 1989. "A Preliminary Settlement Pattern Study of a Prehistoric Cultural Corridor: The Comayagua Valley, Honduras." *Journal of Field Archaeology* 16(3):257–271.

Drennan, Robert D. 1996. "One for All and All for One: Accounting for Variability without Losing Sight of Regularities in the Development of Complex Society." In *Emergent Complexity: The Evolution of Intermediate Societies*, ed. Jeanne E. Arnold, 25–34. Ann Arbor: University of Michigan.

Drennan, Robert D., and Christian E. Peterson. 2004. "Comparing Archaeological Settlement Systems with Rank-Size Graphs: A Measure of Shape and Statistical Confidence." *Journal of Archaeological Science* 31(5):533–549.

Drennan, Robert D., and Christian E. Peterson. 2005. "Early Chiefdom Communities Compared: The Settlement Pattern Record for Chiefing, the Alto Magdalena, and the Valle de Oaxaca." In *Subsistence, Settlement, and Social Complexity: Essays Honoring the Legacy of Jeffrey R. Parsons*, ed. Richard E. Blanton, 119–154. Los Angeles, CA: Costen Institute of Archaeology, UCLA.

Drennan, Robert D., Christian E. Peterson, Gregory G. Indrisano, Mingyu Teng, Gideon Shelach, Yanping Zhu, Katheryn M. Linduff, and Zhizhong Guo. 2003. "Approaches to Regional Demographic Reconstruction." In *Regional Archaeology in Eastern Inner Mongolia: A Methodological Exploration*, 152–165. Beijing, China: Science Press.

Epstein, Jeremiah F. 1957. "Late Ceramic Horizons in Northeastern Honduras." Unpublished PhD dissertation, Department of Anthropology, University of Pennsylvania, Philadelphia, PA.

Epstein, Jeremiah F. 1975. *Survey of the Island of Roatan, Bay Islands, Honduras.* Manuscript on file. Tegucigalpa, Honduras: Archives of the Instituto Hondureño de Antropología e Historia.

Espinoza Perez, Edgar, Laraine Fletcher, and Ronaldo Salgado Galeano. 1996. *Arqueología de Las Segovias: Una Sequencia Cultural Preliminar*. Managua, Nicaragua: Instituto Nicaragüense de Cultura.

Hasemann, George E. 1987. "Late Classic Settlement on the Sulaco River, Central Honduras." In *Chiefdoms in the Americas*, ed. Robert D. Drennan and Carlos A. Uribe, 85–102. Lanham, MD: University Press of America.

Hasemann, George E. 1995. *Informe del Proyecto Arqueológico Talgua 1995*. Manuscript on file. Tegucigalpa, Honduras: Archives of the Instituto Hondureño de Antropología e Historia.

Hasemann, George E. 1998. "Regional Settlement History on the Lower Sulaco River, West Central Honduras: Rural Settlement Theory and Ancient Settlement Pattern in the Honduran Highlands." Unpublished PhD dissertation, Department of Anthropology, University of Kentucky, Lexington, KY.

Hasemann, George E., and Gloria Lara-Pinto. 1993. "La Zona Central: Regionalismo e Interacción." In *Historia Antigua*, Volume 1, *Historia General de Centroamérica*, ed. Robert Carmack, 135–216. Madrid, Spain: Facultad Latinoamericana de Ciencias Sociales.

Healy, Paul F. 1974. "The Cuyamel Caves: Preclassic Sites in Northeast Honduras." *American Antiquity* 39(3):435–447.

Healy, Paul F. 1975. "The H-CN-4 (Williams Ranch) Site: Preliminary Report on a Selin Period Site in Northeast Honduras." *Vínculos* 1(1):61–71.

Healy, Paul F. 1976. "Informe preliminar sobre la arqueología del período Cocal en Colón, Noreste de Honduras." *Yaxkin* 1(2):4–9.

Healy, Paul F. 1978a. "Excavations at Rio Claro, Northeast Honduras: Preliminary Report." *Journal of Field Archaeology* 5:15–28.

Healy, Paul F. 1978b. "Excavations at the Selin Farm Site (H-CN-5), Colon, Northeast Honduras." *Vínculos* 4(2):57–79.

Healy, Paul F. 1980. *Archaeology of the Rivas Region, Nicaragua*. Ontario, Canada: Wilfrid Laurier University Press.

Healy, Paul F. 1984a. "The Archaeology of Honduras." In the *Archaeology of Lower Central America*, ed. Frederick W. Lange and Doris Z. Stone, 113–161. Albuquerque: University of New Mexico Press.

Healy, Paul F. 1984b. "Northeast Honduras: A Precolumbian Frontier Zone." In *Recent Developments in Isthmian Archaeology*, ed. Frederick W. Lange, 227–241. Oxford, UK: BAR.

Healy, Paul F. 1992. "Ancient Honduras: Power, Wealth, and Rank in Early Chiefdoms." In *Wealth and Hierarchy in the Intermediate Area*, ed. Frederick W. Lange, 85–108. Washington DC: Dumbarton Oaks.

Helms, Mary. 1979. *Ancient Panama: Chiefs in Search of Power*. Austin.: University of Texas Press.

Henderson, John. 1977. "The Valley of Naco: Ethnohistory and Archaeology in Northwestern Honduras." *Ethnohistory* 24(4):363–377.

Henderson, John S., Ilene Sterns, Anthony Wonderley, and Patricia A. Urban. 1979. "Archaeological Investigations in the Valle de Naco, Northwestern Honduras: A Preliminary Report." *Journal of Field Archaeology* 6(2):169–192.

Hirth, Kenneth G. 1988. "Beyond the Maya Frontier: Cultural Interactions and Syncretism along the Central Honduran Corridor." In *The Southeast Classic Maya Zone*, ed. Elizabeth Boone and Gordon R. Willey, 297–334. Washington, DC: Dumbarton Oaks.

Hirth, Kenneth G., Gloria Lara-Pinto, and George Hasemann. 1989. *Archaeological Research in the El Cajón Region*, Vol. 1. Pittsburgh, PA: Department of Anthropology, University of Pittsburgh.

Hoopes, John W. 1993. "A View from the South: Prehistoric Exchange in Lower Central America." In *The American Southwest and Mesoamerica: Systems of Prehistoric Exchange*, ed. J. E. Ericson and T. G. Baugh, 247–282. New York: Plenum Press.

Johnson, Gregory A. 1977. Aspects of Regional Analysis in Archaeology. *Annual Review of Anthropology* 6(1):479–508.

Johnson, Gregory A. 1980. "Rank-Size Convexity and System Integration: A View from Archaeology." *Economic Anthropology* 56(3):234–247.

Johnson, Gregory A. 1981. "Monitoring Complex System Integration and Boundary Phenomena with Settlements Size Data." In *Archaeological Approaches to the Study of Complexity*, ed. Sander Van der Leeuw, 144–189. Amsterdam, Netherlands: University van Amsterdam.

Joyce, Rosemary A. 1991. *Cerro Palenque: Power and Identity on the Maya Periphery*. Austin: University of Texas Press.

Lange, Frederick W. 1984. "Cultural Geography of Pre-Columbian Lower Central America." In *The Archaeology of Lower Central America*, ed. Frederick W. Lange and Doris F. Stone, 33–62. Albuquerque: University of New Mexico Press.

Lange, Frederick W., ed. 1992. *Wealth and Hierarchy in the Intermediate Area*. Washington, DC: Dumbarton Oaks.

Lentz, David L., Carlos R. Ramirez, and Bronson W. Griscom. 1997. "Formative-Period Subsistence and Forest-Product Extraction at the Yarumela Site, Honduras." *Ancient Mesoamerica* 8(1):63–74.

Murdock, George Peter. 1949. *Social Structure*. New York: McMillan.

Murillo Herrera, Mauricio. 2009. *Social Change in Pre-Columbian San Ramón de Alajuela, Costa Rica, and Its Adjacent Regions*. Pittsburgh, PA: University of Pittsburgh.

Parkinson, William A., ed. 2002. *The Archaeology of Tribal Societies*. Ann Arbor: University of Michigan.

Peterson, Christian. 2006. *Crafting Hongshan Communities? Household Archaeology in the Chifen Region of Eastern Inner Mongolia*. Pittsbugh, PA: University of Pittsburgh.

Peterson, Christian, and Robert D. Drennan. 2005. "Communities, Settlements, Sites, and Survey: Regional-Scale Analysis of Prehistoric Human Interaction." *American Antiquity* 70(1):5–30.

Pope, Kevin O. 1987. "The Ecology and Economy of the Formative-Classic Transition Along the Ulua River, Honduras." In *Interaction on the Southeast Mesoamerican Frontier: Prehistoric and Historic Honduras and El Salvador*, ed. Eugenia J. Robinson, 95–128. Oxford, UK: BAR.

Salgado, Silvia. 1996. "Social Change in a Region of Granada, Pacific Nicaragua (1000 BC–AD 1522)." Unpublished PhD dissertation, Department of Anthropology, State University of New York, Albany, NY.

Sanders, William T. 1977. "Environmental Heterogeneity and the Evolution of Lowland Maya Civilization." In *The Origins of Maya Civilization*, ed. Richard E. W. Adams, 287–298. Albuquerque: University of New Mexico Press.

Sanders, William T. 1984. "Pre-Industrial Demography and Social Evolution." In *On the Evolution of Complex Societies: Essays in Honor of Harry Hoijer*, ed. Timothy Earle, 7–39. Malibu, CA: Undena Publications.

Schortman, Edward M., and Patricia A. Urban. 1987. "Survey within the Gualjoquito Hinterland: An Introduction to the Investigations of the Santa Barbara Archaeological Project." In *Interaction on the Southeast Mesoamerican Frontier: Prehistoric and Historic Honduras and El Salvador*, ed. Eugenia J. Robinson, 5–27. Oxford, UK: BAR.

Schortman, Edward M., and Patricia A. Urban. 1992. "Current Trends in Interaction Research." In *Resources, Power, and Interregional Interaction*, ed. Edward M. Schortman and Patricia A. Urban, 225–235. New York: Plenum Press.

Sheets, Payson. 1992. "The Pervasive Pejorative in Intermediate Area Studies." In *Wealth and Hierarchy in the Intermediate Area*, ed. Frederick Lange, 15–42. Washington, DC: Dumbarton Oaks.

Steward, Julian. 1955. *Theory of Culture Change: The Methodology of Multilinear Evolution*. Urbana: University of Illinois Press.

Stone, Doris Z. 1941. *Archaeology of the North Coast of Honduras*. Cambridge, MA: Harvard University Press.

Stone, Doris Z. 1954. *Estampas de Honduras*. Mexico City, Mexico: Impresora Galve.

Strong, William Duncan. 1934. *An Archaeological Cruise Among the Bay Islands of Honduras*. Washington, DC: Smithsonian Institution.

Strong, William Duncan. 1935. *Archaeological Investigations in the Bay Islands, Spanish Honduras.* Washington, DC: Smithsonian Institution.

Winemiller, Terance, and Virginia Ochoa-Winemiller. 2009. *The Telica Connection: Community and Lifeways at Chichicaste and Dos Quedradas, Honduras.* Paper presented at the 74th Annual Meeting of the Society for American Archaeology, Atlanta, GA.

7

In the Mosquitia region of eastern Honduras, a long-distance relationship of a noneconomic nature (i.e., not commodity based) appears to have played a critical part in the sociopolitical development of the local polities as complex societies emerged around AD 500, during late Period IVb or Period V (AD 500–1000). Research presented here demonstrates a long-distance relationship that was manifested most clearly in symbolically and ritually important elements, coincident with the first evidence of complex social organization, suggesting that an interaction based on prestige rather than economics was an integral part of the emerging complex society. Data suggest that the prestige associated with traversing both geographical space and cultural distance is clearly a factor in strategies adopted by eastern Honduran elites during the time in which their societies achieved increasing complexity. This long-distance exchange is examined in order to contextualize and understand the internal dynamics of sociopolitical development and change in eastern Honduras. Ultimately, the focus turns away from external factors to exploring the negotiations and machinations within eastern Honduran society through which elites acquired, applied, and maintained power.

In an attempt to elucidate the actual mechanisms utilized in these elite power-acquisition strategies, I discuss some specific ways in which the long-distance connections were manifested as concrete changes in material culture, as well as ways in which these manifestations

Ancient Mosquito Coast

Why Only Certain Material Culture Was Adopted from Outsiders

CHRISTOPHER BEGLEY

DOI: 10.5876/9781646420971.c007

supported an increasing power differential within eastern Honduran society. Specifically, I examine the adoption of ballcourts and related rituals by the nascent elite of eastern Honduras through the interpretation of data collected via survey, excavation, and analysis of archaeological materials from the Culmí and Olancho Valleys and the Paulaya and Plátano watersheds of eastern Honduras. By adopting that ritual complex, the elite associated themselves with powerful and prestigious polities to the west, provided an arena to negotiate social relations with competitors, and appropriated existing cosmological concepts, thereby making their increasingly differentiated position in the hierarchy seem "natural" or inevitable.

THE MOSQUITIA OF EASTERN HONDURAS

The Mosquitia, or Mosquito Coast, of eastern Honduras is positioned just beyond the limits of Mesoamerica, along the northern frontier of Lower Central America (figure 7.1), whose cultures were oriented more towards South America than towards the north. Significant differences between the material culture of eastern and central/western Honduras have been widely noted (Hasemann et al. 1996; Healy 1984a; Stone 1941; Strong 1948). While the rest of Honduras shares many features with Mesoamerica, the eastern part looks distinctly different and non-Mesoamerican in terms of its material culture. Because of this difference, the prehistoric societies of eastern Honduras have been regarded as northern extensions of essentially South American cultures (Healy 1984a:156). Despite the presence of items like obsidian, greenstone, and exotic ceramics in eastern Honduras, which suggest trade connections with Mesoamerica (Healy 1984a, 1992), the fundamental non-Mesoamerican quality of eastern Honduran populations has been consistently noted. Mesoamerican traits such as "stepped pyramids, ball courts, Mesoamerican deities, or other traditional hallmarks" were thought absent in eastern Honduras (Healy 1984a:159), although a complex heterogeneity has long been recognized in the region, and relationships with neighboring regions were not homogenous over space and time. While I documented ballcourts and other "Mesoamerican" traits at various places in eastern Honduras, they have not been documented in some neighboring areas (see Martínez, chapter 6, this volume; MacFarlane and Suri, chapter 5, this volume).

Despite the common description of the Mosquitia region as "unexplored" (e.g., Preston 2013, 2015), archaeologists have worked in the area since the 1920s. While my archaeological research represents the first long-term, extensive projects in the region, notable work has been conducted there previously.

FIGURE 7.1. *Map of Lower Central America with the northeast region of Honduras shaded.*

I have conducted archaeological research in the Mosquito Coast of Honduras since 1991, completing my doctoral dissertation fieldwork there (Begley 1999, 2004), and written about the lost-city legends of the region (Begley 2016; Begley and Cox 2007). Previous to this, important work had been conducted by Strong (1934), Stone (1941), Healy (1984a, 1984b), and Lara-Pinto and Hasemann (1988; Hasemann and Lara-Pinto 1992). Newer research in the Mosquito Coast recently includes work by Christian Wells and his students (Goodwin 2011; Mihok 2013; Mihok et al., chapter 8, this volume), the work related to the sites found with LiDAR (Fisher et al. 2016; Preston 2015), and some restudies of museum collections (e.g. Cuddy 2007; Dennett 2007, 2008).

One of the most persistent problems with the focus on interaction along the Southeastern Mesoamerican frontier has been the tendency to view the periphery with what has been termed a "pervasive pejorative" (Sheets 1992), relegating it to the status of a miniature, quasi-developed version of the core. Sheets and others (Graham 1993; Joyce 1993) lament the definition of cultures along the periphery in terms of their more-complex neighbors and the resulting misreading of the past that can arise from a failure to define these cultures in their own terms. This "pervasive pejorative" is compounded by the tendency to dichotomize theoretical frameworks dealing with sociocultural development into (1) those that emphasize local adaptation to the physical and social environment, and (2) those that place primary importance on intersocietal interaction of various sorts (trade, warfare, migration) as impetus for change. While most would agree with Schortman and Urban (1986:8) that local developments are almost always affected by outside contacts, and that societies do not comprise closed systems, this dichotomy nevertheless has created a *de facto* privileging of one over the other. Internal developments are often overshadowed or explained in terms of external connections. However, the focus on interregional interaction in the present study is not an emphasis on the external over the internal. In this case, while preliminary evidence suggests that some sort of interaction with Mesoamerica was associated with the emergence of complexity in eastern Honduras, it is the *transforming* effects of that intersocietal interaction at the local level that are important. In other words, it is how this interaction is translated into *local adaptations* to the changing social environment that is of interest. Ultimately, in order to understand the role of interaction on the historical trajectory of eastern Honduras, the *actual on-the-ground changes* that took place within eastern Honduran society must be examined, looking at the effects on the nonelites and exploring the ways in which these changes fit into a larger strategy. The focus here, then, starts with the "intersocietal interaction" but ultimately moves to and emphasizes the internal response or "local adaptation" and the impact of this interaction on the eastern Honduran population, emphasizing the *internal* use of this *external* connection by emerging elites.

FIELD RESULTS

My research in eastern Honduras recorded many "Mesoamerican" elements during Periods V (AD 500–1000) and VI (AD 1000–1530). These "Mesoamerican" elements included not only portable trade items but also some of the "traditional hallmarks" of Mesoamerica, including ballcourts, plazas, and patio groups (Begley 1992, 1999, 2004). Such architectural elements, particularly the ballcourts formed by twin, parallel mounds at sites such as La Cooperativa and Suyapita (figures 7.2 and 7.3), have been called "diagnostic" features of Mesoamerican sites, and have been assumed to indicate the presence of Mesoamerican peoples (Kirchhoff 1943; Messenger 1987:398–399).

Mesoamerican elements in eastern Honduras first appear during Period V (AD 500–1000), which is the first period for which we have enough data to recognize any patterns (Healy 1984a, 1984b). Archaeological indicators of

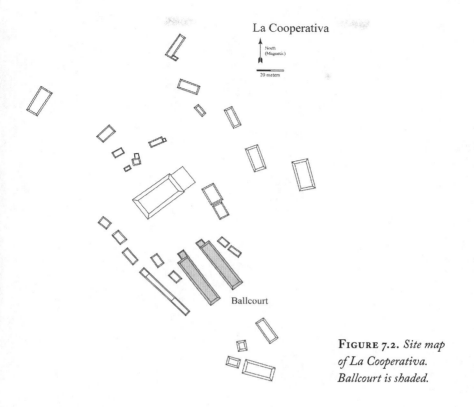

La Cooperativa

North
(Magnetic)

20 meters

Ballcourt

FIGURE 7.2. *Site map of La Cooperativa. Ballcourt is shaded.*

complex social organization or institutionalized inequality (such as monumental construction and a hierarchical settlement pattern) appear at this time in Mesoamerican-like form with orthogonal plazas and patio groups. Although there were a number of Mesoamerican elements of material culture in eastern Honduras, these were mainly confined to an architectural complex, primarily public architecture such as the ballcourts. Most material culture was not, however, reminiscent of Mesoamerica and therefore does not support the conclusion of an intrusive population during the occupation of any known archaeological sites (Period V and early Period VI).

Regional settlement systems in eastern Honduras were investigated both systematically and non-systematically. One hundred percent of an approximately 100-km² section of the central section of the Culmí Valley was surveyed. This area, referred to as the Culmí project area, traversed the valley from east to west and included the three largest known sites in the valley. Additionally, 13 other areas of 1 km² each, selected at random, were surveyed in

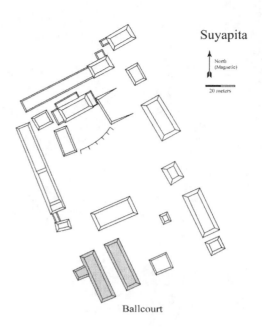

Suyapita

North
(Magnetic)

20 meters

Ballcourt

FIGURE 7.3. *Site
map of Suyapita.
Ballcourt is shaded.*

order to examine a sample of the valley outside of the area surveyed systematically. In addition to this, non-systematic surveys, primarily utilizing local
informants, were conducted in the Culmí Valley and throughout the Paulaya,
Plátano, Pao, and Wampú watersheds to the east. One hundred and twenty-
five sites were located throughout eastern Honduras. Thirty sites in the Culmí
Valley project area were investigated with shovel probes, and nine of those
sites were excavated. The earliest settlements identified in eastern Honduras
date to around AD 250–300, the beginning of Period IVb (Healy 1984a). After
this date, open-air sites occur with great frequency, possibly representing an
increase in population around this time. Even the earliest sites from the present project display evidence of supralocal political organization as far back as
the end of Period IVb or the beginning of Period V, after AD 250 and probably
before AD 600. While most sites are dated via temporally diagnostic artifacts,
a series of ^{14}C assays were done on sites throughout the Culmi Valley. The
earliest date came from the site of Altas de Subirana at 1510 BP ± 130 (I-18095;

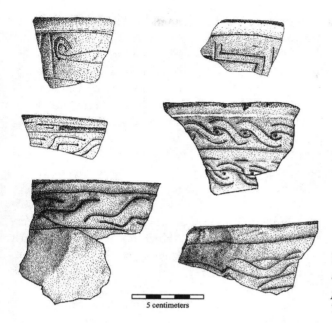

FIGURE 7.4. *Dorina abstract incised-punctate ceramic type: Tome variety.*

wood charcoal) associated with structures over 2 m high and over 50 m long. From the earliest evidence of complexity there is evidence of some degree of contact with Mesoamerica, seen most clearly in the formal, orthogonal site plans and in imported materials such as obsidian. This early interaction with northern groups appears to focus on elite paraphernalia and symbols, including jade, obsidian, and templates for public constructions.

A significant change appears to have taken place near the beginning of Period VI. Shortly after the Maya "collapse" and concomitant population declines or decentralization in central Honduras, the cultures of eastern Honduras (somewhat predictably) began showing fewer connections to the north, and stylistically began to resemble their southern neighbors. This is most clearly visible in the ceramics (Healy 1993). Period V ceramics were painted in many cases, whereas Period VI ceramics (figure 7.4) are firmly in the incised-punctate tradition seen throughout the rest of Lower Central America. In other ways, however, eastern Honduran societies showed more Mesoamerican-like elements. Unlike most societies to the south, for instance, the eastern Honduran polities built large public constructions, and appear either to have been organized in complex ways not seen elsewhere in Lower Central America or to have expressed it in a radically different manner.

It is unclear when societies in eastern Honduras reached their height. Healy (1984a) suggests an apogee in early Period VI, sometime after AD 1000. Data from the present project suggest that Period V settlements are more numerous and larger than Period VI sites in at least some parts of eastern Honduras, such as the Culmí Valley (Begley 1999). This variation within eastern Honduras may indicate that the region did not reach its zenith at the same time in all places. While the Culmí Valley seems to have many Period V occupations, with few sites dating to Period VI, most large sites previously reported in the northeast are primarily Period VI (Begley 1999; Healy 1984a). Important areas of eastern Honduras, particularly the Paulaya River drainage that contains numerous large sites, remain temporally undefined.

There appears to have been a widespread demographic collapse or a radical decentralization of the population in Honduras during Period VI, affecting western and central Honduras (Healy 1984a; Hirth 1989; Messenger 1991). Eastern Honduran populations continued strong during early Period VI. Late Period VI occupations are scarcer, hardly represented in the archaeological record of the Culmí Valley and throughout the Paulaya and Platano Valleys. It may be that late Period VI materials are difficult to distinguish from those of early Period VI, or it could be that a demographic shift happened during this period. This could have been a population decline, or a dispersal of formerly nucleated populations into smaller sites with a greater chance of underrepresentation in the sample.

Judging from the artifactual assemblage, which yields little late Period VI material, many of the larger archaeological sites had been abandoned by the time the Spanish arrived. Early chroniclers, however, report large polities that declined radically in less than a century. No archaeological site has yet been identified with these large villages described by the Spanish, although Healy (1984a:153) suggests that the site of Río Claro in the Aguan Valley may be the village of Chapagua, the center of one of these polities.

The two important periods in the development of identified eastern Honduran societies were around AD 500–600 and AD 1000. The earlier date marks the date by which complexity had emerged in this area, while significant stylistic changes and a possible increase in population and the size of some regional centers occurred at the latter date. These may be related to events within Mesoamerica. The first date, AD 500–600, corresponds roughly to the hiatus in the Maya area associated with the decline of Teotihuacan as well as the reopening of the southern trade route through El Salvador after the catastrophic eruption of the Ilopango volcano (Sharer 1984). The second date is about a century after the Maya transformation or "collapse" and concurrent demographic declines in central Honduras, as well as the increase in long-distance trade at the beginning of Period VI (Andrews 1985; Chapman 1957). In both cases, the decline of powerful polities with extensive trade and communication networks is temporally correlated with an increase in sociopolitical complexity or population in eastern Honduras. While it cannot be demonstrated that these events offered new opportunities for eastern Honduran elites or resulted in greater opportunities for trade and interaction by eastern Honduran groups, it seems unlikely that the correlation is completely spurious.

Many of the differences between Period V and VI, such as the increasing emphasis on incision as a decorative technique on ceramics, appear around AD 800. This may relate to the transformation or collapse in the Maya area. Other related phenomena, like the migrations of groups like the Pipil and Nicarao into El Salvador and Nicaragua at the end of Period V, probably affected these developments in eastern Honduras (Fowler 1989a, 1989b). The appearance of what may be feathered-serpent motifs on ceramics and rock art throughout the region may be related to these migrations. There is no archaeological evidence, however, for the migration of these or other foreign populations directly into eastern Honduras (Lara-Pinto 1991). Since no site occupied by Nahua-speakers at contact has been identified archaeologically, the material correlates that would mark the posited Nahua occupation of some parts of eastern Honduras at the time of contact remain unknown.

LONG-DISTANCE ACQUISITION OF ESOTERIC KNOWLEDGE

In eastern Honduras, a long-distance relationship of a noneconomic nature appears to have been an important part of the sociopolitical development of the region. Helms's (1979, 1988, 1992) study of power-attainment through the acquisition of esoteric knowledge in contact-period Panama provides a good exemplar for the present study. In Panama, long-distance connections were associated with the acquisition of esoteric knowledge, which played a significant role in the political power of elites. Helms laments the fact that "the ethnohistoric and archaeological data directly pertinent to the pre-Columbian Intermediate Area do not allow for clear substantiation of this hypothesis" (1988:xi). A similarity exists between the power-acquisition strategies in use by emerging elites in eastern Honduras during Period V and those proposed by Helms for contact-period Panamanian chiefs. Helms focuses on the symbolic value of external relationships, recognizing the connection between geographical distance and power. Helms (1988:13) defines esoteric knowledge as "knowledge of the unusual, the exceptional, the extraordinary." She associates the "successful operation of rank societies" with the "ability of the elite, especially chiefs, to generate and sustain the belief that they can control all facets of life, including people, natural resources, and the supernatural" (Helms 1979:70). She suggests that one of the essential ways in which elites demonstrate or verify their sanctity or control over the supernatural, and by extension, control over the quotidian world is through ritual. This would require special "esoteric knowledge," which translated to political and social power. Helms suggests that

> the fundamental mode of verification evidenced by ritual emphasized the high degree of esoteric knowledge controlled by the rulership, that is, knowledge of the meaning of sacred symbols, insights into the "meaning" of life, and understanding of the mystical origins and operations of the cosmos whose creative-destructive energies could be controlled for human use by the application of uniquely human intellect. Whatever other activities were required of the political elite, essentially it was by developing and displaying a store of exceptional knowledge and understanding that the [elite] of this nonliterate society were able to authenticate and legitimize their positions. (Helms 1979:119–120)

Helms also suggests that "sanctity" or the ability to wield esoteric knowledge in an effective way is a particularly important element in social control in small or nascent complex societies, "where authorities have little secular power to achieve compliance with social norms" (Helms 1979:176). In these small groups without a powerful state apparatus, "sanctity becomes a vital element of political power since it is largely by virtue of their aura of sanctity [that is, of association with 'ultimate truth'] that the leaders of such societies control the people and material resources under their charge" (Helms 1979:176).

One way in which this sanctity or sacred power was gained was through travel to or associations with geographically distant areas. Helms emphasizes the parallels between the geographically distant and the supernaturally distant, noting "that this association was succinctly stated by the acquisition from distant geographical regions of elite prestige items with sacred significance" (Helms 1979:109–110). Helms suggests that the acquisition of esoteric knowledge or the association with a geographically distant land was always an important part of interregional interaction, especially by small chiefdoms like those found in eastern Honduras, since it was parlayed into sociopolitical power or legitimization of power at home.

Helms warned against the application of her model to other situations without the specific documentation of particulars that she has for Panama. A lack of particulars leaves unanswered the central question of how the acquired esoteric knowledge was utilized or acted upon. Helms provides an important example of how the ideological significance of geographic space and distance can contribute to a significant, non-commodity-based interaction, but, as she noted, this idea may lack explanatory power if generalized. One must, as she does, demonstrate the particular ways in which this significance is turned into political power.

Even with a specific mechanism identified, another necessary step remains. It is not enough to explain how this "functioned" for the elite. Ideology, in order to have functioned for the elite, must also have immediacy or some other compelling quality for the rest of society. Here, I invoke Bourdieu's (1977, 1991) concept of *doxa*, or the perceived "natural" way of the world. Ideology must form part of a "doxic experience"; that is, the socially constructed must seem natural in order to reflect an order inherent in nature. With that in mind, I suggest that the ballcourt-related ritual complex would have been incorporated in the existing *doxa*, while at the same time transforming the doxic experience, naturalizing a new and increasingly complex hierarchy.

UNDERSTANDING THE RELATIONSHIP WITH MESOAMERICA

The connection with Mesoamerica (direct or indirect) was varied over time, but at all times a clear qualitative difference existed between the eastern Honduran populations and the Mesoamerican folk. At some point near the end of Period IVb or the beginning of Period V (roughly AD 250–650), complex societies developed in the interior region of eastern Honduras, the population was drawn into increasingly nucleated settlements, and large-scale construction projects were undertaken for the first time. The individuals or groups who designed and organized these construction projects clearly emulated the patterns present in the large societies to the north, the closest and possibly only exemplar available to them.

This interaction with Mesoamerica is most evident in elements of site planning. Today, the most obtrusive features of archaeological sites in eastern Honduras are architectural. Foremost among the indicators of a connection with Mesoamerica are the ballcourts, whose shape, size, orientation, and placement within the site leave little doubt that they are ballcourts of the type found throughout Mesoamerica. This is in contrast to other ballcourt styles, such as those from the Caribbean and from the southwest United States, which are substantially different from the Mesoamerican type and do not indicate the same sort of significant interaction with Mesoamerica suggested by the parallel-mound type. Additionally, other proxemic elements appear with the ballcourts, such as formal plazas and plazuelas, which are architectonic templates common throughout Mesoamerica.

While evidence for the use of economic or military power in eastern Honduras is not clear, the role of ideological power is suggested by the nature of the imported elements. Why should it be that the most notable imported elements are symbols and templates? Why were material markers of a relationship with the powerful polity to the west so few? And above all, why were Mesoamerican elite symbolic complexes being used in a tradition that does not seem to use these symbols normally? Helms suggests that the acquisition of knowledge, especially esoteric knowledge, is important to the goals of an emerging elite, but how is acquired esoteric knowledge acted upon? Why was this strategy adopted? That is, why were the spatial templates and symbols used while the portable material markers, such as ceramics and obsidian so often traded around Mesoamerica, not? Helms (1979, 1988) provides an important start in demonstrating that "in traditional societies space and distance are not neutral concepts, but are accorded sociological, political, and especially ideological significance" (1988:4), allowing for a significant, non-commodity-based interaction, but the particular ways in which this significance is turned into political power remains to be demonstrated. Stating that geographical space is in some way equivalent or associated with mythical space is one thing. Explaining how and why foreign symbols were used successfully by elites in eastern Honduras is something else.

ELITE POWER STRATEGIES

Because the basic question here concerns the acquisition and application of power by elites, it seems prudent to turn to theorists concerned explicitly with power. Bourdieu (1977) and Foucault (1980) are the foremost modern theorists who have offered "sustained, conceptually focused perspectives on power and status formation in social life" (Marcus 1992:299). While many of these theorists offer a useful conceptual framework, an element of Foucault's work proved to be the most interesting or applicable. Foucault stresses that, in an analysis of power, "the analysis should not concern itself with power at the level of conscious intention or decision . . . Instead, it is a case of studying power where its intention, if it has one, is completely invested in real and effective practices" (Foucault 1980:97). In this instance, explaining the introduction of ballcourts and other Mesoamerican elements as an attempt by emerging elites to gain and maintain social and political power seemed unsatisfactory, since it did not explain how these changes resulted in increased power. In some ways it begs the question by not addressing the specific mechanism by which the long-distance relationship and the introduction of these foreign elements served to increase the political power of the elite.

In order to go beyond general statements linking long-distance exchange and prestige, I attempt to ascertain a way in which long-distance relationships were converted to political power. Power is approached from another angle, examining the "real and effective practices" by which the will to power of the elite was manifested. With this in mind, the search does not begin with an abstraction of possible strategies used by elites but with an examination of the kinds of concrete changes that accompanied the rise of elites, which allow for the demonstration of the ways in which power was played out in everyday life. This ultimately leads back to a discussion of the strategies of the elites, but it is a discussion of strategy informed by the examination of the concrete manifestations of power. What is drawn from Foucault, then, is largely methodological. In heeding his "methodological precaution" that the concrete application of power should be the object of study, I focus on one of the few visible changes associated with the emergent elite that are evident in the archaeological record—the introduction of Mesoamerican-style site planning, especially the introduction of ballcourts—and attempt to reconstruct the societal changes these material changes would have represented.

It is evident that the real transformations, at their most manifest and physical level, involved manipulating an existing cosmological complex and associating it with corporate architecture, which requires a certain amount of political power to create. These manipulations make critical elements of what Foucault calls "the production of truth" inaccessible to the masses (Foucault 1980:93–95, 130–132). Rappaport (1971:37–39) describes this process as a display of "sanctity" by elites, associating themselves with "ultimate truths." Earle (1997:142) warns that, in order to be effectively parlayed into political power, the elite association with ideological concepts "must be made concrete in forms such as ceremonies, symbols, and monuments." What we see in eastern Honduras is the elite in the process of concretizing their association with the ideological, creating a permanent reminder of their "sanctity" and appropriating that which is needed to produce "truth." The process of "controlling the production of truth" left detectable traces in the archaeological record. Thus, the focus of the inquiry ultimately shifts from the strategic use of elite interactions with Mesoamerica to the "internal" role of such interaction, with the "production of truth" as agent of legitimization.

Eastern Honduras was an area undergoing important sociopolitical developments that are understandable not in terms of interaction so much as in the internal power-plays of the emerging elite. The emerging elite were in the process of "materializing" their claim to ideology-based power, to use a term from DeMarrais et al. (1996). Contact with Mesoamerica, whatever the form, provided these elite with the esoteric knowledge by which they were able to continue the "production of truth" in Foucault's terms, or to maintain their sanctity or "association with ultimate truth," to use Rappaport's (1971) concept. The sites with ballcourts date to late Period V, with one possibly in Period VI, but temporal resolution is poor. Excavation in and around the ballcourts did not yield any information on the specific use or function of the ballcourts.

Giddens (1979) and Mann (1986) have suggested that there are a variety of ideologies in a given society, including ideologies of resistance held by those not in power. Ideology becomes a strategic tool, which, according to DeMarrais et al. (1996), must be "materialized" into practices and objects that can be controlled or manipulated by the elite as a way to gain political power. Creating ritual out of ideology would be a first step in the materialization process. Earle (1997:153) notes that public ceremonial events "create the symbolic nexus for a society" and are "probably the most basic and simple form of materialized ideology." The participation in rituals can be controlled or limited (Earl 1997:153), or the elite may increase the "organizational complexity [of the rituals], that is, the specialized nature and number of component elements required for their performance" (Earle 1997:154), making the elite increasingly indispensable.

Earle (1997) and DeMarrais et al. (1996) emphasize that this process of materialization must go beyond the creation of practices or rituals. Earle describes public ceremonial events as "not an ideal basis for power . . . they are not capital investments like the construction of a ceremonial place or the creation of ritual paraphernalia. Events are performed and then are over and done with. They cannot be 'owned' or passed on to the succeeding generations" (Earle 1997:154). A ritual monument, on the other hand, can be owned, inherited, and experienced by great numbers of people at once. Whereas an event may be seen as a weak, transitory investment, ballcourts are a more permanent manifestation of that ceremonial event. The ballcourts and related architecture, then, represent the fully materialized elite ideology.

In addition to the authority embodied in a public, ideologically important structure commissioned by the local elite, there must also have been a benefit to using an established and relatively powerful template (including orthogonal plazas and ballcourts) linked with the powerful polities to the west. This would imbue the elite with another sort of authority based in both might and precedent, drawing on the manifest power of Mesoamerican polities.

BALLCOURTS

The discussion to this point has focused on the adoption of an architectural complex that included ballcourts as part of a power-gathering strategy on a somewhat abstract level, dealing with issues of legitimization and the materialization of ritual knowledge. A more concrete level of discussion is needed here to address the question, why ballcourts? Why were ballcourts and associated rituals an effective or appropriate means for an emerging elite to consolidate power? Merely explaining the presence of ballcourts in eastern Honduras as an elite strategy to convert long-distance relations with Mesoamerica into political and social capital or power, though accurate, is incomplete and unsatisfactory because it does not confront the question of how this long-distance relationship was converted into power. Why should imitating foreign elites be the strategy of choice? Why was it effective? By looking closely at the transformation related to interregional interactions and the emergence of an elite, an attempt is made to identify not only the strategy but also the mechanisms by which at least part of the strategy worked.

The emerging elite in eastern Honduras would have adopted the rituals associated with the ballcourt as a means of establishing, rearranging, or reinforcing a set of social relations, placing themselves in a position of power, or justifying the inequality that existed. Ballcourts served as more than mere playing fields, and were often the site of a number of different rituals. For instance, Fox (1996) argues that ballcourts in the Cuyumapa drainage of west-central Honduras are associated with feasting and "may be viewed as public arenas in which power relations were negotiated, reproduced, and occasionally transformed through rituals in which the layered symbols of ballgames and feasts were alternately invoked" (Fox 1996:493). Ethnohistoric, ethnographic, and archaeological evidence support the association of ballcourts with multistage rituals.

The fact that part of the ritual complex associated with ballcourts involved a game must not be overlooked. Lévi-Strauss (1966:32) suggests that games constitute a unique ritual category that "end in the establishment of a difference between individual players or teams where originally there was no indication of inequality." Fox (1996:493) notes this "disjunctive" quality of the ballgame, citing Lévi-Strauss, and also stresses the unpredictability of the outcome of rituals involving games and sports. Fox argues that the games, in concert with associated feasting, provide an arena where local "aggrandizers" could increase their prestige through a public display of "pomp and pageantry" (Fox 1996:494). He suggests that the feast would have followed the game as "an attempt to transform competition and conflict into coordination and allegiance." Seen in this way, the ballgames would provide sponsors with a means of self-aggrandizement, at least part of which (the feast) was predictable. The game itself was presumably less predictable and would have interested challenging factions as a means of increasing prestige relative to the sponsoring faction, since the challengers would have a chance to gain ground relative to the sponsors.

Recent research suggests that monumentality does not necessarily signal elite behavior, but rather that many other forms of organization can result in the creation of monumental architecture (e.g., Burger and Rosenwig 2012). Monumental architecture provides a visible and permanent means of communication between elites and nonelites, and it is tempting to think of the ballcourts as an elite project designed to influence the nonelites. Another possibility, however, is that ballcourts were less a means of communicating between elites and the *hoi polloi*, but rather served as part of a corporate strategy meant primarily as a means of contact or communication between competing groups of elites. Or perhaps it represents communication between competing communities. In any case, there have been numerous suggestions that there exists an inverse relationship between the number of sites with ballcourts and the degree of political centralization in a region (Fox 1996; Kowalewski et al. 1991; Santley et al.1991), suggesting that ballcourt-related rituals played a part in the competition for political hegemony. In eastern Honduras, I have identified four sites with ballcourts, and two other sites have structures that are less obviously ballcourts. Fox (1996) argues that ballcourt-related rituals were one means of reordering the political landscape in nearby west-central Honduras. This precedent would have been another factor in the adoption of ballcourts and associated rituals by eastern Honduran elite. It is not surprising that a ritual complex already associated with the negotiation of this kind of social relations would be adopted by nearby emerging elites who were beginning the process of solidifying their place in the social order. Here, the dangers of reification of the Mesoamerican/non-Mesoamerican dichotomy become clear. While the linguistic and biological heritage of the eastern and western Honduran groups may be different, this may not reflect, in any meaningful way, the relationships during the first millennium AD. They were, after all, neighbors. Sites located at the interface of these groups show a blend of material culture (for instance, ballcourts with an incised and punctated ceramic tradition), and although this may not be a reliable indicator of the degree to which these groups thought of themselves as distinct, it suggests a degree of communication and familiarity that could be obscured by the Mesoamerican/non-Mesoamerican dichotomy.

Much of the discussion to this point has concentrated on the role of ideology as a tool of the elite. This is not intended as naive functionalism, which explains ideological phenomena as if they functioned *in order to* anchor or reinforce inequalities. It is unlikely that the ballcourt-related ritual complex would have been perceived by the rank and file of eastern Honduran society solely as a means of legitimization for elites. Rather, the ballgames would have had some real meaning, completing a necessary negotiation of cosmological issues, although it seems unlikely that the implications the game held for the elites or the competition between factions would not go unnoticed by the general populace. Demonstrating that the ballcourts "function" as an arena to negotiate social relations is, in one sense, only a step away from earlier functional explanations of ideology, a problem that has plagued recent attempts to place ideology as a "prime mover" in social change (e.g., Conrad and Demarest 1984). Here, this tendency is mitigated to some degree by focusing not only on the way in which the ballcourts and associated rituals functioned as tools of the elite, but also on the ways in which the ballcourts fit within the existing cosmology. The ballcourt-related rituals would have been presented and understood as much as a negotiation between society and the supernatural as a negotiation between competing elite factions. They would have been compelling in both their cosmological and sociopolitical role.

CONCLUSIONS

Our limited data suggest that complex sociopolitical organization developed sometime between AD 250 and 600, in which interaction with Mesoamerican groups is evident. The emerging eastern Honduran elite utilized certain Mesoamerican architectural templates as part of a strategy to "materialize" their ideology, visibly and permanently putting themselves at the center of the "production of truth." This was undoubtedly not the only power strategy employed in eastern Honduras, but one of the only for which there is evidence.

It is not suggested that eastern Honduras was unified in any way beyond a basic internal cultural affiliation indicated by a similarity in material culture. Linguistic, ideological, and other differences probably existed, as suggested by the multiethnic, multilingual situation in the sixteenth century. If there were Nahua populations in eastern Honduras during the sixteenth century (see Lara-Pinto 1991), the timing of their arrival remains unknown. Given the lack of evidence for intrusive populations during Period IVb, Period V, and early Period VI, the most likely time seems to be late Period VI, for which there is little archaeological evidence. In making any generalization, however, we should note that significant differences between the interior and coastal populations could exist.

The focus here is ultimately on internal development rather than external connections. While external connections existed, and interregional interactions were certainly important, it is important not to overemphasize external influences. Here, a particular part of the mechanism by which the elite power strategies were put into action is explored. Admittedly, the part identified must have been only a part of the total mechanism, but it provides a starting point for understanding eastern Honduras in its own terms. By exploring the internal aspect of external affiliations, it is possible to examine internal processes without assuming that these societies constituted closed systems, and to discuss Mesoamerican influence without oversimplifying the power strategies of eastern Honduran elites. The vision of elite power strategies presented here represents an attempt to balance the role of external factors with an emphasis on internal events.

WORKS CITED

Andrews, A. P. 1985. "The Role of Trading Ports in Maya Civilization." In *Vision and Revision in Maya Studies*, ed. F. S. Clancy and P. D. Harrison, 159–168. Albuquerque: University of New Mexico Press.

Begley, Christopher T. 1992. *Informe preliminar sobre las excavaciones en Difficulty Hill, Isla de Roatán, Honduras*. Manuscript on file, Tegucigalpa, Honduras: Archives of the Honduran Institute of Anthropology and History.

Begley, Christopher T. 1999. "Elite Power Strategies and External Connections in Ancient Eastern Honduras." Unpublished PhD dissertation, Department of Anthropology, University of Chicago, IL.

Begley, Christopher T. 2004. "Intercambio Interregional, Conexiones Externas, y Estratégias de Poder en el Oriente de Honduras durante Periódos V y VI." In *Memoria VII Seminario de Antropología de Honduras "Dr. George Hasemann,"* ed. Carmen Julia Fajardo and Kevin Ávalos, 287–302. Tegucigalpa, Honduras: Instituto Hondureño de Antropología e Historia.

Begley, Christopher T. 2016. "The Lost White City of the Honduras: Discovered Again (and Again)." In *Answering Pseudoarchaeology: Proactive Dialogue and Research in Response to Extraordinary Popular and Esoteric Archaeological Claims*, ed. Jeb J. Card and David S. Anderson, 35–45. Tuscaloosa: University of Alabama Press.

Begley, Christopher T., and Ellen Cox. 2007. "Reading and Writing the White City: Allegories Past and Future." *Southwest Philosophy Review* 23(1):179–186.

Bourdieu, Pierre. 1977. *Outline of a Theory of Practice*. Cambridge. UK: Cambridge University Press.

Bourdieu, Pierre. 1991. *Language and Symbolic Power*. Cambridge, UK: Polity Press.

Burger, Richard, and Robert Rosenwig, eds. 2012. *Early New World Monumentality*. Gainesville: University of Florida Press.

Chapman, Anne M. 1957. "Port of Trade Enclaves in Aztec and Maya Civilizations." In *Trade and Market in the Early Empires*, ed. Karl Polanyi, C. M. Arsenberg, and H. W. Pearson, 114–153. New York: Free Press.

Conrad, Geoffrey W., and Arthur A. Demarest. 1984. *Religion and Empire: The Dynamics of Aztec and Inca Expansionism*. Cambridge, UK: Cambridge University Press.

Cuddy, Thomas. 2007. *Political Identity and Archaeology in Northeast Honduras*. Boulder: University Press of Colorado.

DeMarrais, Elizabeth, Luis Jaime Castillo, and Timothy Earle. 1996. "Ideology, Materialization and Power Strategies." *Current Anthropology* 37(1):15–31.

Dennett, Carrie. 2007. "The Rio Claro Site (AD 1000—1530), Northeast Honduras: A Ceramic Classification and Examination of External Connections." Unpublished MA thesis, Department of Anthropology, Trent University, Peterborough, Ontarion, Canada.

Dennett, Carrie. 2008. "A Modal Analysis of Vessel Appendages from Río Claro (AD 1000–1530), Northeast Honduras." *La Tinaja* 19(2):12–16.

Earle, Timothy. 1997. *How Chiefs Come to Power: The Political Economy in Prehistory*. Stanford, CA: Stanford University Press.

Fisher, Christopher T., Juan Carlos Fernández-Diaz, Anna S. Cohen, Oscar Neil Cruz, Alicia M. Gonzáles, Stephen J. Leisz, Florencia Pezzutti, Ramesh Shrestha, and William Carter. 2016. "Identifying Ancient Settlement Patterns through LiDAR in the Mosquitia Region of Honduras." *PloS one* 11(8):e0159890.

Foucault, Michel. 1980. *Power/Knowledge*. New York: Pantheon.

Fowler, William R. 1989a. *The Cultural Evolution of Ancient Nahua Civilizations: The Pipil-Nicarao of Central America*. Norman: University of Oklahoma Press.

Fowler, William R. 1989b. "Nuevas Perspectivas sobre las Migraciones de Los Pipiles y Los Nicaraos." *Arqueologia* 1:89–98.

Fox, John G. 1996. "Playing with Power: Ballcourts and Political Ritual in Southern Mesoamerica." *Current Anthropology* 37(3):483–509.

Giddens, Anthony. 1979. *Central Problems in Social Theory*. London: Macmillan.

Goodwin, Whitney. 2011. *Archaeology and Indigeneity, Past and Present: A View from the Island of Roatan, Honduras*. Unpublished MA thesis, Department of Anthropology, University of South Florida, Tampa, FL.

Graham, Mark Miller, ed. 1993. *Reinterpreting Prehistory of Central America*. Niwot: University Press of Colorado.

Hasemann, George, and Gloria Lara-Pinto. 1992. Regionalismo e Interacción: Historia Social de la Zona Central. In *Historia Antiqua de America Central:*

Del Poblamiento a la Conquista, ed. Robert Carmack. San José, Costa Rica: Facultad Latinoamericana de Ciencias Sociales.

Hasemann, George, Gloria Lara-Pinto, and Fernando Cruz Sandoval. 1996. *Los Indios de Centroamerica*. Madrid, Spain: Editorial Mapfre.

Healy, Paul F. 1984a. "The Archaeology of Honduras." In *The Archaeology of Lower Central America*, ed. F. W. Lange and D. Z. Stone, 113–161. Albuquerque: University of New Mexico Press.

Healy, Paul F. 1984b. "Northeast Honduras: A Precolumbian Frontier Zone." In *Proceedings of the 44th International Congress of Americanists*, ed. F. W. Lange, 227–241. Manchester, UK.

Healy, Paul F. 1992. "Ancient Honduras: Power, Wealth and Rank in Early Chiefdoms." In *Wealth and Hierarchy in the Intermediate Area*, ed. F. W. Lange, 85–108. Washington, DC: Dumbarton Oaks.

Healy, Paul F. 1993. "Northeastern Honduras." In *Pottery of Prehistoric Honduras: Regional Classification and Analysis*, ed. John S. Henderson and Marilyn Beaudry-Corbett, 194–213. Los Angeles, CA: Cotsen Institute of Archaeology, UCLA.

Helms, Mary W. 1979. *Ancient Panama: Chiefs in Search of Power*. Austin: University of Texas Press.

Helms, Mary W. 1988. *Ulysses' Sail: An Ethnographic Odyssey of Power, Knowledge, and Geographical Distance*. Princeton, NJ: Princeton University Press.

Helms, Mary W. 1992. "Thoughts on Public Symbols and Distant Domains Relevant to the Chiefdoms of Lower Central America." In *Wealth and Hierarchy in the Intermediate Area*, ed. Frederick Lange, 317–330. Washington, DC: Dumbarton Oaks.

Hirth, Kenneth. 1989. "Observations about Ecological Relationships and Cultural Evolution in a Prehistoric Tropical Subsistence System." In *Archaeological Research in the El Cajon Region*, Volume 1: *Prehistoric Cultural Ecology*, ed. K. Hirth, G. Lara-Pinto, and G. Hasemann, 233–251. Pittsburgh, PA: University of Pittsburgh, Department of Anthropology.

Joyce, Rosemary. 1993. "The Construction of the Mesoamerican Frontier and the Mayoid Image of Honduran Polychromes." In *Reinterpreting Prehistory of Central America*, ed. Mark Miller Graham. Niwot: University Press of Colorado.

Kirchhoff, Paul. 1943. "Mesoamerica." *Acta Americana* 1(1):92–107.

Kowalewski, Stephen A., Gary M. Feinman, Laura Finsten, and Richard E. Blanton. 1991. "Pre-Hispanic ballcourts from the Valley of Oaxaca, Mexico." In *The Mesoamerican Ballgame*, ed. V. L. Scarborough and D. Wilcox, 25–44. Tucson: University of Arizona Press.

Lara-Pinto, Gloria. 1991. "Change for Survival: The Case of the Sixteenth-Century Indigenous Populations of Northeast and Mideast Honduras." In *Columbian*

Consequences, Volume 3, ed. D. H. Thomas, 227–243. Washington, DC: Smithsonian Institution Press.

Lara-Pinto, Gloria, and George Hasemann. 1988. "La Sociedad Indigena del Noreste de Honduras en El Siglo XVI: Son La Ethnohistoria y La Arqueologia Contradictorias?" *Yaxkin* 11(2):5–28.

Lévi-Strauss, Claude. 1966. *The Savage Mind*. Chicago, IL: University of Chicago Press.

Mann, Michael. 1986. *The Sources of Social Power*. Cambridge, UK: Cambridge University Press.

Marcus, George E. 1992. "The Concern with Elites in Archaeological Reconstructions: Mesoamerican Materials." In *Mesoamerican Elites: An Archaeological Assessment*, ed. D. Chase and A. Chase, 292–302. Norman: University of Oklahoma Press.

Messenger, Lewis C., Jr. 1987. "Community Organization of the Late Classic Southern Periphery of Mesoamerica: 'Expressions of Affinity.'" In *Interaction on the Southeast Mesoamerican Frontier: Prehistoric and Historic Honduras and El Salvador*, ed. E. J. Robinson, 385–420. Oxford, UK: BAR.

Messenger, Lewis C., Jr. 1991. "Climatic Settings and Prehistoric Social Complexity: The Central American Isthmus." In *The Formation of Social Complexity in Southeastern Mesoamerica*, ed. William Fowler, 237–275. Boca Raton, FL: CRC Press.

Mihok, Lorena D. 2013. "Unearthing Augusta: Landscapes of Royalization on Roatan Island, Honduras." Unpublished PhD dissertation, Department of Anthropology, University of South Florida, Tampa, FL.

Preston, Douglas. 2013. "The El Dorado Machine: A New Scanner's Rain-Forest Discoveries." *New Yorker*, May 6, 2013.

Preston, Douglas. 2015. Exclusive: Lost City Discovered in Honduran Rain Forest. *National Geographic*, http://news.nationalgeographic.com/2015/03/150302 -honduras-lost-city-monkey-god-maya-ancient-archaeology/.

Rappaport, Roy A. 1971. "The Sacred in Human Evolution." *Annual Review of Ecology and Systematics* 2(1):23–43.

Santley, Robert S., Michael J. Berman, and Rani T. Alexander. 1991. "The Politicization of the Mesoamerican Ballgame and Its Implications for the Interpretation of the Distribution of Ballcourts in Central Mexico." In *The Mesoamerican Ballgame*, ed. V. L. Scarborough and D. R. Wilcox, 3–24. Tucson: University of Arizona Press.

Schortman, Edward M., and Patricia A. Urban. 1986. "Introduction." In *The Southeast Maya Periphery*, ed. P. A. Urban and E. M. Schortman, 1–14. Austin: University of Texas Press.

Sharer, Robert J. 1984. "Lower Central America as Seen from Mesoamerica." In *The Archaeology of Lower Central America*, ed. Frederick Lange and Doris Stone, 63–84. Albuquerque: University of New Mexico Press.

Sheets, Payson. 1992. "The Pervasive Pejorative in Intermediate Area Studies." In *Wealth and Hierarchy in the Intermediate Area*, ed. Frederick Lange, 15–42. Washington, DC: Dumbarton Oaks.

Stone, Doris Z. 1941. *Archaeology of the North Coast of Honduras*. Cambridge, MA: Peabody Museum of Archaeology and Ethnology.

Strong, William Duncan. 1934. *An Archaeological Cruise among the Bay Islands of Honduras*. Washington, DC: Smithsonian Institution.

Strong, William Duncan. 1948. "The Archeology of Honduras." *In The Circum-Caribbean Tribes*, Volume 4, *Handbook of South American Indians*, ed. Julian H. Steward, 71–120. Bureau of American Ethnology, Bulletin No. 143. Washington, DC: Smithsonian Institution.

8

Tucked away in a corner of the Caribbean Sea, the Bay Islands were visited in July of 1502 by Christopher Columbus on his fourth and final voyage to the "New World." Sighting an island covered by pine trees ("Bonacca" or Guanaja), he named it "Isla de Pinos" and claimed it for Spain. Bartolomé de Las Casas (1951), the Spanish Dominican priest and editor of Columbus's published journal, further tells us that Guanaja, "had three or four neighboring islands . . . they were all very well populated." While this story was subsequently retold by early colonial historians (Anghiera 1812; Herrera y Tordesillas 1944; Las Casas 1951), none deny that this was a historical moment of great significance for the Bay Islanders, a moment of culture contact and perhaps divine appearance (Clendinnen 1987:4). Other eyewitness accounts of this event tell the story with great emotion (Harrisse 1866:473; Major 1847:169–234; Navarrete 1825:I:283–284, III:556). What did the indigenous inhabitants of the island think about this exchange? How did their culture, language, and history shape their interpretations? What happened after Columbus and crew departed? What kinds of stories and histories emerged? How did those ideas change the (re)production of their culture on the islands? These kinds of unanswered questions are immensely important for understanding the culture history of the Bay Islands and the various populations that came to settle there as well as the long-term consequences for today's residents.

The Royalization of Roatán

Colonial Encounters with the Pech and Miskitu

LORENA D. MIHOK,
E. CHRISTIAN WELLS, AND
WHITNEY A. GOODWIN

DOI: 10.5876/9781646420971.c008

179

The sixteenth-century Bay Islanders and their descendants continued to interact with the Spanish and other Europeans for another 150 years (Muñoz 1639; see also Strong 1935:14–15). Through enslavement to Cuba and resettlement to Guatemala, the Bay Islands were reported to be depopulated of "natives" by 1650 (Conzemius 1928:59–66; see also Newson 1986). Captain Nathaniel Uring's (1727:341–361) description of his visit to the islands in 1719 makes no mention of native peoples, only the English logwood cutters who had occupied Port Royal since the mid-1600s. Yet today on the islands, some people claim "native" ancestry. Clearly, ancestry and indigeneity are complex phenomena in this part of the Caribbean and people today continue to live with the legacy of these past dynamics (Figueroa et al. 2012).

In this chapter, we draw on the concept of "royalization" (Mihok 2013) to better understand the population trajectories of indigenous groups in the Bay Islands and their long-term sociopolitical and economic consequences. *Royalization* refers to the processes that both Spain and England deployed to engender the loyalty of indigenous groups in southern Mesoamerica to their burgeoning empires (Mihok and Wells 2014:102–105). In Honduras, Spain's strategy to royalize indigenous groups emphasized forceful resettlement and Christianization, among other authoritarian practices. In contrast, English strategists recognized that successful infiltrations into Spanish territory would require some degree of cooperation from indigenous allies. They believed that partnerships with local peoples as a strategy for royalization would help English colonists cope successfully with the many challenges of settling in foreign territory, such as inadequate labor, limited knowledge of the environment, and insufficient resources for defense. In addition, English interests in acquiring access to valuable commodities and trade routes around the Bay of Honduras prompted the English Crown to encourage partnerships of various kinds between colonists and the native inhabitants. However, the relationships that the English Crown forged with its colonists and with local indigenous populations, including the Pech and Miskitu, both enabled and constrained their efforts toward royalizing the region's populations because such relations not only impacted commodity distributions but also structured everyday living environments and the activities that encompassed them. As such, we argue that royalization was not limited to practices of consumption (e.g., McConville 2006) but instead can be viewed more broadly as a "negotiated and contested process of meaning making" (Mihok and Wells 2014:102; see also Offen 2007).

In this chapter, we draw from archaeological and historical research over the past decade, including our own investigations on Roatán Island, to consider microdemographic trends in the Bay Islands from ca. AD 600 to 1788. Our research indicates that the Pech might not have been completely removed from the Bay Islands in the seventeenth century, as Spanish records suggest, and that Miskitu groups were settled on Roatán for a short period during the eighteenth century to aid English military efforts. The royalization of the Bay Islands involved implementing a degree of cohesion and allegiance to these colonial powers over the lives of all the islands' inhabitants. We argue that the different processes of royalization early in the colonial histories of indigenous groups had significant consequences for descendent populations, including political access and economic development.

ROATÁN AND THE BAY ISLANDS, CA. 600–1501

Little is known about the peoples that Columbus met at Guanaja, but scholars have proposed that the Bay Islanders spoke Pech (Davidson 1974:20; 1991:205, 208–209; Lehmann 1920:629, 631) or Tol (formerly Jicaque; Thomas and Swanton 1911:73–81) and possibly some dialect of Mayan (Conzemius 1927:245–246; 1928:68; Sauer 1966). Very few descriptions of their material culture are available (Conzemius 1927:283–293; 1928:62–63; Joyce 1983:167; Squier 1858:610; Stone 1939:227–230) and these are mostly from the historian Antonio de Herrera y Tordesillas (1944:dec.IV,lib.I, cap.VI), who transcribed and possibly merged original accounts, particularly those of Las Casas.

The earliest descriptions of prehispanic ruins on the Bay Islands come from Thomas Young (1847, cited in Squier 1858:123–124), who visited Plan Grande on Guanaja in 1841, and from Captain Mitchell (1850, cited in Squier 1858:118) of the British Navy, who visited Roatán in 1850. Since these initial descriptions, several visits, collections, and studies have been made of the prehistory of the Bay Islands, which provide detailed but largely incomplete cultural, historical, and archaeological information (see Cervallos 1919; Conzemius 1927; Rose 1904; Spinden 1925). Under the auspices of the Museum of the American Indian/Heye Foundation, Frederick Mitchell-Hedges visited the islands in 1930 and 1931 and amassed a large collection of prehispanic artifacts by gift and purchase (Houlson 1934; Mitchell-Hedges 1954a, 1954b; Strong 1935:1). In 1931, Junius Bird led the Boekelman Shell Heap Expedition to Roatán, Utila, and Guanaja for the American Museum of Natural History (results reported in Strong 1935). In 1935, William Duncan Strong of the Bureau of American Ethnology at the Smithsonian Institution published an account of his explorations (Strong 1935; published in Spanish as Strong 1939; see also Montgomery 2004:27–28, 71). In 1937, Lord Moyne of the Royal Geographic Society at the

University of Cambridge briefly visited the Bay Islands for three weeks where he collected over 3,000 artifacts (Feacham and Braunholtz 1938). Moyne supported a second expedition to the islands in 1939, led by R. W. Feacham and accompanied by Derek Leaf (Feacham 1940).

On the heels of several important syntheses of the archaeology and history of northwest Honduras (Stone 1941; Strong et al. 1938; Valladares 1939; Yde 1938), the year 1950 saw some of the first scientific excavations in the Bay Islands. A. V. Kidder, Gordon Eckholm, and Gustav Stromsvik excavated at the 80-Acre site on Utila, revealing two distinct occupation horizons. Jeremiah Epstein (1957, 1959) studied these materials and those obtained by the Boekelman Expedition and applied the terms *Selín Horizon* to the Late Classic period (roughly AD 600–1000) and *Cocal Horizon* to the Postclassic (ca. AD 1000–1520). Subsequent analyses by Paul Healy (1978, 1993) and others (Begley 1999a; Cuddy 2007; Dennett 2007) of collections from eastern mainland Honduras support this division, but push the earliest date of settlement in the region back to AD 300 on the mainland.

The Bay Islands were first surveyed with modern archaeological techniques in the early 1970s (Davidson 1974). On Roatán, these surveys collectively recorded over 30 sites, most identified as small villages (Epstein 1978; Epstein and Véliz 1977; Véliz et al. 1976, 1977). Cocal-period (Postclassic) settlements were more numerous, marked by plain and simply decorated (incised or punctate) bowls and jars. Examples of Ulúa-style and lowland Maya–style pottery were also encountered, indicating Late Classic trade with mainland groups in northern Honduras and possibly coastal Belize or Guatemala as well as possible tradewares from Costa Rica. Surveys on Utila resulted in the first scientific map and comprehensive description of the 80-Acre site (Goodwin et al. 1979; Hasemann 1975, 1977). A decade later, in 1985, Mark Horton of Oxford University and Fiona Wilmot of Cambridge University (in coordination with the Operation Raleigh Project), carried out the most extensive survey to date of the entirety of the Bay Islands (Horton 1985). A total of 246 sites were identified and recorded, 99 alone on Roatán. More recently, limited salvage excavations on Roatán and Guanaja were performed by both Christopher Begley (1992, 1999b) and Oscar Cruz Castillo (1999) on behalf of the Honduran Institute of Anthropology and History.

All of this research, while piecemeal over a century, allows us to make a few observations about the occupation of Roatán from roughly AD 600 to 1501. Based on the existing archaeological data, it appears that the largest communities were located on Utila (80-Acre) and Guanaja (Plan Grande and Marble Hill), while Roatán may have been largely, though not exclusively, reserved for special functions, including burial and ceremonial activities (Goodwin 2011). Evidence for population on the islands stretches back to about the seventh century AD, when the occupants maintained economic connections with groups in the Maya and Ulúa regions of Southeastern Mesoamerica and possibly Nicaragua and Costa Rica (based on pottery, jade, and obsidian imports). Populations increased over the next few hundred years, while interregional interactions appear to have contracted. However, access to materials from other parts of Mesoamerica did not cease altogether, judging by the presence of green (possibly Pachuca) obsidian and Tohil Plumbate pottery. When Columbus arrived in the early sixteenth century, these and other trade goods from the Maya region were clearly in transit among the islands.

ROATÁN AND THE BAY ISLANDS, 1502–1788

Spain claimed the Bay Islands of Honduras in 1502 after Columbus arrived at the chain of islands during his fourth voyage to the New World. Governed by the Spanish from the city of Trujillo, then the capital of Honduras, island inhabitants engaged actively in communication and exchange with the Spanish as part of the royalization process. However, despite Spanish claims to the islands, English, French, and Dutch buccaneers began arriving in the Bay Islands during the early seventeenth century who "did not recognize the Spanish claim to the whole New World" (Conzemius 1928:64). The Bay Islands provided these sailors with a strategic position from which to disrupt Spanish commerce routes and to attack Spanish settlements along the coast of mainland Honduras, suggesting resistance to royalization on behalf of the Bay Islanders. Free from an immediate threat of attack, buccaneers established temporary settlements on the islands and took advantage of the plentiful resources by either buying or stealing food from indigenous inhabitants (Conzemius 1928; McBride 2006). As demand for slaves increased after the settlement of Cuba, many of the Bay Islands were targeted by slave-hunting parties and drained of their populations.

As the English gained control of the Bay Islands in the early seventeenth century, the English government recognized three categories of colonies: charter, proprietary, and crown (or royal). The plans for a charter colony, like the one established by the Providence Company on Providence Island off the coast of Nicaragua, often revolved around profit. The investors of the Providence Island Company received a royal patent from the King in 1629 to search for profitable tropical commodities and to participate in privateering efforts aginst Spain (Kupperman 1993:25). Proprietary colonies became more common during the seventeenth century as the Crown gave out land grants as a way to repay debts to loyal supporters. The King issued proprietary grants to individuals in the "nature of feudatory principalities" (Blackstone 1766:108). Referred to as proprietary governors, these individuals were given land and the right to oversee the property as they wished. The grants were made to "well-connected patron proprieters" who held strong connections to the King and the ability to assemble the capital and settlers necessary for the growth of the colony (Elliott 2006:118).

The earliest proprietary colony founded in the Bay Islands was established on Roatán in 1638 by William Claiborne, a planter from Virginia, through a patent from the Providence Company (Naylor 1989:33). The company renamed the island Rich Island in honor of Henry Rich, the Earl of Holland and the brother of Robert Rich, the Earl of Warwick (Newton 1966:267). According to Davidson (1974:49), the location of the Puritan settlement may have been just north of Old Port Royal on the eastern end of the island near the Pech village of Roata, which would have allowed colonists to "farm and trade with the Indians" (Davidson 1974:50). These colonists appear to have had only a few years at the site because civil-war conditions in England damaged the country's connections to its colonists in the Caribbean and left the Puritan settlement without protection from England. The settlers remained on Rich Island until 1642, when Spanish forces drove them away from the region and destroyed the settlement (Kupperman 1993; Newton 1967; Sorsby 1997).

While the Crown granted a considerable amount of administrative freedom to the recipients of charter and proprietary patents, the English government transitioned to the establishment of royal colonies by the end of the seventeenth century. In accordance with the growing political and economic concerns of the country, the Crown created royal colonies in the Americas, colonial provinces under the "direct government of the crown," and governed them with his advisory committees (Labaree 1967:vii). The replacement of charter and proprietary patents with royal colonies began during the 1670s when Charles II's administration recognized the lack of uniformity among the country's colonial territories as the King sought to build an empire. Early reforms included the introduction of royal colonies either by revoking older charter or proprietary patents or by creating original colonies. Stanwood (2011:26) believes these changes helped "pave the way for the royalization of New England, the most argumentative and independent of the colonies, and eventually all of the American plantations."

Throughout the establishment of English colonies in Central America and continued Spanish penetration of interior Honduras during the sixteenth and seventeenth centuries, the Pech and Miskitu experienced demographic fragmentation and contraction to interior and remote regions of mainland Honduras, largely away from colonial enterprises (Newson 1986). At the time of Spanish contact, the Pech occupied the Bay Islands and a wide territory in northeast Honduras, from the Aguán Valley near Trujillo (Department of Colón) in the west to Puerto Lempira (Department of Gracias a Dios) in the east, and potentially as far south as the Juticalpa Valley (Department of Olancho). Spanish activities in the region largely avoided confrontation with Pech groups, except for the Bay Islands, which they reported to have completely depopulated in 1650. After a series of colonial incursions into their territory, today the Pech occupy two small settlements zones: one in Colón and one in northeastern Olancho. With the aid of the British, the Miskitu expanded onto the northeast Honduran coast (Departments of Gracias a Dios and Colón) in the late seventeenth century from northern coastal Nicaragua, and subsequently forced Pech communities to retreat to the mountainous interior. Through alliances with the British, the Miskitu settled throughout the north coast of Honduras and perhaps as far north as southern coastal Belize throughout the early eighteenth century. Today, Miskitu communities occupy various settlements throughout Gracias a Dios in Honduras, but concentrate along the eastern border between Honduras and Nicaragua.

PECH AND MISKITU DYNAMICS ON ROATÁN

Archaeological research in the Bay Islands by the University of South Florida since 2008 has focused on two settlements: El Antigual and Augusta on Roatán Island (figure 8.1). Here we summarize our findings concerning Pech and Miskitu settlement on Roatán.

PECH

When Hernán Cortés arrived in Trujillo in 1526, the islanders requested protection and upon "hearing that new expeditions were fitting out in Cuba and Jamaica, he at once dispatched a vessel to order them away, notwithstanding they had a license from the Governor of Cuba" (Squier 1858: 606). Relations between the Spanish and the islanders developed as the capital began receiving supplies from the indigenous populations at the request of Cortés during his stay in Trujillo in 1526–1527. After his initial request for quantities of fish from the Bay Islands, the "aborigines supplied this town, with fish, cassava and maize, and were employed as laborers on the public works" (Conzemius 1928:62).

FIGURE 8.1. *Map showing sites mentioned in the text.*

According to Squier (1858:606), while Spanish expeditions in Mexico and Peru diverted attention away from the Bay Islands during the early part of the sixteenth century, the "islands appear to have been quietly occupied by their inhabitants, and governed by the authorities of Honduras as dependencies of the port of Truxillo." In his report to the president of Guatemala in 1639, Don Francisco de Avila y Lugo, governor and captain general of Honduras described "four towns of Indians in the Guanaja Islands, namely, Guanaja, Masa, Roata, and Utila" (Squier 1858:609). He described the towns of Masa and Roata as separated by "a narrow canal not admitting navigation, even by vessels of the lightest draft, so that the two parts are considered as one island" (Squier 1858:609). Governor Avila also described the inhabitants of Roata. He states that "the Indians, though few, are good, less easily reduced than those of Guanaja, especially those of Roata, who are laborious and faithful. In both towns the inhabitants suffer much from musquitoes, and are greatly reduced in consequence, notwithstanding the island is as fertile as Guanaja, yielding the same fruits and dye-woods" (Squier 1858:611).

In 1577 English Captain Francisco de Acles arrived with two ships on the island of Guanaja and overtook an indigenous community to use as a short-term base for supplies and ship repair. Upon hearing about the English occupation, Spanish Captain Diego López and his men sailed from Trujillo to attack the camp and drive out the invaders. During the battle the English captain was killed but several English sailors escaped. In a letter to the Spanish

Crown from 1578, Captain López wrote that one of his soldiers had found an English frigate that had "looted the neighboring island of Ruatan, and took a bark from its natives, and captured them." Captain López sent the letter to request the Crown's compassion for failing to "put an end to the damage these people are inflicting" (Wright 1932:196–198).

Tensions over the control of the Bay Islands' ports and resources prompted the Spanish to consider ways to diminish the appeal of the islands to other European powers. The Spanish considered removing the inhabitants as early as 1639 "in order to deprive the buccaneers of this asylum where it was so easy for them to obtain food and guides" (Conzemius 1928:5). Squier (1858:607) reports that a decision was made "to withdraw them [aboriginal inhabitants] to the main land, and, by destroying the towns and plantations, deprive the corsairs of an asylum, and of the means of prosecuting their lawless enterprises on the adjacent coasts." After launching the steps for removal in the 1640s, the Spanish claimed in 1650, to have removed the Pech—the indigenous population of the Bay Islands—possibly to the vicinity of Livingston or Puerto Barrios, Guatemala (Wells 2008). Royalization of the Pech thus relied on direct intervention in Pech communities rather than collaboration.

Despite the destruction of the Providence Company settlement at Old Port Royal and the removal of the indigenous populations from the island, the Spanish continued to experience problems with English pirates in the Caribbean well into the seventeenth century. Both large and small groups of pirates were attracted to the Bay Islands "as a secluded place to careen and refit ships, to cut logwood, to hunt the feral hogs, and to catch turtles" (Davidson 1974:51). The cays along the coastlines of Guanaja, Utila, and Roatán provided pirate fleets with shelter and escape routes if attacked while at anchor. After the expulsion of the Puritan settlers from Old Port Royal, buccaneer activity in the Bay Islands prevented the establishment of permanent settlements until the early eighteenth century.

El Antigual

From 2008 to 2012, the University of South Florida investigated the late prehispanic Pech settlement of El Antigual and the surrounding region, located in roughly the center of the island (figure 8.2). The site spreads across two small hilltops and the saddle that connects them, covering about 800 m² of sometimes steep and uneven terrain. The hilltops are currently covered with grass and other low-lying vegetation, while the saddle is completely forested, largely with palms and ferns. From either hilltop, one can clearly see both bay and

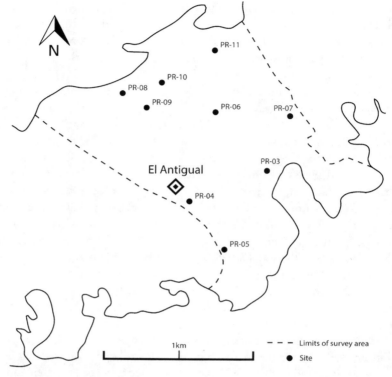

FIGURE 8.2. *The survey region surrounding El Antigual.*

ocean sides of the island and a clear view of the mainland of Honduras. The site was last formally inspected by Epstein, who observed "plain pottery and one 'monkey' lug similar to that found on the handles of San Marcos ware." After his visit, he concluded that "the hilltop seems to have served as an offertory or burial area since it is too small to have contained a single family unit. It is possible that a small population lived further down the slope" (1975:39).

Today, the site has no observable architecture, although much of it is under overgrown brush and so it is presently impossible to determine if there are mounds. There are numerous areas along the slopes of the hills with high concentrations of small boulders, suggesting the possibility that part of the site was artificially terraced in the past. Numerous artifacts—as isolated finds and in concentrations indicative of activity areas—can be observed throughout the site. Artifacts from the site include mostly plainware and incised pottery of the Dorina Abstract Incised Punctate type (Epstein 1957:91–98; Healy

1993:209–212). Illustrations of this type are numerous (Epstein 1957:figures 10, 11g–p; Healy 1993:figures 11.17–11.19; Stone 1941:figures 9, 36f–h; Strong 1935:plates 5e–g, 18d, 28a, 31f, 73). The most-common forms are open-mouth jars and shallow outcurving and flaring-wall bowls with smoothed surfaces. No paint was present. The ceramics, along with the discovery of a green obsidian blade segment, strongly suggest that the latest occupation of the site dates to the Postclassic (Cocal period, ca. AD 1000 to 1530) (Healy 1993; Véliz et al. 1977:11) and that these residents had access to materials from mainland Mesoamerica.

Excavations at the site focused on the northern hilltop to provide an uninterrupted profile of the site. Concentrated and spatially discrete midden deposits suggest that certain areas at the summit were swept clean. Artifacts collected during excavation did not include the full range of materials encountered during the preliminary site visit, indicating that surface materials do not necessarily represent the variety of subsurface deposits (Klassen 2010). In spite of this, the ceramic assemblage provides supporting evidence for the chronological cross-ties suggested during analysis of the existing collections of pottery from Roatán formerly curated by the University of South Florida (Moreno Cortés and Wells 2006).

Compared to historical descriptions and depictions of Pech pottery, it is possible that the ceramic materials found at Antigual were used by *watas* (shamans) and other participants in *kesh* ceremonies, carried out after the death of a community member (Aguilar 2006; González et al. 1995; Lanza et al. 1992). These practices involved the consumption of fermented beverages made from yucca (*munia*) and corn (*ostia*) and special foods such as tamales made of yucca (*sasal*). The beverages were consumed from *guacales*, small clay bowls, and the tamales and other foods were served on small, shallow ceramic dishes or wooden plates. Today, Pech communities in northern Honduras continue this tradition, although participants often use plastic dishware instead of the traditional *guacales*.

Parallel to excavations at El Antigual, Project Roatán also carried out an intensive pedestrian survey of the immediate vicinity of the site (Figueroa 2011), stretching to both the north and the south shores of the island, and identified nine additional sites (see figure 8.2 above). Most of these sites appear to have been used for special purposes, such as ceremonies or burials. Pottery recovered from surface collections has provided important information for cross-tie dating (figures 8.3–8.8). This has allowed us to establish occupation of the central part of Roatán from ca. AD 600 to at least 1600 (Goodwin 2011). Thus, when the English settled in the vicinity of the Pech village of Roata on the eastern end of the island in the early seventeenth century, we now have evidence that other parts of the island were either in use or occupied contemporaneously.

MISKITU

Contact between English colonists and the Miskitu of eastern Nicaragua and northern Honduras began during the seventeenth century as England attempted to establish a foothold in the Spanish-claimed territory of Central America. Although the Mosquito Coast (the eastern coastline region of eastern Honduras and Nicaragua) was included within the Viceroyalty of New Spain, Spanish jurisdiction and occupation of the area was minimal. The rugged landscape appeared to lack the precious-metal sources that Spanish conquistadors had found in central Mexico and South America (Naylor 1989). Without any incentive to establish outposts or transportation routes in this area, Spain left the coastline relatively unoccupied and unprotected except for the town of Trujillo, a colonial shipping port for gold and silver export to Europe (Helms 1969; Naylor 1989). This absence of a Spanish presence along the coastline attracted the attention of English, French, and Dutch buccaneers and pirates seeking secluded ports around the Bay of Honduras in which to repair ships, restock resources, and reorganize for their attacks against Spanish ships and towns. English merchants early on took notice of many of the Mosquito Coast's natural resources, such as dyewoods and mahogany, which could be used for trading ventures and other economic purposes. This growing interest in the Mosquito Coast led to the gradual emergence of small European settlements along the coastline's lagoons and river deltas. While it seems that the Miskitu and other indigenous groups remained hostile toward the Spanish, they developed agreeable relations with English buccaneers and settlers as an English presence grew around the Bay of Honduras.

According to Noveck (1988:19), the group referred to as the Miskitu was not named or distinguished from other indigenous groups along the Mosquito Coast prior to the introduction of English colonial settlements in the 1630s. Published references to Miskitu settlements appear in popular books and maps from the late seventeenth and early eighteenth centuries, but the history of these people and the origin of their name prior to contact is not well documented (Freeland 1988; Offen 2007). According to Helms (1971:15–16), seventeenth-century pirates called the natives of Cape Gracias the "Mosqueto," but buccaneer accounts of mulattoes living with the indigenous people of this area add to the "problem of the origin of the Miskito as an identifiable ethnic

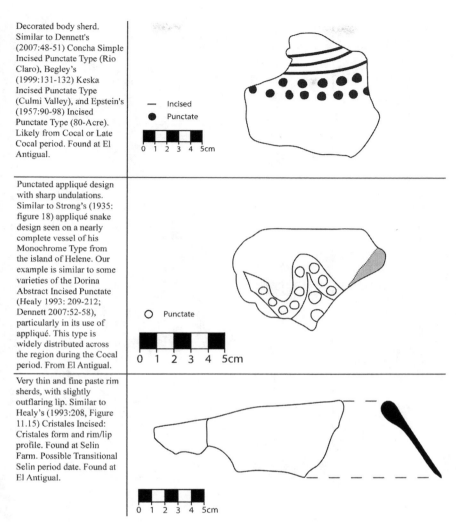

Decorated body sherd. Similar to Dennett's (2007:48-51) Concha Simple Incised Punctate Type (Rio Claro), Begley's (1999:131-132) Keska Incised Punctate Type (Culmi Valley), and Epstein's (1957:90-98) Incised Punctate Type (80-Acre). Likely from Cocal or Late Cocal period. Found at El Antigual.

— Incised
● Punctate

0 1 2 3 4 5cm

Punctated appliqué design with sharp undulations. Similar to Strong's (1935: figure 18) appliqué snake design seen on a nearly complete vessel of his Monochrome Type from the island of Helene. Our example is similar to some varieties of the Dorina Abstract Incised Punctate (Healy 1993: 209-212; Dennett 2007:52-58), particularly in its use of appliqué. This type is widely distributed across the region during the Cocal period. From El Antigual.

○ Punctate

0 1 2 3 4 5cm

Very thin and fine paste rim sherds, with slightly outflaring lip. Similar to Healy's (1993:208, Figure 11.15) Cristales Incised: Cristales form and rim/lip profile. Found at Selin Farm. Possible Transitional Selin period date. Found at El Antigual.

0 1 2 3 4 5cm

FIGURE 8.3. *Ceramic cross-ties from pottery at El Antigual.*

group." Noveck (1988:20; see also Bulnes 2012) argues that a "process of colonial transformation" occurred among one of the region's indigenous groups as a result of English contact, a process that resulted in the creation of the cultural identity of the Miskitu. From this point of view, Miskitu identity, as recognized by a European audience, materialized through their contact and interactions with the English. This perspective is shared by Helms (1969:76),

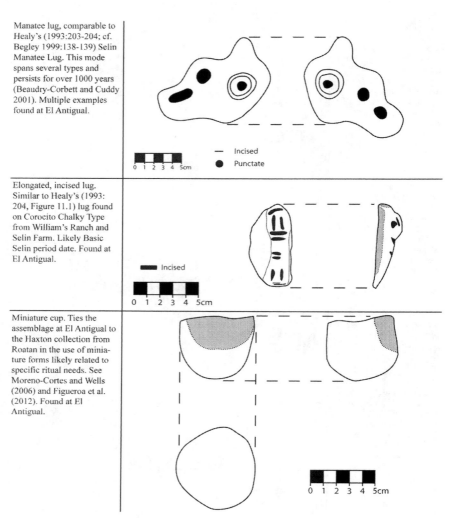

Manatee lug, comparable to Healy's (1993:203-204; cf. Begley 1999:138-139) Selin Manatee Lug. This mode spans several types and persists for over 1000 years (Beaudry-Corbett and Cuddy 2001). Multiple examples found at El Antigual.

— Incised
● Punctate

0 1 2 3 4 5cm

Elongated, incised lug. Similar to Healy's (1993: 204, Figure 11.1) lug found on Corocito Chalky Type from William's Ranch and Selin Farm. Likely Basic Selin period date. Found at El Antigual.

■ Incised

0 1 2 3 4 5cm

Miniature cup. Ties the assemblage at El Antigual to the Haxton collection from Roatan in the use of minia-ture forms likely related to specific ritual needs. See Moreno-Cortes and Wells (2006) and Figueroa et al. (2012). Found at El Antigual.

0 1 2 3 4 5cm

Figure 8.4. *Ceramic cross-ties from pottery at El Antigual, continued.*

who believes that Miskitu-European relations—specifically contact with English colonists—are "solely" responsible for the production of Miskitu cultural identity. As more and more English colonists began to settle in small communities along the Mosquito Coast, a "new coastal Indian population" appeared in close proximity to these settlements (Noveck 1988:20). Prior to English contact, most indigenous groups inhabited interior locations within

Basin. Similar in aspects of incised and punctate designs to Healy's (1993:205-206; esp. Figure 11.13c) Orion Orange Incised: Orion from Selin Farm and Williams Ranch on the mainland. Dates to Basic Selin period. From PR05.

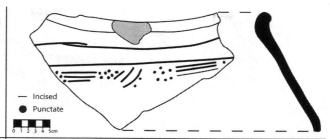

— Incised
● Punctate

0 1 2 3 4 5cm

Basin with ring stand base. Similar to Healy's San Antonio Variety of the San Antonio Carved Type (1993:208) at Selin Farm. The scroll design seen here and associated "El Rey" lug (see Dennett 2007:72; Healy 1993: 208, Figure 11.16a; Stone 1941:33) suggest ties to the Ulua style marble vases, a connection first made by Strong (1935:100). Also shares characteristics with a variety of this type described by Dennett from Rio Claro which features, "simple linear and often undulating incised lines" (2007:64) and is closely tied to the later Arena Variety of the Dorina Abstract Incised Punctate at that site, particularly in the use of the "lazy-8" motif (Dennett 20007:57-58). Two complete vessels of this type found by Strong (1935: Pl. 24, see also Pl. 26) at the Indian Hill site on Helene and classified as Elaborate Monochrome vessels. Dates to Transitional Selin period. From PR05.

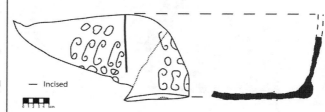

— Incised

0 1 2 3 4 5cm

FIGURE 8.5. *Ceramic cross-ties from pottery at survey site PR05, Selin period.*

the region and used areas along the coastline for temporary seasonal camps. By the beginning of the eighteenth century, Miskitu villages appeared along the coastline in close proximity to English settlements, unlike the nomadic living patterns of other hunter-gatherer groups in the area. The communities of Black River (Honduras) and Bluefields (Nicaragua) were two of the largest settlements with European, Indian, and African residents (Helms 1983).

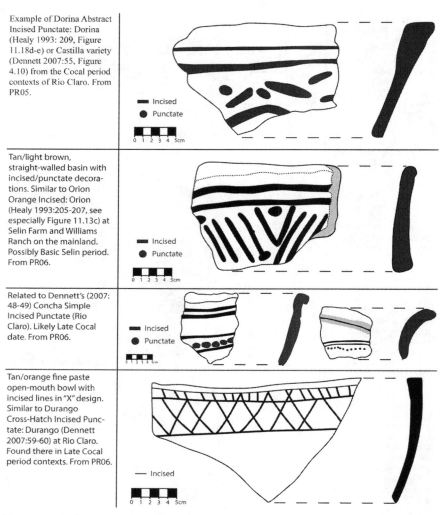

Example of Dorina Abstract Incised Punctate: Dorina (Healy 1993: 209, Figure 11.18d-e) or Castilla variety (Dennett 2007:55, Figure 4.10) from the Cocal period contexts of Rio Claro. From PR05.

- ▬ Incised
- ● Punctate

0 1 2 3 4 5cm

Tan/light brown, straight-walled basin with incised/punctate decorations. Similar to Orion Orange Incised: Orion (Healy 1993:205-207, see especially Figure 11.13c) at Selin Farm and Williams Ranch on the mainland. Possibly Basic Selin period. From PR06.

- ▬ Incised
- ● Punctate

0 1 2 3 4 5cm

Related to Dennett's (2007: 48-49) Concha Simple Incised Punctate (Rio Claro). Likely Late Cocal date. From PR06.

- ▬ Incised
- ● Punctate

0 1 2 3 4 5cm

Tan/orange fine paste open-mouth bowl with incised lines in "X" design. Similar to Durango Cross-Hatch Incised Punctate: Durango (Dennett 2007:59-60) at Rio Claro. Found there in Late Cocal period contexts. From PR06.

- — Incised

0 1 2 3 4 5cm

FIGURE 8.6. *Ceramic cross-ties from pottery at survey sites, Selin and Cocal periods, continued.*

While managing to remain independent of Spanish colonial authority, the Miskitu developed amicable trading relationships with English colonists during the seventeenth and eighteenth centuries (Helms 1983; Long 1774; M. W. 1744; Naylor 1989; Olien 1983; Pares 1936). English traders provided clothing and tools to the Miskitu in exchange for natural resources such as cacao,

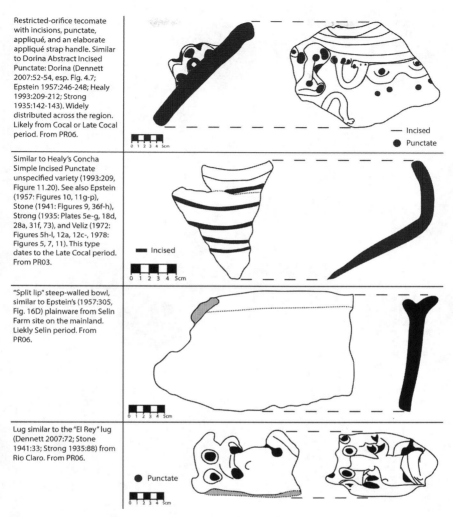

Restricted-orifice tecomate with incisions, punctate, appliqué, and an elaborate appliqué strap handle. Similar to Dorina Abstract Incised Punctate: Dorina (Dennett 2007:52-54, esp. Fig. 4.7; Epstein 1957:246-248; Healy 1993:209-212; Strong 1935:142-143). Widely distributed across the region. Likely from Cocal or Late Cocal period. From PR06.

— Incised
● Punctate

Similar to Healy's Concha Simple Incised Punctate unspecified variety (1993:209, Figure 11.20). See also Epstein (1957: Figures 10, 11g-p), Stone (1941: Figures 9, 36f-h), Strong (1935: Plates 5e-g, 18d, 28a, 31f, 73), and Veliz (1972: Figures 5h-l, 12a, 12c-, 1978: Figures 5, 7, 11). This type dates to the Late Cocal period. From PR03.

■ Incised

"Split lip" steep-walled bowl, similar to Epstein's (1957:305, Fig. 16D) plainware from Selin Farm site on the mainland. Liekly Selin period. From PR06.

Lug similar to the "El Rey" lug (Dennett 2007:72; Stone 1941:33; Strong 1935:88) from Rio Claro. From PR06.

● Punctate

FIGURE 8.7. *Ceramic cross-ties from pottery at survey sites, Selin and Cocal periods, continued.*

sarsaparilla, and tortoise shells (Helms 1983:187). In addition to these items, the acquisition of European firearms quickly gave this population a techno-logical advantage over rival communities. Miskitu identity became linked to their ownership of English weaponry and tools as these types of European objects became symbols of their "military and cultural superiority" (Noveck

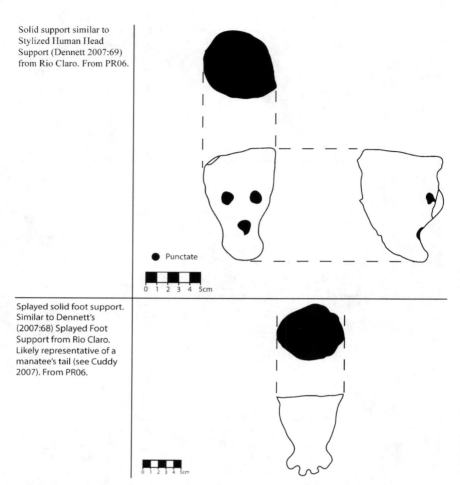

Solid support similar to Stylized Human Head Support (Dennett 2007:69) from Rio Claro. From PR06.

Punctate

0 1 2 3 4 5cm

Splayed solid foot support. Similar to Dennett's (2007:68) Splayed Foot Support from Rio Claro. Likely representative of a manatee's tail (see Cuddy 2007). From PR06.

0 1 2 3 4 5cm

FIGURE 8.8. *Ceramic cross-ties from pottery supports at survey sites.*

1988:18). The Miskitu used this military superiority during slave raids on neighboring indigenous communities. As plantation economies shifted from indentured servants to African-slave workforces, indigenous peoples from the Central American mainland were sent to Jamaica to work. The Miskitu conducted slave raids among their "wild Indian" neighbors and included slaves among their other trade goods (Helms 1983). Naylor (1989:36) argues that the Miskitu not only created their identity and this localized hierarchy based on their involvement with the English, but that their leaders also began to emulate their European allies by incorporating material symbols of English authority into their daily lives. This process of royalization demonstrates how consumption of both utilitarian goods and items with symbolic value contributed to the transformation of Miskitu identity.

The Miskitu's close association with the peoples and practices of England fostered not only their sense of an ethnic identity, one separate and distinct from other indigenous groups living in the Mosquito Coast, but also encouraged their identification as English citizens themselves (Olien 1983). Offen (2007:262) argues that as the Miskitu began to formally define their territory as separate from the areas inhabited by their wild Indian enemies, they "came to see themselves as a nation among nations, as co-equals in the western Caribbean." A key factor to this identification existed in their perceived relationship with the English and the classification of themselves as subjects of the English Crown (Offen 2007). By the end of the seventeenth century, those Miskitu rulers formally recognized by the English government as leaders began to use the title of "king" after the governor of Jamaica referred to the chief as the "King of Mosquitia" in 1687 (Freeland 1988:18; Olien 1983). Again, the Miskitu differentiated themselves from their "wild" neighbors by incorporating the "modern" English concept of a king into their lives (Helms 1969:79). M. W.'s (1744) writings include a description of Mosqueto King Jeremy, one of the earliest historical references to an officially acknowledged Miskitu king (Olien 1983). Miskitu kings expressed their elevated positions by adopting English clothing and objects as symbols of authority. Kings wore pieces of English military uniforms and carried scepters to confirm their status and power (Naylor 1989; Noveck 1988). By officially acknowledging the authority of local rulers, England established its claim to the Mosquito Coast in "acceptable" European political terms and helped the Miskitu to assert their identity of superiority and political standing over neighboring coastal groups (Helms 1969; Olien 1983).

Augusta

Archaeological and historical research conducted by the University of South Florida from 2009 to 2012 at the English settlement of Augusta on the eastern end of Roatán demonstrates a Miskitu presence in the mid-1700s, and suggests the possibility for a slightly longer period of occupation, perhaps until the late 1700s. Augusta was founded as an English stronghold in New Port Royal harbor from 1742 to 1748, toward the end of the Anglo-Spanish War of Jenkins's Ear—England's first international "trade war" (Young and Levy 2011). After capturing the island of Jamaica from Spain in 1655, the English

Crown issued a royal charter in 1661 naming Jamaica a royal colony. Under the supervision of the royal governor of Jamaica, the island of Roatán was named a dependency of Jamaica in 1742. The Augusta community included English militia from Jamaica, English settlers from the Black River settlement on the Mosquito Coast of Honduras, and local Miskitu peoples from northeastern Honduras and Nicaragua. This unique, integrated settlement was a result of the 1740 Treaty of Friendship and Alliance between King George II and King Edward, the leader of the Miskitu "kingdom," designed to royalize the Miskitu territory in exchange for English military protection against the Spanish.

The archaeological data recovered from the site of Augusta (Mihok 2013) corroborate the Council of War's orders (Grant et al. 2005; Rolt 1749–1750) to send a combined group of English soldiers and Miskitu to Roatán Island to construct a military outpost. Recognized by the English Crown as subjects of Great Britain, Augusta's occupants participated in the royalization process by utilizing English materials such as tin-glazed earthenware, hand-wrought iron nails, and glass bottles in daily practice. Through survey and excavation we found a variety of artifact types including bottle glass, hand-wrought nails, coarse earthenwares, decorated delftware, *bajareque*, ceramic pipestems, and miscellaneous firearm components. We identified five diagnostic European ceramic types at Augusta: Staffordshire-style slipware, Astbury-type earthenware, blue-on-white delftware, polychrome delftware, and delftware with powdered-over stencils (figure 8.9).

However, the presence of *mano* and *metate* fragments, indigenous ceramics, and *bajareque* in archaeological deposits suggests that the English and Miskitu utilized indigenous objects and building materials while having access to English products. Archaeological investigations show that European and Miskitu artifacts were intermixed across the settlement (Mihok and Wells 2014). For example, excavations revealed the remains of a collapsed structure built from a combination of English and Miskitu building materials. This structure was made primarily of *bajareque* (wattle and daub). Hundreds of large pieces of *bajareque* were collected with visible stick striations from the wooden frame to which they were originally applied. Hand-wrought iron nails embedded in *bajareque* fragments and covered with a plaster coating were also recovered. Nail holes were observed and noted in several *bajareque* pieces. Since *bajareque* structures do not require iron nails and a plaster finish for completion, the existence of plaster-covered nails in the remnants of *bajareque* walls suggests that Augusta's English and Miskitu occupants chose to design buildings that took advantage of multicultural knowledge of construction. In this case, these diverse building materials were combined to create a

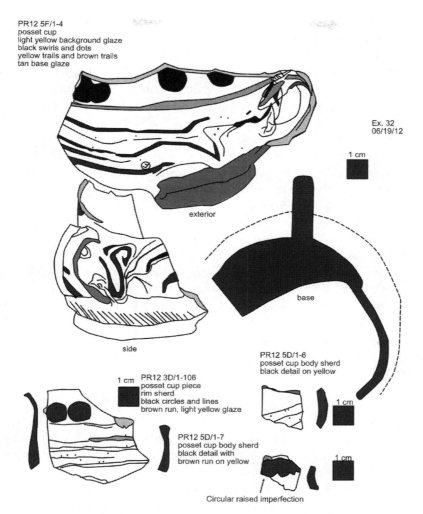

FIGURE 8.9. *Staffordshire-type slipware: posset cup from Augusta.*

workshop or storage facility. While these assemblages do not reveal the degree or the nature of interaction, we believe that the juxtaposition of European and indigenous artifacts indicate that Augusta's occupants chose to use material culture representative of both English and Miskitu origins. We further believe the archaeological data show that the English royalization process was not fluid or universally enforced among the Crown's colonial territories.

Suppositions that simply ask whether Augusta's occupants participated in the royalization process do not consider the intentions behind the use of objects. One possibility is that, because the archaeological evidence recovered from Augusta dates to the initial period of the English treaty with the Miskitu, perhaps the impact of the 1740 treaty on Miskitu identity had not yet permeated through Miskitu society. As Offen (2007:280) notes, "the Mosquito forged a shared identity through a diversity of colonial encounters that empowered them." Another possibility is that Augusta's occupants chose to use objects in ways that differed from the artifact's original purpose. They may have also used any available artifacts or building materials in their daily lives as the result of convenience or adaptation to environmental conditions with little or no concern for the Crown's intentions behind royalization.

These findings may reveal Augusta's uniqueness compared to other English Caribbean settlements, namely plantations and other resource-extraction ventures, where boundaries and partitions (social and material) actively segregated natives and slaves from the English (Clement 1997; Delle 1999, 2009). We have been unable to detect any patterning in the spatial distribution of artifacts or assemblages, which may suggest that residential spaces at Augusta were used or occupied by more than a single group. However, we must acknowledge that much of what we know about Augusta derives from English documents, maps, and artifacts, and so our understanding of labor and residential occupation of the settlement has yet to be evaluated by archaeological excavation.

CONCLUSION

Documentary and archaeological data suggest that multifaceted relationships emerged among European colonists and indigenous populations around the Bay of Honduras. These interactions, like those proposed at Augusta, played a pivotal role in the effectiveness of Spanish and English royalization and these countries' attempts to pursue their political and economic interests in the Caribbean. While this research contributes to broader themes in culture-contact studies by investigating the motivations and consequences of English and Spanish colonization on the landscapes and peoples of the Americas, here we have attempted to enhance national and local knowledge of the ancestral heritage of northern Honduras by examining the legacy of the royalization process.

Given the evidence for demographic shifts among the Pech and Miskitu, we speculate that contemporary settlement for both groups may be largely a product of early twentieth-century colonialism and modernism, and not a specific consequence of royalization. However, royalization processes appear to have created the conditions conducive to colonial intrusion by decimating populations and, in some cases, relocating them (such as in the case of the Pech). Members of Miskitu communities along the eastern coast of Honduras experienced a period of relocation to the Bay Islands as they joined English colonists to construct and occupy the settlement of Augusta. While the royalization process was intended to instill a sense of loyalty and English identity into the lives of colonists, enforcement of the use of material goods and space may have proved difficult or impractical. In the end, it appears that royalization led to long-term processes of fragmentation, contraction, and isolation that continue today.

Stonich's (2000) discussion of recent comments made about the questionable identity of Bay Islanders highlights the importance of this research to Honduras and the contemporary communities of Roatán. The complicated history of the islands contributes to the diversity found in their populations and to the difficulty of defining "who are the Bay Islanders?" (Stonich 2000:49). For example, residents of several communities on Roatán, especially Jonesville, Oak Ridge, and French Harbour (Evans 1966), still identify as "English" or "of English heritage." If the Honduran government does not consider Bay Islanders either "Honduran" or "indigenous," or recognize their ancestral history that includes English descent, how can local populations recognize and preserve their past in the present?

ACKNOWLEDGMENTS

The work reported here was conducted with the permission and under the supervision of the Instituto Hondureño de Antropología e Historia. We would like to thank Virgilio Paredes, Darío Euraque, Eva Martínez, and Aldo Zelaya of that institution for their support and advice. The research was carried out in collaboration with various units at the University of South Florida, including the Department of Anthropology, the Office of Education Abroad, and the Humanities Institute, which provided both logistical and financial support for the work. We especially appreciate the kindness and generosity of Dr. David Evans of Wake Forest University for sharing his deep knowledge of the island's history and his extensive contacts, without which we could not have accomplished our research. We thank the numerous students who participated in the excavations and are also thankful for the support and advice of several Roatán residents, including Eric Anderson, Mayor Perry Bodden, Bill and Irma Brady, Bill and Daine Etches, Errol and Mary Jackson, and Doc Radawski.

WORKS CITED

Aguilar, Juan Carlos Vargas. 2006. *Etno-demografía de la étnia pech, Honduras*. San José, Costa Rica: Centro Centroamericano de Población, Universidad de Costa Rica.

Anghiera, Pietro Martire. 1812. "The History of the West Indies." In *A Selection of Curious, Rare and Early Voyages*, ed. R. Hakluyt, 366–688. London: R. H. Evans and R. Priestly.

Begley, Christopher T. 1992. *Informe preliminar sobre las excavaciones en Difficulty Hill, Isla de Roatán, Honduras*. Tegucigalpa, Honduras: Archives of the Honduran Institute of Anthropology and History.

Begley, Christopher T. 1999a. "Elite Power Strategies and External Connections in Ancient Eastern Honduras." Unpublished PhD dissertation, Department of Anthropology, University of Chicago, IL.

Begley, Christopher T. 1999b. *Investigación de Plan Grande, Guanaja, Islas de la Bahía, Honduras: Ideología y vida cotidiana en la frontera de Mesoamérica*. Manuscript on file. Tegucigalpa, Honduras: Archives of the Honduran Institute of Anthropology and History.

Blackstone, William. 1766. *Commentaries on the Laws of England*. Volume 1. London: Clarendon Press, Eighteenth Century Collections Online, http://find.galegroup .com.ezproxy.lib.usf.edu, accessed November 13, 2013.

Bulnes, Miralda. 2012. *Latwan Laka Danh Takisa: Los pueblos originarios y la guerra de baja intensidad en el territorio de La Moskitia*, Tegucigalpa, Honduras: Honduran Institute of Anthropology and History.

Cervallos, Fernando P. 1919. *Reseña histórica de las Islas de la Bahía*. Tegucigalpa, Honduras: Tipografía Nacional.

Clement, Christopher O. 1997. "Settlement Patterning on the British Caribbean Island of Tobago." *Historical Archaeology* 31(2):93–106.

Clendinnen, Inga. 1987. *Ambivalent Conquests: Maya and Spaniard in Yucatan, 1517–1570*. Cambridge, UK: Cambridge University Press.

Conzemius, Eduard. 1927. "Los Indios Payas de Honduras: Estudio geográfico, histórico, etnográfico y lingüístico." *Journal de la Societé des Americanistes de Paris*. 19(1):245–302.

Conzemius, Eduard. 1928. "On the Aborigines of the Bay Islands (Honduras)." *Atti del XXII Congresso Internazionale degli Americanisti* 2:57–68.

Cruz Castillo, Oscar Neill. 1999. *Informe de inspección a los sitios arqueológicos de Plan Grande y Marble Hill, Guanaja, Islas de la Bahía, Honduras*. Manuscript on file. Tegucigalpa, Honduras: Archives of the Honduran Institute of Anthropology and History.

Cuddy, Thomas W. 2007. *Political Identity and Archaeology in Northeast Honduras*. Boulder: University Press of Colorado.

Davidson, William V. 1974. *Historical Geography of the Bay Islands, Honduras: Anglo-Hispanic Conflict in the Western Caribbean*. Birmingham, AL: Southern University Press.

Davidson, William V. 1991. "Geographical Perspectives on Spanish-Pech (Paya) Indian Relationships in Sixteenth Century Northeast Honduras." In *Columbian Consequences*, Volume 3, ed. David Hurst Thomas, 205–226. Washington, DC: Smithsonian Institution Press.

Delle, James A. 1999. "The Landscapes of Class Negotiation on Coffee Plantations in the Blue Mountains of Jamaica: 1790–1850." *Historical Archaeology* 33(1):136–158.

Delle, James A. 2009. "The Governor and the Enslaved: An Archaeology of Colonial Modernity at Marshall's Pen, Jamaica." *International Journal of Historical Archaeology* 13(4):488–512.

Dennett, Carrie L. 2007. *The Río Claro Site (AD 1000–1530), Northeast Honduras: A Ceramic Classification and Examination of External Connections*. Unpublished MA thesis, Department of Anthropology, Trent University, Peterborough, Ontario, Canada.

Elliott, John H. 2006. *Empires of the Atlantic World: Britain and Spain in America 1492–1830*. New Haven, CT: Yale University Press.

Epstein, Jeremiah F. 1957. "Late Ceramic Horizons in Northeastern Honduras." PhD dissertation, University of Pennsylvania, Philadelphia.

Epstein, Jeremiah F. 1959. "Dating the Ulua Polychrome Complex." *American Antiquity* 25(1):125–129.

Epstein, Jeremiah F. 1975. Reconocimiento arqueológico de las Islas de la Bahía: R1 a R33. Manuscript on file. Tegucigalpa, Honduras: Archives of the Honduran Institute of Anthropology and History (IHAH).

Epstein, Jeremiah F. 1978. "Problemas en el estudio de la prehistoria de las Islas de la Bahía." *Yaxkin* 2(3):149–158.

Epstein, Jeremiah F., and Vito Véliz. 1977. "Reconocimiento arqueológico de la Isla de Roatán, Honduras." *Yaxkin* 2(1):28–39.

Evans, David K. 1966. "The People of French Harbour: A Study of Conflict and Change on Roatán Island." Unpublished PhD dissertation, Department of Anthropology, University of California, Berkeley.

Feacham, R. W. 1940. "The Bay Islands, Gulf of Honduras." *The Geographical Journal* 96(3)181–189.

Feacham, R. W., and H. J. Braunholtz. 1938. "Exhibition of Antiquities and Photographs." *Man* 38:73–74.

Figueroa, Alejandro J. 2011. *The Clash of Heritage and Development on the Island of Roatán, Honduras*. Unpublished MA thesis, Department of Anthropology, University of South Florida, Tampa, FL.

Figueroa, Alejandro J., Whitney A. Goodwin, and E. Christian Wells. 2012. "Mayanizing Tourism on Roatán Island, Honduras: Archaeological Perspectives on Heritage, Development, and Indigeneity." In *Global Tourism: Cultural Heritage and Economic Encounters*, ed. S. Lyon and E. C. Wells, 43–60. Lanham, MD: AltaMira Press.

Freeland, Jane. 1988. *A Special Place in History: The Atlantic Coast in the Nicaraguan Revolution*. London: Spiderweb.

González, Silvia, C. Mumford, E. Martínez, and A. Corrales. 1995. "La cultura Pech: Un acercamiento a su estado actual." *Yaxkin* 13(1–2):37–56.

Goodwin, R. Christopher, Cyd Heymann, and Glen T. Hanson. 1979. "Archaeological sampling on Utila, Bay Islands, Honduras." *Journal of the Virgin Islands Archaeological Society* 7:3–26.

Goodwin, Whitney A. 2011. *Indigenous Populations of the Island of Roatán, Honduras, and Their Mainland Neighbors: Implications for the Future of Heritage Tourism on the Bay Islands*. Unpublished MA thesis, Department of Anthropology, University of South Florida, Tampa, FL.

Grant, William L., J. Munro, and A. W. Fitzroy, eds. 2005. *Acts of the Privy Council of England*, Colonial Series, Vol. 3. Burlington, Ontario, Canada: Tanner Richie Publishing,

Harrisse, Henry. 1866. *Bibliotheca Americana Vetustissima, A Description of Works Relating to America Published between theYyears 1492–1551*. New York: G. P. Philes.

Hasemann, George E. 1975. Survey Report of Utila Island. Manuscript on file. Tegucigalpa, Honduras: Archives of the Honduran Institute of Anthropology and History.

Hasemann, George E. 1977. "Reconocimiento arqueológico de Utila." *Yaxkin* 2(1):41–76.

Healy, Paul F. 1978. "La arqueología del noreste de Honduras: Informe preliminar de la investigación de 1975 y 1976." *Yaxkin* 2(3):159–173.

Healy, Paul F. 1993. "Northeastern Honduras." In *Pottery of Prehistoric Honduras: Regional Classification and Analysis*, ed. J. S. Henderson and M. Beaudry-Corbett, 194–213. Los Angeles: Cotsen Institute of Archaeology, UCLA.

Helms, Mary W. 1969. "The Cultural Ecology of a Colonial Tribe." *Ethnology* 8(1):76–84.

Helms, Mary W. 1971. *Asang: Adaptations to Culture Contact in a Miskito Community*. Gainesville: University Press of Florida.

Helms, Mary W. 1983. "Miskito Slaving and Culture Contact: Ethnicity and Opportunity in an Expanding Population." *Journal of Anthropological Research* 39:179–197.

Herrera y Tordesillas, Antonio de. 1944. *Historia general de los hechos de los Castellanos en las islas y tierra-firme de el mar océano*. Asunción del Paraguay, Paraguay: Editorial Guarania.

Horton, Mark. 1985. Preliminary Report: Archaeological Survey of the Bay Islands (Proyecto Operación Raleigh), April–June 1985. Manuscript on file. Tegucigalpa, Honduras: Archives of the Honduran Institute of Anthropology and History.

Houlson, Jane Harvey. 1934. *Blue Blaze: Danger and Delight in Strange Islands in Honduras*. Indianapolis, IN: Bobbs-Merrill.

Joyce, Rosemary A. 1983. "Ceramic Traditions and Language Groups of Prehispanic Honduras." *Journal of the Steward Anthropological Society* 15(1–2):158–186.

Klassen, Sarah. 2010. El Antigual: A Test of Surface Collection Methods. Unpublished BA thesis, Department of Anthropology, Dartmouth College, Hanover, NH.

Kupperman, Karen O. 1993. *Providence Island, 1630–1641: The Other Puritan colony*. New York: Cambridge University Press.

Labaree, Leonard Woods, ed. 1967. *Royal Instructions to British Colonial Governors, 1670–1776*. 2 volumes. New York: Octagon Books.

Lanza, Roberto de Jesús, Marcio Julio Escobar, Mauren Denise Carias Moncada, and Rosa Carminda Castellanos. 1992. *Los Pech (payas): Una cultura olvidada*. Tegucigalpa, Honduras: Editorial Guaymuras.

Las Casas, Bartolomé de. 1951. *Historia de las Indias*. Mexico City, Mexico: Fondo de Cultura Económica.

Lehmann, Walter. 1920. *Zentral-Amerika*. Berlin, Germany: D. Reimer.

Long, Edward. 1774 [2002]. *The History of Jamaica: Reflections on Its Situation, Settlements, Inhabitants, Climate, Products, Commercy, Laws and Government*. Vol. 1. London: McGill-Queen's University Press.

M. W. 1744. "The Mosquito Indian and his Golden River, being a Familiar Description of the Mosqueto Kingdom in America . . . written in or about 1699." In *A Collection of Voyages and Travels*, ed. Awnsham Churchill, 297–312. London, UK.

Major, R. H., ed. and trans. 1847. *Select Letters of Christopher Columbus, with Other Original Documents Relating to his Four Voyages to the New World*. London: Hakluyt Society.

McBride, J. David. 2006. "Contraband Traders, Lawless Vagabonds, and the British Settlement and Occupation of Roatan, Bay Islands, Honduras." In *X Marks the Spot*, ed. R. K. Skowronek and C. R. Ewen, 44–63. Gainesville: University of Florida Press.

McConville, Brendan. 2006. *The King's Three Faces: The Rise and Fall of Royal America, 1688–1776*. Chapel Hill: University of North Carolina Press.

Mihok, Lorena D. 2013. "Unearthing Augusta: Landscapes of Royalization on Roatán Island, Honduras." Unpublished PhD dissertation, Department of Anthropology, University of South Florida, Tampa, FL.

Mihok, Lorena D., and E. Christian Wells. 2014. "Miskitu Labor and English Royalization at Augusta, Roatán Island, Honduras." *International Journal of Historical Archaeology* 18(1):100–121.

Mitchell, R. C. 1850. "A Statistical Account and Description of the Island of Roatán." *Colburn's United Service Journal and Navy and Military Magazine*, Part II, August.

Mitchell-Hedges, Frederick A. 1954a. *Danger My Ally*. London: Elek Books.

Mitchell-Hedges, Frederick A. 1954b. "Some Problems of Middle American Research: The Bay Islands." *New World Antiquity* 9:1–3.

Montgomery, Robert. 2004. Register to the papers of William Duncan Strong. Washington, DC: National Anthropological Archives, Smithsonian Institution.

Moreno Cortés, José E., and E. Christian Wells. 2006. Explaining Standardization without Explaining It Away: Inferring Production Scale from Ancient Pech Pottery of Roatán Island, Honduras. Paper presented at the 105th Annual Meeting of the American Anthropological Association, San Jose, CA.

Muñoz, Juan Bautista. 1639. "Descripción de las islas Guanajas (Audiencia de Guatemala)." *Colección de Juan Bautista Muñoz*, Volumen 23. Madrid, Spain: Archivo de la Real Academia de la Historia.

Navarrete, Martín Fernández de. 1825. *Colección de los viages y descubrimientos, que hicieron por mar los Españoles desde fines del siglo XV, con varios documentos inéditos concernientes a la historia de la Marina Castellana*. Madrid, Spain: Madrid Imprenta Nacional.

Naylor, Robert A. 1989. *Penny Ante Imperialism: The Mosquito Shore and the Bay of Honduras, 1600-1914*. London: Associated University Presses.

Newson, Linda. 1986. *The Cost of Conquest: Indian Decline in Honduras under Spanish Rule*. Boulder, CO: Westview Press.

Newton, Arthur P. 1966. *The Colonising Activities of the English Puritans: The Last Phase of the Elizabethan Struggle with Spain*. Port Washington, NY: Kennikat Press.

Newton, Arthur P. 1967. *The European Nations in the West Indies 1493–1688*. New York: Barnes and Noble.

Noveck, Daniel. 1988. "Class, Culture, and the Miskito Indians: A Historical Perspective." *Dialectical Anthropology* 13(1):17–29.

Offen, Karl H. 2007. "Creating Mosquitia: Mapping Amerindian Spatial Practices in Eastern Central America, 1629–1779." *Journal of Historical Geography* 33:254–282.

Olien, Michael D. 1983. "The Miskito Kings and the Line of Succession." *Journal of Anthropological Research* 39(2):198–241.

Pares, Richard. 1936. *War and Trade in the West Indies, 1739–1763*. New York: Barnes and Noble.

Rolt, Richard. 1749–1750. *An Impartial Representation of the Conduct of the Several Powers of Europe, Engaged in the Late General War: . . . from . . . 1739. to . . . 1748,*

volume 2. Eighteenth Century Collections Online, http://find.galegroup.com
.ezproxy.lib.usf.edu, accessed on November 13, 2013.

Rose, Richard H. 1904. *Utilla: Past and Present*. Dansville, NY: F. A. Owen
Publishing.

Sauer, Carl O. 1966. *The Early Spanish Main*. Berkeley: University of California Press.

Sorsby, Karen R. 1997. The Puritans of Providence Island, the Cape-Continent
and the Mosquito-Jamaica Connection. Paper presented at the 29th Annual
Conference of the Association of Caribbean Historians (ACH), Fort-de-France,
Martinique.

Spinden, Herbert J. 1925. "The Chorotegan Culture Area." *Proceedings of the International Congress of Americanists, 21st Session, 1924* 2:528–545.

Squier, Ephraim George. 1858. *The States of Central America*. New York: Harper and
Brothers.

Stanwood, Owen. 2011. *The Empire Reformed: English America in the Age of the Glori-
ous Revolution*. Philadelphia: University of Pennsylvania Press.

Stone, Doris Z. 1939. "A Delimitation of the Paya Area in Honduras and Certain
Stylistic Resemblances Found in Costa Rica and Honduras." *Vigesimoseptimo
Congreso Internacional de Americanistas: Actas de la Primera Sesion, Celebrada en la
Ciudad de Mexico en 1939*. Mexico City, Mexico: Instituto National de Antropolo-
gia e Historia.

Stone, Doris Z. 1941. *The Archaeology of the North Coast of Honduras*. Cambridge, MA:
Peabody Museum of Archaeology and Ethnology.

Stonich, Susan. 2000. *The Other Side of Paradise: Tourism, Conservation, and Development in the Bay Islands*. New York: Cognizant Communication Corporation.

Strong, William Duncan. 1935. *Archaeological Investigations in the Bay Islands, Spanish
Honduras*. Washington, DC: Smithsonian Institution.

Strong, William Duncan. 1939. Investigaciones arqueológicas en las Islas de la Bahía.
Revista del Archivo y Biblioteca Nacionales de Honduras 17(12):837–840; 18(1):37–41;
18(2–3):106–109; 18(4):176–178.

Strong, William Duncan, Alfred Vincent Kidder III, and A. J. Drexel Paul. 1938.
*Preliminary Report on the Smithsonian Institution-Harvard University Archaeologi-
cal Expedition to Northwestern Honduras*. Smithsonian Miscellaneous Collections
Volume 97, Number 1. Washington, DC: Smithsonian Institution.

Thomas, Cyrus, and John R. Swanton. 1911. *Indian Languages of Mexico and Central
America and Their Geographical Position*. Bureau of American Ethnology, Bulletin
44. Washington, DC: Smithsonian Institution.

Uring, Nathaniel. 1727. *A History of the Voyages and Travels of Capt. Nathaniel Uring,
with New Draughts of the Bay of Honduras and the Caribee Islands*. London: John
Clarke.

Valladares, Abel Arturo. 1939. *Monografía de Departamento de las Islas de la Bahía.* Tegucigalpa, Honduras: Talleres Tipograficos Nacionales.

Véliz, Vito. 1972. "An Analysis of Ceramics from the Piedra Blanca Site, Northeastern Honduras." Unpublished MA Thesis, Department of Anthropology, University of Kansas.

Véliz, Vito. 1978. *Análisis arqueológico de la cerámica de Piedra Blanca.* Instituto Hondureño de Antropología e Historia, Tegucigalpa, Honduras.

Véliz, Vito, Gordon R. Willey, and Paul F. Healy. 1976. "Una clasificación preliminar descriptiva de cerámica de la Isla de Roatán, Honduras" *Revista de la Universidad (Honduras)* 6(11):19–29.

Véliz, Vito, Gordon R. Willey, and Paul F. Healy. 1977. "Clasificación descriptiva preliminar de cerámica de Roatán." *Yaxkin* 2(1):7–18.

Wells, E. Christian. 2008. "La arqueología y el futuro del pasado en las Islas de la Bahía." *Yaxkin* 24(1):66–81.

Wright, I. A. 1932. *Documents Concerning English Voyages to the Spanish Main 1569–1580.* Cambridge, UK: Cambridge University Press.

Yde, Jens. 1938. *An Archaeological Reconnaissance of Northwestern Honduras: A Report of the Work of the Tulane University-Danish National Museum Expedition to Central America, 1935.* Copenhagen, Denmark: Levin and Munksgaard.

Young, Patricia T., and Jack S. Levy. 2011. "Domestic Politics and the Escalation of Commercial Rivalry: Explaining the War of Jenkins' Ear, 1739–48." *European Journal of International Relations* 17:209–232.

Young, Thomas. 1847. *Narrative of a Residence on the Mosquito Shore, with an Account of Truxillo, and the Adjacent Islands of Bonacca and Roatán, and a Vocabulary of the Mosquitian Language.* London: Smith, Elder.

9

Archaeological research in Honduras is predominantly focused on the period before European colonization. This emphasis has contributed to an impression of a discontinuity between the late prehispanic-period peoples of Honduras and the histories that came after colonization. I have maintained elsewhere that this perceived break is artificial and leads us to expect discontinuities that do not exist in the archaeological record (Joyce and Sheptak 2014; Sheptak 2013). Here I reconsider our current understandings of colonial-period sites (those dating between 1502 and 1821) reached through excavation and research on archival documents and point out a number of implicit and often overlooked challenges to creating archaeological understandings of colonial Honduras.

There is a major disconnect between the way archaeologists conceptualize their units of analysis as linguistic or ethnic groups with a wide geographic distribution, and how the same people were described in the first generations of colonization (Sheptak 2007, 2013; see also Gómez, chapter 11, and Lara-Pinto, chapter 10, this volume). Furthermore, a lack of newly introduced materials in indigenous communities, material that is demonstrably European in origin, creates challenges in dating colonial indigenous assemblages (Joyce and Sheptak 2014). Archaeologists working in Honduras have employed a default assumption that sites of the colonial period will yield European-tradition materials, whereas excavations so far have shown that these

Historical Archaeology in Honduras

RUSSELL SHEPTAK

DOI: 10.5876/9781646420971.c009

are only rarely found in Honduran indigenous communities until late in the eighteenth century.

Further, there are contradictions between the rich material world described in colonial documents, and the more modest material remains found in those few colonial sites that have been explored. This is, in part, due to retention of objects as property transmitted to successors. Finally, most colonial-period archaeology has been focused on individual sites. If we are to come to a rich understanding of indigenous communities in a colonial setting, we will have to look at them in the broader context of networks of interaction across the landscape.

In the remainder of this chapter, I use the material record of Ticamaya and Candelaria/Masca, two indigenous colonial communities located in northern Honduras (figure 9.1), as instructive examples of how to address these challenges. In order to place the archaeology of the town of Ticamaya in a regional context, I begin with a brief overview of archaeological research conducted to date on sites dating after Europeans entered the area. I then consider three challenges for historical archaeology—establishing chronology, addressing the relatively modest Honduran material record, and working at a landscape scale—using the archaeology of Ticamaya and its relations to the indigenous town of Masca and the Spanish fort and town of Omoa as an example. I return in the end to the question of appropriate units of analysis, suggesting it is the town, rather than the ethnic or linguistic group, that serves better for understanding the colonial period.

HISTORICAL ARCHAEOLOGY IN HONDURAS: AN OVERVIEW

Historical archaeology in Honduras began with the investigation of the institutions and apparatus of Spanish colonization. There have been four foci of such work: the Santa Barbara region missionized by Mercedarians; the city of Comayagua; and the forts and settlements on the Río Tinto of both English and Spanish origin, and at Omoa. The earliest intentional historical archaeological work took place at the fortress of San Fernando de Omoa when George Hasemann (1986) excavated within several rooms in the Omoa fortress and in the earlier El Real fort beside it. His work was meant both to establish chronology and to determine the construction history of the fort. Secondarily, he tried to look at the uses of each of the rooms he excavated. He recovered abundant Spanish colonial ceramics, metal, and glass, but also plain ceramics, obsidian, and flaked glass indicative of an indigenous presence in this late eighteenth-century outpost. In 2008, Oscar Neil Cruz Castillo

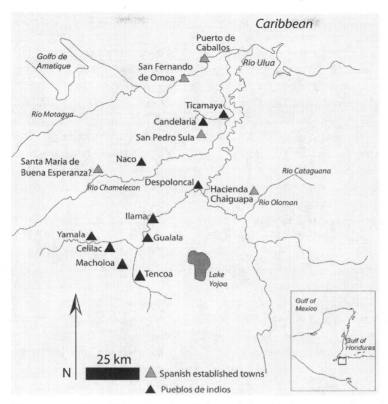

FIGURE 9.1. *Map showing locations of sites mentioned in text.*

and Ranferi Juárez Silva (2009) performed additional test pitting and selected excavation in the town and in the fortress of San Fernando de Omoa as a result of a reconstruction project. They documented standing colonial architecture within the modern town and identified some subsurface colonial remains outside of the fort.

In the 1980s, John Weeks and Nancy Black (Weeks 1997; Weeks and Black 1991; Weeks et al. 1987) undertook a survey of archaeological sites in the Department of Santa Barbara. Their investigation focused on the Mercedarian missions and associated indigenous towns and churches that were affected by missionization. They documented a number of colonial churches in towns that still today bear indigenous names: Gualala, Machaloa, Tencoa, Celilac, Ojuera, and Yamala. They described their expectations for seeing a transition from the protohistoric to colonial periods marked in the archaeological record by the introduction of Spanish glazed ceramics and a change in the settlement system (Weeks and Black 1991:255).

However, with the exception of the colonial churches they documented, Weeks and Black did not identify the expected transformations in indigenous life that they were relying on to indicate colonial sites. In the region of Yamala, they did identify one site as an indigenous town that the Spanish burned in the 1530s, based on its description in colonial documents and the location and layout of the ruins there. Yet they note that, at this Site 503, "ceramics excavated . . . indicate a predominant Late Post-Classic occupation" (Weeks and Black 1991:255). This is just one of many places they investigated that is described in Spanish colonial documents yet was found to lack clear colonial or European materials.

Several projects have looked at traces of the British presence in eastern Honduras, especially along the Black River. The first project of note that explored this area was that of Clark et al. (1982), who excavated in the English cemetery and fort on the Black River (Río Tinto, known as Palacios today). The fort, constructed in 1740, was burned in 1800. While Clark, Dawson, and Drake identified the English fort, for the most part they failed to find signs of occupation or living features within it. They reported finding glass bottles along with locally made, sand-tempered pottery.

Both this project and a later one at the site by Valles Perez (2002) reported remains of likely residential buildings in the cemetery area. These consisted of buried brick walls and part of a colonial oven, accompanied by porcelain, glass, and iron fragments that dated these features to the mid-eighteenth century. Valles Perez (2002) identified the oven as part of the reported Sambo-Miskito settlement outside of the English Black River town.

In all three of these pioneering investigations, archaeologists were able to identify materials that allowed identification of the European institutions of colonial society, but had more difficulty with, or failed to clearly identify, indigenous components that historical documents suggest would have been present. Some archaeological research on the Spanish colonial period has focused entirely on the institutions of the colony. In Comayagua, Oscar Neil Cruz (2003, 2009) has explored the Casa de Contratación, the Plaza de La Merced, and the Cathedral, preparatory to renovation/reconstruction of these colonial facilities to encourage tourism, which limited both the time available and the scope of the work performed.

Other projects have explored the practices of colonial, indigenous, and African-descendant people, primarily along the north coast (See Mihok et al., chapter 8, this volume). The most extensive record comes from excavations of Ticamaya, a site in the lower Ulúa Valley occupied from at least the thirteenth century to the nineteenth century (Blaisdell-Sloan 2006). A total of six likely household areas were sampled in this entirely buried riverbank site, three occupied during the sixteenth century, and the latest from the late eighteenth to early nineteenth century. No European-tradition material culture was associated with the sixteenth-century households. Extensive evidence of burning and the construction of an oven directly over an earlier burial show discontinuities in use of space after the early sixteenth century.

Ticamaya survived a demographic crash that left 90 percent of the indigenous towns in the region abandoned by the end of the sixteenth century (Sheptak 2013). Later colonial occupation was evident in all six areas sampled (most dating to the late eighteenth century), but European-tradition materials came from only two areas. In one household, residents discarded majolica ceramics, cow and sheep bones, and bottle glass (Wonderley 1984). The majority of the materials used even in eighteenth-century Ticamaya were consistent with indigenous traditions, including chipped stone, both obsidian and chert, and low-fired slipped and unslipped earthenware ceramics. The metal, glass, and glazed ceramics used here represent types made between 1780 and 1830, when documentary records show Ticamaya was engaged closely with the fortress of San Fernando de Omoa.

Excavations at Omoa in 2009 documented remains of houses that formed the front line of buildings facing the fort across a large open plaza (Gómez et al. 2010; Joyce and Sheptak 2016). The most-deeply buried materials were remains of an indigenous settlement, possibly of indigenous laborers who worked on building the fort. These remains included indigenous-tradition earthenware, obsidian flakes and blades, and an indigenous-style net weight. Covering this component were the remains of at least three late eighteenth-century structures with brick floors and foundations, perishable walls, and ceramic tile roofs. These collapsed buildings yielded majolica and other glazed Spanish wares, costume jewelry, and small bits of metal. Based on the documentary record for Omoa, the most likely residents of these houses would have been members of the commercial elite of the free African-descendant population of the town (Joyce and Sheptak 2016).

While less developed than either the archaeology of Spanish institutions or that of colonial indigenous communities, the archaeology of African-descendant peoples was the focus of a significant project by Charles Cheek (1997). He examined material from three settlements near Trujillo to look at acculturation and identity formation by African-descendant immigrants to Honduras in a region undergoing intense conflict between the Spanish and

English. Campamento, just west of Trujillo, was settled in 1799. Site 8, southwest of Trujillo, was probably occupied from about 1800 to 1830. Finally, Site 1, in Cristales, on the western edge of Trujillo, was occupied from the 1830s to 1880s. Cheek (1997) characterized the ceramics at all three sites as being either Hispanic (wheel-thrown redwares and majolicas), English (Staffordshire wares), or indigenous (handmade red-painted water jars). Cheek looked at changes through time in the use of tea-serving wares as implying Garifuna adoption of English foodways as a way to distinguish themselves from surrounding indigenous populations.

While work on colonial and Republican-era (post-1821) sites has demonstrated the potential for historical archaeology in Honduras, several issues have to be addressed to fully develop this potential. The first of these is moving away from using European goods as the main basis for chronology, a practice that has made it more difficult to identify colonial settlements occupied by people with less access to European goods. Because indigenous people maintained use of traditional earthenware ceramics and used obsidian as cutting material until quite late, overreliance on the presence of European goods can lead to failing to recognize colonial indigenous sites (Joyce and Sheptak 2014).

The materials from sites investigated by historical archaeologists are better employed to understand specific practices, as Cheek (1997) and Mihok et al. (chapter 8, this volume) did. Yet the excavated assemblages need to be treated as partial, with attention given to another material register, documents, to build up a clearer image of the material lives of indigenous, African-descendant, and Spanish-identified residents. We need to pay attention to site-formation processes at a landscape scale. Rather than treat individual sites on their own, the future of historical archaeology of Honduras lies in considering sites connected with each other through a variety of processes, a potential I illustrate below through a discussion of the relationships materially evident between Ticamaya, Omoa, and a third place, Masca, intimately connected to the other two.

FIRST CHALLENGE: ESTABLISHING CHRONOLOGY IN COLONIAL ARCHAEOLOGY

Historical archaeologists in Latin America have typically relied on the presence of European goods within the sites they investigate to establish chronology. The temporal distribution of various types of majolicas, European tin-glazed ceramics, and Chinese porcelain are reasonably well understood. This chronology has held up remarkably well, even in Latin America, as long as the focus of excavation has been a Spanish or other European-derived community. It breaks down in places like Honduras, especially when one is examining indigenous communities.

An illustrative example comes from the report on the investigation of Yamala, where the excavators found a colonial church at the center of what they described as a Late Postclassic community, based on the presence of European-tradition ceramics and metals in the remains of the church, but absence of the same in the surrounding households (Weeks 1997; Weeks and Black 1991). The households around the church used obsidian and plain and red-slipped domestic ceramics that were similar in form and finish to late-prehispanic domestic ceramics. The excavators of the site were uncomfortable saying the community surrounding the church was contemporary with it, based on the absence of Spanish-introduced materials. I have argued elsewhere that this reflects the archaeologist's perspective that separates pre-Spanish indigenous archaeology disjunctively from colonial indigenous archaeology as two separate specializations, unrelated beyond sharing excavation as a technique (Joyce and Sheptak 2014).

The expectation that colonial sites will have European goods appears to be invalid for indigenous colonial Honduras. Ticamaya, an indigenous community in northern Honduras with continuous occupation from the thirteenth century through the nineteenth century (Blaisdell-Sloan 2006), might easily have been identified as primarily a late-prehispanic community using the criteria applied to Yamala. The domestic ceramics of Ticamaya's inhabitants continued the forms and finishes familiar in late-prehispanic pottery known from the region. Indeed, after Spanish colonization, only the polychrome ceramics of the late Postclassic drop out of the ceramic assemblage. No metal, glass, or European- or Chinese-origin ceramics were found except in deposits from the late eighteenth century, and even then, not in all households. Obsidian blades continued to be used throughout the colonial period as the preferred cutting tool in the household.

At Ticamaya, Blaisdell-Sloan (2006) collected and ran radiocarbon samples from houses, ovens, hearths, and other features within the site. It was fine-grained control of stratigraphy that allowed her to confidently assign house floors and their associated material remains to various episodes. Radiocarbon samples established which of these episodes dated to the Postclassic and early-colonial time periods. Once that sequence was established, a detailed study of the apparently unchanging domestic ceramics revealed subtle variations in the way domestic pots were finished, the vessel rim was shaped, and the vessel body was constructed on otherwise visually similar red-slipped and plain pots of the late eighteenth century, for which no radiocarbon or European-object-based dates could be developed. This shows the importance of stratigraphic excavations as the basis for establishing chronologies, even in time periods when it might be assumed that documentary histories and the constructed histories of European goods supercede such basic archaeological methods.

SECOND CHALLENGE: UNDERSTANDING SITE-FORMATION PROCESSES

Archaeologically documented material remains of colonial households give only a partial description of the colonial material world. There is a vast difference between the richness of households described in colonial documents and the material remains found in the colonial sites investigated so far in Honduras.

Part of this is due to cultural practices. Nothing of value was left in a colonial household when it was abandoned. Rich colonial individuals left estates with or without wills, which document what was owned, and document the disposition of these belongings. The things people owned continued to circulate. Some goods, like saint's images, jewelry, and clothing, were the subject of bequests (see Sheptak 2009). Everything not specifically gifted to someone was auctioned off, with the proceeds going to carry out cash bequests, the remainder being given to heirs. The inventories of goods and the prices paid for them were duly recorded in the executor's accounting of the estate. This information needs to be included in historical archaeological studies to complement excavated materials.

The archaeology of indigenous households also shows that little of value remained behind even in houses that were destroyed by fire. While indigenous people did not leave estates that required the appointment of an executor, or wills, their property clearly also continued to circulate in indigenous society. Colonial documents can still provide a better idea of what the property of indigenous households once was. Legal cases and petitions show that along the north coast, indigenous people were a crucial part of the contraband trade, bringing alcohol, vinegar, clothing, and British and French ceramics into the Spanish colony, and their towns were often the locus of sale of such goods to the Spanish population (Sheptak 2013). With few exceptions, these goods apparently did not remain within indigenous communities, but rather passed into the hands of Spanish and Afro-descendent people through transactions taking place in indigenous spaces.

The most valuable materials are likely to be least often recovered in excavation. Even in late eighteenth-century Ticamaya, when contemporary documents suggest there were resident ladinos or people identifying with the

Spanish-majority population, only a small amount of metal (mostly non-cutting artifacts), and six fragments of majolica ceramics were recovered, all from a single household. More abundant were fragments from glass bottles, possibly pointing to breakage from such things as the contraband alcohol stored at Ticamaya after one ship was confiscated (Sheptak 2013). Only by constructing histories of circulation of materials that join accounts from documents and excavation data can we provide a realistic sense of life in colonial settings.

THIRD CHALLENGE: INVESTIGATING THE
COLONIAL PERIOD AT THE LANDSCAPE SCALE

Once chronological control is established and documents are integrated as another source of material evidence, colonial and Republican-period archaeology needs to treat sites in relation to each other in order to understand regional processes and interactions. In the following pages, I discuss how the indigenous communities of Ticamaya and Candelaria/Masca can be better understood by exploring their relationships with the other indigenous, Afro-descendent and Spanish communities that surrounded them, particularly Omoa.

I view the people of Ticamaya, Candelaria/Masca, and Omoa as part of shared *communities of practice* in the late eighteenth and early nineteenth centuries (see Lave and Wenger 1991 and 2005 for the concept). At Ticamaya and Omoa, this is evident in the reproduction of specific ways of doing things that are the result of persistence of a viable community of practice. The concept of community of practice allows me to identify archaeological traces of new social relations like those recorded in historical documents, providing evidence of the emergence of new social identities in communities where indigenous and Afro-descendent people were intermarrying in the late eighteenth century.

Ticamaya and Candelaria/Masca were indigenous communities with long histories. Omoa consisted of a Spanish town and a military fort founded in 1745. The town had a large Afro-descendent population, both free and enslaved (Cáceres Gómez 2003). From 1745 until 1760 Omoa also had a dislocated indigenous work force that came from both the lower Ulúa Valley and highland western Honduras (Sheptak 2013). After 1760, only indigenous service from the Ulúa Valley continued, specifically people from Ticamaya and Masca who worked and lived at the fort.

To establish the existence of a shared community of practice, we compared archaeological data from Ticamaya with similarly dated materials from Omoa (Blaisdell-Sloan 2006; Gómez et al. 2010; Joyce et al. 2008; Sheptak 2013). Elsewhere I have offered a reanalysis of the postcolumbian Ticamaya material

FIGURE 9.2. *Flaked European glass recovered from features dated to AD 1740–1760 at the fort at Omoa.*

deposits in light of our work at Omoa (Sheptak and Blaisdell-Sloan 2014). This comparison allowed for the definition of shared communities of practice with respect to ceramic production, foodways, and use of lithic materials. Within the fort at Omoa, indigenous-tradition ceramics, worked obsidian, and European glass worked into flakes were recovered from subfloor levels, construction features that can be securely dated to between AD 1740 and 1760 (figure 9.2; Gómez et al. 2010; Joyce et al. 2008). Indigenous tradition ceramics also form part of later assemblages recovered from between floors likely dating to remodeling between AD 1760 and 1790.

Excavations in 2009 in an area of the colonial town of Omoa across from the main gate of the fort also yielded indigenous tradition material (Gómez et al. 2010). The earliest colonial houses documented here, provisionally dated to AD 1780–1800 by European-tradition ceramics and household goods, had prepared brick floors, wall foundations of several rows of brick bonded together with mud, that apparently supported more perishable upper walls, and tile roofs. Just below the former ground surface associated with these Spanish-tradition houses, we recovered an assemblage of indigenous-tradition ceramics, obsidian, and fired-clay artifacts comparable to those from Ticamaya. These most likely were from short-term habitation of this area by indigenous labor forces brought to Omoa during the construction of the fort, a practice recorded historically as early as 1750 (Sheptak 2013), before the construction of the substantial houses of the wealthy townsfolk that replaced them by 1780.

It is very likely that the resident indigenous group in this area between 1750 and 1780 would have been from one of the two northern Ulúa Valley *pueblos de indios*, Ticamaya or Candelaria (formerly Masca), that owed continuing labor to Omoa (Sheptak 2013). We know from colonial documents that men from Candelaria were living in Omoa in 1781 (Sheptak 2013). However, at that time, the substantial Spanish houses had replaced the more ephemeral indigenous settlement we sampled.

There are two other possible origins for the indigenous-tradition materials we recovered in Omoa. One alternative, that this was the remains of the indigenous community known to have been there in the sixteenth century, is inconsistent with the indigenous-tradition pottery, which included details of form and finishing technique only found in eighteenth-century contexts at Ticamaya. The other alternative is that the indigenous materials buried by the first houses of the town were left by indigenous people brought in as labor from central and western Honduras. Documents from the 1750s attest to the presence of laborers from central and western Honduras at Omoa, but also record their objection to working there (Sheptak 2013). The documents confirm that this practice of importing labor from far afield was discontinued around 1760. Without archaeological materials from colonial indigenous communities in central and western Honduras to compare to those from Omoa, it is impossible to securely relate the Omoa occupation with indigenous people from central Honduras. At present, the closest links for the Omoa materials are to the late eighteenth-century contexts excavated at Ticamaya.

ARCHAEOLOGICAL CONTEXTS AT TICAMAYA

At Ticamaya, Blaisdell-Sloan (2006:122, 182–183) identified traces of eighteenth-century surfaces at depths of 29–30 cm in Operation 1, Operations 2A and 2B, Operation 3, Operation 4, and Operation 5. Wonderley's excavations that yielded an eighteenth-century assemblage with European-tradition materials terminated at around 35 cm (Blaisdell-Sloan 2006:141; Wonderley 1984). In addition, material from the uppermost 35 cm in Operations 2C and 2D was comparable to that recovered in the other eighteenth-century operations, even though a corresponding surface was not detected in excavation. None of the eighteenth-century materials was associated with construction features. Nonetheless, the associated ceramics, lithics, and faunal and floral remains reflect everyday life in what were likely perishable houses of indigenous tradition.

In Operation 1, the top 20 cm of material excavated covered a structure that Blaisdell Sloan (2006) dated to the sixteenth century through radiocarbon dating. Ceramics recovered included red-slipped, incised, brushed, burnished, and plain types that appear to be of local manufacture. There is significant diversity in the paste and finish of the plain and brushed ceramics, sufficient to allow the definition of multiple types. A range of bowl and jar forms were represented, and notably, incurved rim bowls (*tecomates*) that may have served as multipurpose transport vessels, which are typical of the eighteenth-century occupation. Distinctive brushed and plain types may represent a seventeenth-century occupation preceding an eighteenth-century one.

In Operation 2A/2B, a surface at 50 cm yielded artifacts with sixteenth-century dates. Traces of a later colonial surface were detected at 30 cm (Blaisdell-Sloan 2006:182). Ceramics from the upper levels here include a mixture of earlier types and typical red-slipped, unslipped, and brushed types of the eighteenth century. Notable among unslipped sherds recovered here are some that were "formed using a different, much more precise forming technique" than previously, and had rims that were described by Blaisdell-Sloan (2006) as "crisply formed, with distinctive hard edges."

In Operation 2C/2D a burned oven, dated by radiocarbon to the sixteenth century, was overlain by two later surfaces (at 48 and 45 cm deep) with traces of burning probably related to cooking that Blaisdell-Sloan (2006:182) suggested might date to the seventeenth century. This suggestion was supported by the recovery of ceramics of three distinctive varieties not present in sixteenth-century or eighteenth-century deposits at the site. The sediments over these seventeenth-century surfaces thus date to the eighteenth century. The eighteenth-century ceramics here are comparable to those from Operation 2A/2B, including multiple plain types, red-slipped, and rarer burnished wares. The only identified brushed types are more likely of seventeenth-century date. A single fired-clay spindle-whorl came from this operation (Blaisdell-Sloan 2006:243–244).

In Operation 3, Blaisdell-Sloan encountered remnants of a burned structure at a depth of 33–39 cm, dated to the sixteenth century by radiocarbon dating. Above this was a surface at 30 cm. The upper 20 cm of deposits here were recognized as eighteenth century. Ceramics included the same range of red-slipped, unslipped, and brushed bowls and jars seen in eighteenth-century deposits elsewhere on the site. An uncommon but distinctive burnished ceramic type diagnostic of the eighteenth century elsewhere appears to be absent here. The eighteenth-century residents in this area of the site also left a distinctive collection of remains of hunted land animals, including both artiodactyls and opossum.

Operation 4 encountered remains of two sixteenth-century structures that were covered by a surface at 29 cm depth. Eighteenth-century materials were recovered in the upper 20 cm of deposits. An early nineteenth-century date is suggested by the presence of lead fragments (Blaisdell-Sloan 2006:242). Plain and burnished ceramics comparable to eighteenth-century wares in other units were reported, but none of the common red-slipped or brushed types seen in other areas.

Operation 5 yielded late-prehispanic surfaces at 80, 60, and 40 cm. These were covered by a later surface formed at 30 cm (Blaisdell-Sloan 2006:183). Blaisdell-Sloan recovered a number of items of European tradition, including a piece of lead shot, in this excavation. The top 20 cm of deposits yielded historic bottle glass, at least one piece made in a three-part mold, a technology in use by about 1814 in England, the source of much of the imported European material in eighteenth-century deposits at Omoa. The European-tradition glass from this deposit was found alongside worked obsidian in the form of blade fragments. Also present were indigenous-tradition ceramics comparable to those recovered from Omoa. They included plain, brushed, and red-slipped types found in other eighteenth-century deposits at Ticamaya. One unslipped type included examples of a distinctive smoothing technique leaving crisp marks— innovative in eighteenth-century assemblages. A notched fishing-net weight made of fired clay came from this operation as well (Blaisdell-Sloan 2006:243).

Finally, the excavation by Wonderley (1984), which ended at 35 cm deep, produced European-tradition majolica ceramics dating to the 1780s or later, fragments of glass, and pig and cow bones, the only evidence of European domesticates from the site. Blaisdell-Sloan (2006:248) notes that even beyond being the sole area with European domesticates, the fauna from this excavation "is distinctive . . . While the contexts [Wonderley] excavated were midden-like, they contained no *Pachychilus* (jute) shell, a species present in all of the other midden contexts at the site." The glass recovered included at least one piece from the base of a bottle. Despite their distinctive culinary practices, the residents in this area also used typical eighteenth-century indigenous-tradition ceramics, including red-slipped, brushed, and plainwares.

CERAMIC COMMUNITY OF PRACTICE

Hand-made pottery from Ticamaya shows the repeated reproduction of specific ways of making vessels that is evidence of a community of practice. Indigenous-tradition ceramics from Omoa show a range of variation comparable to that seen at Ticamaya, even while they form part of household inventories with constant, diverse, and high frequencies of European-tradition ceramics (majolica from a variety of sources, lead-glazed ware, and in the latest colonial deposits, creamwares and pearlwares likely imported from England).

What distinguishes the indigenous-tradition ceramics from late eighteenth-century contexts at Omoa and Ticamaya as products of participants in a shared community of practice are details of manufacture. Vessel forms entirely overlap, including the use of a sharply demarcated lip on some vessels that was described as "crisply finished" at Ticamaya. The thin red slip used in both sites is matte in texture, and ranges to the orange end of the spectrum. Many examples are blackened. The principal distinctive surface treatment on both unslipped and red-slipped vessels is brushing, with a very small number of sherds showing individual shallow incised lines (figure 9.3).

Forming techniques on burnished, brushed, and plain vessels leave areas of vessel walls of uneven thickness. In the Omoa assemblage, Joyce recorded several examples that clearly show a central impact zone in the thinner part of sherds consistent with paddle and anvil techniques of forming (Gómez et al. 2010; Joyce and Sheptak 2016). This characteristic was also noted at Ticamaya by Blaisdell-Sloan (2006:205–206). These same vessels often have distinctive "crisp" smoothing lines. Some plainware sherds at Ticamaya were described as slab built. At Omoa, overlapping segments of adjacent clay slabs were also noted.

While on a typological level vessel forms do not vary greatly from those in Late Postclassic deposits at Ticamaya, and the colonial assemblages exhibit continuity in surface-treatment techniques, innovations in forming techniques occurred in the eighteenth century at both Ticamaya and Omoa. These reflect changes in fundamental ways of forming vessels: the use of new forming methods and of new ways of smoothing vessels and terminating vessel rims. This is consistent with the documentary record that indicates that the people of Ticamaya circulated into work at Omoa and then returned to their homes, illustrating the need to consider these places together as part of a single landscape.

DISCUSSION

Combining data from documents with detailed analysis of artifact manufacture and use we can begin to understand how indigenous communities in colonial and early Republican Honduras reproduced and reshaped traditional practices. Integration of data from excavation in colonial indigenous communities and related Spanish settlements, combined with extensive analysis of the documents providing windows into the histories of the people who

FIGURE 9.3. *Examples of indigenous-tradition ceramics recovered from contexts at Omoa and Ticamaya.*

moved between these places, demonstrates that the level of analysis required to understand colonial society needs to be the landscape across which people moved between communities.

Documentary research as part of historical archaeology needs to be extensive, not selective. All the resources mentioning each individual town should be used to gain a clearer idea of the colonial social and material world, which would seem impoverished if we relied exclusively on excavation alone. Using the concept of *communities of practice* provides a way of understanding similar material assemblages and seeing them as evidence of networks of interacting people and things at the local and regional scale.

Taking the regional scale as the focus will have the effect of moving us away from developing separate archaeologies of Spanish colonial institutions and of indigenous groups, and instead will lead to a focus on how new ways of surviving and thriving in the colonial world were created. This is what historical archaeologists of the Spanish world elsewhere, such as Barbara Voss (2008), Kojun Sunseri (2014), and Joel Palka (2005) have called *ethnogenesis* in their studies of the emergence of Californio, *genizaro*, and Lacandon identities in different parts of the Spanish colonial world. The concept is defined by Terrance Weik (2004:36) as "the formation of *new or different* sociocultural groups from the interactions, intermixtures, and antagonisms among people who took part in global processes of colonialism and slavery."

Ethnogenesis in colonial Honduras was facilitated by a variety of practices that have left material traces in documents and excavated sites (Joyce and Sheptak 2021). We can say that ethnogenesis began in the sixteenth century with sexual relations that crossed boundaries between the racialized indigenous, black, and European groups that the Spanish sought to define and police with increasing effort and decreasing success throughout the colonial period (Sheptak et al. 2011a). This produced a population that, as in Voss's (2008) example of *californio* identity, could not really maintain sharp distinctions based on kinship or blood and instead emphasized practical engagement as a shared identity.

Arguably, for indigenous people in colonial Honduras, the focus of identity was the town, whereby Spanish-law residents had a degree of autonomy, and where families with long-established histories of community leadership continued to dominate new Spanish roles such as *alcalde* and *regidor* (Sheptak 2007, 2013). The process of ethnogenesis in indigenous towns was facilitated by the creative incorporation of Catholic religious practices, objects of worship, and architecture, again beginning in the sixteenth century and ultimately providing indigenous communities with one of their best ways of maintaining town-level identities through the thorough reworking of what archaeologists have taken as European practices indicating assimilation (Sheptak et al. 2011b; Joyce and Sheptak 2014; compare Hanks 2010).

The residents of indigenous towns used the Spanish language they learned as a way of promoting their own survival in the colonial world, a practice that indigenized Spanish in Honduras not through the incorporation of loan words, but through the incorporation of indigenous arguments and logic represented in petitions from towns like Masca (Sheptak 2013). From this perspective, the abandonment of indigenous languages in the lower Ulúa Valley should not be seen as a loss of indigenous identity, but as an effect of the emergence of a new identity through ethnogenesis. In the same way that Hanks (2010) argues that modern Yucatec originated in the colonial period, we can say that Honduran

Spanish, as spoken by indigenous people, originated through its use by the new Honduran population.

The expectation that material culture might be easily interpreted as a sign of the presence of specific groups also is questionable once we consider colonial Honduras as a site of ethnogenesis, a place where a specifically *hondureño* identity emerged (Joyce and Sheptak 2021). The materials that continued to be used—locally produced, red-slipped and unslipped earthenware ceramics, chipped obsidian, food sources like *jute*—were not the same as they had been prior to Spanish colonization. Their significances shifted. In some cases, material practices reproduced during ethnogenesis reinforced existing indigenous values. For example, cultivation of cacao—prized for community rituals—continued into the eighteenth century (Sheptak 2013), In others, such as the production of red-slipped and unslipped domestic pottery using new techniques, practices that appeared to be representative of continuity in existing identity, actually promoted the emergence of a new identity in communities made up of racially complex households (Sheptak et al. 2011a; Sheptak and Blaisdell-Sloan 2014). Even the use of imported European trade goods can provide evidence of ethnogenesis, as when newly arrived African-descendant people, the ancestors of the Garifuna, took up the service of tea as a way to mark their distinction from other African-descendants in northern Honduras (Cheek 1997).

One thing that made ethnogenesis a necessity in other parts of the Spanish colonial world was mobility, the movement of people to new locations where they had to forge means of coping. For *californios*, this involved the establishment of the Presidio of San Francisco, a fort that, like Omoa, encouraged the growth of a commercial town with complicated labor relations to preexisting people (Voss 2008). For the *genizaros* on the New Mexican frontier, this involved their forced resettlement in new communities ordered by the colonial authorities, mixing indigenous people from different communities along with people of mixed *casta* status (Sunseri 2014). In the same way, labor demands for Omoa would have mixed indigenous Hondurans from the interior of the country with others from the coast, in a multiracial working environment. In the case of the Lacandon (Palka 2005), the mobility in question is that of indigenous people fleeing colonial jurisdiction and then using their location outside controlled territory as a basis for economic exchanges with the colonized societies, a situation like that of the independent Miskitu of eastern Honduras (Mihok and Wells 2014; Mihok et al., chapter 8, this volume).

At first glance, the colonial archaeology of Honduras does not appear to illustrate such mobility, but in fact, in every case documentary evidence shows that there were movements of people into and out of the settlements that have often been taken as sites to be understood on their own. Even Ticamaya—where excavations and documentary evidence combine to indicate occupation from the fourteenth century AD through to the nineteenth century—had a history of mobility that affected its material record. This began with violent movement into the town by Spanish soldiers, possibly reflected in elevated numbers of dart points and burned features found in sixteenth-century deposits (Blaisdell-Sloan 2006; Sheptak et al. 2011b). Around 1700, a second indigenous community, Masca, moved to within close proximity and its residents began to intermarry with those of Ticamaya (Blaisdell-Sloan 2006; Sheptak 2013; Sheptak et al. 2011a). Soon after, Ticamaya was the site of detention for English renegades who sailed a boat there from Roatán (Sheptak 2013). In the second half of the eighteenth century, men from Ticamaya traveled to Omoa to live and work, and some returned with wives of African descent (Sheptak 2013; Sheptak et al. 2011a; Sheptak et al. 2011b). By 1780, the population residing in the town included people self-identified as *ladinos* and indigenous people labeled *forasteros*, meaning they were born somewhere else.

Even the most apparently stable settlement in colonial Honduras was a site of movement of people and things, and an opportunity for the kind of creative reshaping of things and identity that the concept of ethnogenesis implies. The red-slipped and unslipped pots discarded in late eighteenth-century Ticamaya were made to look like the kind of pots that had been made and used for generations. The people who made these pots, and the equivalent ceramics used at Omoa, did not share the same understanding of how to make a pot as earlier generations of potters. They were developed and used by members of a community of practice that stretched across northern Honduras, a community of practice that documentary evidence suggests joined African-descendant and indigenous people. Understanding the archaeology of Ticamaya requires addressing the archaeology of Omoa, and ideally, many other places that formed the landscape of colonial Honduras. Doing so will require us to begin with a more appropriate concept of the social processes shaping the colonial world, questioning how we know who was where, what they were doing, and why.

WORKS CITED

Blaisdell-Sloan, Kira. 2006. "An Archaeology of Place and Self: The Pueblo de Indios of Ticamaya, Honduras (1300–1800 AD)." Unpublished PhD dissertation, Department of Anthropology, University of California, Berkeley.

Cáceres Gómez, Rina. 2003. "On the Frontiers of the African Diaspora in Central America: The African Origins of San Fernando de Omoa." In *Trans-Atlantic Dimensions of Ethnicity in the African Diaspora*, ed. Paul Lovejoy and David Trotman, 115–137. London: Continuum,

Cheek, Charles D. 1997. "Setting the English Table: Black Carib Archaeology on the Caribbean Coast of Honduras." In *Approaches to the Historical Archaeology of Mexico, Central, and South America*, ed. Janine Gasco, Greg Smith, and Patricia Fournier Garcia, 101–109. Los Angeles: Institute of Archaeology, UCLA.

Clark, Catherine., M., Frank G. Dawson, and Jonathan C. Drake.1982. *Archaeology on the Mosquito Coast: A Reconnaissance of the Pre-Columbian and Historic Settlement along the Rio Tinto*. Cambridge, UK: Centre of Latin American Studies, University of Cambridge.

Cruz Castillo, Oscar Neil. 2003. "Un ejemplo de arqueología histórica en Honduras: La Catedral de Comayagua." *Yaxkin* 22(1):104–125.

Cruz Castillo, Oscar Neil. 2009. Un ejemplo de arqueología Histórica en Honduras: la catedral de Comayagua. *Boletín AFEHC* 40. http://afehc-historia-centroameri cana.org/index.php?action=fi_aff&id=2137.

Cruz Castillo, Oscar Neil, and Ranferi Juárez Silva. 2009. "El Asentamiento Colonial de Omoa, últimos resultados." *Boletín AFEHC* No. 40, http://afehc-historia -centroamericana.org/index.php?action=fi_aff&id=2133.

Gómez, Esteban, Rosemary A. Joyce, Russell Sheptak, Kira Blaisdell-Sloan, and Laurie Wilkie. 2010. The Archaeology of San Fernando de Omoa. Paper presented at the 43rd annual meeting of the Society for Historical Archaeology, Amelia Island, FL.

Hanks, William F. 2010. *Converting Words: Maya in the Age of the Cross*. Berkeley: University of California Press.

Hasemann, George. 1986. *Investigaciones Arqueológicas en la Fortaleza de San Fernando y el Asentamiento Colonial de Omoa*. Estudios Antropologicos e Historicos No. 6. Tegucigalpa, Honduras: Instituto Hondureño de Antropología e Historia.

Joyce, Rosemary A., and Russell N. Sheptak. 2014. "History Interrupted: Doing 'Historical Archaeology' in Central America." In *The Death of Prehistory*, ed. Peter Schmidt and Steve Mrozowski, 161–182. Oxford, UK: Oxford University Press.

Joyce, Rosemary A., and Russell N. Sheptak. 2021. "Becoming One or Many: Material Mediation of Difference." In *Material Hybridity: Archaeologies of Cultural Contact*, ed. Timothy Clack and Marcus Brittain. In press. Oxford University Press.

Joyce, Rosemary A., and Russell N. Sheptak. 2016. "Queering Being in the Colonial Pueblo de San Fernando de Omoa, Honduras." Under review for *Historical Archaeology*.

Joyce, Rosemary A., Russell N. Sheptak, and Laurie Wilkie. 2008. "Arqueología y la comunidad y la Fortaleza de Omoa: un informe sobre la marcha de los trabajos." Simposio Internacional *Esclavitud, Ciudadania y Memoria: Puertos Menores en el Caribe y el Atlantico*, November 13–16, 2008. Honduras: Museo de Antropología e Historia de San Pedro Sula, y Fortaleza San Fernando de Omoa.

Lave, Jean, and Etienne Wenger. 1991. *Situated Learning: Legitimate Peripheral Participation*, Cambridge, UK: Cambridge University Press.

Lave, Jean, and Etienne Wenger. 2005. "Practice, Person, Social World." In *An Introduction to Vygotsky*, ed. Harry Daniels. London: Routledge.

Mihok, Lorena, and E. Christian Wells. 2014. "Miskitu Labor and English Royalization at Augusta, Roatán Island, Honduras." *International Journal of Historical Archaeology* 18:100–121.

Palka, Joel. 2005. *Unconquered Lacandon Maya: Ethnohistory and Archaeology of Indigenous Culture Change*. Gainesville: University Press of Florida.

Sheptak, Russell N. 2007. "Los Toqueguas de la costa Norte de Honduras en la época colonial." *Yaxkin* 13:140–157.

Sheptak, Russell N. 2009. Untangling Words: Dialogic Analysis and Social Fields in Historical Documents. Paper presented at the 43rd annual meeting of the Society for Historical Archaeology, Amalia Plantation, Florida.

Sheptak, Russell N. 2013. "Colonial Masca in Motion: Tactics of Persistence of a Honduran Indigenous Community." Unpublished PhD dissertation, Faculty in Archaeology, Leiden University, Netherlands.

Sheptak, Russell N., and Kira Blaisdell-Sloan. 2014. "Indigenous Lifeways in Colonial Honduras: Communities of Practice at Omoa and Ticamaya." Prepared for *Between Worlds: Ancient Lifeways in Honduras and the Intermediate Area*, ed. Virginia Ochoa-Winemiller and Terance L. Winemiller. Under review by University of Alabama Press.

Sheptak, Russell N., Kira Blaisdell-Sloan, and Rosemary A. Joyce. 2011a. "In-Between People in Colonial Honduras: Reworking Sexualities at Ticamaya." In *The Archaeology of Colonialism: Intimate Encounters and Sexual Effects*, ed. Barbara L. Voss and Eleanor Casella, 156–172. Cambridge, UK: Cambridge University Press.

Sheptak, Russell, Kira Blaisdell-Sloan, and Rosemary A. Joyce. 2011b. "Pragmatic Choices, Colonial Lives: Resistance, Ambivalence, and Appropriation in Northern Honduras." In *Enduring Conquests*, ed. Matthew Liebmann and Melissa Murphy, 149–172. Santa Fe, NM: School for Advanced Research.

Sunseri, Kojun. 2014. "Hiding in Plain Sight: Engineered Colonial Landscape and Indigenous Reinvention on the New Mexican Frontier." In *Rethinking Colonial Pasts through Archaeology*, ed. Neal Ferris, Rodney Harrison, and Michael Wilcox, 173–190. Oxford, UK: Oxford University Press.

Valles Perez, Erick. 2002. Excavaciones en Black River, La Mosquitia. Un Asentamiento Colonial Inglés En Honduras. Paper presented at the 6th Congreso Centroamericano de Historia, Panama City, Panama. http://www.hcentroamerica .fcs.ucr.ac.cr/Contenidos/hca/cong/mesas/cong6/docs/HistCol/evallesp.rtf.

Voss, Barbara. 2008. *The Archaeology of Ethnogenesis: Race and Sexuality in Colonial San Francisco*. Berkeley: University of California Press.

Weeks, John. 1997. "The Mercedarian Mission System in Santa Bárbara de Tencoa, Honduras." In *Approaches to the Historical Archaeology of Mexico, Central and South America*, ed. Janine Gasco, Greg Smith, and Patricia Fournier-Garcia, 91–100. Los Angeles: Cotsen Institute of Archaeology, UCLA.

Weeks, John, and Nancy Black. 1991. "Mercedarian Missionaries and the Transformation of Lenca Society in Western Honduras, 1550–1700." In *Columbian Consequences*, Volume 3: *The Spanish Borderlands in Pan American Perspective*, ed. David H. Thomas, 245–261. Washington, DC: Smithsonian Institution Press.

Weeks, John, Nancy Black, and J. Stuart Speaker. 1987. "From Prehistory to History in Western Honduras: The Care Lenca in the Colonial Province of Tencoa." In *Interaction on the Southeast Mesoamerican Frontier*, Part 1, ed. Eugenia J. Robinson, 65–94. Oxford. UK: BAR.

Weik, Terrance. 2004. "Archaeology of the African Diaspora in Latin America." *Historical Archaeology* 38:32–49.

Wonderley, Anthony. 1984. "Rancho Ires Phase (Colonial) Test Excavations." In *Archaeology in Northwestern Honduras: Interim Reports of the Proyecto Arquologico Sula*, Volume 1, ed. J. Henderson, 67–73. Ithaca, NY: Cornell University Archaeology Program–Latin American Studies Program.

10

The Politics of Ethnic Identity in the Context of the "Frontier"

Ethnohistory of the Lenca, Chortí, and Nahua Peoples of Honduras

Gloria Lara-Pinto

DOI: 10.5876/9781646420971.c010

UNDERSTANDING THE PRESENT THROUGH THE PAST . . .[1]

For precolumbian native populations in Honduras on the eve of the Spanish contact, migrations, invasions, conquests, and the imposition—or even welcome reception—of new religious ideologies, technologies, and languages were commonplace. The ethnohistory of the Lenca peoples is relatively well documented; on the other hand, however, much less is known about the Chortí[2] or the later-arriving Nahua groups. Any attempt to isolate the Chortí and Nahua data gets tangled up, sooner rather than later, with events concerning the ancient Lenca territory. Therefore, the search for an explanation requires an in-depth analysis of the context of the "frontier," even before the rise of the historical social formation of Mesoamerica as such. Furthermore, the late Nahua juxtaposition in the borderland shared with today's El Salvador, as well as in the lower Motagua and Chamelecón Rivers, tempered the ancestry of the "original native people"—say, the proto-Lenca population. Hence, the aim here is to contribute to the understanding of the scenario of the Lenca-Chortí-Nahua-Pipil "frontier" at the time of the conquest.

Even after decades of studying the primary documents of the contact period in Honduras and its neighboring regions, this remote past continues to be quite elusive. Whilst the landscape has certainly changed over the past five centuries, and even more over the last millennia, many revealing features remain in the human and physical geography that can attest to the past. Of course, I am referring to an imperfect approximation to that reality, which will surely become itself the subject of future revisions. Moreover, "the past is, by definition, a datum which nothing in the future will change. But the knowledge of the past is something progressive which is constantly transforming and perfecting itself" (Bloch 1953:58).

The evidence discussed below has been systematically collected (Lara-Pinto 1980, 1983, 1985, 1986, 1991, 1996, 2001, 2009, 2011), yet is by no means exhaustive, in search of alternative explanations of the facts concerning indigenous life as described in historical documents. These documents are fraught with contradictions, the products of the diverging interests guiding their notation and the temporal distance between the events and their transcription. Furthermore, in Honduras there is an absence of documents written by native protagonists during the Spanish contact. Thus, these accounts still raise a series of questions: Who were these natives, ethnically and linguistically speaking? How long ago had they settled in their territories? How complex was their political organization? What circumstances favored their unified mobilization against the Spanish invasion? What internal factors contributed to the fragmentation of the indigenous social structure? What endogenous and external causes contributed to the loss of native languages?

Certain similarities between the populations circumscribed within the territories of modern Honduras and neighboring Guatemala and El Salvador allow for comparisons. However, in the spirit of Marc Bloch, this common ground also highlights the unique cultural elements of the populations converging in it (Sewell 1967:209). Thus, within a strictly "local" vision may lie a tendency to extrapolate apparently explanatory causes to broader phenomena, while in turn, a converse danger is that generalizations across phenomena may obscure the fundamental aspects and causes of local events (Sewell 1967:210). Consequently, the guideline to follow—in an apparently straightforward manner—consists of sketching an adequate comparative framework that allows for the recognition of phenomena of a general order, without underestimating the explicative power of local conditions (Sewell 1967:211). How do we decide, then, upon adequate units of comparison? How do we establish the appropriate geographic context within which these units could be subject to comparison? Bloch suggests geographic proximity and historic contemporaneity as starting points, under the consideration that social systems can and do interact with each other and may even have common roots (Sewell 1967:214–215). The interest here lies in how far Bloch's proposal can take us in widening our understanding of the sociopolitical native structures in pre- and postconquest Honduras.

In accord with Fredrik Barth, boundaries are the very fertile ground for the maintenance of ethnic groups or, more concretely, of their differences. Geographic and social isolation have not been the critical factors in sustaining cultural diversity, for "ethnic distinctions do not depend on an absence of social interaction and acceptance, but are quite to the contrary often the very foundations on which embracing social systems are built" (Barth 1998:9–10). Furthermore, Barth argues that "the cultural contents of ethnic dichotomies would seem analytically to be of two orders: (i) overt signals or signs . . . and (ii) basic value orientations . . . [However,] one cannot predict from first principles which features will be emphasized and made organizationally relevant by the actors" (Barth 1998:14).

The resilience exhibited by Lenca people until the present day is manifested in the retention of the core of their ancestral territory—central and southwest Honduras. Their common origin was reinforced by very distinct cultural patterns, implemented by mechanisms that regrouped the Lenca in times of crisis despite all the possible internal conflicts. While the boundaries to the east seem to have risen gradually on shared ground over millennia, to the west the natural barrier represented by the Motagua River might have signaled the extent of their territory, especially during the last three millennia BC. This may have been the case given the historical formation—Mesoamerica—that was emerging in the neighboring highlands and beyond (see Campbell 1997; Campbell and Kaufman 1985; Campbell et al. 1986; England 1994). The dispersal of proto-Mayan speakers began at least ca. 2000 BC, initially to the far northwest, followed by steady migrations to the south, north, and finally the southeast and east, creating a frontier as they approached and eventually entered the boundaries of proto-Lenca territory. The concept of a *floating frontier*, defined as a "social space of cultural hybridization, a space where the identity of oneself transforms very rapidly accordingly to the inherited perspectives and the changing forces that affect social reality" (Giménez 2007:26), seems adequate to characterize this state of things.

The frontier under discussion is known in the literature as the *Southeastern Mesoamerican frontier*, a term that introduces the notion of subordination of the original ancient Lenca settlers, traditionally undetermined by research, by new immigrants, namely the Maya. This approach has reduced the possible outcomes of this encounter: conquest and active resistance, formalized complementary commercial transactions, negotiation of the interactions to certain times and locations, and of course domination and passive resistance.

In each case, "boundaries may persist despite what may figuratively be called the 'osmosis' of personnel through them" (Barth 1998:21).

THE GENERAL CONTEXT: THE "LENMICHI" AS
THE ORIGINAL NATIVE PEOPLE

The extension and limits of the ancestral Lenca territory continues to be an unfinished discussion. So far, archaeological research has reinforced the perspective of the relatively recent arrival of Ch'ol speakers (proto-Ch'orti) to the Copán Valley and eastern El Salvador in the year AD 100 (e.g., Sharer 2009:131) from the central and northern regions of what is currently Guatemala. Given that they did not arrive in a vacant space, the immediate question is with whom these Ch'ol speakers might have shared this territory with, or, conversely, who might have been displaced from it upon their arrival. Adolfo Constenla's (2011:136) posthumous legacy in linguistic research provides a more cogent outlook. He argued for the millennia-old presence of the "Lenmichi" microphylum (Lencan, Misumalpan, and Chibchan languages) in Central America, from which the Lencan language family separated around 5000 BC. This thesis propounds the deep historic origins of the Lenca people in Honduras and El Salvador. The Nahua migrations are far later than the Maya, and there is ample consensus that the Nahua first enter this territory as early as AD 800 until AD 1300 (Fowler 1989).

Constenla (2011) postulated that the Lenmichi microphylum separated 10,000 years ago, into proto-Misulencan and proto-Chibchan; furthermore, proto-Misulencan split into proto-Lencan and proto-Misumalpan about 7,000 years ago. His cumulative research (1987, 1991, 2002, 2008, 2011) disproved, once and for all, the notion that the Lenca was a language isolate (figure 10.1). Finally, Constenla also highlighted the role played by Honduras in the following terms: "In the Central American territory, Honduras, being the region where languages of the three groups [Lencan, Misumalpan and Chibchan] were present, it would have been the original settlement of the proto-Lenmichi speakers; from here, their descendants would have dispersed toward the south" (2011:136).

Besides historical linguistics, paleoecological "dates overlap with previous genetic dates suggesting Chibchan populations originated between 14,000 and 8000 ya" (Barrantes et al. 1990 in Melton 2008:189); more accurately, they diverged from earlier Paleoindian groups between 10,000 and 8,000 years ago (Melton 2008:iii). Constenla also saw his argument reinforced by archaeological research at the El Gigante rockshelter in southwest Honduras which is, so far, the most ancient locus of occupation in the northern part of the isthmus

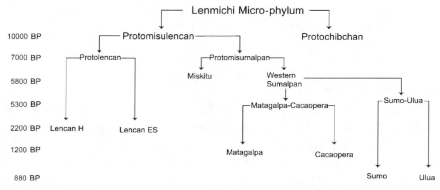

Figure 10.1. *Lenmichi microphylum. (Elaborated by the author from Constenla 2011 and Moreira González 2010.)*

(Scheffler 2008; Scheffler et al. 2012; see also Figueroa and Scheffler, chapter 2, this volume), in the heart of the ancestral Lenca territory.

The earliest document to be discussed here is the so-called Egerton Map (Denucé 1910). It was drawn ca. 1514, based on the 1508–1509[3] voyage of discovery along the coast of Honduras, in which the place names Chavana, Petegua, and Poton were pinpointed along the coast. Rudolf Schuller proposed, nearly a century ago (1929:318), that toponyms endings in *-hua, -gua,* and *-wua* in northwest Honduras originated from the Lenca language: for instance *Petegua, Omoa, Ulua/Oloa,* but also *Chavana, Tolian, Amatique,* and *Manabique.* Schuller's rather straightforward conclusion was that Lenca people had originally occupied the region around the Ulúa River and into the Amatique Gulf, and that Lenca speakers would have been superseded by Maya groups before the Spanish invasion. For his part, Walter Lehmann also pointed carefully to the affinity of Lenca with Cacaopera, Matagalpa, Sumo, and Miskito, and further with Paya and other Chibchan Languages (1920:641). Besides, Lehmann acknowledged, "a certain relationship between Lenca and Xinca, maybe based on loans, especially by the numerals, [which] speak for a former spatial context of both peoples" (1920:646). In addition, he hinted that Xinca and Lenca people were the original inhabitants of northern Central America (1920:643).

In accordance with William Gates's map (1934), Ch'olti' was spoken from the Lake Izabal to the sea. The Ch'orti' language covered from the east shore of the lower Motagua River, including Zacapa and Copán to the south, and the complete course of the Chamelecón River[4] to the lower Ulúa River. These limits were proposed for a period relatively late between AD 1000 and 1500, and may correspond to the maximal extension of the influence of the Maya around AD 1000. Lehmann also agreed with a historic Ch'orti' occupation in the lower Motagua (1920:719), but was puzzled by the existence there of a town named *Amatique*, then he assigned all the place names ending in *-tique*, *-quin/aiquin*, and *-guara* to the Lenca (1920:636). In fact, this very place name *Amatique*, together with *Quelepa* and *Sensembra*, were also identified in eastern El Salvador by Lehmann as definitely Lenca, despite his reluctance to award ethnic identity based solely on toponyms (1920:719, 722). Were these Indians of Amatique themselves the survivors of the proto-Lenca population, the "original native people," as Lehmann called them (1920:643)?

Later works (e.g., Campbell 2013; Joyce 1991; Sheptak 2007; Thompson 1970) revisited this proposal from different perspectives. Thompson added to this list additional *-gua* toponyms present in Honduras, El Salvador, and even Nicaragua, and stressed their connection with the Misumalpan language family (1970:98–99). Joyce argued that "the language of this area was a dialect of Lenca, with a long history of contact with Cholan, specifically Chortí . . . and a less extensive history of contact with Nahuatl-influenced Yucatec as a language of status" (1991:17). Following Feldman (1975), Joyce (1991) further states that "Toquegua, a language recorded for the northern Motagua Valley . . . is a comparable example. Lists of Toquegua personal names[5] include some with Cholan, some with Nahuatl, and a majority not interpretable as either. Toquegua itself may be identifiable as a Lenca word." The evasive Toquegua emerged in 1536 in the town name *Touqueba* (Repartimiento de San Pedro 1911 [1536]) on the eastern shore of the Motagua River. This is confirmed for 1598 by an official report informing that, three leagues before the site called Quiriguá, the land between the Techin River[6] (a tributary of the Motagua) and the bays of Manabique and Amatique belonged to the Toquegua (Criado de Castilla 1605 in Feldman 1998:8). Lehmann expressed doubts that Toquegua was a language by itself and suspected it could represent the remains of Nahua warriors[7] (1920:635–636). Even Nahua merchants might have sought refuge among the Lenca population in response to the Spanish invasion.[8] On the other hand, Campbell (2013:437) is more cautious: "It is interesting in this case that J. Eric S. Thompson . . . concluded from places names ending in *-agua*, *-ahua*, *-gua* and *-hua*, that there had been what he called an '*Agua* people' in the region, a non-Mayan people who were displaced by invading lowland Maya (Chortí speakers) . . . On closer inspection, however, many of Thompson's *-agua* place names appear to be based on Xincan."

Sheptak (2007:150–153) contests this argument by analyzing the personal name *Çoçumba*, the main overlord in the Ulúa Valley[9] at the time of contact, with the information provided by Campbell himself (1976) on the Lenca of Honduras and El Salvador.[10] Yet, another piece of information provided by Campbell is of relevance here: "it is assumed that names which are not analyzable are older and that toponyms which can be analyzed into component morphemes are younger. [Sapir] explains the logic of this: the longer a country has been occupied, the more do the names of its topographical features and villages tend to become purely conventional and to lose what descriptive meaning they originally possessed" (Campbell 2013:437).

This background suggests that the northwestern part of Honduras was also Lenca, a notion that Joyce (1991:18) extends to the Naco Valley, which agrees with research focused directly on this region (Schortman et al. 2001; Schortman and Urban 2011a, 2011b; Urban and Schortman 1999; Wonderley 1986), while others argue for a more nuanced approach to the notion of non-Maya people in the Ulúa Valley, at least in the Classic period (see Hudson and Henderson 2014). However, by the time of the Spanish conquest a more complex frontier situation had already developed there and the Lenca, as well as the Ch'orti', were confronting advances from the south from the already firmly established Nahua-Pipil immigrants.

There is still some discussion that needs to take place concerning the Xinca populations, which currently occupy a reduced portion of Pacific Guatemala near the border with El Salvador, where most toponyms in question are clustered. However, this could be the result of the constriction of the territory by immigrants in prehispanic times. As the author of the most recent and thorough study on the Xinca people and language puts it:

> Given the vagueness of the geographical reconstruction of the language area, the identification of potential contact languages of Xinka is rather problematic. We may assume that at the time of the Spanish conquest Xinka-speaking settlements were surrounded by the Pipil in the west and by Mayan-speaking population . . . The significant number of loanwords from Western and Eastern Mayan languages proves intensive cultural contacts between Xinka and Maya speakers, although the time-depth of these contacts is another matter of discussion . . . East of the Xinka area, the contact situation is even more opaque . . . and the exact expansion of Pipil and Lenka is not known. (Sachse 2010:47)

Campbell and Kaufman (in Sachse 2010:51) had already contested the well-known "Xinca-Lenca hypothesis" based on their estimation that the genetic relation of both languages cannot be proven. Nonetheless, following Sachse, the Xinca can be considered to share some features of material culture with their Lenca neighbors. Additionally, the Xinca language exhibits a few typological proper ties that are not typical for the Mesoamerican linguistic area, and shares several terms with Lenca and Matagalpa; however, "the direction of borrowing is mostly unclear" (Sachse 2010:53, 56). Constenla's (2011) proposal about the common origin of Lenca and Matagalpa (Misulencan) has bearing on this discussion. This evidence suggests provocative questions: Could the Lenca along with the Xinca and the Matagalpa indeed be the "Agua people"? Furthermore, did they constitute the ancestry of the elusive "Agua country" in the ancient past?

THE LOCAL CONTEXT: SOCIAL ORGANIZATION AND ETHNIC AFFILIATION AT THE TIME OF CONTACT

The Spanish exploration of Honduras began in 1502 and continued into the decade of 1520 with expeditions arriving from the Antilles, Panama, and Mexico. This stage of exploration is characterized by short expeditions into the territory, at times with devastating effects. Although these initial explorations seemed erratic, the conquest mobilizations—from Mexico and Guatemala—resumed in 1524 and slowly revealed the prevailing native political geography (figure 10.2). During these expeditions, some of the territorial units, designated by the Spanish as "provinces," progressively began to emerge as significant. These provinces were disarticulated shortly after, as in the case of the Papayeca-Chapagua, Peiçacura, and Olancho provinces in the northeastern and eastern valleys, along with the Choluteca-Malalaca province in the southern lowlands. The conquest and colonization activities taking place in the coast and alluvial plains in the northwest (1530–1536) led to the emergence of the Naco and Çoçumba provinces. Before long, incursions were organized into the western mountain range, which encountered the limits of the Cerquín province. Subsequent conquests resulted in the delimitation of the provinces of Los Cares and Sulaco-Maniani in the central depression and its surroundings (Hasemann and Lara-Pinto 1993; Lara-Pinto 1980; Lara-Pinto 1991). In 1540, the conquest's enterprises had been consummated, leaving untouched for the time being the objective of the evangelizing mission in the ancestral territories inhabited by the protohistoric Jicaques as well as by the Misumalpan peoples, the historic Taguzgalpa (Lara-Pinto 1980; Lara-Pinto and Hasemann 1995) (figure 10.3).

In sum, the available evidence points to an ethnic affiliation shared by the provinces in central and southwestern Honduras—Sulaco-Maniani, Los Cares, and Cerquín—which are identified as Lenca (Lara-Pinto 1991:225; compare with Chapman 1978:25). Naco and Çoçumba, in the northwest, while

FIGURE 10.2. *Entries into Honduras and neighboring regions during the Spanish conquest, 1524–1536.*

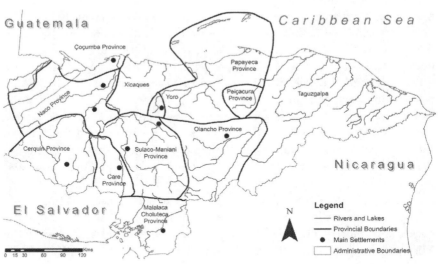

FIGURE 10.3. *Indigenous provinces in Honduras, ca. 1500. (From Lara-Pinto 1980.)*

maintaining their primary Lenca affiliation, seem to have been immersed in an ongoing frontier situation (Lara-Pinto 2001; Sheptak 2007).

To understand the local dynamics that led to the complex formation processes indigenous societies went through before conquest, a regional perspective proves necessary. The regionalism favored by the rough topography of Honduras was counteracted by the fact that this same territory was an obligatory north–south route, and vice versa. Therefore, while maintaining political control over their provinces, the Lenca established trading networks amongst each other and with external agents. Whereas neighboring Nahua-Pipil political entities in El Salvador maintained armies (Fowler 1988:86–96) to inhibit any latent external menace, the Lenca employed ritualized means to secure internal peace—the *guancasco*—through "peace accords in certain times of the year," effective among groups that shared a common language but who belonged to different factions, towns, or even political entities (Herrera, in Chapman 1978:17). This very mechanism proved to be instrumental in confronting external interference.

INDIGENOUS *SEÑORÍOS*

Documentary sources dating to the contact period (1502–1550) confirm the existence of political units of the kind known as *señoríos* or *cacicazgos*. This refers to ranked societies, also called chiefdoms (see Drennan and Uribe 1987:vii–xii), which in Honduras at the time of contact very likely consisted of three differentiated levels of political control. The overlord or *cacique general* (indigenous Lenca terms are unknown) exercised authority over regions defined by certain geographic features. The political centers and seat of an overlord in these territorial jurisdictions were generally found at the core of alluvial valleys, surrounded by subordinate settlements or *pueblos sujetos*, and an indefinite number of smaller localities called *barrios* or *estancias*, all of them administered by *principales* or minor-ranking *caciques* (Lara-Pinto 1980:76; 1991:220; Lara-Pinto and Hasemann 1995:183).

Ostensibly, the premises for the political configuration of an indigenous province would have been the recognition of a shared ethnicity, reinforced by use of a common language (Herrera, in Chapman 1978:17; Lara-Pinto 1991:222–225; compare with Gómez, chapter 11, this volume). However, this does not imply that these provinces or *señoríos* remained static in their arrangements. In fact, they must have experienced a series of fluctuations in their composition and extension as the result of multiple factors. Moreover, historic sources point to the existence of smaller political units incorporated into greater geopolitical territories due to marriage alliances (Lara-Pinto 1991:226–231). Conversely, dissidence and armed conflict may have also ensued due to expansionist endeavors, and there are strong indications that this was the case, as suggested by the custom of peace accords in certain times of the year. In fact, it is very likely that conflict between rival lineages within the same *señorío* escalated to armed confrontations (Herrera, in Chapman 1978:22; Fuentes y Guzmán 1933:203–209).[11] This capacity to establish strategic alliances by appealing to a shared Lenca ethnicity functioned as a means to maintain a "floating frontier," particularly to the south of the Cerquin province, which faced the powerful Nahua-Pipil state of Cuscatlán (Fowler 1989) that sought to expand into Lenca territory, as will be evident later. Shifts of the Chortí populations away from their enclave in El Salvador[12] and from nuclear territory on the eastern bank of the Motagua River in Guatemala seem to have responded, in part, to the same population pressures provoked by the Nahua-Pipil prior to the Spanish conquest (Van Akkeren 2007).

In the end, the administrative districts of early Spanish settlements were superimposed over indigenous territorial jurisdictions to consolidate their control over these native provinces. The incipient colonial administration took advantage of the native geopolitical setting to justify the breadth of indigenous towns entrusted in *encomiendas*. Further, this very strategy also contributed to co-opting the allegiance local populations had to their *señores naturales*, while progressively imposing a new logic of administration, order, and subordination. The changes that ensued in the original settlement patterns of native populations took place relatively late in the case of the conquest and colonization of Honduras in comparison to other regions (see Fernández and Urquijo 2006). As a result, it is still possible today to corroborate the locations of a great majority of the native towns that were allocated in 1536 among the Spanish conquerors, and their identification on the ground allowed for the sketching out of the borders of the ancient Lenca political entities (Lara-Pinto 1980) (table 10.1). The two principal allocations of *encomiendas* took place in mid-1536, within five-day intervals. That is the case of the provinces of Çoçumba and Naco, both corresponding to the administrative district of the Spanish foundation of San Pedro, and of the province of Cerquín, belonging to the city of Gracias (Repartimiento de San Pedro 1911; Repartimiento de Gracias a Dios 1911).

TABLE 10.1. Lenca, Maya, and Nahua-Pipil toponyms in the lower Motagua and Chamelecón Rivers

Geographic Orientation	1514 [1508–1509] Egerton Map	1536 Repartimiento of San Pedro	1605 [1598] Report of Criado de Castilla
On the coast.	Chivana, Pentigua, Poton	Techuacan, Tecucaste, Comoa, Chichiagual	
In the mountain ranges by the sea.		Quelepa, Chabana, Tolian, Petegua, Yama, Xocolo, Maxcaba	
On the Río Balahama (Choloma).		Choloma, Teocunitad, Milon, Conta, Chulula, Pocoy, Lama	
Valley of Naco.		Naco, Quimistan, Tapalampa, Tetacapa, Copáninque, Coluta, Tenestepat, Conalagua, Acapusteque	
Town subordinated to Naco.		Ilamatepet	
Next to the town of Naco.		Chapoapa, Motochiapa	
In the mountain ranges by the Valley of Naco.		Chumbagua, Palapa, Maciguata, Petoa, Acachianyt	
On the road to Guatemala.		Laque, Chapoli/Chapulco, Chinamin	
On the tributaries of Río Laula (Motagua).		[Nahuapochteca]*	
Near to Chapulco.		Abalpoton	
Towards and on the Río Laula (Motagua).		Culuacán, Lalaco	
Towards the road to Guatemala.		Cecatan, Temaxacel, Caxeta, La Guela	
On the other side of the Ulúa River, towards the sea.		Touqueba	
Three leagues before the site called Quiriguá, and the land between the Techin River (a Motagua tributary), and the bays of Manabique and Amatique.			Land of the hostile Toquehua Indians

*Naoponchota in the original.

THE GEOPOLITICAL PANORAMA AT THE TIME OF
CONTACT: FROM THE *LONGUE DURÉE* TO THE EVENTS[13]

Prior to Spanish contact, the established transit of populations from different ethnic origins gave way to a frontier situation in the southwestern corner of Lenca territory. Nahua-Pipil speakers dominated the westernmost region of El Salvador and simultaneously advanced north towards the Lempa River, reducing the spaces colonized earlier by the Ch'orti' population, who had ventured as far as the Sensenti Valley within ancestral Lenca territory in the previous centuries. At the same time, it is especially interesting how a settlement in the northern part of present-day Quimistán Valley, to the northwest, surfaced in the records, a place where Nahua-Pipil and "Chontal" speakers—the latter a generic appellative for unidentified peoples (Molina 1970:21)—coexisted. This settlement, called *Naco* in the chronicles, was at its peak on the eve of the Spanish contact (Hasemann 1996:75). It is known that the designation *Chontal* was used in this epoch to refer to Lenca populations (García de Palacio 1983:24); and there is indication that, by extension, it also referred to the Chortí located between Chiquimula and Gracias (Marroquín 1968). Even in the middle of the twentieth century the lowland Ch'orti' referred to the mountain dwelling Chortí as *Chontal* (Girard 1949:5).

Indigenous war tactics provide some clues to understanding the events and the processes interrupted by the Spanish invasion. The fortifications constructed in precontact time—particularly fortified outcrops known as *peñoles*—found in mountain ranges or strategic river fords, were now hindering the access of Europeans and their Mexican allies. This seems to have been the norm among the mountain-dwelling Lenca of Honduras at Cerquín (Gelliot et al. 2011) and the Xinca of El Salvador at Cinacantán (Gallardo Mejía 2014:75; Sachse 2010:46). In the plains, fortifications recorded as *albarradas*—barricaded palisades—were more common, as was the case of the Chortí at Copantes (Lara-Pinto 2014), the Lenca at Ticamaya (Sheptak 2007),[14] and, apparently, among the Lenca of El Salvador at Chaparrastique (Herrera, in Larde y Larín 1958).[15]

The credibility of the names assigned to the Indian lords and *caciques*, and their actual existence, has been widely discussed, and certainly mistakes have been made under the auspices of mestizo nation-building efforts (Alvarenga 2011; Amaroli 1991). Nonetheless, a few names have survived, regardless of their arbitrary spelling, in relation to some indigenous provinces, which supports the existence of native organizational systems. Such considerations also apply to the nomenclature of settlements in the territories demarcated through 1536, and support claims to their actual locations (see Blaisdell-Sloan 2006;

Lara-Pinto 1980; Sheptak 2013). Additionally, the knowledge obtained by Spanish conquistadors, either through direct experience or mediated by their allied informants, proves accurate. Multiple factors play a role here. On the one hand, the conquest campaigns were prolonged over a decade (1523–1536). On the other, the conquest of neighboring territories in El Salvador and Guatemala was accomplished by 1530. The *indios amigos* or "allied Indians" from central Mexico—Tlaxcaltecas, Tenochtecas, and Cholultecas (Restall and Asselbergs 2007)—and those recruited among the Nahua-Pipil of El Salvador were native speakers of Nahua languages, which were at the very least utilized in commercial interactions in the frontier, reaching as far as Lake Izabal. In 1539, the lords and *principales* in the Quimistán Valley had Nahua-Pipil names, some also with calendric attributes (Cereceda 1539 in Lara-Pinto 1980:198–207), and Nahua-Pipil influence probably extended into the Copán Valley (Lara-Pinto 2001).

A COMPARATIVE EXERCISE: GEOGRAPHIC VICINITY AND HISTORIC CONTEMPORANEITY

Sometime around 1530, once the conquest campaigns had ceased in the region of Chiquimula de la Sierra in the Province of Guatemala (Brewer 2009:139, 141), Spanish attention was briefly directed towards Honduras. This is when the quasi-mythical tale of the Indian *cacique* Copán Calel[16] comes to life. Following the invasion, Copán Calel, along with "armed peoples" and provisions (Fuentes y Guzmán 1972:145), assisted the Chortí *cacique* of Esquipulas in battle on the southern frontier. Historic narratives introduce some confusion by calling Copán Calel's *señorío* Copán, which will later be interpreted as referring to the Copán Valley, whereas the very same chronicler clearly states that Citalá was the seat of this *cacique*'s domain (Fuentes y Guzmán 1972:145, 149), a town located immediately across the modern border between Honduras and El Salvador. In other words, this *señorío* encompassed the south of the modern Department of Ocotepeque. Also, the river next to which Copán Calel built his fortification or *albarrada* was called Copán, though it was in fact the Lempa River.[17] The Spanish attacks against Copán Calel's palisade must have encountered serious difficulties, since this *cacique* had allied himself with the *señores* from Zacapa in the northwest, from Sensenti towards the interior of Honduras, as well as Ostua and Guijar in the modern borders between El Salvador and Guatemala, all of whom sent reinforcements (Fuentes y Guzmán 1972:145–146). Later, Copán Calel would also seek, unsuccessfully, support from the towns of Jocotán and Jupilingo,[18] both located further north, near the Copán Valley. After his defeat,

Copán Calel sought refuge in Citalá (figure 10.4). The key point of this discussion is the character of the geopolitical conditions that allowed these alliances to take place within such a large territory. Was it a common language? Was it a shared history in a frontier zone prior to the Spanish conquest? Was it the shared foreign threat they all faced? There is no straight answer to these questions given the actions taken later by the *cacique* Copán Calel against Jocotán and Jupilingo: Copán Calel "decided to disturb those towns with theft, the death of many Indians cultivating the fields, and with hostility, cutting down their crops, taking a great number of creatures for barbaric sacrifices in his public and famous shrine [Guijar?]" (Fuentes y Guzmán 1972:150).

What were the reasons for such aggressions towards Jupilingo and Jocotán? Let us not forget that in the Honduran Lenca territory, the customary practice known as *guancasco* has been documented along the territories neighboring the *señorío* of Copán Calel. But this aggressive behavior raises the following questions: Did they not speak the same language as Citalá, Ostua, Guijar, or Sensenti? If so, did they not share this very Lenca institution of peace treaties, an apparently generalized Chontal custom? Could the estrangement of Jupilingo and Jocotán from Copán Calel be because his *señorío* had closer ties to the neighboring Lenca territory, given that it was on the margins of the Chontal-Chortí territory? Did Jocotán consider Copán Calel's *señorío* a Chontal-Chortí (lencanized) domain rather than a proper Ch'orti' polity? Was Jupilingo under Nahua-Pipil influence, as it seems was the case in the Copán Valley?[19] After these events, Copán Calel suddenly disappears from the written records of the time, and his memory becomes legendary. Yet, a Chortí enclave remained in El Salvador until the end of the eighteenth century (figure 10.4), and Guijar (Lake Güija) remained a place of ritual in the frontier that Nahua-Pipil, Pokoman, Lenca, and Chortí frequently visited still in 1770 (Amaroli 2006; Cortés y Larraz 1958:I:254).

In El Salvador, the Spanish colonization prospered early to the extent that in 1532 it was possible to generate a registry of 90 *encomienda* towns. This record distinguished tributary from nontributary towns, as well as towns that were up in arms, or both. The record also identified which of these towns-in-resistance were located beyond the jurisdiction of the city of San Salvador, or outside of the indigenous province of Cuscatlán. A third of these *encomienda* towns (33) were classified as Chontal—understood as Lenca or Chortí (see *Relación Marroquín* 1532 in Amaroli 1991:45–48, note 16, figure 1), and it seems some of them had been conquered or were in the process of being conquered by the Nahua-Pipil. Although only two of these Chontal-Chortí towns were at war, none of them paid tribute; the remaining Lenca towns, on the contrary,

FIGURE 10.4. *Location of the main settlements on the Lenca-Chortí-Nahua-Pipil frontier, 1530–1539. (Taken from Lara-Pinto 2009 with modifications.)*

were all rebellious. Twelve of the Chontal towns identified by Amaroli are located on the northern and eastern shores of the Lempa River, in the remaining Chortí enclave and in El Salvador's Lenca territory. An effort was made here to complete the identification of towns (e.g., Coatamagaz, Cocoyagua, Colopele, and El Asistente), which Amaroli could not identify, as well as those towns that remained uncertain (e.g., Tepegualpoton, Xocoyuco) in his description. These towns were part of the Repartimiento of San Pedro (1) and the Repartimiento of Gracias (5) in Honduras, along with Tomalá and Corquín, already identified by Amaroli (1991). The towns identified as Chontal-Chortí (7) were all located within the Chortí enclave that endured into the turn of the eighteenth century, which was situated between the northern limits of the Lempa River and the present-day border between El Salvador and Honduras. Most towns identified as Chontal-Lenca (12) were situated in the Province of Cerquín in Honduras, and two more to the south and east of the Lempa River towards the Province of Chaparrastique in El Salvador (figure 10.5).

On the one hand, independently from Honduran documentary sources, the *Relación Marroquín* corroborates the veracity of the frontier context in southwest Honduras described above, including its geopolitics, particularly evident in the *Repartimiento de Gracias*. On the other, it supports the evidence

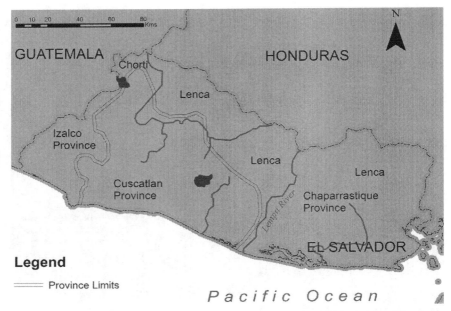

FIGURE 10.5. *Indigenous provinces in El Salvador around 1500. (Adapted from Fowler 1989:140–141, figure 5, with additional information from Lehman 1920:719, with modifications by the author.)*

concerning the permanent indigenous resistance and upheaval against Spanish conquistadors and their allies sustained in Honduras already taking place in 1532. In fact, this state of things continued without a definite Spanish intervention until 1536. This would be the year in which El Asistente or Ocotepeque became the first town in Honduras under colonial governance—a Chontal-Chortí town already under Nahua-Pipil influence (Lehmann, in Girard 1949:7); maybe the same reason Spaniards called it "the adjutant." From here, one can trace the path of destruction followed by Hispanic-Mexican troops into Lenca territory, this time without retreat.

The particularity of these assault troops was their multiethnic composition. This was an army minimally composed of Spanish soldiers and outnumbered by an infantry and logistics provided by hundreds of *indios amigos* coming from faraway places such as Chalco-Tlamanalco or Texcoco (Oudijk and Restall 2008:133; Torres 2011:129). The great majority were simply identified as Tlaxcalteca or Mexica (Lenkersdorf, in Oudijk and Restall 2008:135), and even a small number as Zapoteca (Matthew 2010:127).

IDENTITIES IN THE LENCA-CHORTÍ-PIPIL FRONTIER, 1530–1540: SOME CONCLUSIONS

The panorama sketched out in this chapter demonstrates the resilience of Lenca territory from remote times to the present day, first facing the early advance of Classic Maya populations into the Motagua and Copán Valleys (AD 100–200) followed by a less forceful and short-lived occupation in the Sensenti Valley (AD 600–1000) (Sánchez 2003; see Johnson, chapter 3, this volume, for another approach). The nucleus of Lenca territory also withstood the test of time, enduring five centuries of immigrant Nahua-Pipil populations who established and consolidated complex societies in today's El Salvador, and who had begun to expand into the westernmost bounds of the Chontal-Chortí and Lenca territory towards Ocotepeque, the Quimistán-Naco Valley, and the Copán Valley, maybe with aims to reach the Tencoa Valley. In 1530, Copán Calel's war campaign evidenced the withdrawal of the Chontal-Chortí into the northwestern region of El Salvador, as they had been separated centuries ago from the Ch'orti' core in Guatemala through the Nahua-Pipil wedge. This would explain why Jocotán and Jupilingo did not support Copán Calel against the new invaders, and his ensuing retribution. Copán Calel apparently was a Chontal-Chortí, "a mountain" Chortí, indeed closer to the Lenca by means of centuries of coexistence. Except for Esquipulas, the towns that assisted Copán Calel were in the northwesternmost corner of El Salvador, a Chontal-Chortí stronghold until the end of the eighteenth century. However, one town in the Lenca territory responded, probably Xocuyuco in the Sensenti Valley. This native war campaign also reveals the steady advance of the Nahua-Pipil from El Salvador, as validated by the *Relación Marroquín* of 1532. By then, Ocotepeque was a Nahua-Pipil colony, and so were some towns in the Quimistán-Naco Valley and even the Copán Valley. Hence, Ocotepeque and the Copán-Jupilingo Valley did not participate in battle alongside Copán Calel against the Spanish conquerors.

Western Honduras has been a contested space at least since the separation of proto-Lencan and proto-Misulpan 7,000 years ago, and even more when a wedge was driven between Lenca speakers by Maya immigrants circa 2,000 years ago. We are before a "floating frontier" where decision-makers adopted, when needed, a belligerent position, and differences could be elucidated in open combat or mediated by commerce and diplomacy, or both, depending on the circumstances. However, at the time of contact in the Lenca territory, a Chontal country from the point of view of the Nahua-Pipil neighbors, custom dictated the enactment of peace agreements. Consequently, it made sense that Copán Calel would call upon the general Chontal population—both Lenca and Chortí in the frontier—to set aside their differences and unite against a common enemy (e.g., Xocoyuco-Sensenti, a Lenca town within this porous border attended to his calling). This implies that the Chortí at the time of Copán Calel were already incorporated in this Lenca tradition, which would partially explain why the Lenca and Chortí are all subsumed under the generic term *Chontal* in the *Relación Marroquín* of 1532.

In geopolitical terms, the Spanish invasion interrupted the Nahua-Pipil advance into Honduras. However, the use of Nahua variants as a sort of lingua franca prior to the Spanish contact, facilitated later on by the presence of "Mexican" contingents in the Spanish army, was further reinforced by the permanence of these Mexicans in Honduras. The Spanish conquistadors made use of their Nahuatl interpreters; perhaps among them were Nahua-Pipil recruited directly from El Salvador. Subsequently, colonizers and authorities institutionalized the Nahua-Pipil or "corrupt Mexican," as it was called, as the main language of communication with Lenca speakers (Lara-Pinto 2011), especially among men. This eventually relegated the Lenca language to exclusive use within native communities, private spaces, and in processes of evangelization (Samayoa 1957). This would partly explain how the native language spoken by the majority in Honduras during the sixteenth century fell into disuse within a relatively short period. Indeed, similar reflections would apply to the case of the Chontal-Chortí north of the Lempa River in El Salvador, and by extension in the Ocotepeque region. This was a region once part of the expansion of the nuclear Ch'orti' territory, which later became a Chontal-Chortí enclave in Lenca territory, and was gradually encroached upon by the old Nahua-Pipil state of Cuscatlán during its advance into western Honduras.

ACKNOWLEDGMENTS

Thanks to the Universidad Pedagógica Nacional Francisco Morazán (Tegucigalpa, Honduras), which sponsored the field research and additionally provided me with the time to write this chapter. Thanks also to Ana Hasemann-Lara, who made the initial translation of this chapter and helped me with her many pointed questions to improve the text. Of course, all mistakes are fully my responsibility.

NOTES

1. "Misunderstanding of the present is the inevitable consequence of ignorance of the past. But a man may wear himself out just as fruitlessly in seeking to understand

the past, if he is totally ignorant of the present" (Bloch 1953:43; see also Bloch 1949 in Bédarida 1998:25).

2. The orthographic form *Ch'orti'*, according to the version adopted by the Academia de Lenguas Mayas de Guatemala, is not standardized across Honduras. The Consejo Nacional Indígena Maya Chortí de Honduras (CONIMCHH) website employs the following written forms: *ch'orti, ch'orti', ch'ortí, chortí,* and *Chortí'.* Additionally, in the Honduran Office of Indigenous Peoples and Afrodescendants' (DINAFROH) website the single term utilized is *chortí.* Hence, in this chapter, given the Honduran context, the nomenclature *Chortí* will be used for the historic people in the enclave of El Salvador and its extension in Honduras, and *Ch'orti'* for the people in the nuclear territory of today's Guatemala.

3. Exploration voyage of Vicente Yáñez Pinzón and Juan Díaz de Solis (Schuller 1929:316).

4. Until the end of the seventeenth century, the Chamelecón River was registered in the maps as "Río Pecha, Piche, Puche, Pechey" (e.g., Sanson D'Abbeville 2006).

5. See Feldman (1998:19) for a list of personal names collected among the Toquegua people in 1598.

6. To this day, the Río Techín is also known as the Río Chinamito (http://www .tageo.com/index-e-gt-v-oo-d-m1672354.htm, accessed January 4, 2017), which coincides precisely with the town's name *Chinamin* in the Repartimiento de San Pedro (1911), on the road to Guatemala.

7. In 1605 it was reported that in the main Toquegua settlement were four large houses, each with twenty-four adult male warriors ruled by three lords (Criado de Castillo, in Feldman 1998:16). This statement suggests the survival of some Nahua customs, namely a reminiscence of the war captains called *tequihua* (Gran Diccionario Nahuatl 2012; Lehmann 1920:636).

8. Conclusion prompted by the existence near "Touqueba" and "Chinamin," on the same road to Guatemala, of a town called *Naopochonta* (Repartimiento de San Pedro 1911 [1536]), for which the author proposes the spelling *Nauapochteca.*

9. Cozumbra: "province between the town of San Pedro and Puerto de Caballos" (Pedraza 1868); Río Cozumba: "between Playa Baja and Cabo Tres Puntas, 5 or 6 leagues away from it" (López de Velasco 1971:159).

10. In the Lenca of El Salvador *sho* means "rain" and *camba* or *yamba* is a gerund verb form; *sho* changes in the Lenca of Honduras to *so,* meaning "it is raining" (Sheptak 2007:153).

11. Among the Lenca, men captured in battle became slaves and their noses were cut off (Herrera, in Chapman 1978: 22). The description provided by Fuentes y Guzmán (1933:203–209) is allusive in this context, since the legendary Chortí *cacique*

Copán Calel applied the same procedure to prisoners. This passage reveals this custom prevailed among the Lenca and Chortí as well.

12. The Chortí refuge territory was delimited by the Lempa River to the south and followed part of its course to the east; towards the west, it reached the Güija Lagoon.

13. "[I]t seems that Braudel's longue durée may contain events, if they are produced within adequate narrations, if the suitable queries are made to discover these undisclosed events" (Fogelson 2001:46).

14. Another example would be the *albarrada* of the Chortí *señorío* in Esquipulas (Fuentes y Guzman 1933:178–183), and the fortified site known as Rincón del Jicaque in Ocotepeque, near the border with Guatemala (Girard 1944; Lara-Pinto 2014).

15. Chaparrastique confederated with Quelepa and Moncagua, among others, following the Lenca custom of the *guancasco*.

16. The name *Copán Calel* gives way to two interpretations; the first from Nahuatl, *quauhpantli/quappantli*, and from *cale*, which results in [*Quauhpantli Cale*]: "owner or lord of the house on the wooden bridge" (Molina 1970:85, 93). The second interpretation conserves the term *quauhpantli*, but the second term corresponds to a nobility title in Quiche-Maya, *q'alel*, "he who shines" (Van Akkaren 2007:17). This name composed of terms originating from different languages in the Lenca-Chortí-Nahua-Pipil frontier is quite evocative.

17. The troops starting their journey in Esquipulas probably followed an indigenous path later converted into a *camino real* and now fallen into disuse, leading into a location in Honduras preserved in oral history as *Llano de la Conquista*. On this small plain, on the north shore of the Lempa River, the author argues the battle against the Spanish invaders took place (Lara-Pinto 2014). To the present day, the site called *Rincón del Jicaque* has been associated with Copantes, Copán Calel's fortification. In the author's opinion, this does not yet correspond with the geographic features first described in Fuentes y Guzmán (1972:149). Rincón del Jicaque is situated on a margin high over the riverbed (compare with Girard 1949:65 and Brewer 2009:139; see also Ubico et al. 2001).

18. This name is preserved today as *Jupilingo River*, which merges with the Copán River in a point located just west of the border between Honduras and Guatemala. Although the name *Copán* still designates this river on Guatemalan territory, the valley associated with it is called indistinctly *Copán* or *Jupilingo*.

19. The word *Jupilingo* is quite suggestive; from *Xopilli-n-co*. Xopilli was the name of one of the flags used by Aztec military/warriors/armies (Torres 2011:149).

WORKS CITED

Alvarenga, Patricia. 2011. "El futuro y la lectura del pasado: Historias dignas de naciones dignas." *Cuadernos Intercambio* 8(9):57–83.

Amaroli, Paul. 1991. "Linderos y geografía económica de Cuscatlán, provincia pipil del territorio de El Salvador." *Mesoamérica* 21:41–70.

Amaroli, Paul. 2006. *Informe sobre el sitio arqueológico de Igualtepeque y la amenazas que enfrenta.* Manuscript on file. San Salvador, El Salvador: Archives of the Fundación Nacional de Arqueología de El Salvador.

Barth, Fredrik. 1998 (1969). *Ethnic Groups and Boundaries: The Social Organization of Culture Difference.* Long Grove, IL: Waveland Press.

Bédarida, François. 1998. "Definición, método y práctica de la historia del tiempo presente." *Cuadernos de Historia Contemporánea* 20: 19–27.

Blaisdell-Sloan, Kira. 2006. "An Archaeology of Place and Self: The Pueblo de Indios of Ticamaya (AD 1300–1800)." Unpublished PhD dissertation, Department of Anthropology, University of California, Berkeley.

Bloch, Marc. 1953. *The Historian's Craft: Reflections on the Nature and Uses of History and the Techniques and Methods of Those Who Write It.* New York: Vintage Books.

Brewer, Stewart. 2009. "The Ch'orti' Maya of Eastern Guatemala under Imperial Spain." In *The Ch'orti' Maya Area: Past and Present,* ed. Brent Metz, Cameron L. McNeil, and Kerry M. Hull, 137–149. Gainesville: University of Florida Press.

Campbell, Lyle. 1976. "The Last Lenca." *International Journal of American Linguistics* 42(1):73–78.

Campbell, Lyle. 1997. *American Indian Languages: The Historical Linguistics of Native America.* Oxford Studies in Anthropological Linguistics. 4. New York: Oxford University Press.

Campbell, Lyle. 2013 [1998]. *Historical Linguistics: An Introduction.* Edinburgh, UK: Edinburgh University Press.

Campbell, Lyle, and Terrence Kaufman. 1985. "Mayan Linguistics: Where are We Now?" *Annual Review of Anthropology* 14(1):187–198.

Campbell, Lyle, Terrence Kaufman, and Thomas C. Smith-Stark. 1986. "Meso-America as a Linguistic Area." *Language* 62(3):530–570.

Cereceda, Andrés de. 1539. *Bienes de Andrés de Cereceda. San Pedro del Puerto de Caballos,* 17 de septiembre-24 de octubre de 1539. Contaduría 987 (27 f.). Sevilla, Spain: Archivo General de Indias.

Chapman, Anne. 1978. *Los Lencas de Honduras en el Siglo XVI.* Tegucigalpa, Honduras: Instituto Hondureño de Antropología e Historia.

Constenla Umaña, Adolfo. 1987. "Elementos de fonología comparada de las lenguas misumalpa." *Revista de Filología y Lingüística de la Universidad de Costa Rica* 13(1):129–161.

Constenla Umaña, Adolfo. 1991. *Las lenguas del Area Intermedia: Una introducción a su estudio areal.* San José, Costa Rica: Universidad de Costa Rica.

Constenla Umaña, Adolfo. 2002. "Acerca de la relación genealógica de las lenguas lencas y las lenguas misumalpas." *Revista de Filología y Lingüística de la Universidad de Costa Rica* 28(1):189–205.

Constenla Umaña, Adolfo. 2008. "Estado actual de la subclasificación de las lenguas chibchenses y de la reconstrucción fonológica y gramatical del protochibchense." *Estudios de Lingüística Chibcha* 27:117–135.

Constenla Umaña, Adolfo. 2011. "Estado de la conservación y documentación de las lenguas de América Central pertenecientes a las agrupaciones jicaque, lenca, misumalpa, chibchense y chocó." *Revista de Filología y Lingüística de la Universidad de Costa Rica* 37(1):135–195.

Cortés y Larráz, Pedro. 1958 [1770]. "Descripción Geográfico-Moral de la Diócesis de Goathemala, 1770." *Biblioteca* Goathemala Library. Guatemala City: Sociedad de Geografía e Historia de Guatemala.

Denucé, Jean. 1910. "The Discovery of the North Coast of South America according to an Anonymous Map in the British Museum." *Geographical Journal* 36:65–80, 128.

Drennan, Robert D., and Carlos A. Uribe, eds. 1987. *Chiefdoms of the Americas*. Lanham, MD: University Press of America.

England, Nora C. 1994. *Autonomia de los idiomas mayas: Historia e identidad. (Ukuta'miil Ramaq'iil Utzijob'aal ri Maya' Amaaq')*. Guatemala: Cholsamaj.

Feldman, Lawrence H. 1975. *Riverine Maya: The Toquegua and Other Chols of the Lower Motagua Valley*. Columbia: University of Missouri Museum of Anthropology.

Feldman, Lawrence H. 1998. *Motagua Colonial*. Raleigh, NC: C&M Online Media.

Fernández Chistlieb, Federico, and Pedro S. Urquijo Torres. 2006. "Los espacios del pueblo de indios tras el proceso de congregación, 1550–1625." *Investigaciones Geográficas* 60:145–158.

Fogelson, Raymond D. 2001. "La etnohistoria de los eventos y de los eventos nulos." *Desacatos* 7:36–48.

Fowler, William, Jr. 1988. "La población nativa del El Salvador al momento de la conquista española." *Mesoamérica* 9(15):80–106.

Fowler, William, Jr. 1989. *The Cultural Evolution of Ancient Nahua Civilizations: The Pipil-Nicarao of Central America*. Norman: University of Oklahoma Press.

Fuentes y Guzmán, Francisco A. 1933. *Recordación Florida*. Guatemala: Biblioteca Goathemala. Sociedad de Geografía e Historia, Guatemala.

Fuentes y Guzmán, Francisco A. 1969–1972. *Obras Históricas de Don Francisco Antonio de Fuentes y Guzmán*. I–III. Madrid, Spain: Ediciones Atlas.

Gallardo Mejía, Francisco R. 2014. "El sitio arqueológico de Zinancantán: Primer levantamiento indígena de Cuscatlán." *Revista de Museología Kóot* 4(5):61–85.

García de Palacio, Diego. 1983 [1576]. *Carta-Relación, Relación y Forma de Diego García de Palacio Oidor de la Audiencia de Guatemala 1576*. Mexico City, Mexico: Universidad Nacional Autónoma de México.

Gates, William. 1934. *Map of the Mayance Nations and Languages (AD 1000–1500) Prepared for the Maya Society Quarterly*. Columbus Memorial Library (World Digital Library. Library of Congress). Washington, DC: Panamerican Union. https://www.wdl.org/en/item/11311/, accessed January 3, 2017.

Gelliot, Eric, Philippe Costa, Simon Mercier, and Sebastian Perrot-Minot. 2011. *Informe Final del Proyecto Arqueológico Lempira*. Manuscript on file. Tegucigalpa, Honduras: Archives of the Instituto Hondureño de Antropología e Historia.

Giménez, Gilberto. 2007. "La Frontera Norte como Representación y Referente Cultural en México." *Territorio y Frontera* 2(3):17–34.

Girard, Rafael. 1944. "Descubrimiento de un importante sitio histórico." *Anales de la Academia de Geografía e Historia de Guatemala* 19 (4):279–284.

Girard, Rafael. 1949. *Los chortís ante el problema maya: Historia de las culturas indígenas, desde su origen hasta hoy*. Tomo I. Mexico City, Mexico: Antigua Librería Robredo.

Gran Diccionario Náhuatl [en línea]. 2012. Mexico City: Universidad Nacional Autónoma de México [Ciudad Universitaria, México DF] http://www.gdn.unam.mx, accessed August 25, 2016.

Hasemann, George. 1996. "La prehistoria de la Baja Centroamérica." In *Los Indios de Centroamérica*, ed. George Hasemann, Gloria Lara-Pinto, and Fernando Cruz Sandoval, 19–98. Madrid, Spain: Editorial MAPFRE.

Hasemann, George, and Gloria Lara-Pinto. 1993. "Regionalismo e Interacción: Historia Cultural de la Zona Central." In *Historia Antigua de América Central: Del Poblamiento a la Conquista*, ed. Robert Carmack, 135–216, Volumen I de la Historia General de Centroamérica. Madrid, Spain: Facultad Latinoamericana de Ciencias Sociales.

Hudson, Kathryn Marie, and John Henderson. 2014. "Life on the Edge: Identity and Interaction in the Land of Ulúa and the Maya World." In *Sounds Like Theory*. XII Nordic Theoretical Archaeology Group Meeting in Oulu 25–28.4.2012, ed. Janne Ikäheimo, Anna-Kaisa Salmi, and Tiina Äikäs, 157–177. Helsinki, Finland: Helsinki Archaeological Society of Finland.

Joyce, Rosemary A. 1991. *Cerro Palenque: Power and Identity on the Maya Periphery*. Austin: University of Texas Press.

Lara-Pinto, Gloria. 1980. "Beiträge zur indianischen Ethnographie von Honduras in der 1. Hälfte des 16. Jahrhunderts, unter besonderer Berücksichtigung der Historischen Demographie." Unpublished PhD dissertation, Institut of Archaeology, University of Hamburg, Germany.

Lara-Pinto, Gloria. 1983. "La Región de El Cajón en la Etnohistoria de Honduras."
    Yaxkín 5(1):37–50.
Lara-Pinto, Gloria. 1985. "Apuntes sobre la Afiliación Etnica de los Pobladores Indí-
    genas de los Valles de Comayagua y Sulaco. Siglo XVI." *Mesoamérica* 9:45–57.
Lara-Pinto, Gloria. 1986. "El Respeto a las Lenguas Nativas como un Derecho Natu-
    ral de las Comunidades Indígenas." *Yaxkín* 9(2):3–15.
Lara-Pinto, Gloria. 1991. "Sociopolitical Organization in Central Honduras at the
    Time of the Conquest: A Model for the Formation of Complex Society." In *The
    Formation of Complex Society in Southeastern Mesoamerica*, ed. William R. Fowler,
    215–235. Boca Raton, FL: CRC Press.
Lara-Pinto, Gloria. 1996. "La Población indígena a principios del Siglo XVI." In *Los
    Indios de Centroamérica*, ed. George Hasemann, Gloria Lara-Pinto, and Fernando
    Cruz Sandoval, 101–174. Madrid, Spain: Editorial MAPFRE.
Lara-Pinto, Gloria. 2001. *Las tierras de los indios del pueblo de Copán: Conflicto
    agrario y otorgamiento de justicia en el Siglo XVII.* Paper presented at the Congreso
    Internacional de Copán: Ciencia, Arte y Religión de los Mayas, Copán Ruinas,
    Honduras.
Lara-Pinto, Gloria. 2009. *Identidad etnica en el contexto etnohistórico y político de la
    frontera: El caso de los chortís de Honduras, un avance.* Paper presented at VI Con-
    greso del Consejo Europeo de Investigaciones Sociales de América (CEISAL),
    Toulouse, France.
Lara-Pinto, Gloria. 2011. "Dicotomía de una ciudad: Las raíces indígenas de Teguci-
    galpa y Comayagüela." *Paradigma* 20(30):179–204.
Lara-Pinto, Gloria. 2014. Informe preliminar del recorrido en los municipios
    de Santa Fe, Concepción y Ocotepeque, Departamento de Ocotepeque. Manu-
    script on file. Tegucigalpa, Honduras: Archives of the Departamento de Ciencias
    Sociales, Universidad Pedagógica Nacional Francisco Morazán.
Lara-Pinto, Gloria, and George Hasemann. 1995. "Honduras antes del año 1500: Una
    visión regional de su evolución cultural tardía." *Revista de Arqueología Americana*
    8:9–49.
Larde y Larin, Jorge. 1958. "Guistaluzzitt." *Cultura Revista del Ministerio de Cultura*
    13:54–59.
Lehman, Walter. 1920. *Zentral-Amerika. Die Sprachen Zentral-Amerikas in ihren
    Beziehungen zueinander sowie zu Süd-Amerika und Mexiko.* Berlin, Germany:
    Dietrich Reimer,
López de Velasco, Juan. 1971. *Geografía y Descripción Universal de las Indias.* Madrid,
    Spain: Biblioteca de Autores Españoles.
Marroquín, Francisco. 1968 [1532]. El licenciado Francisco Marroquín y una descrip-
    ción y una descripción de El Salvador, Año 1532, Archivo General de Indias,

Sevilla, Audiencia de Guatemala, Legajo 965. Paleographed by Francis Gall. *Anales de la Sociedad de Geografía e Historia de Guatemala* 41:199–232.

Matthew, Laura. 2010. *Memories of Conquest: Becoming Mexicano in Colonial Guatemala.* Chapel Hill: University of North Carolina Press.

Melton, Phillip Edward. 2008. "Genetic History and Pre-Columbian Diaspora of Chibchan Speaking Populations: Molecular Genetic Evidence." Unpublished PhD dissertation, Department of Anthropology, University of Kansas, Lawrence, KS.

Molina, Fray Alonso de. 1970 [1571]. *Vocabulario en Lengua Castellana y Mexicana y Mexicana y Castellana.* Mexico City, Mexico: Editorial Porrúa.

Moreira González, Yamileth. 2010. Análisis léxicoestadístico de las relaciones entre el cacaopera, matagalpa, sumo septentrional, ulua y miskito. *Revista de Lenguas Modernas* 12:167–194.

Oudijk, Michel R., and Matthew Restall. 2008. *La conquista indígena de Mesoamérica: El caso de don Gonzalo Mazatzin Moctezuma.* Puebla, Mexico: Universidad de las Américas.

Pedraza, Cristóbal de. 1868 [1544]. "Relación de la Provincia de Honduras y Higueras." In *Colección de Documentos inéditos relativos al descubrimiento y organización de las antiguas poseciones españolas de América y Oceanía.* Tomo XI:379–434. Madrid, Spain: Imprenta de M. Bernaldo de Quirós.

Repartimiento de Gracias a Dios. 1911 [1536]. "Repartimiento de la ciudad de Gracias a Dios y su fundación por Pedro de Alvarado." In *Guía de agrimensores o sea recopilación de leyes agrarias,* ed. Antonio Vallejo, 23–35. Tegucigalpa, Honduras: Tipografía Nacional.

Repartimiento de San Pedro. 1911 [1536]. "Repartimiento de la villa de San Pedro de Puerto de Caballos y su fundación por Pedro de Alvarado." In *Guía de agrimensores o sea recopilación de leyes agrarias,* ed. Antonio Vallejo, 13–21. Tegucigalpa, Honduras: Tipografía Nacional.

Restall, Matthew, and Florine Asselbergs. 2007. *Invading Guatemala: Spanish, Nahua, and Maya Accounts of the Conquest Wars.* University Park, PA: Pennsylvania State University Press.

Sachse, Frauke. 2010. "Reconstructive Description of Eighteenth-Century Xinka Grammar." Unpublishd PhD dissertation, University of Leiden, Netherlands.

Samayoa Guevara, Héctor. 1957. "Historia del Establecimiento de la Orden Mercedaria en el Reino de Guatemala, desde el año de 1537 hasta 1632." *Antropología e Historia de Guatemala* 9(2):30–43.

Sánchez, Carleen. 2003. "Topographies of Power: The Political Landscape of the Southeast Maya." Unpublished PhD dissertation, Department of Anthropology, University of California, Santa Barbara.

Sanson D'Abbeville, Nicolás. 2006 [1678]. "Mexique, au Nouvelle Espagne, Nouvlle, Gallice, Yucatan: et autres provinces jusques a l'Isthme de Panama, ou sont les Audiences de Mexico, Guadalaiara, et de Guatimala. tables de la Geographie Ancienne et Nouvelle, Pate 25, Paris: Chez l'autheu." In *Atlas de Mapas Históricos de Honduras*, compiled by William V. Davidson, 85. Managua, Nicaragua: Fundación Uno.

Scheffler, Timothy E. 2008. "The El Gigante Rock Shelter, Honduras." Unpublished PhD dissertation, Department of Anthropology, Pennsylvania State University, University Park, PA.

Scheffler, Timothy, Kenneth Hirth, and George Hasemann. 2012. "The El Gigante Rockshelter: Preliminary Observations on an Early to Late Holocene Occupation in Southwest Honduras." *Latin American Antiquity* 23(4):597–610.

Schortman, Edward M., and Patricia A. Urban. 2011a. "Power, Memory, and Prehistory: Constructing and Erasing Political Landscapes in the Naco Valley, Northwestern Honduras." *American Anthropologist* 113(1):5–21.

Schortman, Edward M., and Patricia A. Urban. 2011b. "Networks of Power: Political Relations in the Late Postclassic Naco Valley, Honduras." Boulder: University Press of ColoradoSchortman, Edward M., Patricia A. Urban, and Marne Ausec. 2001. "Politics with Style: Identity Formation in Prehispanic Southeastern Mesoamerica." *American Anthropologist* 103(2):312–330.

Schuller, Rudolf. 1929. "Die Egertonkarte von Ameika und die ehemalige Verbreitung der Lenkaindianer in Honduras." *Petermanns Geographische Mittleilungen* 75:316–319.

Sewell, William H., Jr. 1967. "Marc Bloch and the Logic of Comparative History." *History and Theory* 6(2):208–218.

Sharer, Robert. 2009. "The Ch'orti' Past. An Archaeological Perspective." In *The Ch'orti' Maya Area. Past and Present*, ed. Brent Metz, Cameron L. McNeil, and Kerry M. Hull, 124–133. Gainesville, FL: University Press of Florida.

Sheptak, Russell N. 2007. "Los toqueguas de la Costa Norte de Honduras en la época colonial." *Yaxkin* XXIII (2):140–157.

Sheptak, Russell N. 2013. "Colonial Masca in Motion: Tactics of Persistence of a Honduran Indigenous Community." Unpublished PhD dissertation, Faculty in Archaeology, Leiden University, Netherlands.

Thompson, J. Eric S. 1970. *Maya History and Religion*. Norman: University of Oklahoma Press.

Torres Servin, Evelia. 2011. La participación de los indígenas mexicanos en la conquista de las tierras altas de Guatemala 1524–1547. Undergraduate thesis, Department of Latin American Studies, Universidad Nacional Autónoma de México, México City, Mexico.

Ubico, Mario, Carlos Batres, Lucrecia de Batres, Marlen Garnica, Ramiro Martínez y Luis Rosada. 2001. "Jupilingo: Un pequeño asentamiento probablemente relacionado con la periferia de Copán." In *XIV Simposio de Investigaciones Arqueológicas en Guatemala, 2000,* ed. J. P. Laporte, A. C. Suasnávar, and B. Arroyo, 592–602. Guatemala City, Guatemala: Museo Nacional de Arqueología y Etnología.

Urban, Patricia A., and Edward M. Schortman. 1999. "Thoughts on the Periphery: The Ideological Consequences of Core-Periphery Relations." In *World-Systems Theory in Practice. Leadership, Production and Exchange,* ed. P. Nick Kardulias, 125–152. Lanham, MD: Rowman and Littlefield.

Van Akkeren, Ruud. 2007. *La visión indígena de la conquista.* Guatemala City, Guatemala: Serviprensa.

Wonderley, Anthony. 1986. "Material Symbolics in Pre-Columbian Households: The Painted Pottery of Naco, Honduras." *Journal of Anthropological Research* 42(4):497–534.

11

Honduran Lenca Chiefdoms of the Contact Period (1502–1550)

Pastor Rodolfo Gómez Zúñiga

This chapter contributes to the study of Lenca political units of the sixteenth century. To that end, I summarize the most widespread political geography model of the Lenca area, then engage in an epistemological discussion focused on the use of the term *province* in ethnohistorical sources as an indicator of political complexity. I also review the contexts in which this term was used in documentation at the time of the conquest, focusing my analysis on the central eastern region of contemporary Honduras. All English translations of primary sources are my own. The present essay specifically evaluates evidence from the "provinces" that Lara-Pinto (1996) labeled as Cerquin, Care, Sulaco-Maniani, and Olancho in order to more closely explore the political geography of these regions. A closer look at the meaning of the term *province* in historical sources indicates that it was broadly used and sometimes indicated political units but was also often used synonymously with the term *nation* to indicate an area of homogenous linguistic and ethnic identities. Keeping this in mind, a review of ethnohistoric sources from the sixteenth century suggests that a much more fragmented and heterogenous political panorama existed within Cerquin, Care, Sulaco-Maniani, and Olancho than was previously thought (Chapman 1986; Lara-Pinto 1991, 1996).

DOI: 10.5876/9781646420971.c011

THE CURRENT MODEL

The dominant interpretation of the structure of the Lenca political units of the contact period (1502–1550) parts from the work of Chapman (1974) on the Chorotega and Nicarao chiefdoms of Nicaragua, where she established the category of "province" as the key indicator to define certain political units to which she attributed a level of chiefdom. In later works, Chapman studied the central and western Lenca populations of Honduras, describing a space divided into four "partidos, señorios or provinces (Care, Cerquin, Potón and Lenca) each comprising various domains including variable numbers of people" (Chapman 1985:27–28, 1986:67).

The work of Gloria Lara-Pinto is along the same lines as that of Chapman, in that it attaches importance to the word *province* for interpreting the complexity of political units as part of thorough investigations into the Lenca chiefdoms that were settled in the studied region (Hasemann and Lara-Pinto 1993:182–183; Lara-Pinto 1991:220–221; 1996:116–117). The importance attached to the term by Chapman and Lara-Pinto necessitates a discussion of how usages and meanings of the term *province* have varied over time and then a closer examination of how and when the term was used in primary-source material.

HISTORICAL SOURCES

Information on native political units is scattered among numerous documents because the description of indigenous societies was not a priority for colonial authorities. Chapman (1985) and Lara-Pinto (1991) based their research primarily on such sources as the *Repartimientos* of the Indian towns of San Pedro Puerto Caballos and Gracias a Dios (AGI, Patronato 20, N°·4, R.6), and the account of Cerquin written by the royal chronicler Antonio de Herrera y Tordesillas. Additionally, Lara-Pinto analyzed the tax appraisals of the Villa de Santa Maria del Valle de Comayagua (AGI, Guatemala 128), along with other non-serial sources, which allowed her to construct a solid proposal on Lenca political geography. Despite their importance, these pioneer works by Chapman and Lara-Pinto should be revised in light of new data from previously unknown sources.

Among these sources are the account ledgers and letters of the *contaduria* of the government of Honduras, where scribes settled the tributes owed by the Indian towns to the Spanish Crown. These accounting ledgers and letters are the best serial source for the study of the evolution of these native populations. They are ideal for documenting the structure of some sixteenth-century

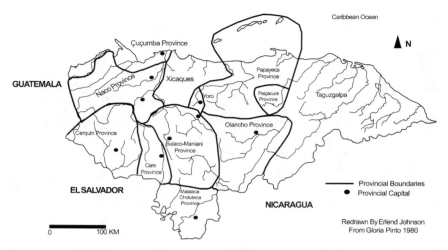

FIGURE 11.1. *Indigenous provinces in sixteenth-century Honduras. (From Lara-Pinto 1980, redrawn by Erlend Johnson.)*

political units because the royal *encomiendas* included the largest indigenous populations found in Honduras during the time of contact, given that there is no evidence of a *congregación* in Honduras, and because the Spaniards tended to manipulate preexisting political units in order to more efficiently collect tribute (RAHM, Relaciones Geográficas, 9/4663, No.16, XLIII). The interpretation of information from letters from the *contaduría* with data from additional sixteenth-century primary sources allows for improved reconstructions based on stronger evidence that also addresses discrepancies in previous political models applied to Lenca population in Honduras.

THE LENCA LANDS

The Lenca territory included most of the western and central region of Honduras, eastern El Salvador, and enclaves in northern Nicaragua (figure 11.1). Most indigenous groups living there spoke languages affiliated with the Lenca family, although the Pacific coast had pockets of Ulúa Indians (possibly Cacaopera speakers), members of the Misumalpan family, as well as Oto-Mangue language speakers. To the east, overlaps with Chibchan-speaking groups such as the Tolupán and Pech would have been frequent; we can also not dismiss some enclaves of speakers of languages of Uto-Aztecan affiliation, such as the Cholutecas of Naco (Gómez Zúñiga 2011:77–155).

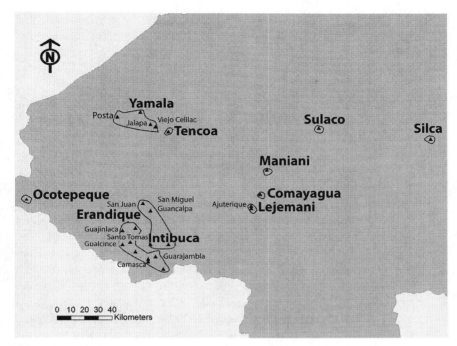

FIGURE 11.2. *Sixteenth-century indigenous political units in Honduras reviewed in this chapter.*

According to the analysis of Lara-Pinto (1980, 1996), the region was divided among six chiefdom-level polities: Care, Cerquin, Sulaco-Maniarí, Olancho, and Chorotega Malalaca in Honduras, and Chaparrastique in El Salvador (figure 11.2). Each of the provinces would have covered several thousand square kilometers and contained multiple indigenous towns. Similarly, many of these provinces would have contained ethnically and linguistically diverse populations (see also Lara-Pinto, chapter 10, this volume).

Information on these provinces in historical sources is often confusing and contradictory, making it difficult to ascertain their existence as political units. Although the names of each province are clearly indigenous terms, their association in colonial sources as political units is opaque because it is not always clear whether they were preexisting native categories or regions created by the Spaniards based on their experiences and imperfect understanding of indigenous political systems. Thus, we can ask if these provinces were political units or alternately broader ethnic and linguistic areas. In this chapter, I argue that part of the difficulty in determining the relevance of these provinces as either political units or ethnic and linguistic units is due to the many meanings of the word *province.*

THE ELUSIVE TERM OF *PROVINCE*

Tracing the semantic overlap that accumulated in the province signifier requires understanding its varied meanings and uses during the contact period (1502–1550). Accordingly, I first turn to definitions from the oldest dictionaries of the Spanish language, and then I study the use that conquistadors made of this concept in the context of the documentation of the first decades of the conquest.

The first dictionaries of the Spanish language document a certain polysemy of the term *provincia* in colonial-period Spanish. The 1611 book *Tesoro de la Lengua Castellana* by Covarrubias (1943), does not analyze this word; however, at the moment of defining *nación*, Covarrubias claims that "it comes from the Latin word *natio*, is valid for the words 'kingdom' or 'larger province', such as the Spanish nation." According to the first edition (1726) of the *Diccionario de Autoridades* (Real Academia Española de la Lengua 1984), *provincia* was "part of a kingdom or state, usually governed on behalf of a prince, by a minister named governor" (Volume V, 1537); *reino*, meanwhile, is defined as "one or many provinces subject to a King" (Volume V, 1737); while *nación* is "the collection of people in any country or province or kingdom" (Volume IV, 1734).

A brief review of documents written in Honduras in the early sixteenth century identified up to three meanings assigned to the term *provincia.* First, it was used to refer to the Honduran governorship as a territory under the Spanish Crown: "at the time that this village of San Pedro was populated . . . that it was the first village in this province to be populated" (AGI, Justicia, 1032, No. 3). It was also used to refer to areas occupied by people of the same ethnic group, regardless of whether they were integrated into one or more independent political units: "and pointed them to the last towns of this jurisdiction of this village the towns of Malcao and Comayagua Canola, which is in the Province of the Canola, and the town of Agalteca, and another Comayagua, and Maniani, and Miambar, and other towns, and that is mainly the towns of the Canola" (AGI, Justicia, 1032, N°3). Third, the Castilians seem to have used this term to refer to political units, differentiating them from physiographic units such as valleys, or from populations: "we have uncovered and taken possession of the valleys, provinces, towns of Zulaco, Maniani, Talanca, Agalta, Quesalpa, Agalteca, Oylanche, and northward along the coast of the Río de los Cristianos, and Río de Tayasal, and up the coast to Golfo Dulce, Tecosyste,

Puerto de Santa Andrés, and Valhama, Pechin, Puerto de Sal, Xagua, Triunfo de la Cruz, the cove of Zoli, Port and Cape Honduras, and many other towns and provinces" (AGI, Patronato, 20, No. 5).

In any case, if we consider the use that Hernán Cortés made of this and other words in his fifth letter to the Spanish King to describe the province of Mazatlan or Quiatleo, south of Mexico, the equivalence of the term *province* with "political unity" is not entirely clear. Cortés mentions the existence of enemy peoples within this province as well as "five or six that are in this province, which are each 'cabeceras de por sí' [capitals in and of itself]" (Cortes 1986:365–366). Despite the doubts arising from the text above, it is desirable to keep in mind the concepts of "provincial," "cabecera de por sí," and "barrio" (neighborhood) because these were used in numerous subsequent documents where Honduran native societies were described, as discussed below. In the following sections, Lenca political traditions are broadly reviewed to provide context for these arguments, and then evidence from specific "provinces" is discussed.

ETHNOHISTORIC INFORMATION ON
LENCA POLITICAL ORGANIZATION

Before exploring the dimensions of individual political units within sixteenth-century Honduras, it is important to more broadly examine evidence for the political institutions of Honduras from historical sources. I focus on data on Lenca institutions gathered about Lempira and the province of Cerquin broadly, since it was one of the largest and most important regions at the time of the conquest. These institutions can reasonably be extended to surrounding regions, such as the Care, Sulaco-Manani, and Olancho "provinces," given the presence of Lenca-speaking populations in these areas. As is explored below, Lenca political structures were made up of limited hierarchies poorly suited for the governance of large territories: they contained segmentary-lineage structures that would quickly have balkanized larger territories and were subject to frequent internal conflict. These features do not seem consistent with the larger political entities proposed by previous investigators (Chapman 1986; Lara-Pinto 1991).

In terms of its social structure, the earliest accounts highlight the military capacity of the leaders and the people of Cerquin, who, entrenched in their natural fortress, endured the siege of Hispanic hosts for years. The testimonies of the conquistadors indicate the existence of several lords in the province, though they never explain their articulation with the rest of society (AGI,

Guatemala, 9A, R.8 No. 15). That work was later undertaken by the chronicler Herrera, who based his writings on an unidentified account of the natives of Honduras.

According to Herrera, each village had its own chief, whose position was hereditary and was transmitted to the eldest son. Although the chiefs could marry several women, their position was inherited exclusively to the offspring obtained from a principal wife, who by obligation had to be the daughter of another chief. The chief had the help of four lieutenants in charge of providing for his home and helping with government affairs. These lieutenants served as a link with the rest of society, and compiled information that was then transmitted and deliberated with their master, along with their opinions on matters. In addition to the lieutenants, the chiefs also consulted priests, who were only allowed to be addressed directly by the chief himself. Among those consulted by the chiefs, the priests stood out, and only the elite could speak to them. The priests were elderly people, with long hair that was braided around the head. They lived in remote, long, narrow houses raised off the ground, where the figures of the gods were kept. Important decisions were made in consultation with the gods through the priests, who were given offerings of food. The population base was composed of commoners, vassals, or *maceguales*, whose main occupation was agriculture. The lower social echelon was occupied by slaves obtained in wars, whose noses were cut off and who were destined for agricultural activities, grinding corn, and other services (Herrera, in Carías 1998:287–288).

The structure of this outlined network was asymmetric, where the greatest power was exercised by the chief, his lieutenants, and the priests. It is not clear, however, if the chief's family held a different rank than the rest of the population. Specific roles are documented only for the eldest son, heir to the position of chief, and for his daughters, who were the only candidates for the position of legitimate wives of other chiefs. The shortage of documented bureaucratic positions suggests a hierarchy that was not well developed, which is indicative of simple chiefdoms.

On a regional level, the interaction between different populations is insinuated, first because the rules of succession of these chiefdoms prescribed exogamous marriage alliances between a chief and another chief's daughters; and secondly, because the onset of hostilities and the establishment of peace were negotiated through embassies (Carías 1998).

Given the cultural affinity between Cerquin and its Care, Poton, and Lenca neighbors, as proposed by Herranz (1996), it is feasible that all had social structures similar to those described in the preceding paragraphs. Therefore, when I discuss cases of populations that today are subsumed under the labels of Care, Sulaco-Maniani, and Olancho by Lara-Pinto (1996), I will try to determine the validity of these provinces as political units as well as reconstruct evidence for any potential chiefdoms that existed within these broader regions. In the following sections, I argue that a number of smaller political units can be identified in each region, suggesting more appropriately sized territories—given the segmentary hereditary structures, lack of bureaucracy, and conflict mentioned above.

THE "PROVINCE" OF CERQUIN

The "province" of Cerquin was one of the larger and better-known regions described by the Spanish, making it an ideal place to begin our examination of individual regions and their political institutions. While there is evidence for an extensive political unit made up of as many as 12 pueblos within the traditional territory of Cerquin (Hasemann and Lara-Pinto 1993), it appears likely, after consulting historical texts, that this territory was much smaller than previously thought. Data from Cerquin broadly suggest that Lenca political units may have been both smaller and less complexly organized than once thought.

The most reliable observation on Cerquin's dimensions suggest that it was much smaller than previously believed, covering, only a portion of the modern department of Lempira, rather than a larger territory made up of the departments of Lempira, Copán, Ocotopeque, and Santa Barbara as Lara-Pinto (1991) proposes. This evidence comes from a dispute over Honduran *encomiendas* between governor Montejo's new administration and previous *encomenderos*, referred to here as *vecinos*, appointed by Pedro de Alvarado in the 1530s:

> Gaspar Juares requested his *repartimiento*, and by mistake (Montejo) gave to him the name of a town, and it is a province, and in it were eleven *vecinos* . . . and writ of possession was given to Gaspar Juares . . . see your Majesty where there were thirty five *vecinos*, and you take out eleven of them, how many can stay, besides five or six others that have also been removed, being this the province of Cerquin as I said, where these eleven had their *encomiendas*, where many hardships have been suffered. (AGI, Guatemala, 9A, R.8, No. 18)

These 11 *encomenderos* were *vecinos* of the city of Gracias, which administered much of Western Honduras during the sixteenth century and contained 35 *vecinos* administering *encomiendas* throughout western Honduras. That 11 of the 35 *vecinos* had *encomiendas* in Cerquin demonstrates the importance of this province to the city of Gracias, but the observation by Montejo also suggests that its limits did not comprise more than one-third of the tributaries of the city of Gracias, and probably less than half of the territorial jurisdiction of Cerquin as projected by Lara-Pinto (1991).

Historical sources add further details as to the identity of the 11 *encomiendas* that made up Cerquin. The engineer Navarro in 1733 indicates that the parish of Cerquin comprised 11 towns separated from each other by 23 leagues, specifying among them Gualcince as its capital, and those of Camasca, Colomoncagua, and Guaranjabaca (possibly Guarajambala, currently Concepción, Intibucá). The bishop of Honduras writing in 1582 indicated that Cerquin included a census of 460 Indians divided into 12 pueblos (Martínez Castillo 1983:132). Finally, the Bishop of Comayagua in 1791, when visiting the parish of Cerquin, said that it was integrated by the populations of Gualcinco, Jocoguera, Piraera, Majatigue, Gualjinlaca, Guasabarque, Gualmoaca, and Erandique. All such populations, as Chapman suggests, are in the center and south of the Honduran departments of Lempira and Intibucá (Chapman 1986:61). The town of Piraera in modern day Lempira may also be considered as part of Cerquin, as the mayor of the town in 1752 indicated that it belonged to the district or *partido* of Cerquín (Leyva 1991:246).

A particular account of Piraera provides the most remarkable depiction of the province, where, according to the chronicler Herrera, there was "a large population whose lord was Entepica, which after his death was divided into many towns" (Carías 1998:302). Although, in saying this, Herrera suggests the existence of a political unit of regional scope, it is not clear whether its domain extended across all of Cerquin, particularly when considering that Lara-Pinto included within its boundaries the town of Ocotepeque (Lara-Pinto 1991:222), the only Pipil population so far documented by historical sources (Herranz 1996:58, 267–269). Therefore, to accept its proposed limits involves not only giving Cerquin a regional dominion over several thousand square kilometers, but also recognizing it as incorporating a multiethnic (Lenca and Pipil) population base.

On the other hand, if Piraera did indeed disintegrate into many villages after Entepica's death, a segmented political power is suggested, indicative of a low level of centralization. The local myth of Comizagual suggests the same. Comizagual, a white woman and expert on magic, founded the capital of Cerquin in Cefalcoquín 200 years before the arrival of the Spanish, from where she expanded her empire with the help of an idol called "the stone of the three points." According to tradition, when Comizagual felt old, she divided her dominions between her three children or siblings, thus dividing the province (Carías 1998:284). Although the story may be based in actual ancient events, for now there is no evidence to endorse its veracity. What the

Comizagual myth does suggest is that, at the arrival of the Spanish, Cerquin was divided among various polities, though for now we lack the sources necessary to determine their number, their extent, or their demographic base.

Based on the abovementioned historical sources, it is possible to say that Cerquin was one of the largest and most complex political units within Honduras at the time of the conquest. However, this "province" was made up of only 12 towns, occupying a territory in the modern-day departments of Lempira and Intibucá that did not cover the entirety of the province of Cerquin as reconstructed by Lara-Pinto (1991). Available documentary sources suggest other political units were present in Tencoa, Yamala, and farther west in Ocotepeque.

Tencoa

Tencoa was an area that was originally identified as part of the larger province of Cerquin by Lara-Pinto (1991) but evidence suggests it was, in fact, an independent region at the time of the conquest. The following sections first demonstrate that the population in Tencoa was Lenca and then explore evidence for political affiliations within this region.

At the time of the conquest, Tencoa was also known as Tequechimal (AGI, Justicia, 1032, No. 4), likely an Uto-Aztecan place name, as suggested by the ending -*chimal*, derived from the Nahuatl root *chimalli*, whose translation to English would be "shield." The historical texts consulted did not indicate the language spoken by its inhabitants, although a document dated to 1600 indicates that part of its population spoke and understood a mother tongue, as well as the Mexican tongue (AGI, Guatemala, 120, No. 8). Several indicators make it likely that the abovementioned mother tongue was Lenca. First, in the late seventeenth century, certain natives of Quelala, Jurla, and Reitoca claimed that the Putun language, a term used to identify Lenca languages in El Salvador by Garcias de Palacios, was spoken in some villages in Tencoa (AGI, Guatemala, 184). Another clue regarding their linguistic affiliation comes from the name *Mayanlepa*, its principal chief, and the name of one of its neighborhoods, called *Lepachichi* (AGI, Patronato, 20, No.4, R.6). In both cases, the linguistic clue is provided by the particle *lepa*, a Lenca word used to denominate jaguars or "tigers." Other Lenca toponyms using *lepa* include *Lepaterique* ("Hill of the Tiger"), *Quelepa* ("Stone of the Tiger"), and *Lepaguare* ("River of the Tiger").

Tencoa was one of the largest villages in the governorate of Honduras but few data exist on its social structure. The *Repartimiento* of Gracias indicates that Pedro de Alvarado reserved this *encomienda* for himself, which comprised "the four *barrios* [neighborhoods] of Tencoa, which are Mayanlepa and Lepachichi and Ocingoscos, village of Malan and the town of Care which are the towns in the middle of that city [of Gracias] with all of their Indian lords and *naborías* and neighborhoods and *estancias* [small farms] and towns subject to them, according to the way that these people organize themselves" (AGI, Patronato, 20, No. 4, R.6). Although limited, the data document a precolonial native elite. In 1539, Alvaro Sandoval said that when Pedro de Alvarado passed by the population studied, "he saw that the people of Tencoa came in peace and it served the Lord Adelantado, and that in the presence of this witness came to give peace and obedience, and the principal chief of this village is called Mayanlepa" (AGI, Justicia, 129, No. 2).

Other later mentions of traditional elites come from the receipt notices of the corregidores, which are acts carried out in the municipal council of Tencoa, and from certain legal documents, such as residences. Thus, in 1562 Alonso Ortiz Delgueta, serving as judge of residence, summoned before him "Diego, principal Indian of the town of Tencoa" (AGI, Justicia, 311, No. 1); nearly two decades later, the Council of the Indies received a letter from the indigenous council of Tencoa, signed by Juan del Valle, as governor, and Don Hernando and Don Andres Vazquez, the latter probably descendants of the original elites of Tencoa, as is evidenced by their signing the letter with the title of *Don* (AGI, Guatemala, 44B, No. 89). A decade later, in 1590, people's governor Don Diego Hernandez and *cacique* Don Nicolas Corella participated in the reception of a new corregidor (AGI, Guatemala, 116, No. 15); while in 1600, a new official was received, among others, by Bartolomé Sánchez, named as principal Indian (AGI, Guatemala, 120, No. 8).

The above data, combined with a lack of sources mentioning Tencoa as part of the territory of Cerquin, suggests that Tencoa was a territory independent from Cerquin that contained its own indigenous Lenca elite. These included chiefs, a post of likely preconquest origin and that persisted into the late sixteenth century. These data suggest that Tencoa had at least a chiefdom-level hierarchy, an interpretation that is consistent with the account of the chronicler Herrera about the native elites of central Honduran societies.

YAMALA

Within the middle basin of the Ulúa River the Spanish conquistadors highlighted Yamala as another prominent town of the "Serranos" or Chontales, which was a "cabecera de por sí" and thus likely an independent political unit. According to the testimony of the local indigenous people indoctrinated by the Mercedarian friars, the Jucap language was spoken in Yamala (AGI, Guatemala, 184), a language affiliated with the Lenca family (Herranz 1996:153–154). As it happened with Tencoa, Lara-Pinto included Yamala within the province of Cerquin. A clue to its relevance and independence can be extracted from the file of the Repartimiento of the towns of Gracias a Dios, where Pedro de Alvarado took the service of the town and its farms and neighborhoods, including the neighborhood of Posta, for himself (AGI, Patronato 20, No 4, R.6).

The texts reproduced, besides supporting the prominence of Yamala in the context of central Honduras, testify to its dominance over other nearby towns, among these Posta. Other documents consulted, especially the letters of the accounts of Honduras's governorship, not only proved that Yamala ruled over Posta but also that it held dominion over the towns of Jalapa and the neighboring town of Celilac (AGI, Justicia, 1032, No. 4, R.1; AGI, Justicia, 299A; AGI, Contaduría, 987, No. 2; AGI, Contaduría, 988). Following the language used by the conquistadors, we can interpret that Yamala was a "cabecera de por sí," and that Jalapa, Celilac, and Posta were the *barrios* and *estancias* alluded to in the *repartimiento*.

Another issue is discerning Yamala's social structure. References about its elite are scarce and limited to Mizquanteite, considered to have been one of the main chiefs of Honduras (AGI, Guatemala, 402, L.2). It is interesting to note the Uto-Aztecan root of the name of this chief, specifically its relationship with the Nicarao language, where the *-teite* particle is equivalent to the Nahuatl *-tecuhtli*. Another likely Uto-Aztecan name in Yamala is Topanteute, possibly referring to a chief if the root *-teute* indicated was due to a scribal error when trying to transcribe *-teite* (AGI, Justicia, 1032, No. 4, R.1). Additional information on Yamala is unknown.

Again, as was the case with Tencoa, no evidence has been located regarding the subordination of Yamala to a larger political entity and Yamala is certainly not mentioned as a town of Cerquin in available historical documents. Therefore, for the purposes of this study, Yamala is considered to be an independent political unit to which the villages of Posta, Jalapa, and Celilac were attached as *barrios* or *estancias*.

THE CARE "PROVINCE"

Among the provinces included in the land of the Chontal, the province of the Cares emerges as a region united in precolumbian times though, unfortunately, testaments to its native ancestry are not accompanied by additional information that clarify the nature of its cohesive ties as political, social, or otherwise.

Establishing the linguistic affiliation of the Care Province with limited sources is difficult. The language spoken was likely Lenca (Chapman 1985:27; Herranz 1996: 281). Two historical documents from the seventeenth century discuss the Care region's linguistic identity. The first is the pastoral visit of Bishop Fray Luis de Cañizares to his diocese, where the prelate sustained the extensive spread of a language called Care, which in his opinion was spoken in the province of the same name. Contrary to the above, the natives interviewed on the record of the dispossession of the doctrines of the Mercedarians never mention a language called Care, and point out that the Putun tongue was spoken in the area (AGI, Guatemala, 184), a language that different specialists catalog within the Lenca family. As several dialects of Lenca have been reported by modern linguists, it is plausible that these two sources do not contradict each other but rather that Care was a dialect within the broader Lenca language family.

The most widespread information about the precolonial origin of the Care Province comes from the chronicler Herrera, who described it as an enemy of the province of Cerquin (Cariías 1998:302). The text of a legal process initiated by Montejo provides further details that support the existence of a Care region. In the first document, the witness Alonso Ortiz, referring to Cares, said that "this name of Care has and is called by three ways: Care, and Cares, and Perutacas, and that therefore this witness believes it is all one." In the same *probanza* the witness Alvaro de Sandoval confirmed that the natives knew the province with this name: "he was asked officially by the lord protector what town Care is . . . he saw certain Indians of the province of Cerquin and Tomala who said that ahead of their towns was a province called Care, that now they are called Caris among the Christians . . . and the Indians put very much fear on Don Pedro de Alvarado saying that it was a very large and very bellicose province" (AGI, Justicia, 129, No. 2).

In the document cited above, the witness Hernando de Saavedra also indicated that the inhabitants of the province recognized themselves under this demonym, thus confirming its prehispanic roots, and that this was a demonym recognized as belonging to the residents of the province being studied: "this declarant has asked the Indians many times about these so-called Cares, where they were from, and they responded that they were Caretaca, which means they were from the province of the Cares, as when someone says I am from the province of Leon or the provinces of Guatemala" (AGI, Justicia, 129, No. 2).

Early documents do not specify the boundaries of the province, whose *encomienda* Pedro de Alvarado reserved for himself when he divided the towns of Gracias in 1536 (AGI, Patronato, 20, No. 4, R.6). Because after Alvarado's death his *encomiendas* passed to the Royal Crown, the towns of the province are surely among those registered in the accounting of the Honduras governorship as Indian villages of the Royal Crown in the *partido* of Gracias a Dios. Setting aside the towns of Tencoa's jurisdiction, the populations of Intibucá, Guarajambala, Guazavazquez, Talgua, Ocotepeque, and Aguarcha remain. Because Ocotepeque, Talgua, and Guazavasquez were all located to the west of Cerquin and the only areas located east of it are Intibucá and its surrounding towns, it is probable that the Care province was located in the vicinity of the town of Intibucá.

According to an account dated to 1611, the pueblo of Gracias a Dios included a parish of the Cares (AGI, Guatemala, 39, R.14, N.95), and, because of a subsequent document, it is known that the so-called parish of Intibucá was located in a province of the Cares (AGI, Guatemala, 164, 1688). Because in 1791 the parish of Intibucá included other surrounding towns, such as Yamaranguila, San Juan, and San Miguel Guancapla (Vallejo 1997:114), all of them settled in the present department of Intibucá, it is plausible to argue that the province of the Cares extended, at least, over the central portion of this department.

The abovementioned sources suggest that a distinct political and ethnic territory referred to as the Care province existed at the time of the conquest. This province was likely made up of the towns surrounding Intibucá east of Cerquin. Its inhabitants likely spoke a dialect of Lenca, and though little can be said about its political organization directly from sources, it was likely a multitown province organized along similar lines to Cerquin.

THE PROVINCE OF THE CANOLA AGAINST THE PROVINCES OF SULACO-MANIANI AND OLANCHO

The final region to be explored here is referred to by some colonial sources refers to as the "Province of the Canola." It provides a clear example of the numerous and often conflicting definitions of the word *province*. Its territory covers the central and northwest quadrants of Olancho, the northern portion of Francisco Morazan, and adjacent territories in Colón, Yoro, and Comayagua, totaling several thousand square kilometers (AGI, Justicia, 1032, No. 3). According to historical records, it seems that the links that bounded this province were linguistic and ethnic instead of political, and that its population belonged to the Lenca family (Gómez Zúñiga 2011:128–131).

The Canola territory overlaps with Lara-Pinto's political units of Sulaco-Maniani and Olancho (Lara-Pinto 1991:223–226; 1996). According to Lara-Pinto, the Sulaco-Maniani polity extended over most of the current Comayagua department, including the southern portion of the Department of Yoro; meanwhile the territory of the Olancho Province covered the western and central region of Olancho (Hasemann and Lara-Pinto 1993). Thus, if the provinces of Sulaco-Maniani and Olancho were unified political units, its leaders would have ruled over an extensive territory. However, a closer look at historical documents fails to support the existence of such a large political entity and paints the picture of an ethnically diverse and fragmented political landscape where five separate smaller chiefdoms may have existed at the time of the conquest.

Traditionally, almost all of the space described is included within Tolupán territory. However, Lara-Pinto (1985:56–57), relying on Richter (1971), showed that Maniani is linked with the Lenca, while Newsom proved the Lenca linguistic identity of Agalteca and Comayagua (Newsom 1992:44–45). Considering that a 1574 source documented a Lenca province in Olancho (AGI, Patronato, 182, Ramo 30) and an earlier source pointed out the existence of Canola Indians there (AGI, Guatemala, 164, 1565), and considering that other sources suggest that these Canola and Lenca of Olancho were the same natives and were settled on central and western Olancho (Gómez Zúñiga 2011:128–131), it can be assumed that the Lenca language provided a shared identity throughout the Canola Province.

However, as I noted earlier, conquerors documented other provinces along this central corridor, among which are those of Olancho and Sulaco-Maniani, currently interpreted as chiefdoms. According to the model of political geography of Lara-Pinto (1991), the population of the valley of Comayagua, as well as several thousand square kilometers of the central region of Honduras, was dominated jointly by Sulaco and Maniani (Dixon 1992:22). These two sites are highlighted in the *repartimiento* of San Pedro de Puerto de Caballos of 1536, where Maniani is described as an important village of about 400 houses (AGI, Patronato, 20, No. 4, R.6). Perhaps because of the relevance of Maniani, conquistadors used it as a reference point to indicate the position of neighboring towns. However, its geographic location and size alone do not demonstrate the political subjection of surrounding populations to it.

According to a document dated to 1593, Don Jeronimo Corella, Indian mayor of Maniani, declared himself to be *cacique* and natural lord of all the Indians of Maniani, and Juan de Guzman made declarations as principal Indian of the town without referring, at any time, to the primacy of Maniani over any population surrounding it (AGI, Escribanía, 344A). One reference to regional political fragmentation comes from Cristobal de Pedraza, protector of the Indians of Honduras and eventually its first bishop: "thus came the said Captain Alonso de Cáceres . . . [with] some people to go conquer the [towns] remaining [to be conquered] to populate the town of Comayagua, a trip during which he populated and pacified all the land and its provinces, which are four or five, until the Olancho Valley" (AGI, Guatemala, 9A, R.8, No. 13). The mention of four or five "provinces" within the territory of Maniani casts doubt on the claim that this area was a single unified political unit. Furthermore, other documents describing the Comayagua Valley also did not document the dependence of that locale on any greater political unit (see Lunardi 1946).

For the Bishop Pedraza, Comayagua was one of the most important towns of central Honduras, and because of this the broader valley took on its name. Thanks to the records of the Royal Accounting Office, it is known that this *encomienda* included Comayagua as a "cabecera de por sí" and Jeto as a *barrio* or *estancia*. That the domain of Comayagua did not cover the whole valley has been proven using old land titles, where natives claimed as their own the land between the Río Grande and the eastern mountains, and from the Canquigue River as far as the valley ends (Lunardi 1946:8).

The most concrete evidence of Comayagua's political organization comes from land disputes of the seventeenth century, whose records include translations of documents of the sixteenth. In these, some notices of 1561–1562 mention an indigenous governor as well as a chief at Jeto, and other men classified as principals (Lunardi 1946:14, 18, 21). Because the post of indigenous governor was imposed by the colonial administration to carry out taxation (AGI, Patronato, 182, R. 46), and as on many occasions the main *cacique* exercised this role, it is probable that Comayagua's precolumbian elite included a principal chief who ruled over the entire political unit, plus another subordinate *cacique* in Jeto, complemented by several principals in each of the towns.

Contact-period chronicles of the Comayagua Valley also highlighted Lejamaní as another powerful town in its vicinity. The Royal Accounting Office of the Honduras governorship provides the most enlightening data on its constitution. Since 1571 royal officials mentioned several *barrios* attached to Lejamaní (AGI, Contaduría, 988, R.10), but their names were not transcribed until 1587, when the towns of Jocola and Ajuterique appear as dependents. Thus, this political unit seems to have been integrated by Lejamaní as a "cabecera de por sí" along with at least two *barrios* or *estancias* (Jocola and Ajuterique). However, given the lack of earlier documents, it is possible that additional *barrios* and *estancias* may have been accorded to Lejamaní at the beginning of the sixteenth century (AGI, Contaduría, 989).

Like Comayagua, Lejamaní seems to have been another simple chiefdom whose territory occupied much of the western portion of the Comayagua Valley, where its capital was found next to two *barrios* or *estancias*. Despite the lack of data on their social organization, it was likely integrated by a group of lords composed of chiefs and principals who ruled over a peasant majority, given the consistent pattern of political organization seen elsewhere in central Honduras, including in nearby Comayagua.

Also within the Province of the Canola was Silca Comayagua, or Comayagua Canola, as it was also called. Silca Comayagua was a town located in a narrow plain west of the Olancho Valley in an area close to the sources of the Guayape River, one of the largest tributaries of the Patuca River. Its geographic location was strategic for the exchange between central Honduras and societies living in Olancho's plains. Regarding the structure of this political unit, a certificate of *encomienda*, dated to 1541, provides evidence of the integration of at least two towns: that of Comayagua, which would be the "capital in itself," and Silca, which would have been its *barrio* or *estancia*.

Texts regarding the rebellion in Olancho (1527) provide the first evidence of Silca's elite when they discuss the figure of its chief Benito, coordinator of the armed uprising of the towns of the Olancho Valley. More comprehensive information is located in the lawsuit for the *encomienda* of Silca Comayagua, where litigants claim to have received the *encomienda* from the hands of members of the local elite. One claimed to have received it from the principal Chicoey Coat, while the other claimed to have taken possession of it from its chief Taususquin and from another chief named Naut Tecacon. The final possession was awarded in 1545 to a native named Quiyaguian, presented as lord and main chief of Comayagua (AGI, Justicia, 1032, No. 3).

The references cited, in addition to documenting various characters of the local elite, called lords, chiefs (*caciques*), or principals, demonstrate the existence of diplomatic channels between Silca Comayagua and its surrounding towns, who were able to join forces to expel the Spanish invaders and later successfully resist their raids for two decades (Gómez Zúñiga 2012:48–49). Outside of the above data, no evidence supports the dependence of Silca Comayagua on a greater political entity, nor is there evidence that it dominated other surrounding towns outside the already-mentioned *barrio* of Silca.

When reviewing sixteenth-century primary-source documents from the area identified as the province of "Canola" by Lara-Pinto, there is stronger evidence for a few chiefdoms, such as Maniani itself, Comayagua, Lejamanai, and Silca Comayagua, than for a single large political entity. The data reviewed suggest that the region may well have been unified by larger ethnic and linguistic ties, which may have led to its being labeled a province by the Spaniards, but it was likely more politically fragmented than previously thought.

CONCLUSIONS

When the term *province* is placed in the context of the ethnohistoric sources of the sixteenth century, the political structure of Lenca political units described in the research of Lara-Pinto (1991:221) is corroborated, in which an elite composed of chiefs and principals ruled over a class of rural commoners. However, if the *encomiendas* discussed here have their origin in original Lenca political units, the political geography of the Lenca territory was probably much more fragmented than has hitherto been assumed. It is therefore essential to pursue this line of research further to determine whether the model of political geography of central Honduras was composed of a greater number of smaller chiefdoms or a small group of large lordships.

The analysis of the data presented here also suggests that the determination of the dimension of the political units of Central America should be elucidated in response to as broad an empirical base as possible, instead of assuming the labels imposed by the authors of these historical documents. Does that mean that the term *province* was not used to refer to political units? It is likely that it was sometimes used with that intention, but on other occasions perhaps it referred to areas occupied by speakers of the same language and thus was closer to the idea of *nation*, regardless of whether the territory was divided among various political units. At other times, it could have been used to describe previously existing political units that were later fragmented, and we cannot rule out that it was also applied to specific geographical areas covering different political units. Given the multiple meanings of the term, and the unsystematic use given to it by the conquerors, it is probable that the "provinces" cited were not always of a similar nature.

WORKS CITED

Carías, Marcos. 1998. *Crónicas y Cronistas de la Conquista de Honduras*. Tegucigalpa, Honduras: Editorial Universitaria.

Chapman, Anne. 1974. *Los Nicarao y los Chorotega según las fuentes históricas*. San José, Costa Rica: Publicaciones de la Universidad de Costa Rica.

Chapman, Anne. 1985. *Los Hijos del Copal y la Candela: Ritos agrarios y tradición oral de los Lencas de Honduras*, Tomo I. Mexico City: Universidad Nacional Autónoma de México.

Chapman, Anne. 1986. *Los Hijos del Copal y la Candela: Ritos agrarios y tradición oral de los Lencas de Honduras*, Tomo II. Mexico City: Universidad Nacional Autónoma de México.

Cortés, Hernán. 1986. *Letters from Mexico*, trans. and ed. Anthony Pagden. New Haven, CT: Yale University Press.

Covarrubias Orozco, Sebastian de. 1943. *Tesoro de la Lengua Castellana*. Reimpresión facsimilar del original de 1611. Barcelona, Spain: Martí de Riquer, Horta de Impresiones y Ediciones.

Dixon, Boyd. 1992. "Prehistoric Political Change on the Southeast Mesoamerican Periphery." *Ancient Mesoamerica* 3(1):11–25.

Gómez Zúñiga, Pastor Rodolfo. 2011. "Los indígenas de la Gobernación de Higueras-Honduras: una visión interdisciplinar sobre la frontera entre el área cultural mesoamericana y el Área Intermedia." Unpublished PhD dissertation, Universidad Nacional de Educación a Distancia, Madrid, Spain.

Gómez Zúñiga, Pastor Rodolfo. 2012. *Minería aurífera, esclavos negros y relaciones interétnicas en la Honduras del siglo XVI (1524–1570)*. Tegucigalpa, Honduras: Instituto Hondureño de Antropología e Historia.

Hasemann, George, and Gloria Lara-Pinto. 1993. "Regionalismo e Interacción: Historia Cultural de la Zona Central." In *Historia General de Centroamérica*, Volumen I: *Historia Antigua de América Central: Del Poblamiento a la Conquista*, ed. Robert Carmack, 135–216. Madrid, Spain: Facultad Latinoamericana de Ciencias Sociales.

Herranz, Atanasio. 1996. *Estado, Sociedad y Lenguaje: la Política Lingüística en Honduras*. Tegucigalpa, Honduras: Editorial Guaymuras.

Lara-Pinto, Gloria. 1980. "Beiträge zur indianischen Ethnographie von Honduras in der 1. Hälfte des 16. Jahrhunderts, unter besonderer Berücksichtigung der Historischen Demographie." Unpublished PhD dissertation, Institut of Archaeology, University of Hamburg, Germany.

Lara-Pinto, Gloria. 1985. "Apuntes sobre la Afiliación Etnica de los Pobladores Indígenas de los Valles de Comayagua y Sulaco. Siglo XVI." *Mesoamérica* 9:45–57.

Lara-Pinto, Gloria. 1991. "Sociopolitical Organization in Central and Southwest Honduras at the Time of the Conquest: A Model for the Formation of Complex Society." In *The Formation of Complex Society in Southeastern Mesoamerica*, ed. William R. Fowler, 215–235. Boca Raton, FL: CRC Press.

Lara-Pinto, Gloria. 1996. "Centroamérica desde la perspectiva indígena, siglos XVI y XVII." In *Los indios de Centroamérica*, ed. George Hasemann, Gloria LaraPinto, and Fernando Cruz Sandoval, 99–277. Madrid, Spain: Editorial MAPFRE.

Leyva, Héctor. 1991. *Documentos Coloniales de Honduras*. Tegucigalpa, Honduras: Centro de Publicaciones del Obispado de Choluteca.

Lunardi, Federico. 1946. *El Valle de Comayagua, Documentos para la Historia: El Tenguax y la Primera Iglesia Catedral de Comayagua.* Tegucigalpa, Honduras: Talleres Tipográficos Nacionales.

Martínez Castillo, Mario Felipe. 1983. *Documentos: Historia de Honduras.* Tegucigalpa, Honduras: Editorial Universitaria.

Newsom, Linda A. 1992. *El Costo de la Conquista.* Tegucigalpa, Honduras: Editorial Guaymuras.

Real Academia Española de la Lengua. 1984 [1726–1739]. *Diccionario de Autoridades, reedición facsimilar 1726–1739, tomos A–C, D–Ñ, O–Z.* Madrid, Spain: Editorial Gredos.

Richter, Ernesto. 1971. "Untersuchungen zum 'Lenca'-Problem." Unpublished PhD Dissertation, Universität Tübingen.

Vallejo, Antonio Ramón. (1997) [1893]. *República de Honduras Primer Anuario Estadístico correspondiente al año de 1889.* Tegucigalpa, Honduras: Editorial Universitaria.

DOCUMENTS

AGI: Archivo General de Indias

Contaduria Section

AGI, Contaduría, 987, No. 2: Cuentas de la Real Hacienda de su Majestad de la Provincia de Honduras, 1554.

AGI, Contaduría, 988: Cuentas de la Real Hacienda de su Majestad de la Provincia de Honduras, 1562.

AGI, Contaduría, 988, R.10, Cuentas de la Contaduría Real de la Gobernación de Honduras, 1572.

AGI, Contaduría, 989, "Cuentas de Martín de Soto Pachón y Antonio Enríquez," Comayagua, 1588.

Escribanía Section

AGI, Escribanía, 344A: "Residencia de Rodrigo Ponce de León, gobernador de Comayagua," Comayagua, 1582–1594.

Guatemala Section

AGI, Guatemala, 9A, R.8, No. 13: "Relación del Licenciado Pedraza a Su Majestad," Gracias a Dios, 1º de mayo de 1539.

AGI, Guatemala, 9A, R.8, No. 15: "Carta de Francisco de Montejo a Su Majestad," Gracias a Dios, 1º de junio de 1539.

AGI, Guatemala, 9A, R.8, No. 18: "Carta de Francisco Montejo a Su Majestad," Gracias a Dios, 15 de agosto de 1539.

AGI, Guatemala, 39, R.14, No. 95: "Don Juan Guerra de Ayala, gobernador de Honduras," 21 de mayo de 1611.

AGI, Guatemala, 44B, No. 89: "Carta del Cabildo de Tencoa," Tencoa, 25 de marzo de 1580.

AGI, Guatemala, 116, No. 15: "Información de Pedro de Paz Quiñónez," Santiago de Guatemala, 3 de mayo de 1604.

AGI, Guatemala, 120, No. 8: "Información de Fernando de Lara," Gracias a Dios, 7 de mayo de 1612.

AGI, Guatemala, 128, No. 136v–150r: "Tasaciones de la villa de Santa María del Valle de Comayagua hecha por los Señores Presidente y Oidores de la Audiencia y Cancillería de los Confines," 1 al 21 de marzo de 1549.

AGI, Guatemala, 164, "Provanza hecha en la provincia de Honduras . . . ante el Señor Gobernador . . . a pedimiento del muy Ilustre Reverendísimo Señor Don Fray Hieronimo Corella, Obispo de dicha Provincia," villa de San Jorge, 28 de febrero de 1565.

AGI, Guatemala, 164, "Carta a S.M. del Obispo fr. Alonso Vargas y Abarca," Valladolid de Comayagua, 14 de febrero de 1688.

AGI, Guatemala, 184: "Información sobre las lenguas de los naturales de los pueblos de doctrina a cargo de la Orden de Nuestra Señora de las Mercedes y de la suficiencia de los religiosos para administrarlos, Comayagua," 1683.

AGI, Guatemala, 402, L.2, "Real Cédula al gobernador de la provincia de Higueras y Cabo de Honduras," Fuensalida, 22 de septiembre de 1541.

Justicia Section

AGI, Justicia, 129, No. 2: "El adelantado don Francisco Montejo, gobernador de las provincias de Yucatán, Higueras y Honduras, con el licenciado Cristóbal de Pedraza, protector de indios, sobre el embargo de sus bienes y la suspensión de su empleo," 1539–1540.

AGI, Justicia, 299A: "Residencia tomada a los licenciados Alonso Maldonado, Pedro Ramírez de Quiñones, Diego de Herrera y Juan Rogel, presidente y oidores de la Audiencia de Guatemala, y a sus oficiales," 1548–1550.

AGI, Justicia, 311, No. 1: "Residencia que se tomó a Pedro de Salvatierra, Alcalde Mayor que fue de la provincia de Honduras, por el Lic. Alonso Ortiz Delgueta, gobernador y justicia mayor de ella," Gracias a Dios, 1562–1563.

AGI, Justicia, 1032, No. 3: "Jerónimo de Sanmartín, vecino de San Pedro, contra Diego Ramírez, sobre ciertos indios" (1544).

AGI, Justicia, 1032, No. 4, R.1: "Alonso García, vecino de Gracias, con el Adelantado Francisco de Montejo, sobre el pueblo de indios de Yamala," Gracias, 1544–1545.

Patronato Section

AGI, Patronato, 20, No. 4, R.6: "Repartimiento general de los pueblos e indios naturales . . . de la jurisdicción de la ciudad de Gracias a Dios," San Pedro de Puerto de Caballos, 20 de julio de 1536; y "Repartimiento General de los Pueblos e Indios Naturales de la Tierra de la Jurisdicción de la Villa de San Pedro de Puerto de Caballos," Jerónimo de Sanmartín, San Pedro de Puerto de Caballos, 15 de julio de 1536.

AGI, Patronato, 20, No. 5, R.2: "Expediente de la fundación de la Villa de la Frontera de Cáceres y de lo sucedido con el gobernador de Nicaragua Pedrarias Dávila," 1526.

AGI, Patronato, 182, Ramo 30, "Renunciación del Obispado de Honduras," San Jorge de Olancho, a 31 de marzo de 1574.

AGI, Patronato, 182, R.46, "Expediente sobre la conveniencia de elevar a arzobispado a la catedral de Guatemala," Guatemala, 1574.

RAHM: Real Academia de la Historia de Madrid

RAHM, Relaciones Geográficas, 9/4663, N°16, XLIII, "Relación de todos los pueblos de la provincia de Honduras y la forma en que se tenía dividida la Administración de Justicia," Alonso Contreras de Guevara, Comayagua, 20 de abril de 1582.

12

Sixteenth–Century Mobility and Interaction in Southeastern Mesoamerica

Clues from Conquistador Routes

WILLIAM R. FOWLER

The historically documented movements of Spanish conquistadors and their allies and interactions between Spaniards and indigenous groups in El Salvador, Honduras, Nicaragua, and Costa Rica in the 1520s indicate routes of communication, networks of interaction, and levels of interconnections continuing from late precolumbian times into the early colonial period (figure 12.1). An examination of early interaction in the region between conquistadors and indigenous groups, and among the Spaniards themselves, reveals specific parameters and possibilities with regard to routes of communication and interaction networks. In addition, the high degree of mobility of the conquistadors and their allies strongly suggests a similar high degree of mobility among precolumbian social groups of the region and for all of Mesoamerica and northern Central America. Put simply, long-distance and rapid transit of large groups must be regarded as possible in precolumbian times when we consider that the movement of early Spanish armies, their logistics, and support depended heavily on indigenous allies.

When studying precolumbian Mesoamerican population movements, we must first address questions of scale. Scale involves three elements: group size, distance, and travel time. Some models of prehispanic Mesoamerican population movements have assumed long distances but have failed to specify group size and travel time. A well-known example

DOI: 10.5876/9781646420971.c012

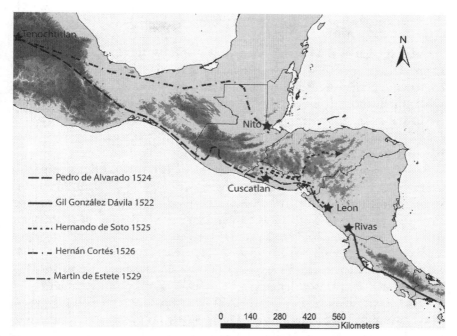

FIGURE 12.1. *Long-distance movements by Spanish conquistadors in Southeastern Mesoamerica during the sixteenth century.*

consists of the arrival of Teotihuacanos in the Maya lowlands, dated by David Stuart (2000:471) through hieroglyphic inscriptions on Tikal Stela 31 to 11 Eb, equivalent to 16 January 378 CE. If this inscription implies a military take-over of Tikal by Teotihuacan, as Stuart believes, many questions remain to be answered on the scale of this military invasion. Ignoring for the moment the possible objections (see Braswell 2003), and following the argument developed here, I suggest that this troop movement could have involved thousands of Teotihuacano warriors.

In this essay I deal exclusively with large groups numbering in the hundreds or thousands, long distances in the range of 500 to 2,000 km, and relatively long travel times of several months or even a few years. To specify further, I discuss large population movements in the form of military mobilizations rather than migrations that often span several generations (Rouse 1986:175–180). Despite their military character, I argue that these movements have the potential to shed light not only on troop movements but also on other kinds of large group movements in preconquest Mesoamerica. I am thinking especially of the movements of long-distance merchants, known as *pochteca*, among the Aztecs.

Other models assume a fairly limited view of the scale of large group mobility in Mesoamerica. Ross Hassig's (1994:15–16, 23–24) calculations of transport constraint and logistical difficulties in Mesoamerican warfare have had a significant influence. He noted that Mesoamerican transport was limited to foot travel and assumed that large groups such as armies had to carry their own food and water or employ specialized porters. The latter would have been the preferred option, since soldiers also had to carry their gear and weapons. At the most favorable ratio of one porter for every two soldiers (known for the case of the Aztecs), each porter carrying a load of 23 kg (50 lbs.), and a consumption of 0.95 kg (2 lbs.) of maize per day (about 24 man/days of food) (he also mentions one-half liter of water per man per day, but this does not enter into his calculation), Hassig calculated that an army could travel for only eight days on its own supplies. Thus, Hassig (1994:16) states, "the time limit that logistics placed on marches meant that armies simply could not go very far." He estimated that Mesoamerican armies marching on poor roads might have traveled about 19 km (12 mi.) per day. This limitation coupled with their logistical constraints led Hassig (1994:16) to conclude that Mesoamerican armies would have had a combat radius of no more than 58 km (36 mi.), assuming a three-days' travel to the destination, one day of engagement, one of recuperation, and three days to return. Arlen Chase and Diane Chase (1998), based on Hassig's calculations, attempt to define warfare arenas in their examination of polity size in the Classic Maya lowlands, concluding that Maya regional polity size was limited by a total military marching distance of 60 km. Yet during the conquest, as I detail below, Spanish armies and their indigenous allies routinely marched 500–1,500 km from their points of departure.

The early Spanish expeditions make appropriate analogs for preconquest travel for the following reasons. The complex societies of Southeastern Mesoamerica and the Greater Chibchan area were immersed in symbolically and cosmologically charged exchange and interaction in which the Spaniards injected themselves (Ibarra Rojas 2001; Lara-Pinto 1996). From an economic perspective, the Spanish conquistadors had much the same interests as powerful indigenous *caciques*: acquisition of wealth (primarily gold and pearls), capturing of slaves, and control of trade routes. The latter for the Spaniards meant "discovery" of indigenous geographical knowledge, gained with the aid of native guides and interpreters. Conquistador troop movements occurred from both north to south and south to north, involving Spanish forces accompanied by substantial numbers of indigenous troops (table 12.1). They followed

TABLE 12.1. Estimated distances and troop numbers of Spanish expeditions across Southeastern Mesoamerica

Expedition Leader	Origin	Destination	Distance (km)	Spaniards	Auxiliaries
Pedro de Alvarado	Tenochtitlan	Cuscatlan	1,500[b]	420–555	5,000–20,000
Gil González Dávila	Panama	Isthmus of Rivas, Nicaragua	1,200[a]	100	400
Hernando de Soto	Leon	Cuscatlan, then Gulf of Honduras	1,445[a]	unknown	unknown
Hernán Cortés	Tenochtitlan	Nito	1,300[b]	380	3,000–20,000
Diego de Rojas	Santiago de Guatemala	San Salvador	unknown[c]	60	300
Martín de Estete	Leon	San Salvador	300[b]	200	4,000

[a] Spanish distances from primary sources in leagues.
[b] Estimate based on projected paths.
[c] There are no available reconstructions of Rojas's path.

well-established prehispanic trade routes that had existed since Classic-period times, if not before, and therefore these movements should be considered an important source of information on interconnectedness of and communication between groups, networks of interaction, migrations of new peoples, and shifts in political structure in the conquest era and precolumbian times.

Spanish incursions into northern Central America radiated north and west from Panama and south and east from Mexico. These two major expansionary thrusts overlapped, and the expeditionary leaders and forces clashed in El Salvador and Honduras. At the conclusion of the Mexica-Spanish war in central Mexico, shortly after the siege and destruction of Tenochtitlan, Hernán Cortés ordered two expeditions to the south and east: one by land to Guatemala and El Salvador, led by Pedro de Alvarado, and the other by sea, sailing around the coast of Yucatán to Honduras, led by Cristóbal de Olid. Cortés's decision to extend the conquest to Guatemala was probably conditioned by a knowledge of the area acquired from Mexica informants (Matthew 2004:74; 2012:36). Alvarado had traveled to the south previously, at least as far as Soconusco. The trade route from central Mexico through Oaxaca and Tehuantepec to Soconusco had been in existence since at least Teotihuacan times, for more than a thousand years before the conquest (Oudijk and Restall

2007:50). Another factor in Cortés's decision to launch these two expeditions at this time consisted of the impending threat that Pedrarias Dávila would expand his conquests northward from Pacific Nicaragua into Honduras and El Salvador (Escalante Arce 2014:42–60; Hackett 1918:47–48).

THE ALVARADO *ENTRADA* TO CUSCATLAN

Alvarado and his troops departed Tenochtitlan in late fall of 1523, very likely November 13 (Lardé 1925:112–113). According to Cortés (1985:193; 1986:317), the captain took with him 120 cavalry, 160 horses, 300 foot soldiers, including 130 crossbowmen and harquebusiers, and four cannon with powder and ammunition. Among the Spaniards figured Pedro de Alvarado's three brothers (Jorge, Gonzalo, and Gómez de Alvarado), three cousins (Hernando de Alvarado, Diego de Alvarado, and Gonzalo de Alvarado y Chávez), and a trusted friend (Pedro Portocarrero, or Puertocarrero). A large number of native lords and warriors from central Mexico accompanied this expedition. Native troops from a number of different polities and regions joined and became *conquistadores indios* or Indian conquistadors (Matthew 2004, 2012; Matthew and Oudijk 2007). Tlaxcaltecs, who had formed the majority of native allies of the Spaniards in the conquest of Mexico, were pressed into service once again. Indigenous troops joined from Tetzcoco, Tenochtitlan, Xochimilco, Coyoacan, Culhuacan, other Aztec city-states in the Basin of Mexico; Cholollan, Huexotzinco, and Tepeaca in the modern state of Puebla (Escalante Arce 2001:18–21; Fowler 1989:135; Indios mexicanos 1564; Matthew 2004:51, 61, 73; 2012:71–73, 76–81; Recinos 1986:64).

As the expedition advanced southward, more native auxiliaries joined: Benizaa (Zapotecs) and Ñuudzavui (Mixtecs) in Oaxaca; Nahua-speaking Pipils in Huehuetan, Soconusco; and Kaqchikels in Guatemala (Escalante Arce 2001:21; Fowler 1989:135; Gasco 2003:286–287; Polo Sifontes 1980). For example, the *artillero mayor* (master gunner) Diego de Usagre brought with him 60 Mixtec warriors from his *encomienda* in the region of Segura de la Frontera in Tutepec, Oaxaca (Kramer 1994:59; Lenkersdorf 1993:85; Probanzas de Diego de Usagre y Francisco Castellón 1564). Estimating the exact number of Indian conquistadors involved in Alvarado's 1524 entrada presents a problem that may never find a fully adequate solution, but some reasonable estimates, or at least parameters, suggest themselves. Alvarado (1924:80) himself put the number of native allies present in the Guatemalan battles at 5,000–6,000. Without specifying an absolute number, Cortés (1985:194; 1986:317) stated that the number of native troops was small because of the length of the journey. Anyone aware of the long-distance troop movements of Mesoamerican armies would know that this statement makes no sense (Hassig 1994), and historical evidence indicates that, contrary to Cortés's claim, very large numbers of native auxiliaries participated in this expedition. Cortés would have had no reason to reveal the large numbers of auxiliaries, and, in fact, he had good motives to suppress their real numbers (Matthew 2004:76; Sherman 1979:124–125). Like Cortés, Bernal Díaz del Castillo (1955:2:121) underestimated the number of Indian auxiliaries on the Alvarado expedition, putting them at 200 Tlaxcaltecs and Chololtecs and 100 Mexicans (i.e., Mexicas or other Aztecs). They did not want to reveal to the Crown the importance of their indigenous allies and their high level of participation in the conquest. Fuentes y Guzmán (1969–1972: bk. 2, ch. 1:82) uncritically accepted the estimate of Bernal (his great-grandfather). It should be noted, however, that Bernal did not participate in this expedition, and his estimate appears extremely low. Furthermore, according to Díaz del Castillo (1955:2:121), the Spanish troops on this expedition numbered 135 cavalry, 300 foot soldiers, and 120 artillery men (*escopeteros* and *ballesteros*), making a total of 555 Spanish troops, or 420 if one prefers Cortés's estimate cited above. It seems highly unlikely, if this expedition followed the pattern of the conquest of Mexico, that Spanish troops would have outnumbered indigenous troops.

Another Spanish conquistador, Pedro González Nájera, a resident of Santiago de Guatemala, declared in an eyewitness account that about 7,000 indigenous allied troops supported Alvarado in Guatemala during the first *entrada* (Escalante Arce 2001:20; Probanza de los indios conquistadores 1573). Going to the other extreme, the Tetzcocan mestizo chronicler Fernando de Alva Ixtlilxochitl (1975–1977:1:487) put the number of indigenous warriors departing with Alvarado on this expedition at 20,000. Interestingly, Bancroft (1883:626), after reviewing the estimates of all of the primary and secondary sources available in his time, also opted for the number of 20,000. Considering the range of numbers in these estimates and the testimony given by the native troops themselves, I see no impediment to accepting Alvarado's estimate of 5,000–6,000 indigenous auxiliary troops, although I would consider this a minimum number. If we apply the 50:1 ratio of indigenous to Spanish troops derived from Mexico (Hassig 1994), the estimated total of indigenous forces in the entrada to Guatemala and El Salvador could rise to more than 20,000, an estimate also suggested independently by William L. Sherman (1979:22).

GIL GONZÁLEZ DÁVILA IN NICARAGUA

A more southerly Pacific network of interaction is attested by documents deriving from the 1522 entrada of the accountant of Hispaniola, Gil González

Dávila, from the Gulf of Chiriquí, Panama, north to the Nicoya Peninsula, passing by Lake Nicaragua, and ending at Nochari, in the Isthmus of Rivas, Nicaragua. Since the arrival of the Chorotegas beginning about AD 800, this Pacific corridor was characterized by Mesoamerican cultural patterns, including expansionist politics, high levels of intergroup conflict, tribute-based political economies, dynamic market exchange of subsistence goods, and intensive exchange of preciosities among elites (Fowler 1992). As reported by the treasurer Andrés de Cereceda and the chroniclers Peter Martyr and Gonzalo Fernández de Oviedo, González and his army, consisting of 100 Spanish troops, 400 native auxiliaries, and four horses, marched 224 leagues (about 1,200 km) (Fowler 1989:17; Incer 1990:56; Lara-Pinto 1996:164–166; Radell 1969:53–56; Sherman 1979:27–28). González Dávila collected gold valued at more than 112,000 pesos from native populations (presumably tumbaga objects from the Chibchan area), sometimes peacefully, other times forcibly, and claimed to have baptized 32,000 indigenous souls on this expedition (Fernández de Oviedo 1959: bk. 29, ch. 21:289; Relación de Gil González Dávila 1522). Though not directly relevant to present concerns, it should be mentioned that while González Dávila was advancing northward by land, his partner and co-expeditionary, the pilot Andres Niño, explored the Pacific coast from Panama, reaching the island of Meanguera in the Gulf of Fonseca on May 31, 1522, and continuing along the Pacific littoral as far north as Tehuantepec, Mexico (Escalante Arce 2014:28–33, 36–41).

HERNANDO DE SOTO IN CUSCATLAN/NEQUEPIO

We turn now to a third case, which bridges the area between the Isthmus of Rivas and central El Salvador and extends to central Honduras: Hernando de Soto's invasion in early 1525 of the Pipil region of Cuscatlan, in central El Salvador. Cuscatlan, known as Nequepio to the Chorotegas in Nicaragua, at this time marked the southeastern frontier of Pedro de Alvarado's extension of the conquest of Mexico (Escalante Arce 2014). From Nicaragua, Francisco Hernández de Córdoba sent Soto, at that time the *alcalde* of León (which had been founded in November 1524), northward to search for a route to the Caribbean and to determine the status of any other Spanish explorations in the area. Doris Stone (1954:87) mentions that another objective was to found a Spanish town, which would fit with the overall strategy of Pedrarias and Hernández de Córdoba. During this expedition, Soto found Pedro de Alvarado's field camp in Cuscatlan, referred to by Pedrarias as "the great city of Nequepio," but Alvarado had withdrawn to his base at Iximche,

Guatemala. Soto reported seeing a lombard cannon and some footwear left behind by Alvarado's army (Carta de Pedrarias a S. M. 1525:20; Escalante Arce 2014:50–52):

> De esta Ciudad de León se fué descubriendo e pacificando hasta la grande Ciudad de Nequepio que decían que era Melaca a donde había llegado Alvarado con su gente de Cortés, v allí se vio donde tuvo el real que tuvo y se vieron algunas cosas de las que allí dejó, en especial una lombarda e algun calzado. (A full English translation of this letter may be found in Lockhart and Otte 1976:7–14.)

In a subsequent letter to the Crown, Pedrarias provided distances from Nicaragua to Nequepio (200 leagues [1070 km]) and from Nequepio to the Gulf of Higueras, Honduras (70 leagues [375 km]), noting that Nequepio was also known as *Cuzcatán* (Carta de Pedrarias a S. M., 1525:2). *Nequepio* was none other than the Mangue place name used by the Chorotegas of Nicaragua and Honduras to refer to the Pipil center and region of Cuscatlan (Duncan 1996:80–81; Escalante Arce 2005; Fernández de Oviedo 1959: bk. 20, ch. 11:252; Guido Martínez 2008; Incer 1990:71; Lardé y Larín 2000:133–135). *Melaca*, or *Malalaca*, referred to the Choluteca region of southeastern Honduras. Daniel Brinton (1895:40) explained it succinctly in his report on the collections exhibited at the Columbian Historical Exposition at Madrid in 1892–1893: "The Chorotegas . . . extended through Nicaragua on the shores of the lakes, and by the way of Nequepio on the gulf of Fonseca or of Chorotega Malalaca, in what now forms the province of Choluteca, in Honduras."

Considering the antecedents and the circumstances, one must assume that Soto's *entrada* into Cuscatlan would not have been peaceable (Escalante Arce 2014:53). From Cuscatlan, Soto pressed northward into the Comayagua mountains north of the border with El Salvador and traveled swiftly to the Olancho region of east-central Honduras where his forces clashed with those of Gil González Dávila (Carta de Pedrarias a S. M. 1525:3; Duncan 1996:81; Incer 1990:72–73; Radell 1969:62–63; Stone 1954:87–88). González Dávila killed several of Soto's men, captured Soto and his surviving soldiers, and confiscated the booty they had acquired in Cuscatlan, estimated at a value of 130,000 pesos of low-grade gold (*oro de baja ley*, presumably tumbaga). González Dávila allowed Soto to return to León. Many of the Spaniards from Nicaragua deserted González Dávila and followed Soto back to León to join forces with Hernández de Córdoba. Meanwhile, González Dávila returned to the north of Honduras where he would form an alliance with Francisco de las Casas against Cristóbal de Olid.

The arrival of Cortés in Honduras the next year with 380 Spaniards and at least 3,000 Mexican warriors (Díaz del Castillo 1955:2:188–193; Milla 1976:119) calmed this chaotic situation, but only briefly. With Matthew (2012:63) and Restall (2003: 51), we note the irony of Cortés campaigning with a largely native Mesoamerican army to quell internal Spanish disputes. Cortés (1985:221) stated simply, "Llevé . . . conmigo todas las personas principales de los naturales de la tierra" ("I took with me all of the principal persons of the natives of the land"), which would imply a small number, but Díaz del Castillo (1955:2:189–190) put the number of indigenous allies at 3,000 plus their servants, and Ixtlilxochitl (1975–1977:1:494) estimated 20,000 indigenous troops (cf. Martínez 1990:422). Cortés returned to Mexico in late 1526 and left proxies to pursue his interests in Honduras and Nicaragua. A second and final stage of the invasion of Honduras-Higueras involved Pedro de Alvarado in 1536 and Francisco de Montejo from 1536–1537 until 1539, both of whom were accompanied by large numbers of Mexican allied troops (Chuchiak 2007:180–181; Fonseca Corrales 1998:70–71).

The struggle for control of eastern El Salvador between the Spanish factions led by Alvarado in Guatemala and Pedrarias in Nicaragua came to a head in late 1529 and early 1530. Captain Diego de Rojas, dispatched by Captain General Francisco de Orduña from Santiago de Guatemala to San Salvador, was already in the region of Usulutan dealing with an Indian uprising when Pedrarias ordered Martín de Estete to Cuscatlan to attempt to seize San Salvador in late December 1529 (Ayón 1993:180; Bancroft 1886:113; Escalante Arce 2014:69–70; Kramer 1994:85–90; Lardé y Larín 2000:129–130). Details of this expedition are sparse, but Rojas, with his troops, estimated at about 60 Spaniards and as many as 300 indigenous allies, organized a sortie to Popocatepet (the Nahua name for eastern El Salvador during the conquest period), stormed a Lenca hilltop fortress in the Usulutan region, and captured and executed the leaders of the uprising (Barón Castro 1996:150–151; Indios Mexicanos 1564; Rubio Sánchez 1979:17–18).

At about the same time, Rojas received notice of a group of Spaniards in the Gulf of Fonseca region, about two days' march from Usulutan, and set out to find them and learn the purpose of their mission. His curiosity was soon satisfied. Estete had entered the region with about 200 men (90 cavalry and 110 infantry) and some 4,000 indigenous Chorotega allies from Nicaragua. He captured Rojas and 17 members of his party, marched into San Salvador, and attempted to persuade the vecinos of San Salvador to shift their allegiance from Alvarado to Pedrarias (Escalante Arce 2001:40–41; 2014:68–72). The *vecinos* rejected Estete's overtures and sent an urgent request to Santiago for assistance. The *cabildo* of Santiago vacillated and referred the request for support from the vecinos of Cuscatlan to the Audiencia of Mexico.

Meanwhile, Estete established a camp or an ephemeral town, Ciudad de los Caballeros (near Perulapan, not far from San Salvador), designating *alcaldes*, *regidores*, and other officials. From this position, near the large Pipil towns of Cojutepeque and Nonoalco, Estete began enslaving Pipil inhabitants of the *encomienda* towns of the San Salvadorans (Barón Castro 1996:152–167; Lardé y Larín 2000:138–140). In March 1530, after a long delay, the *cabildo* of Santiago agreed that Orduña should order forces led by Captain Francisco López from Santiago to expel Estete (Escalante Arce 2014:68–71; Kramer 1994:92–93; Lardé 1925:171–172; Libro de Actas 1932:189; Rubio Sánchez 1979:18–19). López arrived and after some delay drove Estete out, but the latter carried away some 1,000–2,000 Pipil slaves captured from Perulapan, Cojutepeque, and the surrounding region.

CONCLUSION

These accounts comprise a valuable body of data on late precolumbian networks and interaction on the southeastern periphery of Mesoamerica, which continued into the early conquest era. The specific events discussed here occurred through Spanish intervention, but indigenous agency played an important role in these developments and outcomes. Military deployments cannot be regarded as strictly analogous to precolumbian population movements and interaction. Nevertheless, they belie the commonly held assumption that long-distance population movements must have involved only relatively small numbers of people. As we know well from central Mexican native historical manuscripts such as the *Historia Tolteca-Chichimeca*, long-distance travel was rather routine for many Mesoamerican ethnic groups. Likewise, distances meant little to Spanish conquistadors and their indigenous allies who moved in large numbers with alacrity across great spaces when the need arose. With these movements from Tenochtitlan to Cuauhtemallan and Cuscatlan, or from Nicaragua to Nequepio and north to Olancho, we see sizable numbers of people moving long distances at considerable speed. These are important data for the understanding of precolumbian and conquest-period interaction.

ACKNOWLEDGMENTS

I am grateful to Alejandro J. Figueroa, Whitney A. Goodwin, and Erlend M. Johnson for the invitation to present the first version of this essay in the symposium they organized for the 79th annual meeting of the Society for American Archaeology in Austin, Texas. I also thank them for their careful reading of the essay and suggestions for improvement, although all flaws and shortcomings that remain are strictly my own responsibility. The research for this chapter was conducted as part of the Ciudad Vieja Archaeological Project in El Salvador, supported by Vanderbilt University, the National Science Foundation, the Wenner-Gren Foundation for Anthropological Research, the H. J. Heinz III Charitable Fund, and the Foundation for Ancient Meso-american Studies, Inc. The archaeological project is conducted by permission of the Secretaría de Cultura of El Salvador. My friend and colleague Pedro Antonio Escalante Arce first drew my attention to the significance of the term *Nequepio*. I am grateful to Pedro for his advice and support and for his excellent historical research. I dedicate this essay to Pedro with affection and appreciation for his more than 40 years of advocacy for the preservation and investigation of Ciudad Vieja, the first *villa* of San Salvador.

WORKS CITED

Alvarado, Pedro de. 1924. *An Account of the Conquest of Guatemala in 1524 by Pedro de Alvarado*, ed. Sedley J. Mackie, with a facsimile of the Spanish original, 1525. New York: Cortés Society.

Ayón, Tomás. 1993. *Historia de Nicaragua*, volume 1. Managua, Nicaragua: Colección Cultural, Banco Nicaraguense.

Bancroft, Hubert Howe. 1883. *The Works of Hubert Howe Bancroft*, volume 6: *History of Central America*, volume1, *1501–1530*. San Francisco, CA: A. L. Bancroft.

Bancroft, Hubert Howe. 1886. *The Works of Hubert Howe Bancroft*, volume 7: *History of Central America*, volume 2, *1530–1800*. San Francisco, CA: A. L. Bancroft.

Barón Castro, Rodolfo. 1996. *Reseña histórica de la villa de San Salvador desde su fundación en 1525, hasta que recibe el título de ciudad en 1546*, 2nd ed. San Salvador, El Salvador: Consejo Nacional para la Cultura y el Arte.

Braswell, Geoffrey E. 2003. "Introduction: Reinterpreting Early Classic Interaction." In *The Maya and Teotihuacan: Reinterpreting Early Classic Interaction*, ed. Geoffrey E. Braswell, 1–43. Austin: University of Texas Press,

Brinton, Daniel G. 1895. "Report upon the Collections Exhibited at the Columbian Historical Exposition." In *Report of the United States Commission to the Columbian Historical Exposition at Madrid, 1892–93*, 19–89. Washington, DC: Government Printing Office.

Carta de Pedrarias a S. M. 1525. "Carta de Pedrarias Dávila al Emperador, refiriendo el descubrimiento de Nicaragua por su lugarteniente Francisco Hernández de Córdoba." In *Documentos para la historia de Nicaragua. Colección Somoza*, ed. Andrés Vega Bolaños, volume 1, 128–133. Madrid, Spain: Imprenta Viuda de Galo Sáez.

Chase, Arlen F., and Diane Z. Chase. 1998. "Late Classic Maya Political Structure, Polity Size, and Warfare Arenas." In *Anatomía de una civilización: Aproximaciones interdisciplinarias a la cultura maya*, ed. Andrés Ciudad Ruiz et al., 11–29. Madrid, Spain: Sociedad Española de Estudios Mayas.

Chuchiak, John F., IV. 2007. "Forgotten Allies: The Origins and Roles of Native Mesoamerican Auxiliaries and Indios Conquistadores in the Conquest of Yucatan, 1526–1550." In *Indian Conquistadors: Indigenous Allies in the Conquest of Mesoamerica*, ed. Laura E. Matthew and Michel R. Oudijk, 175–225. Norman: University of Oklahoma Press.

Cortés, Hernán. 1985. *Cartas de relación*. Nota preliminar de Manuel Alcalá. Mexico City, Mexico: Editorial Porrúa.

Cortés, Hernán. 1986. *Hernán Cortés: Letters from Mexico*, trans. and ed. Anthony Pagden. New Haven, CT: Yale University Press.

Díaz del Castillo, Bernal. 1955. *Historia verdadera de la conquista de la Nueva España*, ed. Joaquín Ramírez Cabañas. 2 volumes. Mexico City, Mexico: Editorial Porrúa.

Duncan, David Ewing. 1996. *Hernando de Soto: A Savage Quest in the Americas*. Norman: University of Oklahoma Press.

Escalante Arce, Pedro Antoio. 2001. *Los tlaxcaltecas en Centro América*. San Salvador, El Salvador: Consejo Nacional para la Cultura y el Arte.

Escalante Arce, Pedro Antoio. 2005. "Ciudad Vieja, la villa de San Salvador en La Bermuda: Historia y perspectivas." *El Salvador Investiga* 2:43–52.

Escalante Arce, Pedro Antoio. 2014. *Crónicas de Cuzcatlán-Nequepio y del Mar del Sur*, 2nd ed. Antiguo Cuscatlán, El Salvador: Editorial Delgado.

Fernández de Oviedo y Valdés, Gonzalo. 1959. *Historia general y natural de las Indias*, 5 volumes. Madrid, Spain: Ediciones Atlas.

Fonseca Corrales, Elizabeth. 1998. *Centroamérica: Su historia*. San José, Costa Rica: Editorial Universitaria Centroamericana.

Fowler, William R. 1989. *The Cultural Evolution of Ancient Nahua Civilizations: The Pipil-Nicarao of Central America*. Norman: University of Oklahoma Press.

Fowler, William R. 1992. "The Historiography of Wealth and Hierarchy in the Intermediate Area." In *Wealth and Hierarchy in the Intermediate Area*, ed. Frederick W. Lange, 357–377. Washington, DC: Dumbarton Oaks Research Library and Collection.

Fuentes y Guzmán, Francisco Antonio de. 1969–1972. *Recordación florida: Discurso historial, natural, material y político del reino de Goathemala. . .* , 3 volumes. Biblioteca de Autores Españoles, volumes 230, 251, 259. Madrid, Spain: Ediciones Atlas.

Gasco, Janine. 2003. "Soconusco." In *The Postclassic Mesoamerican World*, ed. Michael E. Smith and Frances F. Berdan, 282–296. Salt Lake City: University of Utah Press.

Guido Martínez, Clemente. 2008. "Nequepio: San Salvador y San Miguel en los documentos de historia de Nicaragua." *El Salvador Investiga* 7:21–27.

Hackett, Charles W. 1918. "The Delimitation of Political Jurisdictions in Spanish North America to 1535." *Hispanic American Historical Review* 1:40–69.

Hassig, Ross. 1994. *Mexico and the Spanish Conquest*. London: Longman.

Ibarra Rojas, Eugenia. 2001. *Fronteras étnicas en la conquista de Nicaragua y Nicoya: Entre la solidaridad y el conflicto*. San José, Costa Rica: Editorial de la Universidad de Costa Rica.

Incer, Jaime. 1990. *Nicaragua: Viajes, rutas y encuentros, 1502–1838*. San José, Costa Rica: Libro Libre.

Indios mexicanos. 1564. Los yndios mexicanos, taxcaltecas, zapotecas, mixtecas y consortes con el fiscal de S. M. sobre que pretenden ser libres de pagar tributos. Seville, Spain: Archivo General de Indias, Justicia 291.

Ixtlilxochitl, Fernando de Alva. 1975–77. *Obras históricas*, ed. Edmundo O'Gorman. 2 volumes. Mexico City, Mexico: Instituto de Investigaciones Históricas, Universidad Nacional Autónoma de México.

Kramer, Wendy. 1994. *Encomienda Politics in Early Colonial Guatemala, 1524–1544: Dividing the Spoils*. Boulder, CO: Westview Press.

Lara-Pinto, Gloria. 1996. "Centroamérica desde la perspectiva indígena, siglos XVI y XVII." In *Los indios de Centroamérica*, ed. George Hasemann, Gloria Lara-Pinto, and Fernando Cruz Sandoval, 99–277. Madrid, Spain: Editorial MAPFRE.

Lardé y Larin, Jorge. 1925. "Orígenes de San Salvador Cuzcatlán, hoy capital de El Salvador." In *Boletín Municipal, IV Centenario de la Fundación de San Salvador*, 108–181. San Salvador, El Salvador.

Lardé y Larín, Jorge. 2000. *El Salvador: Descubrimiento, conquista y colonización*, 2nd ed. San Salvador, El Salvador: Consejo Nacional para la Cultura y el Arte.

Lenkersdorf, Gudrun. 1993. *Génesis histórica de Chiapas 1522–1532: El conflicto entre Portocarrero y Mazariegos*. Mexico City, Mexico: Universidad Nacional Autónoma de México.

Libro de Actas. 1932. *Libro de actas del ayuntamiento de la ciudad de Santiago de Guatemala, desde la fundación de la misma ciudad en 1524 hasta 1530, copiado literalmente por Rafael de Arévalo*. Guatemala City, Guatemala: Tipografía Nacional.

Lockhart, James, and Enrique Otte. 1976. *Letters and People of the Spanish Indies*. Cambridge, UK: Cambridge University Press.

Martínez, José Luis. 1990. *Hernán Cortés*. Mexico City, Mexico: Universidad Nacional Autónoma de México, Fondo de Cultura Económica.

Matthew, Laura E. 2004. "Neither and Both: The Mexican Indian Conquistadors of Colonial Guatemala." Unpublished PhD dissertation, Department of History, University of Pennsylvania, Philadelphia, PA.

Matthew, Laura E. 2012. *Memories of Conquest: Becoming Mexicano in Colonial Guatemala.* Chapel Hill: University of North Carolina Press.

Matthew, Laura E., and Michel R. Oudijk, eds. 2007. *Indian Conquistadors: Indigenous Allies in the Conquest of Mesoamerica.* Norman: University of Oklahoma Press.

Milla, José. 1976. *Historia de la América Central.* Guatemala City, Guatemala: Editorial Piedra Santa.

Oudijk, Michel R., and Matthew Restall. 2007. "Mesoamerican Conquistadors in the Sixteenth Century." In *Indian Conquistadors: Indigenous Allies in the Conquest of Mesoamerica*, ed. Laura E. Matthew and Michel R. Oudijk, 28–63. Norman: University of Oklahoma Press.

Polo Sifontes, Francis. 1980. *Los cakchiqueles en la conquista de Guatemala*, 2nd ed. Guatemala City, Guatemala: Ministerio de Educación.

Probanza de los indios conquistadores. 1573. Probanza de los indios conquistadores de Guatemala y San Salvador. Seville, Spain: Archivo General de Indias, Contratación 4802.

Probanzas de Diego de Usagre y Francisco Castellón. 1564. "Probanzas de méritos y servicios de Diego de Usagre y Francisco Castellón. AGCA 4673–40148." *Anales de la Sociedad de Geografía e Historia de Guatemala* 41(1968):141–198.

Radell, David Richard. 1969. "An Historical Geography of Western Nicaragua: The Spheres of Influence of Leon, Granada, and Managua, 1519–1965." PhD dissertation, University of California Berkeley. Ann Arbor: University Microfilms.

Recinos, Adrián. 1986. *Pedro de Alvarado: Conquistador de México y Guatemala*, 2nd ed. Guatemala City, Guatemala: Ministerio de Educación.

Relación de Gil González Dávila. 1522. "Relación del viaje que hizo Gil González Dávila por el Mar del Sur, de las tierras que descubrió, conversiones en ella logradas y donativos que se hicieron, por Andés de Cereceda." *Colección de documentos inéditos, relativos al descubrimiento, conquista y organización de las antiguas posesiones españolas de América y Oceanía, sacados de los archivos del reino, y muy especialmente del de Indias por D. Luis Torres de Mendoza*, 14:20–24.

Restall, Matthew. 2003. *Seven Myths of the Spanish Conquest.* Oxford, UK: Oxford University Press.

Rouse, Irving. 1986. *Migrations in Prehistory: Inferring Population Movement from Cultural Remains.* New Haven, CT: Yale University Press.

Rubio Sánchez, Manuel. 1979. *Alcaldes mayores: Historia de los alcaldes mayores, justicias mayores, gobernadores intendentes, intendentes corregidores, y jefes políticos, de la provincia de San Salvador, San Miguel y San Vicente*, 2 volumes. San Salvador, El Salvador: Ministerio de Educación.

Sherman, William L. 1979. *Forced Native Labor in Sixteenth-Century Central America.* Lincoln: University of Nebraska Press.

Stone, Doris. 1954. *Estampas de Honduras.* Mexico City, Mexico: Impresora Galve.

Stuart, David. 2000. "'The Arrival of Strangers': Teotihuacan and Tollan in Classic Maya History." In *Mesoamerica's Classic Heritage: From Teotihuacan to the Aztecs*, ed. Davíd Carrasco, Lindsay Jones, and Scott Sessions, 465–513. Boulder: University Press of Colorado.

13

In this chapter, I explore an analytical framework for Honduran archaeology that encourages understanding Honduran societies contemporary with those of the Classic Maya (ca. AD 500–1000) as networks of communities of practice, historically connected by traditions of production of things used in practices that linked Honduras with other societies far north and south. My focus is on how social relations were shaped between individual actors, between small groups of coresident actors who occupied compounds of buildings and engaged in everyday face-to-face activities, and between the actors and groups of actors who made up the population of the larger settlements that such household compounds composed. This social framework is an alternative to other ways of approaching the archaeology of Honduras rooted either in culture history or in the archaeology of evolution of chiefdoms and states. Elsewhere, I have laid out the rationale for adopting such a social framework in the study of Central American societies, including those of Honduras (Joyce 2013a, 2017, 2021).

I draw on more than 30 years of fieldwork in an area of western Honduras extending from the lower Ulúa Valley inland to Lake Yojoa, and east into the department of Yoro (figure 13.1) to explore how this social framework transforms our approach to specific categories of evidence: artifacts as small as figurines and as large as settlement patterns. I take the sites in this region as focal points of development of unique

An Alternative Framework for Honduran Archaeology

ROSEMARY A. JOYCE

DOI: 10.5876/9781646420971.c013

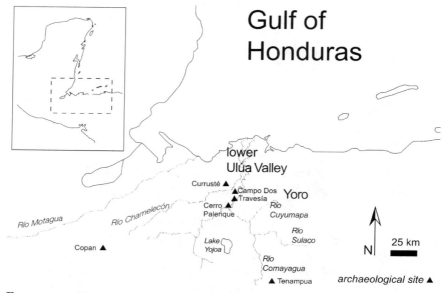

FIGURE 13.1. *Map showing areas and sites discussed.*

histories, and as centers of networks of social relations. The social framework employed highlights the importance of Honduran archaeology as an example where the development of absolute inequality was constrained over long periods of time, even as many of the traditional indicators of social complexity, such as virtuoso craft production, flourished, while enabling large-scale, long-distance exchange of goods, people, and knowledge.

I examine two core characteristics of this alternative framework of social relations, characteristics that also typified many other societies in an area of Central America extending south and west from Honduras to Panama (Joyce 2013a, 2013b). These core features of Central American social formations are the patronage of craft skills and the importance of spirituality as an integrating force. These aspects of Central American social relations are products of the mobilization of groups of people that we can understand as emerging through participation in shared practices, using the framework of communities of practice (Lave and Wenger 1991; Wenger 1998).

Overlapping and at times potentially conflicting communities of practice created different kinds of places whose distributions have been recorded through settlement-pattern studies. Settlement patterns in this area exhibit the kind of patterning that has been recognized in archaeological research as evidence of heterarchy, a form of complexity that presents an alternative to hierarchy. In the final section of this chapter, I turn from discussion of specific Honduran archaeological materials as evidence of heterarchical social relations to consider the significant contribution that can be made by adopting a social framework for archaeology to foregrounding the constraint of inequality as a historical process.

PATRONAGE OF CRAFT SKILLS

In Honduras, as in other zones of Central America, craftworking in a variety of media was developed to a high degree, and products of virtuoso crafters were widely available, not monopolized by a small social segment (Joyce 2013b). Ulúa Polychromes provide one example (figure 13.2). Produced in small-scale workshops in multiple settlements over a period of four to five centuries, they show a strong control of forming and firing technology, command of painting that allowed production of a range of colors, and repeated periods of substantial innovation (Joyce 2017). Ulúa Polychrome vessels are the main food-serving vessels in settlements of all sizes in the lower Ulúa Valley.

When we compare the incidence of Ulúa Polychrome pottery with the restricted distribution of the rarer examples of Classic Maya polychromes found in ruling and noble residences in Belize and the Guatemalan Petén, or the carved black-and-brown vessels that were similarly restricted in distribution at Copán, we can argue that access to craft skill and technical knowledge for the production of ceramics was more widely distributed in the lower Ulúa Valley than at contemporary Classic Maya settlements, including Copán (Joyce 2017). Yet that does not imply that everyone was a participant in ceramic production, or that craft skill was evenly distributed in the settlements where Ulúa polychromes were made and used. Production or patronage of Ulúa Polychrome vases would have differentiated residents in some settlements from those in other settlements, and potentially residents who were crafters or patrons from others within the same settlement who were not patrons or producers of these craft goods.

The potential thus exists that differences in craft skill could have become the basis for difference in social recognition or authority. While Ulúa polychromes are ubiquitous in different sites within their core region of production, and different potters worked to produce pots that conformed to standard layouts and imagery, close examination allows identification of more and less skilled potters (Joyce 2017). In some cases, repeated motifs are not spaced perfectly, leaving an awkward final motif executed smaller, or even rotated to take

FIGURE 13.2. *Early Ulúa Polychrome vessel from the Ulúa Valley, produced by a virtuoso crafter. Dedalos class: Chac subclass. (National Museum of the American Indian 04/3811, collected by J. E. Austin before 1915. Photo by Russell N. Sheptak.)*

up less space. In other instances, a motif has details that are unrecognizable except by comparison with another pot with clearer delineation. The production of both very large and exceptionally small pots otherwise conforming to norms of shape and painted designs suggests command of the standards combined with virtuoso capacity to shape ceramic materials. Potters who produced these large and small versions of the canonical shapes and programs, and those who filled the painted vessel walls with evenly spaced, uniform motifs with highly legible details, would have been recognizable to those using their pots as having greater mastery of craft skill and knowledge.

Conversion of heterogeneity in skill and knowledge into authority is more obvious for the production of carved-stone vases in the Classic Ulúa marble vase style that overlaps in shape and imagery with Ulúa Polychrome pottery (figure 13.3). As Christina Luke has demonstrated, Classic Ulúa marble vases were produced in restricted numbers over several generations in linked workshops in the lower Ulúa Valley, including (and perhaps limited to) workshops

FIGURE 13.3. *Ulúa marble vase typical of Travesia workshops.*
(National Museum of the American Indian, collected by Marco
Aurelio Soto before 1917. National Museum of the American Indian
06/1262. Photo by Russell N. Sheptak.)

at Travesia (Luke 2010; Luke and Tykot 2007; Luke et al. 2006). The technical skill required to produce these objects included knowledge of the location of geological raw materials, understanding of symbolism and meaning, and expertise in carving (Luke and Joyce 2013). The necessary geological knowledge and carving expertise was already present in the lower Ulúa Valley before 1000 BC, when vessels using the same marble sources were first made (Luke et al. 2003). The most innovative feature of development of Classic Ulúa marble vases was the carving on their surfaces of a new symbolic program, which Luke argues incorporates indigenous relations to sacred mountains as ancestral places along with specific conventions of wider Mesoamerican (ultimately Teotihuacan-related) ideologies (Luke 2012).

The patrons of Classic Ulúa marble-vase carving were engaged in long-distance social relations, with examples of this craftwork reaching the Nicoya Peninsula in Costa Rica and into the Petén at Uaxactun (Joyce 1986; Luke 2010). In the Maya lowland sites where they are found, marble vases were recovered from palaces, attesting to connections forged between the patron family or families at Travesia and families at the highest hierarchical levels of Classic Maya polities such as those of Altun Ha, San Jose, and Uaxactun. Ulúa polychromes, while having their own external distribution as far as Nicaragua, El Salvador, eastern Guatemala, and Belize, did not travel as far afield as the marble vessels (Joyce 2017). Patronage of craftwork had the potential to serve as a basis of differential social standing, perhaps authority, and possibly power. Yet within the lower Ulúa Valley, Travesia, site of the development of marble workshops, never consolidated control of a larger hinterland, nor did it come to dominate other neighboring settlements. Other communities made ceramic versions of marble vases, some of them produced using the same mold technology widely employed for figurines (Hendon et al. 2014).

Classic Ulúa marble vases, their ceramic copies, and Ulúa Polychrome ceramics were all used within the lower Ulúa Valley in ritual practices that coordinated activity across multiple independent settlements. The production of Ulúa marble vases may have been part of a strategy intended to create greater distinction for one family at Travesia, both within that settlement and across the lower Ulúa Valley, a possibility discussed in more detail below. But the scale at which the patronage of these objects was effective seems rather to have been interregional, and the audience that accepted them as signs of distinction was not local, but distant. At the local scale of the lower Ulúa Valley, both marble and ceramic vessels were part of assemblages of objects whose primary significance was their incorporation into ritual practices through which activities of people in otherwise independent settlements were coordinated.

SPIRITUALITY AS AN INTEGRATING FORCE

Ritual events in settlements in the lower Ulúa Valley occupied between AD 500 and 1000 left abundant archaeological traces in the form of architecture, buried deposits, and refuse. These events would have included seasonal rituals, some marked by ballgames, as well as life-cycle rituals, especially those in which intermarried families celebrated alliances, births, life passages, and burial. Both kinds of events might have brought residents of different settlements together, regardless of the absence of apparent political integration. Burials at different sites, perhaps the most obvious residues of ritual practice, were oriented toward the same points on the landscape, indicating a shared cosmological framework within which ritual action took place (Joyce 2011; Joyce et al. 2009; Lopiparo 2006, 2007). Trash from consumption of shared meals, or feasting, while slightly different in each settlement, contained overlapping kinds of materials, including well-made serving vessels, musical instruments, incense-burning vessels, and figural sculptures at a variety of scales (Hendon 2010; Hendon et al. 2014; Joyce 2017).

Such patterns can be described quasi-typologically as representing a "ritual mode of production" (Spielmann 2002). This presents residents of settlements like Travesia as bound by a pragmatic logic based on a different rationality than classic economics, not seeking to minimize cost and maximize gain, but to realize a required level of expertise to make a sacred event effective. From another perspective, we might emphasize that the investment in producing objects for ritual practice serves as evidence of the significance of spirituality as a binding force in Central American societies like those of the lower Ulúa Valley (Joyce 2013b). If we turn to the content of that spirituality, we can discern an emphasis on the animate nature of ancestors; the importance of origin places associated with specific settlements or families; and the location of ancestral beings in specific locations in a sacred geography in which caves in the surrounding mountains played key roles (Hendon et al. 2014; Joyce 2017; Lopiparo 2003, 2007; Luke 2012). Where Classic Maya texts indicate that ritual leadership was vested in members of a ruling family and other nobles, ritual leadership in lower Ulúa Valley sites may have followed lines of seniority in families, or been associated with specialist roles not unlike those of craft producers, carried out by a practitioner group. Craft production itself may have been understood as a practice of shaping spiritual forces into animate matter (Joyce 2017; Lopiparo 2006; compare Mills and Ferguson 2008).

Understanding craftworking and spirituality as factors requires attention to groups of human actors who operate at the level of the event, within an individual settlement, and who support the reproduction of certain kinds of activities over multiple generations. It is in the social relations among these groups, and between them and other individuals or groups, that differences in social identity, authority, and power were shaped. These are not easily explained in terms of political categories such as chiefdoms and states, in ethnic or linguistic categories such as Maya or Lenca, or even simply in terms of kinship groups such as lineages or houses. The group of people that forms to enact a particular set of practices, and to reproduce the conditions for the continued performance of those practices, may be smaller than a household, or more extensive than a localized territorial group. It may cross linguistic and political boundaries. There is a social concept that fits this description: the *community of practice*. By taking communities of practice as the model for social relations in Honduras between AD 500 and 1000, we can create a way to talk about the richness of the data as evidence of a form of complexity that is underemphasized in archaeological analyses, which in turn facilitated a historically significant limitation of the growth of absolute inequality.

COMMUNITIES OF PRACTICE

The concepts of communities and constellations of practice developed by Jean Lave and Eliot Wenger (1991; Wenger 1998) are exceptionally useful in understanding Honduran and other Central American societies (Joyce 2021; see also Bowser and Patton 2008; Joyce 2012). For example, at least four distinct communities of practice are implied by archaeological patterns of production and use of Ulúa polychromes, even without taking into account communities of practice that might be formed around interpreting the imagery painted on these pots (Joyce 2017). None of these can be easily mapped onto a typology of settlements, bounded regions, or individual sites.

Chronologically the earliest communities of practice to emerge were centered around production of these pots, formed by groups of people who created the first Ulúa polychromes prior to AD 600 through innovations in imagery and use of clay-slip paints. These innovations took place within workshops, at a scale smaller than the individual settlement. Through intergenerational learning, the innovations involved were reproduced by the community of practice.

With compositional analyses suggesting multiple workshops for production of these objects, and regionalized variants becoming clearly defined between AD 600 and 700, Ulúa Polychrome production implies shared understandings of ceramic materials, communication between decentralized producers at different settlements maintaining relatively uniform imagery, and yet highly localized demand for pots as objects of everyday and special-purpose use. The materials used in their production (and the knowledges they imply about geological resources and technologies), the purposes to which pots were put by the humans whose demands fueled their production, and the learning process through which production was sustained, shaped the community of practice of production. While the community of practice operated at a scale below that of the settlement as a whole, different workshops must have coordinated their actions to account for the regional uniformity that we find. This is an outcome of the formation of what Wenger (1998:127) called *constellations of practice*: in effect, networks of linked communities of practice.

One way that communities of practice of production of Ulúa Polychrome pottery could have been linked is through participation by members in communities of practice of consumption that brought together people from different settlements. The consumption of pots requires knowledge of what constitutes a proper meal, knowledge of and access to still other resources (plants and animals), and coordination of events (daily meals and special-occasion meals). The intersection of one community of practice responsible for the creation of Ulúa Polychromes with another community of practice formed by those whose pragmatic demands structured the proportions of pots of different kinds that were made, allows us to recognize that the distribution of similar pottery (in this case, Ulúa Polychromes) does index groups of people, but not simply people who shared genealogy or language. It allows us to explore the nature of these groups of people independently, rather than forcing us to assign the production and use of these pots to something like a cultural, ethnic, or linguistic group. The Ulúa Polychrome–making group may have overlapped with speakers of multiple languages; it may cross-cut other cultural practices that differentiated people living in settlements in the lower Ulúa Valley from those along Lake Yojoa and in Comayagua, or even differentiated between people in one settlement and another.

When Classic Ulúa marble vases began to be created, they exhibited forms and subsidiary motifs drawn from contemporary Ulúa polychromes (Luke and Joyce 2013). This, along with the presence of workshop debris at Travesia, suggests that a community of practice responsible for the production of marble vases existed alongside, perhaps overlapping with, a community of practice for Ulúa Polychrome production. Yet the imagery of Ulúa marble vases includes divergent elements that show that there is a distinction between these two communities of practice. The consumption of Ulúa marble vases diverges even more from the consumption of Ulúa polychromes than does their production, as marble vases circulated among a limited group of people in a series of neighboring societies. In Honduras, Ulúa marble vases normally are disposed of differently than the polychromes they initially mimic in form. The community of practice that was formed by the circulation and use of Ulúa marble vases was cosmopolitan: multilingual, multiregional, and multicultural, including people at Uaxactun, Altun Ha, San Jose, Travesia, and Guanacaste (as well as people from other sites in Belize, Honduras, and Nicaragua). It cannot be understood in terms of ethnic, linguistic, or traditional cultural groups. The members of this community of practice constituted a significant network of actors whose shared consumption of carved-marble vases produced an identity across settlements and regions.

Even if we assumed that the dominant painted pottery styles of Classic western and central Honduras did map onto ethnic/linguistic groups (Copador for Chortí, Ulúa Polychrome for Lenca), we would be left with problems raised by the series of similar yet distinct substyles or closely related styles in neighboring areas. In El Salvador, Arambala Polychrome closely follows shape, motif, and layout norms more familiar in Copador, without the specific pigment and locally distinctive paste, while the Chamelecon Bichrome and Polychrome (Trichrome) types of the Department of Santa Barbara have demonstrable similarities in vessel forms, some motifs, and design structure. In El Salvador, a local substyle of Ulúa polychromes has been defined as Salua Polychrome.

The differences between these closely related but technologically, morphologically, and iconographically distinct series of painted pottery styles cannot easily be attributed to subdivisions within culture areas or ethnic/linguistic groups. They can be modeled as another example of constellations of practice (see Roddick and Stahl 2015). Wenger suggested that such related yet divergent series of communities of practice could result from communities of practice sharing common historical roots, having members in common, sharing particular artifacts, or using overlapping styles or discourses. From this perspective, Copador and Arambala resemble each other because their independent makers—members of different communities of practice—nonetheless shared practices that required similar artifacts and employed similar rhetorical representations in those practices. They may have been linked by some individuals who moved between the areas where each community of practice was localized: for example, through travel for trade, ritual participation, or kinship-based connections such as marriage and fostering of children. Salua Polychrome and the comparable localized groups of Ulúa polychromes found in the Comayagua Valley, near Lake Yojoa, and in the lower Ulúa Valley are, I have argued, products of different communities of practice linked by engagement in similar social ceremonies in which eating and drinking from pots bearing signs related to ancestral origin were required, events at which people from any one of these areas might have been visitors and participants (Joyce 2017).

The notion of a constellation of practice turns explanation toward historical and pragmatic causes of similarities that exist at scales impossible to explain in terms of traditional models of cultural or ethnic groups within bounded territories. It allows us to address the lack of coherence among different patterns of distribution of things by viewing each as evidence of a community of practice with its own goals, organization, and engagements. Ultimately, communities of practice provide a better language to translate distributions in space of traces of human activity such as those found in Honduras into social terms, by allowing us to recognize the heterogeneity of settlement at the landscape scale.

HETEROGENEITY ON THE LANDSCAPE

As an example, consider sites located in the zone of production and use of Ulúa Polychrome ceramics (Joyce 1993a, 2017). In this area, the largest settlements occupied during the period from AD 500 to 1000—Cerro Palenque in the lower Ulúa Valley and Tenampua in the Comayagua Valley—grew to contain 400–600 buildings (Dixon 1989; Joyce 1985, 1991). In each of these well-studied regions, only one settlement reached such an exaggerated size. In both cases, this larger site emerged as a sole center, very late in the period under consideration (after AD 800). Previous to that, both regions had a number of sites reaching a maximum size of between 100 and 200 structures. In the lower Ulúa Valley, Travesia and Currusté are examples of these smaller towns that have been subject to modern excavations (Hasemann et al. 1977; Hendon et al. 2014; Joyce 1987). The majority of sites in these areas had much smaller counts of buildings. A number of these have been extensively explored through excavation, with Campo Dos (CR 132) serving here as my main example of smaller villages (Hendon et al. 2014; Lopiparo 1994, 2003).

A similar settlement pattern marks the area immediately east of the lower Ulúa Valley. This was the region of production of Sulaco polychrome ceramics, which were also used in some of the settlements in the lower Ulúa Valley (Hirth et al. 1993; Joyce 2017). In the Sulaco River valley itself, George Hasemann (1987) identified one very large regional center, Salitrón Viejo, with over 400 structures; five towns with between 40 and 210 structures; and 36 villages with up to 35 structures. Hasemann (1987) noted a tendency for settlement distribution along the Sulaco River to correspond to the distribution of arable land. In the drainage of the Río Cuyumapa, north of the Sulaco Valley, where a mix of Ulúa and Sulaco-related polychromes were used, Julia Hendon and I found that it was impossible to draw tight boundaries around sites, as there was a continuous, loosely dispersed distribution of small groups of structures along the rivers, punctuated by at least seven, and possibly eight, groups that included a ballcourt (Hendon 2010; Joyce and Hendon 2000).

In fact, while archaeological research has heuristically defined sites in the lower Ulúa Valley as if they were nucleated or bounded, detailed settlement survey there also shows continuous distribution of small mound groups along streams (Joyce et al. 2009; Joyce and Sheptak 1983; Robinson 1989; Sheptak 1982). Settlements with clusters of larger architectural features are more identifiable in the lower Ulúa Valley than in the Cuyumapa drainage, and towns, including Travesia, Cerro Palenque, and Currusté, are evenly spaced and surrounded by equal-sized hinterlands (Lopiparo 2003, 2007). The settlement pattern of Comayagua also features clusters of buildings located in proximity to arable land, along the river courses, with most sites small, having fewer than 100 structures (Dixon 1989:262).

Thus, in the areas that I am discussing, where Ulúa and Sulaco polychrome ceramics were produced, circulated, and used, during the majority of the equivalent of the Maya Late Classic period, most people lived in household compounds located in proximity to arable land, along the secondary and primary streams (figure 13.4). Ballcourts were maintained and used in some small villages in the Cuyumapa and Ulúa Valleys, including Campo Dos. In Comayagua, some smaller sites included monumental buildings (Dixon 1989:262). In the Sulaco Valley, Hasemann (1987:65) identified a group of six villages in which monumental scale platforms were found, despite the absence of formalized plazas, which was his criterion for a more central place. While the form of the larger buildings in these two areas does not tell us as much about their use, like the ballcourts distributed independently of nucleated sites in the Cuyumapa and Ulúa Valleys, these buildings do not follow a simple pattern of centralization of special-purpose architecture. The lower Ulúa Valley has the most centralized pattern of distribution, in which larger towns contain significant clusters of larger buildings arranged around larger open spaces, but this should be seen as part of a continuum in regional settlement patterns that resulted from the simultaneous operation of multiple motivations for settlement development.

These Honduran settlement patterns match the characteristics of what has been called *heterarchical organization* (Hendon 2010; Hendon et al. 2014; Joyce and Hendon 2000; Joyce et al. 2009; Lopiparo 2007). Heterarchy was developed as a concept to explain a region in which multiple principles of organization—political, economic, and religious—were operating simultaneously, shaping settlement distribution (Crumley 1987; Crumley and Marquardt 1987). The simultaneous operation of different organizational structures produced different effects that overlapped.

In the region comprising the lower Ulúa Valley, Comayagua, and the adjacent Sulaco and Cuyumapa drainages, one principle of organization reflected everywhere is likely the demands of an agricultural economy: most people lived close to arable land and water, producing continuous distributions of house compounds along streams. These agrarian communities constituted a community of practice, in which knowledge of how to cultivate specific plants in specific environments was inculcated through the practices of farming.

In each area, some other activities were enabled by the construction of distinct architectural complexes, ballcourts in the lower Ulúa Valley and the

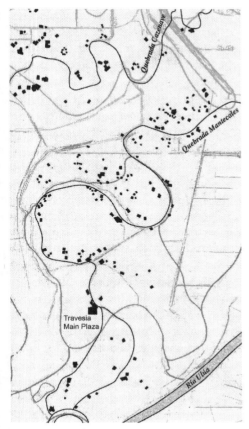

FIGURE 13.4. *Detail of settlement distribution along the Quebradas Cazenave and Mantecales in the central floodplain of the lower Ulúa Valley, with the location of the main plaza of Travesia marked. (Based on air photo survey by Russell Sheptak, and ground survey directed by Rosemary Joyce.)*

Cuyumapa drainage, and structures simply labeled "monumental" in the Sulaco and Comayagua Valleys. In the Cuyumapa drainage, we have demonstrated that the distribution of ballcourts is consistent with possible seasonal (summer and winter) use of ballcourts located on more and less central waterways (Joyce and Hendon 2000). In the lower Ulúa Valley, ballcourts, whether located in larger towns or in villages, were oriented toward a locally important mountain (Joyce et al. 2009; Lopiparo 2003, 2006, 2007).

In each area, we can understand the builders of ballcourts as forming part of communities of ritual practice. Yet, while in both areas enabling the playing of ballgames was the goal of the community of practice, these communities of practice were quite different. In the lower Ulúa Valley, we see a single community of practice spanning multiple sites that shared an understanding of the cosmological significance of the game, enacted in the orientation of different courts. In the Cuyumapa drainage, the builders of summer ballcourts and winter ballcourts may better be thought of as forming a constellation of practice with two distinct communities of practice. This is evident not only in the difference in orientation between the courts each created, but in the size and shape of the ballcourts in the two groups, and the kind of game each would have facilitated.

What could have been taken as a trait allowing definition of a single regional culture area that united the lower Ulúa Valley and the Cuyumapa drainage becomes instead the evidence of multiple communities of practice. All three communities of practice of the ballgame could be considered part of a very cosmopolitan constellation of practice that extended across the territory of Mesoamerica, reaching the southwest United States on the north, and reaching into Central America and the Caribbean. At the same time, the conceptualization of these architectural assemblages as evidence of participation in practices draws our attention to sites occupied in the same territory at the same time where ballcourts were absent, such as Salitrón Viejo, and suggests thinking of them as participants in a different community of practice, perhaps actually formed in opposition to the practices promulgated by ballgame communities of practice.

By foregrounding practices and their heterogeneity, the use of communities of practice as a social framework for understanding archaeological data from Honduras allows us to see and represent the region as incredibly complex, if not complex in the same way as Maya neighbors, such as Copán. This is significant because the kind of complexity evident in Honduras during the five centuries of the Maya Late/Terminal Classic was marked by greater stability and constraint on the development of inequality. This can now be seen as a positive outcome of the way that Honduran societies between AD 500 and 1000 managed social heterogeneity.

CONSTRAINING INEQUALITY

What archaeology normally privileges as the emergence of "complexity" is in effect increasing inequality. This is not a particularly new observation; decades ago, Randy McGuire (1983) provided an excellent analysis of inequality and cultural complexity by identifying a distinction between absolute inequality and relative inequality that is particularly relevant for Honduras. *Relative inequality* takes into account not just the specific differences between two individuals, but the scale of difference: whether "the rich have 100 times the wealth of the poor or only 3 times . . . the greater the relative inequality, the more a small number of individuals can dominate a society, and the greater the disparities in social resources within the society" (McGuire 1983:103).

A number of social resources might be subject to differential control. For example, Elliot Abrams (1994) undertook work to estimate the labor that was harnessed by noble families at Copán for the construction of residential architecture. The degree of labor investment in cut-stone and plastered architecture, when compared to the opposite end of the spectrum, the relatively modest houses of the majority of the rural Copán population, suggests that there was substantial inequality in access to labor between the rural farming population and the nobility at Copán. This exemplifies McGuire's concept of *absolute inequality*, here differentiating between nobles and commoners.

There is nothing like the range of variation in investment of labor seen at Copán in contemporary residential architecture in the settlements of the lower Ulúa Valley. Yet this does not mean there was no inequality evident in this index of differential access to labor. While most residential structures at sites like Travesia and Cerro Palenque are similar in dimensions, at both sites a few residential structures show a greater degree of labor investment through the use of cut stone in place of perishable materials, and the application of plaster and architectural stone sculpture. If we take into account the larger apparent population size at Copán (where settlement mapping documented about 1,000 Classic-period structures) than at Cerro Palenque (where around 500 Terminal Classic residential structures were mapped) or at Travesia (with an estimated 200 Classic residential structures), then we can see that, not only is the degree of labor investment in a few residences much higher at Copán, these few residences made up a smaller proportion of the overall universe of house compounds at Copán than at Cerro Palenque or Travesia, and at Cerro Palenque than at Travesia. In terms of absolute inequality, each settlement shows that a privileged group had differential access to resources. In relative terms, however, the degree of inequality was much higher at Copán than at Cerro Palenque, and at Cerro Palenque than at Travesia, evident in the proportional control of larger absolute resources by a smaller segment of population in each case.

The demonstration of differences in relative inequality does not of itself establish a way to understand usefully the differences between the power exercised by the ruling family of Copán, and the power that might have been exercised by the dominant families of Cerro Palenque or of Travesia. In each case, the exercise of power was lodged in a group of people considered to be kin, whose right to make decisions was based at least in part on their distinction from others in the same society who were not-kin. The kinds of decisions being made might have differed (with Copán's ruling family directing military action against neighbors, for example, an activity not evident in the cases of Cerro Palenque or Travesia). The number of people whose lives were affected in each case differs.

McGuire (1983) paired inequality with a second characteristic, heterogeneity, as two intertwined but fundamentally independent dimensions of complexity. *Heterogeneity*, McGuire (1983:93) said, "refers to the distribution of populations between social groups." The kinds of social groups McGuire considered were such things as classes, families, and age- and gender-based strata. In the Honduran case, coresidential groups or families can be identified archaeologically, based on the definition of house compounds, and provide potential measurable units of heterogeneity, based on age and sex (Hendon 1991, 1997, 2003; Joyce 1993b; Lopiparo 2006). Some coresidential groups at both Copán and Cerro Palenque included individuals engaged in some forms of activity that distinguished those coresidential groups from others. Not all house compounds at Copán yielded evidence of textile production, for example (Hendon 1997). At Cerro Palenque, firing of specialized ceramics took place in the vicinity of one centrally located household (Hendon 2010). The products of this workshop were found in low frequencies in all tested outlying house compounds (Joyce 1991).

Heterogeneity, McGuire argued, could change in three ways. The first would be through an increase in hierarchical levels. At Copán, an apparent increase in political agency of a number of non-ruling noble families occurs late in the history of the site (Webster 1999). This could be seen as increasing heterogeneity through the creation of an interstitial hierarchical level between rulers and ruled. An attempt to increase the number of hierarchical levels is implied by novel strategies that Travesia's centrally located family engaged in late in the Classic period, which included developing unique patronized craft production of marble vases, orienting the house compound of one family as a central point in a symbolic geography, and greatly increasing investment in residential architecture in this centrally located house compound (Joyce et al. 2014; Lopiparo 2007; Luke 2010, 2012; Luke and Tykot 2007). These three linked developments can be read as the attempt to create a higher level of hierarchy above two existing levels of more and less wealthy families. The family living next to Cerro Palenque's ballcourt appears to have successfully created such a third hierarchical level, attracting a higher population than any previous or contemporary site in the lower Ulúa Valley to the site, patronizing the use of the site's monumental ballcourt, which was physically linked to the household compound by a pavement, and monopolizing imported obsidian, marble, and shell, while also producing distinctive craft products (Hendon 2010).

Here is where we can see the utility of separating analyses of inequality and heterogeneity: the way that multiplication of hierarchical levels proceeded at Travesia and Cerro Palenque between AD 700 and 900 was arguably more transformative of existing social life than the coalescence of a non-ruling noble group at contemporary Copán. In the lower Ulúa Valley sites, what was promulgated at Travesia and successfully developed for a few generations at Cerro Palenque was the existence of a more powerful, more limited stratum of society. At Copán, the authority of a single ruling family remained intact, with some noble families asserting more control within the existing structure of nobles and commoners. While the absolute degree of inequality at Cerro Palenque and Travesia was lower than at Copán, the change in the heterogeneity of social complexity might be viewed as more significant, and as producing greater relative inequality.

McGuire (1983:107–109) defined a second means by which complexity could increase through changes in heterogeneity, by adding dimensions of differentiation. He described these as "multiple hierarchies of power," as in religious or secular domains, for example. By 1987, this idea would become permanently identified as *heterarchy* (Crumley 1987; Crumley and Marquardt 1987). McGuire (1983:107) argued that "the more complex the society, the greater the number of multiple hierarchies of power (or routes to power) that exist." A multiplicity of hierarchies can exist as an alternative form of complexity or heterogeneity. Multiplying hierarchies can form greater complexity, contrasting with but of equal interest to multiplying levels of a single hierarchy.

This leads to the third way McGuire (1983:107) argued that heterogeneity can increase: by increasing independence of different social parameters. *Independence* here means that a person may be able to take up positions in different social groupings, in which he or she will have different perceived rank and actual authority or power. In the accepted model of political organization at Copán, multiple routes to power were concentrated in a single hierarchy that controlled resources, labor, status, the production of history, and ritual, to name just a few potential "routes to power" (Webster 1999). In the lower Ulúa Valley at the same time, in contrast, a more complex heterarchy developed, and people might have been recognized as authorities in some arenas but not in others. The independence of different domains of heterogeneity created the conditions for constraint of the development of greater absolute and relative inequality.

DISCUSSION

The social framework for analysis of complexity described here seeks to understand the ongoing reproduction of practices as localized traditions, histories, and identities that are not pre-given, but formed via alliances, exchanges, and symbolic production of meanings that allowed cross-societal linkages and intrasocietal distinctions to be formulated and naturalized. It adds back into traditional models the agency of a variety of social actors, placing a premium on recovering evidence from a wide spectrum of social positions. It makes archaeological research in places that have been less examined, less understood, and where the mechanisms of social complexity are those underemphasized in Western social theory more significant than repeated documentation of pathways to greater hierarchy and inequality. In Honduras, mechanisms of social complexity produced and maintained heterogeneity, even in the face of pressures promoting increasing inequality. As we broaden our examination of the past to encompass a more contentious, multiple set of actors engaged in dynamic, ever-changing communities of practice that must have produced contradictions, we transform archaeological research into something that could produce surprising results. It may be harder to do, but it is also much more important.

WORKS CITED

Abrams, Elliot. 1994. *How the Maya Built Their World: Energetics and Ancient Architecture*. Austin: University of Texas Press.

Bowser, Brenda J., and James Q. Patton. 2008. "Learning and Transmission of Pottery Style: Women's Life Histories and Communities of Practice in the Ecuadorian Amazon." In *Cultural Transmission and Material Culture: Breaking Down Boundaries*, ed. Miriam T. Stark, Brenda J. Bowser, and Lee Horne, 105–129. Tucson: University of Arizona Press.

Crumley, Carole L. 1987. "A Dialectical Critique of Hierarchy." In *Power Relations and State Formation*, ed. Thomas Patterson and Christine W. Gailey, 155–169. Washington, DC: American Anthropological Association.

Crumley, Carole L., and William Marquardt, eds. 1987. *Regional Dynamics: Burgundian Landscapes in Historical Perspective*. Orlando, FL: Academic Press.

Dixon, Boyd. 1989. "A Preliminary Settlement Pattern Study of a Prehistoric Cultural Corridor: The Comayagua Valley, Honduras." *Journal of Field Archaeology* 16:257–271.

Hasemann, George. 1987. "El patron de asentamiento a lo largo del Río Sulaco durante el Clásico Tardío." *Yaxkin* 10(1):58–77.

Hasemann, George, Lori van Gerpen, and Vito Veliz. 1977. *Informe preliminar, Curruste: Fase 1*. Manuscript on file. Tegucigalpa, Honduras: Archives of the Instituto Hondureño de Antropología e Historia.

Hendon, Julia A. 1991. "Status and Power in Classic Maya Society: An Archeological Study." *American Anthropologist* 93:894–918.

Hendon, Julia A. 1997. "Women's Work, Women's Space and Women's Status among the Classic Period Maya Elite of the Copán Valley, Honduras." In *Women in*

Prehistory: North America and Mesoamerica, ed. Cheryl Claassen and Rosemary A. Joyce, 33–46. Philadelphia: University of Pennsylvania Press.

Hendon, Julia A. 2003. "Feasting at Home: Community and House Solidarity among the Maya of Southeastern Mesoamerica." In *The Archaeology and Politics of Food and Feasting in Early States and Empires*, ed. Tamara L. Bray, 203–233. New York: Kluwer Academic/Plenum Publishers.

Hendon, Julia A. 2010. *Houses in a Landscape: Memory and Everyday Life in Mesoamerica*. Durham, NC: Duke University Press.

Hendon, Julia A., Rosemary A. Joyce, and Jeanne Lopiparo. 2014. *Material Relations: The Marriage Figurines of Prehispanic Honduras*. Boulder: University Press of Colorado.

Hirth, Kenneth, Nedenia Kennedy, and Maynard Cliff. 1993. "El Cajon Region." In *Pottery of Prehistoric Honduras: Regional Classification and Analysis*, ed. John S. Henderson and Marilyn Beaudry-Corbett, 214–232. Institute of Archaeology Monograph 35. Los Angeles: University of California Press.

Joyce, Rosemary A. 1985. "Cerro Palenque, Valle de Ulua, Honduras: Terminal Classic Interaction on the Southern Mesoamerican Periphery." Unpublished PhD dissertation, Department of Anthropology, University of Illinois at Urbana-Champaign.

Joyce, Rosemary A. 1986. "Terminal Classic Interaction on the Southern Mesoamerican Periphery." *American Antiquity* 51(2):313–329.

Joyce, Rosemary A. 1987. "Intraregional Ceramic Variation and Social Class: Developmental Trajectories of Classic Period Ceramic Complexes from the Ulua Valley." In *Interaction on the Southeast Mesoamerican Frontier: Prehistoric and Historic Honduras and El Salvador*, ed. Eugenia J. Robinson, 280–303. International Series 327. Oxford, UK: BAR.

Joyce, Rosemary A. 1991. *Cerro Palenque: Power and Identity on the Maya Periphery*. Austin: University of Texas Press.

Joyce, Rosemary A. 1993a. "The Construction of the Maya Periphery and the Mayoid Image of Honduran Polychrome Ceramics." *Reinterpreting Prehistory of Central America*, ed. Mark Miller Graham, 51–101. Boulder: University of Colorado Press.

Joyce, Rosemary A. 1993b. "Women's Work: Images of Production and Reproduction in Pre-Hispanic Southern Central America." *Current Anthropology* 34:255–273.

Joyce, Rosemary A. 2011. "In the Beginning: The Experience of Residential Burial in Prehispanic Honduras." In *Residential Burial: A Multiregional Exploration*, ed. Ron L. Adams and Stacie King, 33–43. Arlington, VA: American Anthropological Association.

Joyce, Rosemary A. 2012. "Thinking about Pottery Production as Community Practice." In *Potters and Communities of Practice: Glaze Paint and Polychrome Pottery in the American Southwest, AD 1200–1700*, ed. Linda S. Cordell and Judith A.

Habicht-Mauche, 149–154. Anthropological Papers No. 75. Tucson: University of Arizona Press.

Joyce, Rosemary A. 2013a, ed. *Revealing Ancestral Central America*. Washington, DC: Smithsonian Institution Latino Center/National Museum of the American Indian.

Joyce, Rosemary A. 2013b. "Surrounded by Beauty: Central America Before 1500." In *Revealing Ancestral Central America*, ed. Rosemary A. Joyce, 13–22. Washington, DC: Smithsonian Institution Latino Center/National Museum of the American Indian.

Joyce, Rosemary A. 2017. *Painted Pottery of Honduras: Object Lives and Itineraries*. Leiden, Netherlands: Brill.

Joyce, Rosemary A. 2021. "Central America: Time for a Paradigm Shift." In *Toward an Archaeology of Greater Central America*, ed. Colin McEwan, Bryan Cockrell, and John Hoopes, 35–47. Washington, DC: Dumbarton Oaks.

Joyce, Rosemary A., and Julia A. Hendon. 2000. "Heterarchy, History, and Material Reality: 'Communities' in Late Classic Honduras." In *The Archaeology of Communities: A New World Perspective*, ed. Marcello-Andrea Canuto and Jason Yaeger, 143–159. London: Routledge.

Joyce, Rosemary A., Julia A. Hendon, and Jeanne Lopiparo. 2009. "Being in Place: Intersections of Identity and Experience on the Honduran Landscape." In *The Archaeology of Meaningful Places*, ed. Brenda J. Bowser and María Nieves Zedeño, 53–72. Salt Lake City: University of Utah Press.

Joyce, Rosemary A., Julia A. Hendon, and Jeanne Lopiparo. 2014. "Working with Clay." *Ancient Mesoamerica* 25(2):411–420.

Joyce, Rosemary A., and Russell N. Sheptak. 1983. *Settlement in the Southwest Hills and Central Alluvium, Valle de Ulúa*. Manuscript on file. Tegucigalpa and La Lima, Honduras: Archives of the Instituto Hondureño de Antropología e Historia.

Lave, Jean, and Etienne Wenger. 1991. *Situated Learning: Legitimate Peripheral Participation*. Cambridge, UK: Cambridge University Press.

Lopiparo, Jeanne. 1994. *Stones and Bones at Home: Reconstruction Domestic Activities from Archaeological Remains in a Terminal Classic Residence, Ulua Valley, Honduras*. Unpublished senior honors thesis, Department of Anthropology, Harvard University, Cambridge, MA.

Lopiparo, Jeanne. 2003. "Household Ceramic Production and the Crafting of Society in the Terminal Classic Ulua Valley, Honduras." Unpublished PhD dissertation, Department of Anthropology, University of California, Berkeley.

Lopiparo, Jeanne. 2006. "Crafting Children: Materiality, Social Memory, and the Reproduction of Terminal Classic House Societies in the Ulua Valley, Honduras."

In *The Social Experience of Childhood in Ancient Mesoamerica*, ed. Traci Ardren and Scott R. Hutson, 133–168. Boulder: University of Colorado Press.

Lopiparo, Jeanne. 2007. "House Societies and Heterarchy in the Terminal Classic Ulúa Valley, Honduras." In *The Durable House: House Society Models in Archaeology*, ed. Robin A. Beck, 73–96. Occasional Paper No. 35. Southern Illinois University, Carbondale: Center for Archaeological Investigations.

Luke, Christina. 2010. "Ulua Marble Vases Abroad: Contextualizing Social Networks Between the Maya World and Lower Central America." In *Trade and Exchange: Archaeological Studies from History and Prehistory*, ed. Carolyn D. Dillian and Carolyn L. White, 37–58. New York: Springer.

Luke, Christina. 2012. "Materiality and Sacred Landscapes: Ulúa Style Marble Vases in Honduras." In *Beyond Belief: The Archaeology of Ritual and Religion*, ed. Yorke Rowan, 114–29. Arlington, VA: American Anthropological Association.

Luke, Christina, and Rosemary A. Joyce. 2013. "Artisanry in Motion." In *Revealing Ancestral Central America*, ed. Rosemary A. Joyce, 33–44. Washington, DC: Smithsonian Institution Latino Center/National Museum of the American Indian.

Luke, Christina, Rosemary A. Joyce, John S. Henderson, and Robert H. Tykot. 2003. Marble Carving Traditions in Honduras: Formative through Terminal Classic. In *ASMOSIA 6, Interdisciplinary Studies on Ancient Stone: Proceedings of the Sixth International Conference of the Association for the Study of Marble and Other Stones in Antiquity, Venice, June 15–18, 2000*, ed. Lorenzo Lazzarini, 485–496. Padova, Italy: Bottega d'Erasmo.

Luke, Christina, and Robert H. Tykot. 2007. "Celebrating Place through Luxury Craft Production: Travesìa and Ulua Style Marble Vases." *Ancient Mesoamerica* 18:315–328.

Luke, Christina, Robert H. Tykot, and Robert W. Scott. 2006. "Petrographic and Stable Isotope Analyses of Late Classic Ulúa Marble Vases and Potential Sources." *Archaeometry* 48(1):13–29.

McGuire, Randall H. 1983. "Breaking Down Cultural Complexity: Inequality and Heterogeneity." *Advances in Archaeological Method and Theory* 6:91–142.

Mills, Barbara J., and T. J. Ferguson. 2008. "Animate Objects: Shell Trumpets and Ritual Networks in the Greater Southwest." *Journal of Archaeological Method and Theory* 15:338–361.

Robinson, Eugenia J. 1989. "The Prehistoric Communities of the Sula Valley, Honduras: Regional Interaction in the Southeast Mesoamerican Frontier." Unpublished PhD dissertation, Department of Anthropology, Tulane University, New Orleans, LA.

Roddick, Andrew, and Ann Stahl, eds. 2015. *Knowledge in Motion: Constellations of Learning across Time and Place*. Tucson: University of Arizona Press.

Sheptak, Russell N. 1982. "Fotos aereas y el patron de asentamiento de la zona central del valle de Sula." *Yaxkin* 5(2):89–94.

Spielmann, Katherine A. 2002. "Feasting, Craft Production, and the Ritual Mode of Production in Small Scale Societies." *American Anthropologist* 104:195–207.

Webster, David. 1999. "The Archaeology of Copán, Honduras." *Journal of Archaeological Research* 7:1–53.

Wenger, Etienne. 1998. *Communities of Practice: Learning, Meaning, and Identity.* Cambridge, UK: Cambridge University Press.

14

UNITS OF INTERACTION

The chapters of this volume raise important questions about the units of study we use to describe and understand past human developments. That query, in turn, is directly related to the very basic question of how we imagine that interpersonal dealings are and were structured.

Traditionally in Mesoamerican archaeology, we have assumed that such transactions were organized within a series of nested territorially defined boxes ranging in scale from households to societies to large-scale states. A corollary of this premise is that social interactions were structured hierarchically. Prominent members of, say, households would act as representatives to higher-order bureaucrats residing at secondary political centers who, in turn, were subordinate to paramount elites ruling from regional capitals. The crucial interpersonal ties were those of domination and subordination defined by the extraction of labor, loyalty, and goods from below in return for social, political, and economic direction from above. This approach mirrors the world of nation-states, each with its internal bureaucratic divisions of province, municipality, and village.

An alternative view posits that significant dealings were conducted among people who, while they lived in particular places, engaged with others of varying ranks, occupations, and places of residence, all with a fine disregard for borders (Knappett 2011; Schortman 2014). Such a view does not negate the existence of hierarchies.

Sociopolitical Dynamism, Fluidity, and Fragmentation in Southeast Mesoamerica

EDWARD SCHORTMAN AND PATRICIA URBAN

DOI: 10.5876/9781646420971.c014

It is, however, conducive to modeling past dealings as organized along hierarchical lines (Crumley 1995). From this perspective, diverse alliances among sundry actors extended over varying spatial extents to create a structure of overlapping social networks that is not easily reduced to a single system of straightforward unequal relations. A view of the world as composed of variably intersecting interaction networks is inspired in part by ongoing processes of political, economic, and cultural globalization. (Examples of this approach can also be found in world systems theory [Hall et al. 2011] and various forms of network theory [Brughmans 2010; Campbell 2009; Peeples and Haas 2013; Schortman 2014].) Such complexly interwoven interaction webs, it is argued, are not so much unique products of the modern world as enduring elements of human behavior in all periods. The scale of such transactions may have changed but these sorts of dealings have long defined the sociopolitical and economic structures in which humans operate and through which they create history.

Deciding between these paradigms requires considering how material goods and styles figure in interpersonal transactions of all sorts (Hodder 2012; Knapett 2011; Latour 2005). In both instances, it is assumed that the objects and features we uncover were once parts of dynamic processes through which people accomplished a wide range of objectives. As none of us achieves anything significant on our own, everything from securing food to seeking a spouse to building a pyramid requires regular and predictable forms of cooperation. Depending on the task in question, such collaboration often involves varying numbers of individuals employing a wide array of material goods and styles. Identifying patterned relations among these things and motifs is our primary means of describing ancient interpersonal dealings and discerning the structures that were forever emerging from those interactions.

If the world is composed primarily of relatively distinct territorial groupings that circumscribe most interpersonal transactions, we are predisposed to ask what material forms and styles are diagnostic of these spatially bounded entities. Archaeological research then aims to reconstruct, from spatial patternings recognized among recovered artifacts, the cultural jigsaw pieces that fit together to describe ancient social landscapes. If past transactions were structured according to social webs, our attention shifts to how objects and styles might have been deployed to instantiate connections and materialize affiliations that were enacted through practices occurring at varying spatial scales. No clear disjunctions in material patterns suggestive of territorial boundaries are expected in this approach. Just as social ties variably overlapped, so will the distribution of the goods and motifs through which those transactions were performed appear as a palimpsest.

Unfortunately for theory (and theorists), reality rarely resolves itself into the simple binaries we often find so appealing. For example, one could argue that elites generally seek to control subordinates by drawing clear boundaries around the populations from whom they exact loyalty and goods, thereby denying those resources to competitors in other realms (e.g., Osborn and van Valkenberg 2013). The more powerful these rulers become, the more successful they are at limiting the choices their followers may exercise concerning with whom they can associate. At the same time, subordinates might well strive to escape those constraints by maintaining ties with residents of other polities from whom items and ideas crucial to maintaining some degree of autonomy are secured. Their elite counterparts would also likely seek allies among their peers as they strive to sustain power at home and expand it abroad. Consequently, the spatial patterning of the materials that figured in these interactions will not tell a simple story.

The contributions to this volume convey how complex those interactions can be. Though the authors root their discussions in their detailed knowledge of Southeast Mesoamerican prehistory and history, their research speaks to issues that are equally relevant no matter where in the world we work. In summing up their contributions here, we seek to highlight how the essays challenge all of us to rethink (1) culture areas and the academic specialties built on their study, (2) how past sociopolitical and economic structures emerged from, and were sustained by, diverse interpersonal dealings, (3) the varied ways in which sundry goods and styles were involved in these transactions, and (4) the implications of such approaches for understanding human prehistory.

SOUTHEAST MESOAMERICA AS A CULTURE AREA

As McFarlane and Stockett Suri (chapter 5, this volume) explicitly ask, did Honduras, western El Salvador, and eastern Guatemala comprise a culturally distinct and coherent area at any point in its long history? Alternatively, is the zone simply an ill-considered outcome of scholarly efforts to create the Maya Culture Area to the west?

Much of New World archaeology through the mid-twentieth century was concerned with fashioning systems for categorizing and describing the materials that were coming to light from early archaeological investigations. Researchers had to be able to specify the social units to which their results could be generalized (e.g., Kirchoff 1952; Kroeber 1939). This required grouping settlements within larger entities based on shared material styles. The histories of said groups were then written by identifying temporally distinct phases defined by changes in those common motifs. Archaeologists, largely working within anthropology in the United States, were concerned that their analytical units approximate those used by their disciplinary brethren to categorize the continuum of behavioral variation among living people. Consequently, early research in Mesoamerica focused on identifying its component cultures and culture areas. These units, in turn, became the bases for distinguishing academic specialties devoted to their study.

From Stephens and Catherwood's early reports (1841–1842) onwards, public and archaeological attention has been riveted on the spectacular ancient material remains found across the lowlands of Yucatán, Chiapas, Guatemala, and Belize. These were used to define something called "Maya culture," the history and boundaries of which were to be reconstructed through analyses of spatial and temporal shifts in its component material markers, or traits. The latter included such features as hieroglyphic inscriptions, distinctive forms of polychrome-decorated ceramics, and certain characteristics of monumental architecture ranging from details, such as corbel vaulting, to specific building forms and arrangements, including pyramidal temples and ballcourts. It was in this context that the first systematic archaeological investigations in Southeast Mesoamerica were launched (Canby 1949, 1951; Glass 1966; Gordon 1898; Healy 1984; Longyear 1944, 1947, 1966; Lothrop 1925, 1927, 1939; Popenoe 1934; Sheets 1984; Stone 1940, 1941, 1942, 1957; Strong 1935; Strong et al. 1938; Yde 1938). That research was devoted largely to drawing the limits of the Maya culture area by mapping the distribution of its distinctive traits. In the course of such pioneering work, Maya "outposts" were found at Copán and Quirigua within western Honduras and eastern Guatemala, respectively. They existed, however, within what was taken to be a sea of non-Maya people. The latter were generally thought to have lived in societies that were smaller, less complexly organized versions of those known among the lowland Maya.

Having drawn the southeastern frontier of the Maya lowlands, interest in areas beyond that boundary quickly waned. Truly interesting questions concerning the development of cultural complexity would be addressed in the major lowland Maya capitals that were such dramatic manifestations of hierarchy building and political centralization. There was little to be learned, it was thought, about these processes in the small-scale societies of Southeast Mesoamerica.

No practicing archaeologist adheres wholeheartedly to such views today. It is equally obvious, however, that the legacy of this longstanding approach continues to impact ongoing investigations. For one thing, despite a marked acceleration in the number of research projects initiated in Southeast Mesoamerica beginning in the late 1960s, the pace of study still lags well behind that evinced in putative Mesoamerican cultural cores, including the Maya lowlands.

Nowhere is this tendency more obvious than in the study of the Preceramic. We contend that this situation has much to do with the perception that culturally transformative processes, such as domestication, occurred in core areas like highland Mexico and only later diffused out to their margins. Figueroa and Sheffler's pioneering work at El Gigante cave and elsewhere in southern Honduras reveal this to be, at best, an oversimplification (see chapter 2, this volume). Here niche construction through the intensive management of trees, including the avocado, was part of a stable and very successful adaptation. Those processes of intensive resource-management do not match the inexorable march to corn, beans, and squash cultivation that has long been how domestication was modeled in areas of Mesoamerica to the north and west (Smith 2001). In adapting to their physical settings, as in so much else, people in Southeast Mesoamerica traveled their own varied paths that are not easily subsumed within broader narratives derived from the better-known sequences recorded elsewhere in Mesoamerica. Further, as Figueroa and Scheffler note, domesticating the Mesoamerican triad may not have been so much a triumph of evolutionary progress as an accommodation to meeting the tribute demands of emerging rulers. Incorporating tree production within a broad adaptive strategy of resource management, therefore, possibly faded from southern Honduras not because it was unsustainable. Rather, it did not fit into emerging hierarchically structured political economies.

Another legacy of the culture-historical approach to southern Mesoamerica is that Mayanist archaeology is an acknowledged specialty in which one can be gainfully employed. Meanwhile, those of us working in Southeast Mesoamerica struggle to situate ourselves within the academic landscape, not really Central Americanists but not Mayanists either. These seemingly prosaic matters of employment speak to uncertainties about who we study and what the relevance of that work is to anthropology and academia in general.

The people whose histories we seek to understand are often called the "non-Maya." This is highly unsatisfactory, as it defines them by what they were not. Recent attempts to address this problem, including efforts by contributors to this volume such as Gómez (chapter 11) and Lara-Pinto (chapter 10), take the form of designating Southeast Mesoamerican people by names, such as the "Lenca," that are derived from ethnohistoric records. These moves are promising. At least they allow us to talk about the ancient residents of Southeast Mesoamerica in terms that do not depend on reference to the Maya. Nonetheless, such efforts run the risk inherent in cultural classifications of homogenizing cultural diversity in the search for commonalities of action and belief that are thought to unite widely dispersed populations at particular moments in time.

Juxtaposing "Lenca" and "Maya" culture areas can be advantageous insofar as we realize that we are highlighting the equivalence of both regional entities as valid units of study and academic specialization. As the contributors to this volume point out, however, we must remember the following points. (1) Our categorical creations serve analytical purposes in the present but were not necessarily units that were culturally significant to ancient populations. (2) There was significant economic, political, and cultural variations within what we think of as the Maya and Lenca cultural zones throughout their histories. (3) That variation resulted in large part from the fluid, dynamic interpersonal interactions through which people residing across southern Mesoamerica made their histories as they allied with some and competed with others in trying to achieve their objectives. The latter interactions may well have been pursued with little care for the borders that loom so large in our academic imaginations. As Martínez reminds us in chapter 6 of this volume, we would be well advised to shift from a traditional search for shared material styles thought to be diagnostic of particular cultural groups. Instead, investigations might profitably focus on understanding the social dynamics that were mediated through material items and that occurred at multiple spatial scales.

The contributors to this volume take the first point as axiomatic and devote most of their considerable energies to addressing the last pair of issues. We cannot do justice to the subtlety and details of their reasoning and findings. Instead, we will highlight certain themes that their important work addresses.

CREATING SOUTHEAST MESOAMERICA'S DIVERSE PASTS FROM THE RESOURCES AT HAND

The essays in this volume argue that Southeast Mesoamerica might best be characterized as a mosaic of varied cultural, political, and economic forms rather than as a relatively homogeneous culture area, a point especially stressed in the chapters by McFarlane and Stockett Suri along with Martínez. The people who crafted these different formations, whether classed as Maya or not, were often in contact with each other as evinced by shared material styles. Further, general demographic and political trends that encompass broad areas of the Southeast can sometimes be discerned. Such commonalities suggest that local historical trajectories were impacted by developments in surrounding zones. Nonetheless, contact did not breed slavish imitation and the ways in which history was fashioned, even in neighboring valleys, could diverge considerably. What factors contributed to this diversity?

Several of the authors strongly suggest that the palimpsest of diverse material styles and behavioral forms that characterizes Southeast Mesoamerica was in large part an outcome of political strategies pursued by varied agents seeking their own aims with the assets at hand. The different ways of waging power contests, and the suite of resources employed by variously positioned actors, shifted across time and space. Consequently, it is not surprising that Southeast Mesoamerica's archaeological record is characterized by overlapping distributions of material styles and organizational forms variably inspired by combinations of local precedents and foreign models. The distribution patterns traced by specific architectural styles, pottery designs, cultigens, and settlement forms have, therefore, different, if related, stories to tell.

Johnson (chapter 3, this volume), for example, presents us with the contrasting cases of the neighboring Sensenti and Cucuyagua Valleys in western Honduras. During the Late Classic (AD 650–800), emergent elites at the Cucuyagua center of La Union apparently used their favored relations with Copán's Maya lords to make locally novel claims to power within the basin. These connections were manifest in the sudden appearance of architectural forms and embellishments within elite contexts at La Union that mirror, if they do not exactly replicate, models derived from the nearby Maya center. Contacts instantiated through monumental architecture and stone sculpture, Johnson contends, helped create a valley-wide hierarchy with La Union's rulers ensconced at its apex. At the same time, the adjacent Sensenti Valley experienced no comparable material or political shifts. Their Late Classic residents apparently resisted the siren song of power promised by alliances forged with Copán's divine lords.

Comparable examples of leaders adopting manifestations of lowland Maya rulership abound in these essays. For example, McNeil and her colleagues (chapter 4, this volume) also draw on evidence from architectural and sculptural styles to argue for the close association between Late Classic nobles residing at Río Amarillo and Copán's rulers living a scant 17 km away. Between the reigns of Copán's twelfth and sixteenth paramount lords, the architectural and sculptural similarities between monumental constructions raised at Río Amarillo and Copán were so precise that it seems likely that the former center was incorporated within the Copanec realm (compare with the site of El Paraiso, an apparent outpost of Copanec power in the valley of the same name; Canuto and Bell 2013).

Further afield, Begley (chapter 7, this volume) calls attention to the incorporation of ballcourts within northeastern Honduran political centers during AD 500–1000. Begley chronicles the appearance of a novel architectural arrangement that has no local antecedents but was seemingly inspired by foreign, not necessarily lowland Maya, models, a situation like that of La Union and Río Amarillo. He argues convincingly that these locally unprecedented architectural arrangements were venues for making equally revolutionary claims to power by rulers who used the courts to articulate new self-serving truths.

Ballcourts and architectural sculptures would have formerly been used as traits to define the spread of "Maya culture." They are now productively reimagined as resources strategically deployed in local power contests by magnates who were free to draw on certain ideas and goods in ways that served their parochial interests. Meanwhile, as McFarlane and Stockett Suri note, the Late Classic occupants of the Jesús de Otoro Valley, over 200 km from Copán, were constructing their own political formations without any apparent use of monumental forms or elaborations derived from that Maya capital. In addition, McFarlane and Stockett Suri describe a situation in which multiple, closely spaced, apparently equivalent political foci seemingly coexisted for a protracted span. This arrangement contrasts markedly with the cases described previously where rulers monopolized control over subordinates from their primate centers. At the very least, such patterning implies that the sorts of hierarchical political formations attested to in the Cucuyagua, Río Amarillo, and Copán valleys were not reproduced in the Jesús de Otoro basin (compare to Fox 1996). Located even further along the continuum of sociopolitical variation are the social formations Martínez describes for the Late Classic Jamastrán Valley, about 500 km from Copán. Here she finds yet another form of sociopolitical organization, this time involving distinct settlement clusters that lacked clear signs of political hierarchies.

These five articles alone highlight several important features about Southeast Mesoamerican sociopolitical and cultural processes. For one thing, there is tremendous heterogeneity in the historical trajectories created by the area's populations. Part of what spurred that diversity is the varied ways that different local groups either rejected hierarchical systems or selectively drew inspiration for their political projects from sundry parochial and foreign models. The latter included, but were not limited to, those offered by Copán. The rulers of many Southeast Mesoamerican realms largely operated outside the control of any one political regime as they forged alliances or competed with different actors in pursuit of their political aims. Consequently, as Begley and

Johnson remind us, understanding what observed material patterns have to tell us about ancient interactions and their sociopolitical outcomes depends largely on understanding how those items and motifs figured in the intrasocietal power contests pursued by varied local agents.

Such independence may not have universally been the case. For example, Copán's rulers seemingly exercised direct control over some populations living within about 100 km of that center. In addition to the case of Río Amarillo discussed here, the sites of El Paraiso, 45 km to the north of Copán (Canuto and Bell 2013), and Quirigua, 90 km north of that lowland Maya capital, (Ashmore 2007; Looper 2003; Schortman and Ashmore 2012) were apparently incorporated within the Copanec realm. The apparently successful revolt by Quirigua's ruler K'ak Tiliw Chan Yopaat in AD 738 suggests that Copán's suzerainty was rarely certain and never beyond question (Ashmore 2007; Looper 2003).

In any event, material patterns which were formerly used to define cultural boundaries are now being seen as outcomes of the multiple strategies employed by varied local factions to secure parochial political advantages. This shift is important and exciting in large part because history is now understood as the outcomes of actions initiated by diverse agents pursuing different strategies instantiated through the use of sundry materials and styles. Far from being a homogenous culture area, Southeast Mesoamerica was an arena in which these heterogeneous processes were enacted.

As with any conceptual approach there are some limits to this perspective. Emphasis, for example, remains largely on elite transactions primarily geared to establishing and projecting power through the manipulation of mostly symbolic resources. Economic processes and products are, consequently, given relatively short shrift. There also remains a temptation to see Copán as the major source of those political symbols (though Martínez along with McFarlane and Stockett Suri challenge that tendency). Finally, the time period with which this research deals is primarily restricted to the seventh–tenth centuries AD.

In raising these issues, we are well aware that our own work can be justly criticized in the same terms. There is, in fact, nothing wrong in examining how symbolic resources inspired by Copanec models were deployed in power contests within and across varied Late and Terminal Classic (AD 800–1000) Southeast Mesoamerican polities. The problem is in confusing this particular suite of interaction processes with the full range of intra- and intersocietal dealings in which residents from diverse backgrounds and in different time periods engaged.

RETHINKING UNITS OF ANALYSIS

Gómez and Lara-Pinto take us out of the seventh through tenth centuries to the time of the Spanish conquest in the sixteenth century. In the process, they raise serious questions about the static nature of the sociopolitical and cultural units that existed in Southeast Mesoamerica during that interval. Thus, Gómez questions attempts by Iberian interlopers to rationalize and systematize divisions among the people they encountered using the concept of a "province." The latter was presumed to be a distinct, enduring sociopolitical entity led by a *cacique* with whom the Spanish could deal in diplomacy or subjugate in war. Such attempts to reduce indigenous sociopolitical relations to neat territorial structures were no doubt appealing to Spanish bureaucratic sensibilities. Nonetheless, as Gómez effectively argues, these efforts distorted the dynamic relations among different populations that he and Lara-Pinto summarize.

To convey that complex reality, Lara-Pinto suggests employing the concept of a "floating frontier" to refer to places where hybrid identities take shape in the course of negotiating linguistic, political, and cultural differences. These distinctions in sixteenth-century Southeast Mesoamerica were brokered through various means ranging from war to *guancasco* ceremonies that maintained peaceful relations among potentially competing factions. The picture that Lara-Pinto paints of Southeast Mesoamerica in the sixteenth century is less one populated by perennial territorial groups and more a place where alliances among varied actors were constantly shifting as they adjusted to new circumstances. Such fluidity required the existence of a suite of elite and nonelite identities that could be enacted situationally, depending on who was interacting with whom under what conditions. There is no reason to think that such dynamism was limited to the early historic period. The question remains how to describe and understand the shifting interpersonal dealings that constituted the floating frontier that likely encompassed Southeast Mesoamerica in all periods.

Joyce and Sheptak (chapters 13 and 9, in this volume, respectively) and elsewhere (e.g., Joyce 2012; Joyce et al. 2014; see also Yaeger 2000) offer important suggestions for how to achieve that aim. They propose adapting notions of communities of practice from the sociological and education literature (Lave and Wenger 1991; Wengner 1998) to analyze the nature of human interactions generally. This approach has the salutary effect of not taking the existence of spatially bounded social entities for granted nor does it privilege dealings among the powerful. Instead, these authors encourage us to pay attention to the ways in which the connections instigated by groups of varied ranks, occupations, places of residence, and genders were instantiated through processes of producing, exchanging, and using diverse goods. Rather than seeing ancient landscapes as divided among distinct territorial boxes, a communities-of-practice approach imagines them as matrices cross-cut by variably overlapping social networks. Those nets were, in turn, constituted by people and their actions, through which things (material or ideational) were used, fashioned, and exchanged.

The approach is broad enough to accommodate processes ranging across economic, political, social, and cultural domains. For example, Joyce notes that there were distinct communities of practice defined by shared modes of manufacturing elaborately decorated ceramic and marble vessels during the Late/Terminal Classic in the Ulúa Valley of northwestern Honduras. These communities, however, variably coincided with other social nets constituted by shared understandings of how the vessels were to be used in ritual and more prosaic consumption contexts. None of these social webs was neatly contained within political realms or areas defined by shared languages. Materials, therefore, are not seen here as diagnostics of bounded ethnic, linguistic, or political divisions. Rather, they are traces of those interpersonal dealings in which goods and symbols were intimately implicated. Artifacts are thus perceived as both the means by which past individuals materialized alliances and the resources deployed in collective efforts to make choices and see them carried out.

Sheptak highlights many of the same processes for the colonial and early Republican periods in northwestern Honduras. Here he reminds us that, if our focus is on communities of practice, we cannot attend solely or primarily to developments that occurred at specific sites or in particular regions. Instead we have to examine the landscapes over which ancient people moved and across which they were variably linked by differentially shared practices of consumption, production, and exchange. Fowler indicates just how extensive these landscapes could be. In his contribution (chapter 12, this volume), Fowler points out the detailed knowledge of widely dispersed peoples and places that at least some segments of ancient Mesoamerican populations had. It was this information that enabled them to traverse great distances in prehistory and to guide Spanish invaders across Mesoamerica and beyond during the early colonial period. We cannot simply assume that such topographic features as mountains and rivers were major barriers to significant social interactions or the spread of the knowledge on which these dealings were based.

Sheptak reinforces Fowler's observations and nicely illustrates the importance of contextualizing finds made in specific sites within the variably extensive social webs or communities in which they were embedded. It is only in this way that we can appreciate, for example, the complex cultural interactions that occurred as indigenous populations from various coastal and interior locations were brought together to construct such expressions of Spanish power as the fortress at Omoa.

Mihok and her colleagues (chapter 8, this volume) effectively make many of the same points in their discussion of what they call "royalization" in colonial Southeast Mesoamerica. For example, Augusta was a settlement initiated on the island of Roatán under orders from the English Council of War. Nevertheless, the ways in which it was constructed and how people lived there speak to the intersection of multiple European and indigenous social networks. These communities of practice were enacted through distinctive ways of using and producing various goods from iron nails to stone metates. Asking whether Augusta is English or indigenous misses the point. Similarly, wondering whether La Union is Maya or if the Jamastrán Valley falls within the Maya culture area leads only to intellectual cul-de-sacs. Far more interesting is to follow the leads of Sheptak, Mihok et al., Joyce, and other contributors to this volume and investigate the many ways in which recovered materials were implicated in practices through which people defined themselves and achieved goals as parts of variably extensive social networks or communities of practice.

Accomplishing this ambitious aim requires:

Carefully attending to how a wide array of items—from buildings to pots, obsidian blades to ceramic figurines—were employed in distinct practices of production, consumption, and exchange within specific sites. Comparing those results with the outcomes of similar analyses pursued at settlements in the same and other regions. Using these findings to describe commonalities and differences in the varied ways people made, used, and distributed certain goods. Based on such studies, reconstructing the communities of practice that were constituted by these processes. Outlining the matrix of overlapping social networks that emerged from such oft-repeated social dealings and the sociopolitical and economic structures that these connections constituted.

Complicating this already daunting task is the long-recognized fact that different materials were likely used in practices conducted within distinct social webs. The making and exchanging of obsidian blades, for example, probably defined different social nets than did the fashioning and distributing of ceramic figurines. Equally important, one class of artifacts may tell several different stories about how social webs were created and sustained in antiquity depending on which aspects of that material are examined. For example, our research in the adjoining Naco, middle Chamelecon, and lower

Cacaulapa Valleys of northwestern Honduras revealed that all of the Late/Terminal Classic residents of these basins employed a distinctive red-painted jar in daily practices of food preparation and consumption. These containers are identical in form and decoration. Such commonalities suggest that the people using them engaged in a community of practice defined by shared understandings of the symbols adorning the jars and agreements about what constituted a proper vessel shape for the accomplishment of certain domestic functions. These social webs crossed status distinctions and geographic distances. The red-painted jars are well represented in elite and nonelite households spread across what, based on settlement hierarchies, were three distinct polities. At the same time, investigations in the three valleys indicate that the containers were made in distinct workshops employing different clay recipes and modes of vessel shaping and firing. Consequently, the extensive social net instantiated through the distribution and use of one class of decorated ceramics was fragmented among at least two, possibly three, distinct communities of practice constituted by how these vessels were made. This finding parallels what Joyce reports for the manufacture and use of polychrome and marble vessels in the Ulua Valley. Bear in mind that (1) these are just four basins among the many different areas comprising Southeast Mesoamerica, (2) the analyses involve representatives of only a few categories among the multitude of ceramic taxa defined in each case, (3) they exclude all of the other artifact classes recovered during work here, and (4) the studies encompass materials dating solely to the seventh through tenth centuries AD.

Recognizing the different ways artifacts and features might have figured in the operation of diverse social nets does not exhaust the challenges research in Southeast Mesoamerica must confront. When we see the ancient world as composed of discrete territorial entities we can structure our investigations to sample—through survey, excavation, and data analyses—even the largest of those units as defined by topographic or other features. At the end of these studies we can have some confidence that a substantial proportion of the past behavioral variation that characterized these spatially defined units has been captured. As a result, we can offer reasonably certain assessments of an area's history and propose plausible explanations for the changes we observe. If past social landscapes are imagined to have been matrices constituted by overlapping social webs that spread over varying distances, matters are somewhat different. In this case we begin our analyses without the comforting assumption that we know the general contours and dimensions of the social groups about which we are attempting to make statements. Even sizable valleys, as Fowler reminds us, may not have limited all of the significant interactions in which past people engaged. In addition, as Martínez argues, one basin may have contained multiple, relatively distinct sociopolitical nets. Consequently, we find ourselves in the position of trying to reconstruct diverse communities of practice, or social networks, whose spatial extents we cannot specify beforehand and whose relations to the items we recover are undoubtedly multifarious.

Joyce is quite right, therefore, when she says that adopting a communities-of-practice approach to studying the past anywhere in the world is difficult. As implied in the above remarks, it is also probably beyond the capacities of even the most diligent, energetic investigator or research team to conduct all of the work needed to parse out the multiple social webs that were materialized in any area through the production, use, and exchange of recovered objects. Pursuing such work will require not only what has become the traditional approach of combining survey with extensive excavations and detailed artifact analyses across multiple sites. Investigating the sociopolitical formations constituted by communities of practice will also mandate close coordination among investigators working across multiple areas in how we record and present our findings so that others can glean relevant information from our studies. Such cooperation, in turn, will depend on having free access to full sets of research records from multiple projects. It is only in this way that current and future generations of students can analyze in some detail the materials recovered by others and thus meet McFarlane and Stockett Suri's call for intervalley comparisons of material and sociopolitical patterns.

Nonetheless, as Joyce also notes, difficult as describing ancient communities of practice might be, the potential rewards for pursuing such open-ended studies are great. This is the case if only because the sheer messiness of the resulting picture almost certainly approximates the unbounded, dynamic, contingent reality of the ancient lives we seek to understand.

SOUTHEAST MESOAMERICA AND THE NATURE OF HUMAN INTERACTION

The research reported in this volume gives some sense of the exciting potential offered by further investigations of Southeast Mesoamerican prehistory and early history. These studies, however, have implications for understanding long-term processes of sociopolitical and cultural change in other parts of the world. This is especially the case in those areas where agents from relatively small-scale societies interacted under varying conditions with representatives of extensive, hierarchically structured realms (e.g., Stein 1999, 2002).

Joyce suggests one question that might profitably be asked of this research: How did the actions of people in different places and times thwart the construction of enduring hierarchies in areas adjoining large, expansive states? Addressing this concern has the advantage of (1) foregrounding the social nets, and the strategies enacted through them, of nonelites in their interactions with each other and would-be rulers; (2) providing a strong basis for contrasting developments on the margins and the interiors of so-called core states; and (3) encouraging us all to reimagine social complexity in ways that do not privilege processes of political centralization and hierarchy building.

There are many more questions we can ask of Southeast Mesoamerican societies that are not "Were they Maya?" or "What do their historical trajectories owe to lowland Maya inspiration?" Pursuing those queries requires that we think of the past in different categories, supplementing traditional units such as households, settlements, and realms with the study of the social nets that fragmented these territorial groups even as they transcended their boundaries. The chapters in this volume point the way towards those exciting interpretive horizons. It is now up to the rest of us to follow their lead.

WORKS CITED

Ashmore, Wendy. 2007. *Settlement Archaeology at Quirigua, Guatemala.* Quirigua Reports, Volume IV, Museum Monograph 126. Philadelphia: University of Pennsylvania Museum.

Brughmans, Tom. 2010. "Connecting the Dots: Towards Archaeological Network Analysis." *Oxford Journal of Archaeology* 29(3):277–303.

Campbell, Roderick. 2009. "Toward a Networks and Boundaries Approach to Early Complex Polities." *Current Anthropology* 50(6):821–848.

Canby, Joel. 1949. "Excavations at Yarumela, Spanish Honduras." Unpublished PhD dissertation, Department of Anthropology, Harvard University, Cambridge, MA.

Canby, Joel. 1951. "Possible Chronological Implications of the Long Ceramic Sequence Uncovered at Yarumela, Spanish Honduras." In, *The Civilization of Ancient America*, ed. S. Tax, 79–85. Chicago, IL: University of Chicago Press.

Canuto, Marcello, and Ellen E. Bell. 2013. "Archaeological Investigations in the El Paraíso Valley: The Role of Secondary Centers in the Multiethnic Landscape of Classic Period Copán." *Ancient Mesoamerica* 24(1):1–24.

Crumley, Carole. 1995. "Heterarchy and the Analysis of Complex Societies." *Archaeological Papers of the American Anthropological Association* 6(1):1–5.

Fox, John. 1996. "Playing with Power: Ballcourts and Political Ritual in Southern Mesoamerica." *Current Anthropology* 37(3):483–509.

Glass, John. 1966. "Archaeological Survey of Western Honduras." In, *Handbook of Middle American Indians*, Volume 4, *Archaeological Frontiers and External Connections*, ed. Gordon Ekholm and Gordon Willey, 157–179. Austin: University of Texas Press.

Gordon, George Byron. 1898. *Researches in the Uloa Valley, Honduras*. Cambridge, MA: Peabody Museum of Archaeology and Ethnology.

Hall, Thomas, P. Nick Kardulias, Christopher Chase-Dunn. 2010. "World Systems Analysis and Archaeology: Continuing the Dialogue." *Journal of Archaeological Research* 19(3):233–279.

Healy, Paul F. 1984. "The Archaeology of Honduras." In, *The Archaeology of Lower Central America*, ed. Frederick Lange and Doris Stone, 113–161. Albuquerque, NM: University of New Mexico Press.

Hodder, Ian. 2012. *Entangled: An Archaeology of the Relationships between Humans and Things*. Oxford, UK: Wiley-Blackwell.

Joyce, Rosemary. 2012. "Thinking About Pottery Production as Community Practice." In *Potters and Communities of Practice: Glaze Paint and Polychrome Pottery in the American Southwest, AD 1200–1700*, ed. Linda S. Cordell and Judith A. Habicht-Mauche, 149–154. Tucson: University of Arizona Press.

Joyce, Rosemary, Julia Hendon, and Jeanne Lopiparo. 2014. "Working with Clay." *Ancient Mesoamerica* 25:411–420.

Kirchoff, Paul. 1952. "Mesoamerica: Its Geographical Limits, Ethnic Composition, and Cultural Characteristics." In *Heritage of Conquest*, ed. S. Tax, 17–30. New York: Free Press.

Knapett, Carl. 2011. *An Archaeology of Interaction: Network Perspectives on Material Culture and Society*. Oxford, UK: Oxford University Press.

Kroeber, Alfred L. 1939. *Cultural and Natural Areas of Native North America*. Berkeley: University of California Press.

Latour, Bruno. 2005. *Reassembling the Social: An Introduction to Actor-Network-Theory*. Oxford, UK: Oxford University Press.

Lave, Jean, and Etienne Wenger. 1991. *Situated Learning: Legitimate Peripheral Participation*. Cambridge, UK: Cambridge University Press.

Longyear, John, III. 1944. *Archaeological Investigations in El Salvador*. Cambridge, MA: Peabody Museum of Archaeology and Ethnology.

Longyear, John, III. 1947. "Cultures and Peoples of the Southeastern Maya Frontier." *Theoretical Approaches to Problems* 3:1–12.

Longyear, John, III. 1966. "Archaeological Survey of El Salvador." In *Archaeological Frontiers and External Connections*, ed. Gordon F. Ekholm and Gordon R. Willey, 132–156. *Handbook of Middle American Indians*, Volume 4, gen. ed. Robert Wauchope. Austin: University of Texas Press.

Looper, Matthew. 2003. *Lightning Warrior: Maya Art and Kingship at Quirigua.* Austin: University of Texas Press.

Lothrop, Samuel. 1925. "The Museum Central American Expedition, 1924." *Indian Notes* 2:12–23.

Lothrop, Samuel. 1927. *Pottery Types and Their Sequence in El Salvador.* New York: Museum of the American Indian, Heye Founation.

Lothrop, Samuel.1939. "The Southeastern Frontier of the Maya." *American Anthropologist* 41:42–54.

Osborn, James, and Parker Van Valkenberg, editors. 2013. *Territoriality in Archaeology.* New York: John Wiley.

Peeples, Matthew, and W. Randall Haas. 2013. "Brokerage and Social Capital in the Prehispanic U.S. Southwest." *American Anthropologist* 115(2):232–247.

Popenoe, Dorothy. 1934. "Some Excavations at Playa de los Muertos, Ulua River, Honduras." *Maya Research* 1:61–85.

Schortman, Edward M. 2014. "Networks of Power in Archaeology." *Annual Review of Anthropology* 43:167–182.

Schortman, Edward M., and Wendy Ashmore. 2012. "History, Networks, and the Quest for Power: Ancient Political Competition in the Lower Motagua Valley, Guatemala." *Journal of the Royal Anthropological Institute* 18:1–21.

Sheets, Payson. 1984. "The Prehistory of El Salvador: An Interpretive Summary." In *The Archaeology of Lower Central America,* ed. Frederick W. Lange and Doris Stone, 85–112. Albuquerqu: University of New Mexico Press.

Smith, Bruce D. 2001. "Low-Level Food Production." *Journal of Archaeological Research* 9:1–43.

Stein, Gil. 1999. *Rethinking World-Systems: Diasporas, Colonies, and Interaction in Uruk Mesopotamia.* Tucson: University of Arizona Press.

Stein, Gil. 2002. "From Passive Periphery to Active Agents: Emerging Perspectives in the Archaeology of Interregional Interaction." *American Anthropologist* 104(3):903–916.

Stephens, John, and Frederick Catherwood. 1841–1842. *Incidents of Travel in Central America, Chiapas, and Yucatan.* London: John Murray.

Stone, Doris. 1940. "The Ulua Valley and Lake Yojoa." In *The Maya and Their Neighbors,* ed. Clarence L. Hay, Samuel K. Lothrop, Ralph L. Linton, Harry L. Shapiro, and George C. Vaillant, 386–394. New York: Appleton-Century.

Stone, Doris. 1941. *Archaeology of the North Coast of Honduras.* Cambridge, NA: Peabody Museum of Archaeology and Ethnology.

Stone, Doris. 1942. "A Delimitation of the Area and Some of the Archaeology of the Sula-Jicaque Indians of Honduras." *American Antiquity* 7:376–388.

Stone, Doris. 1957. *The Archaeology of Central and Southern Honduras*. Cambridge, MA: Peabody Museum of Archaeology and Ethnology.

Strong, William Duncan. 1935. *Archaeological Investigations in the Bay Islands, Spanish Honduras*. Washington, DC: Smithsonian Institution.

Strong, William Duncan, Alfred V. Kidder II, and Drexel Paul Jr. 1938. *Preliminary Report on the Smithsonian-Harvard University Archaeological Expedition to Northwestern Honduras, 1936*. Washington, DC: Smithsonian Institution.

Wenger, Etienne. 1998. *Communities of Practice: Learning, Meaning, and Identity*. Cambridge, UK: Cambridge University Press.

Yaeger, Jason. 2000. "The Social Construction of Communities in the Classic Maya Countryside." In *The Archaeology of Communities: A New World Perspective*, ed. Marcello Canuto and Jason Yaeger, 123–142. New York: Routledge.

Yde, Jens. 1938. *An Archaeological Reconnaissance of Northwestern Honduras: A Report of the Work of the Tulane University-Danish National Museum to Central America, 1935*. New Orleans, LA: Middle American Research Institute, Tulane University.

EDY BARRIOS, faculty, Department of Anthropology, Centro Universitario del Petén, Universidad de San Carlos de Guatemala, Guatemala City, Guatemala.

CHRISTOPHER BEGLEY, associate professor, Department of Anthropology, Transylvania University, Lexington, KY.

WALTER BURGOS, affiliated faculty, Department of Anthropology, City University of New York.

MAURICIO DÍAZ GARCÍA, graduate student, Department of Anthropology, City University of New York.

ALEJANDRO J. FIGUEROA, PhD candidate, Department of Anthropology, Southern Methodist University, Dallas, TX.

WILLIAM R. FOWLER, associate professor, Department of Anthropology, Vanderbilt University, Nashville, TN.

PASTOR RODOLFO GÓMEZ ZÚÑIGA, independent researcher.

WHITNEY A. GOODWIN, senior research specialist, Archaeometry Group, University of Missouri Research Reactor, Columbia, MO.

ERLEND JOHNSON, adjunct, Department of Anthropology, Tulane University, New Orleans, LA.

ROSEMARY A. JOYCE, professor, Department of Anthropology, University of California, Berkeley.

GLORIA LARA-PINTO, professor, Social Sciences Department, Universidad Pedagógica Nacional Francisco Morazán, Tegucigalpa, Honduras.

EVA L. MARTÍNEZ, professor, Department of Anthropology, Universidad Nacional Autónoma de Honduras, Tegucigalpa, Honduras.

WILLIAM J. MCFARLANE, professor and chair, Department of Anthropology, Johnson County Community College, Overland Park, KS.

CAMERON L. MCNEIL, assistant professor, The Graduate Center, City University of New York.

LORENA D. MIHOK, instructor, Department of Anthropology, Eckerd College, St. Petersburg, FL.

TIMOTHY SCHEFFLER, affiliate faculty, Department of Anthropology, University of Hawai'i at Hilo.

EDWARD SCHORTMAN, professor, Department of Anthropology, Kenyon College, Gambier, OH.

RUSSELL SHEPTAK, research associate, Archaeological Research Facility, University of California, Berkeley.

MIRANDA STOCKETT SURI, assistant professor, Department of Anthropology, Queen's College, City University of New York.

PATRICIA URBAN, professor emerita, Department of Anthropology, Kenyon College, Gambier, OH.

ANTOLÍN VELÁSQUEZ, faculty, Department of Anthropology, Universidad de San Carlos de Guatemala, Guatemala City, Guatemala.

E. CHRISTIAN WELLS, professor, Department of Anthropology, University of South Florida, Tampa, FL.